LONDON'S GREAT THEATRES

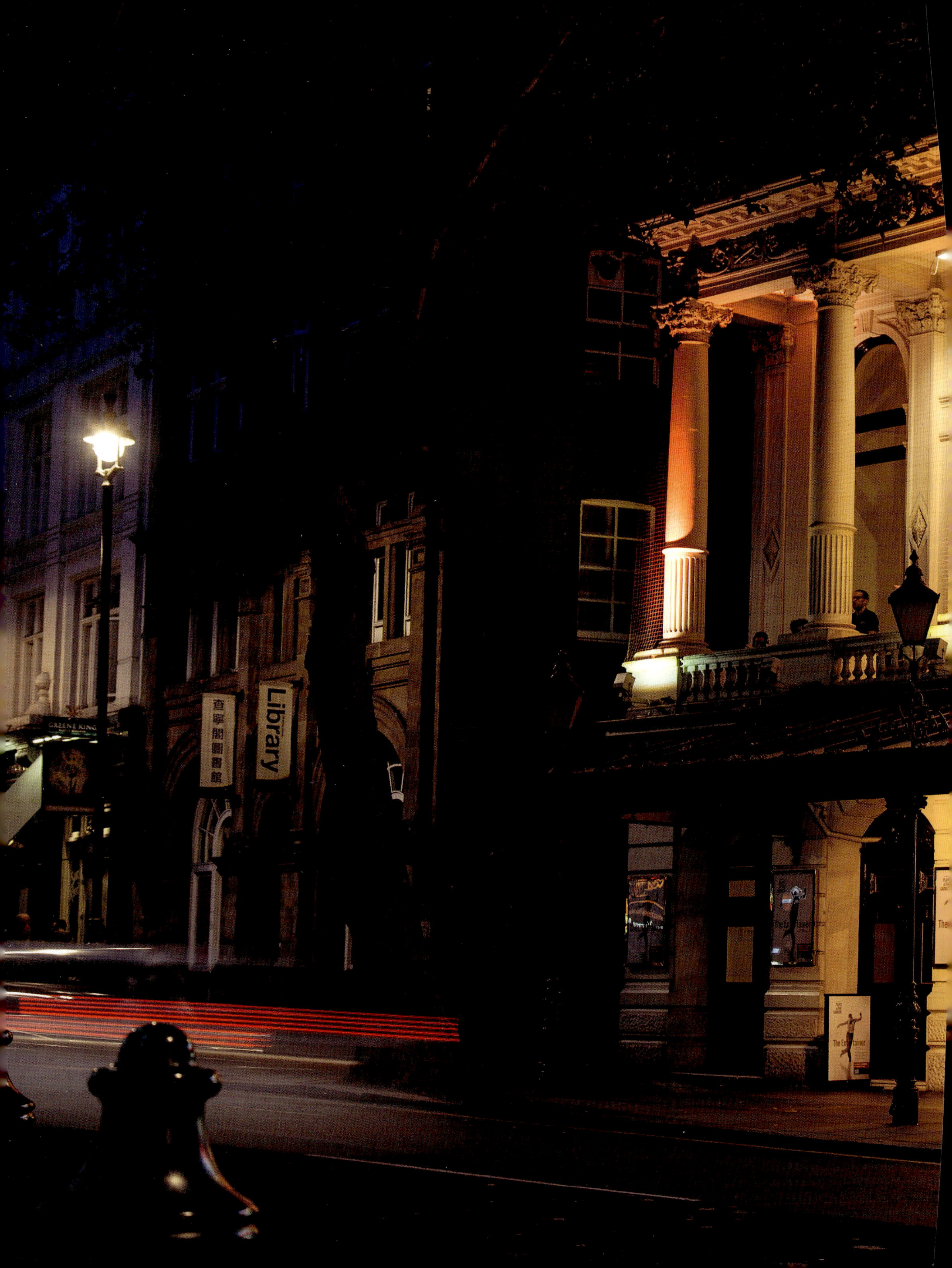
GREENE KING
查寧閣圖書館
Library
The Entertainer

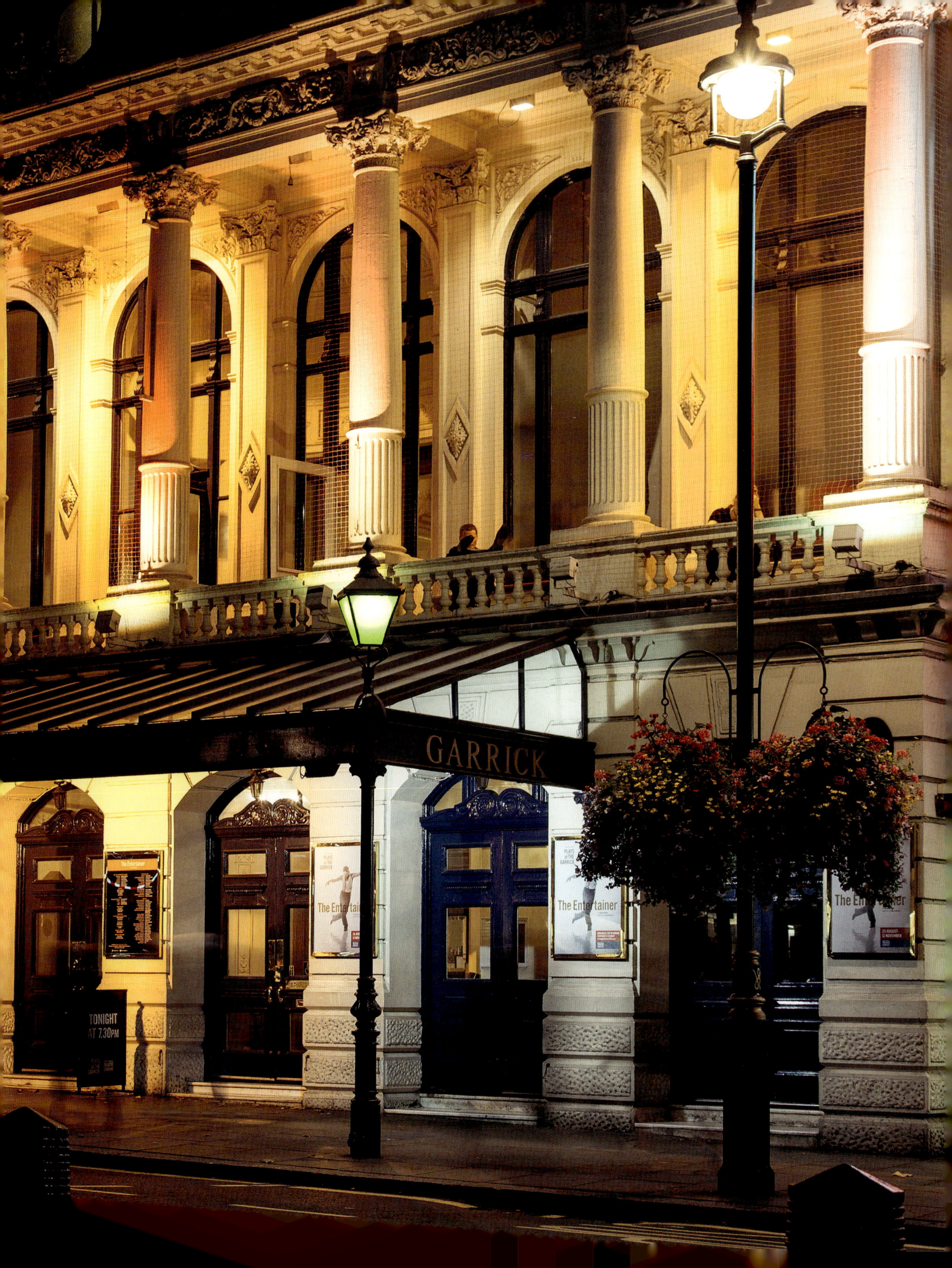
GARRICK
TONIGHT
AT 7.30PM
The Entertainer

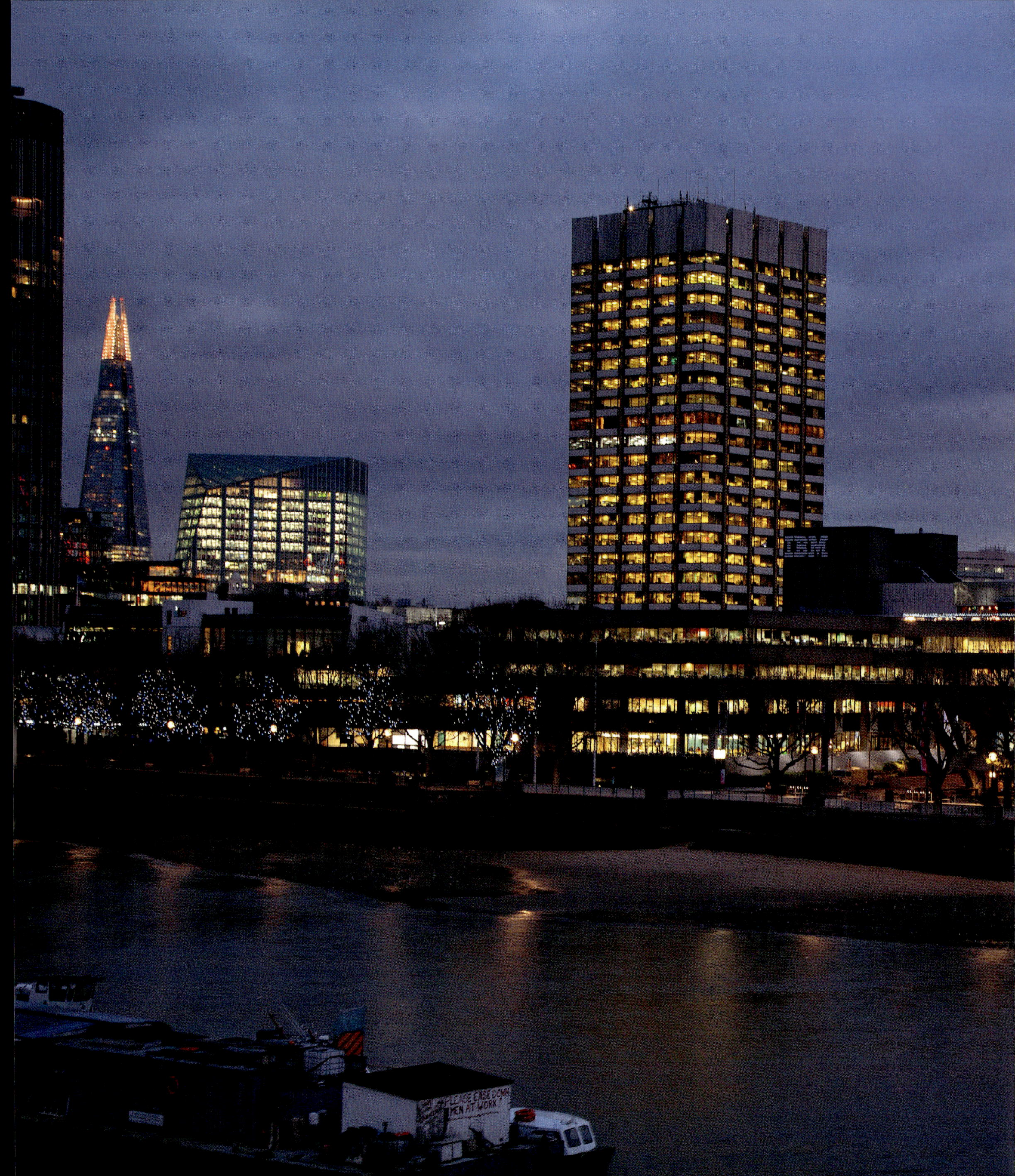
IBM
PLEASE EASE DOWN
MEN AT WORK

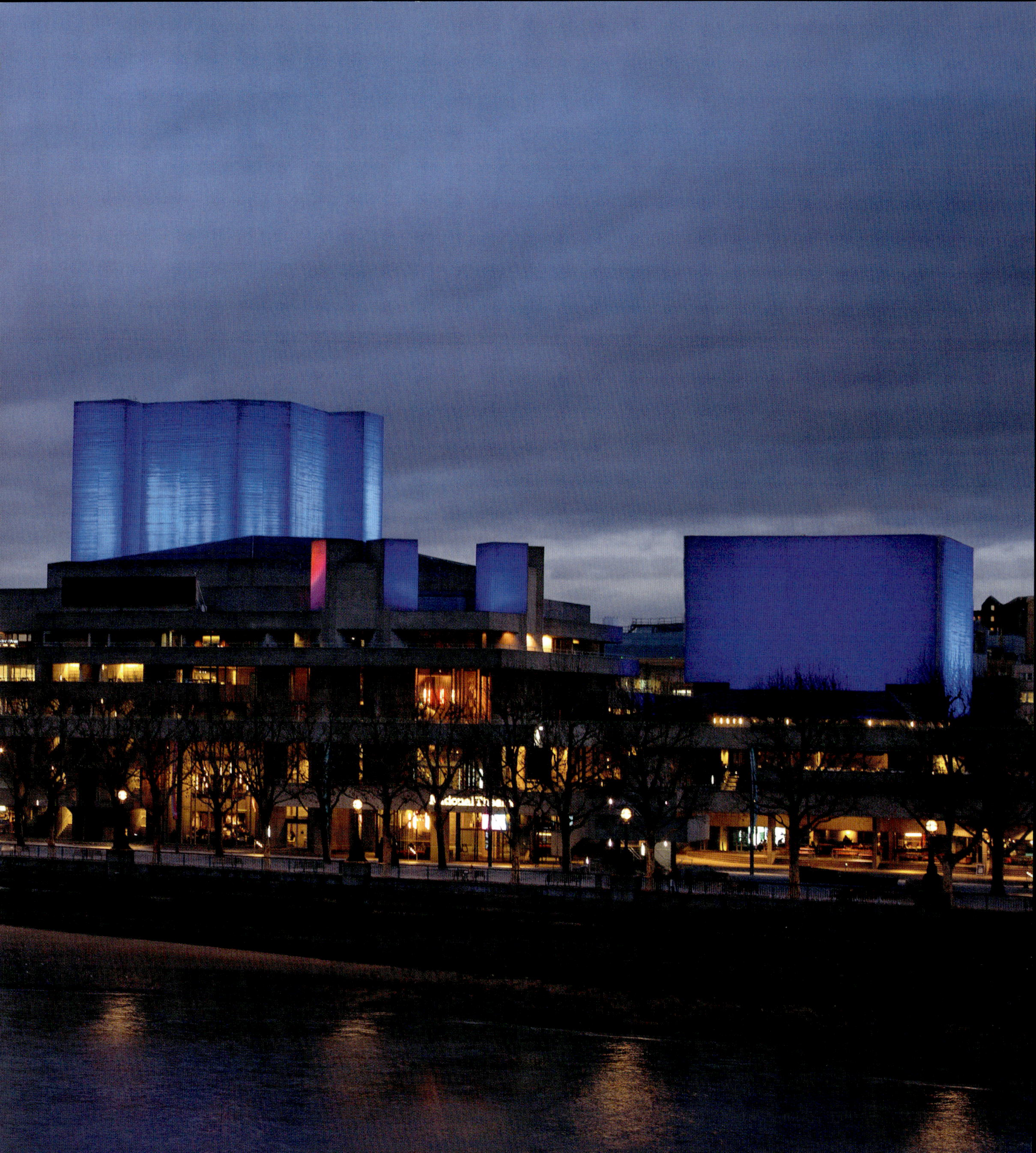

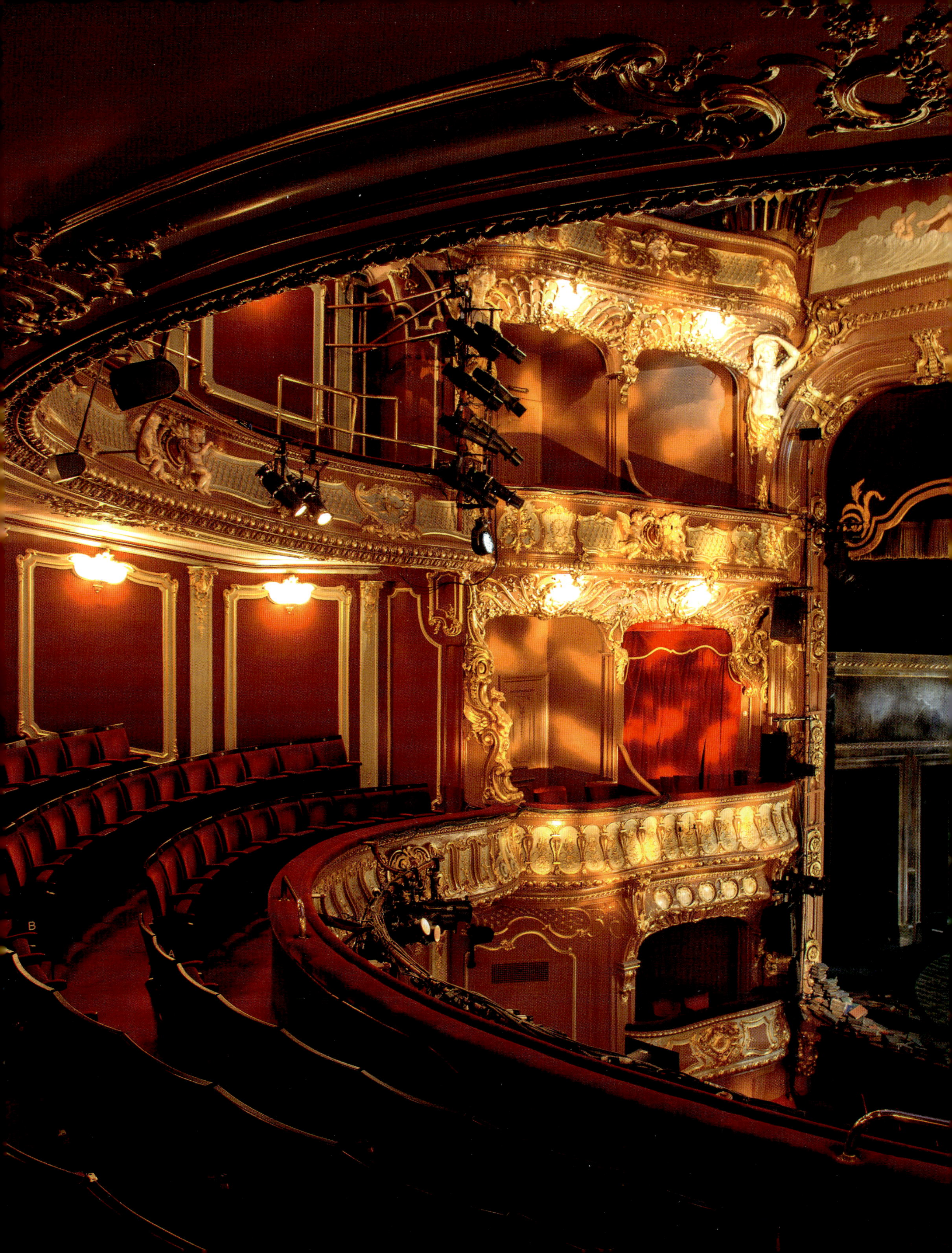

LONDON'S GREAT THEATRES

SIMON CALLOW
AND
DERRY MOORE

To David Drummond,
Theatrical bookseller extraordinaire who kept the flame burning in the heart of the West End for fifty glorious years, and who knows everything in this book much better than its authors.

PRESTEL
MUNICH • LONDON • NEW YORK

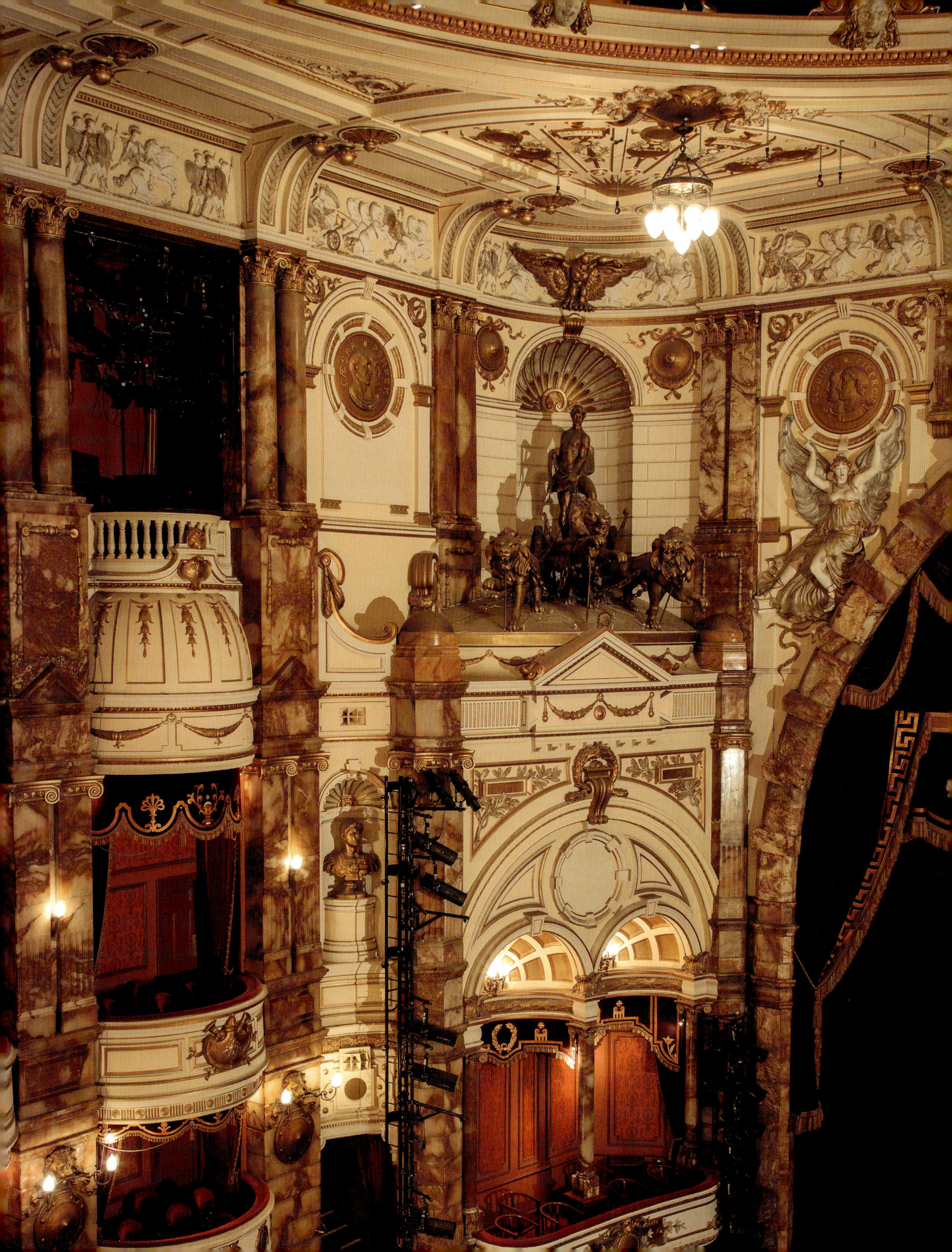

CONTENTS

2–3 The Garrick in the evening, seen from Charing Cross Road.
4–5 View of the National Theatre from Waterloo Bridge.
6 The auditorium of the Apollo Theatre. A feast of red on gold.
OPPOSITE The auditorium of the London Coliseum, showing its hybrid quality.

INTRODUCTION

When Derry Moore told me that he wanted to do a book about London's theatres, I was thrilled. His unique eye, his sense of occasion and responsiveness to atmosphere seemed to me to qualify him perfectly for the task. When he then asked me to provide little introductory texts to each theatre, I was more than thrilled. I have loved the West End, and particularly Theatreland (as it has been known, rather surprisingly, since the mid-nineteenth century), from the time that I was old enough to take a bus from suburban south London on my own and venture all the way up West, as we called it.

I explored the prodigious number of theatres one after another from my vertiginous vantage point in the gods – not a bad place from which to see the auditorium, though not always ideal for seeing the play. What did it matter? It was the atmosphere of each theatre that was so intoxicating, the voluptuousness of their names, the gods and goddesses, nymphs and shepherds that cavorted along the proscenium arches and over domed ceilings, the posters of past productions lining the foyers, the red and the gold, the velvet and the shot silk. I had a strong sense of the history of all these places: I always bought a programme and keenly studied the roll-call of fabled artistes and directors and writers. This meant something to me: I was already familiar with the names of long-vanished performers which my grandmothers could occasionally, if pestered long and hard enough, dredge up from half a century ago.

So when Derry came to me with his innocent invitation to write little introductions to his photographs of the theatres, he unwittingly touched a nerve of some magnitude. His idea was that I would write a few paragraphs about each theatre, a sort of verbal sketch as a complement to his photographs. I thought that this was a splendid notion, easily knocked off in a few days: I'd barely need to consult a book, just trawl through my memories. So off I went, with a spring in my heel, and soon started the first piece – on the Aldwych, as I remember. Almost idly, I started to do a little research. It immediately became apparent that there was a vast amount of information on the subject of these theatres in books and, notably, on the internet, which is teeming with facts, pictures and analysis on the subject.

As I was gulping at the magnitude of what I felt sure was needed, Derry was producing ravishing photographs of the theatres with indecent speed and brilliance. I quickly fell far behind him, but his images focused my mind and relieved me of some of my more grandiose aspirations. Although one would almost by default be telling the story of the British theatre since the return of the Stuarts and the reopening of the theatres after the collapse of the Cromwellian Commonwealth (but not before, since no theatre from Britain's greatest period of theatre, under Elizabeth I and James I, survives), the focus would be on the individual theatres, each of which tells a unique story. The juxtaposition of these stories might create some sort of a developing panorama of what the theatre has been to the city over the last

OPPOSITE Simon Callow, suitably dressed, in a box at the London Coliseum.

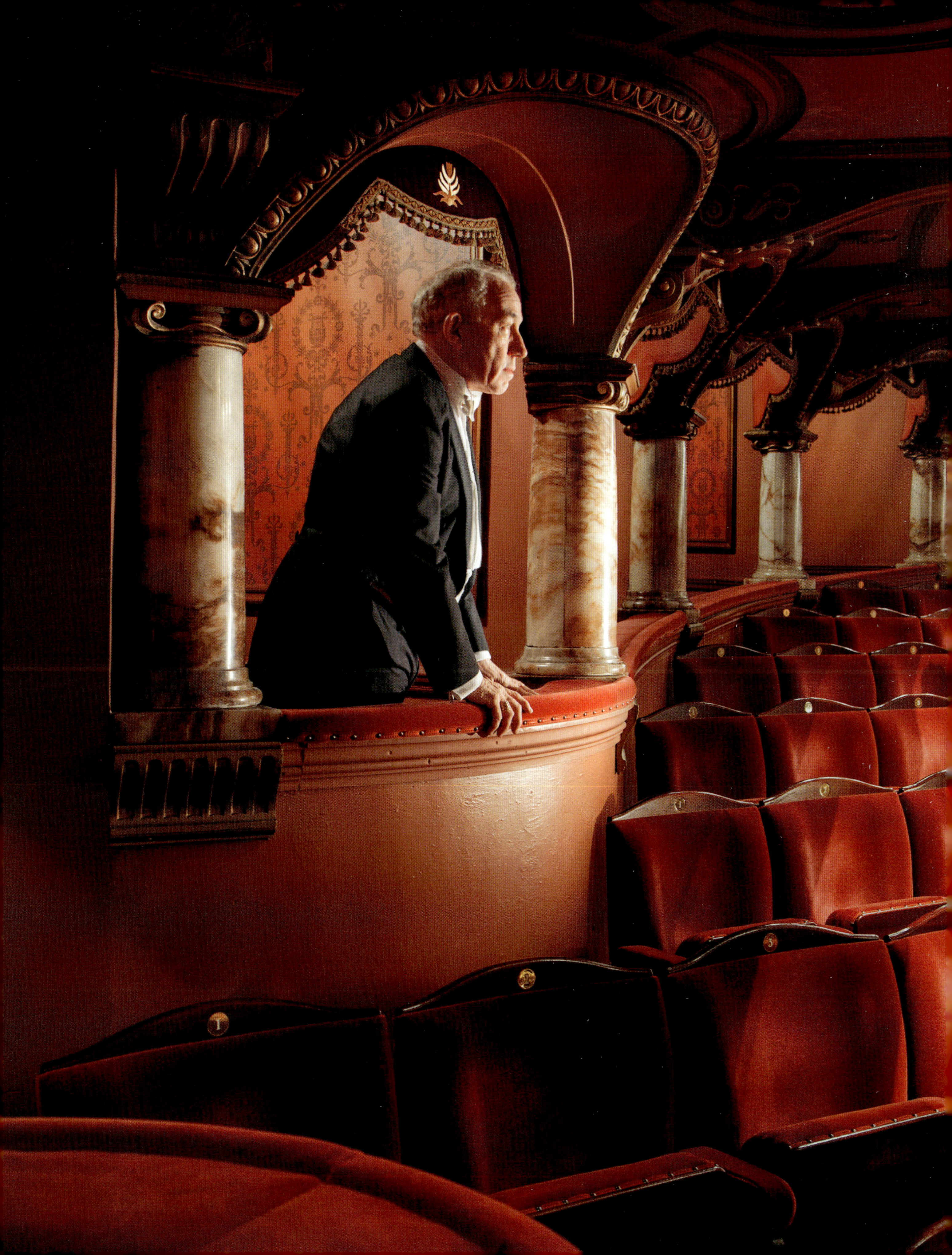

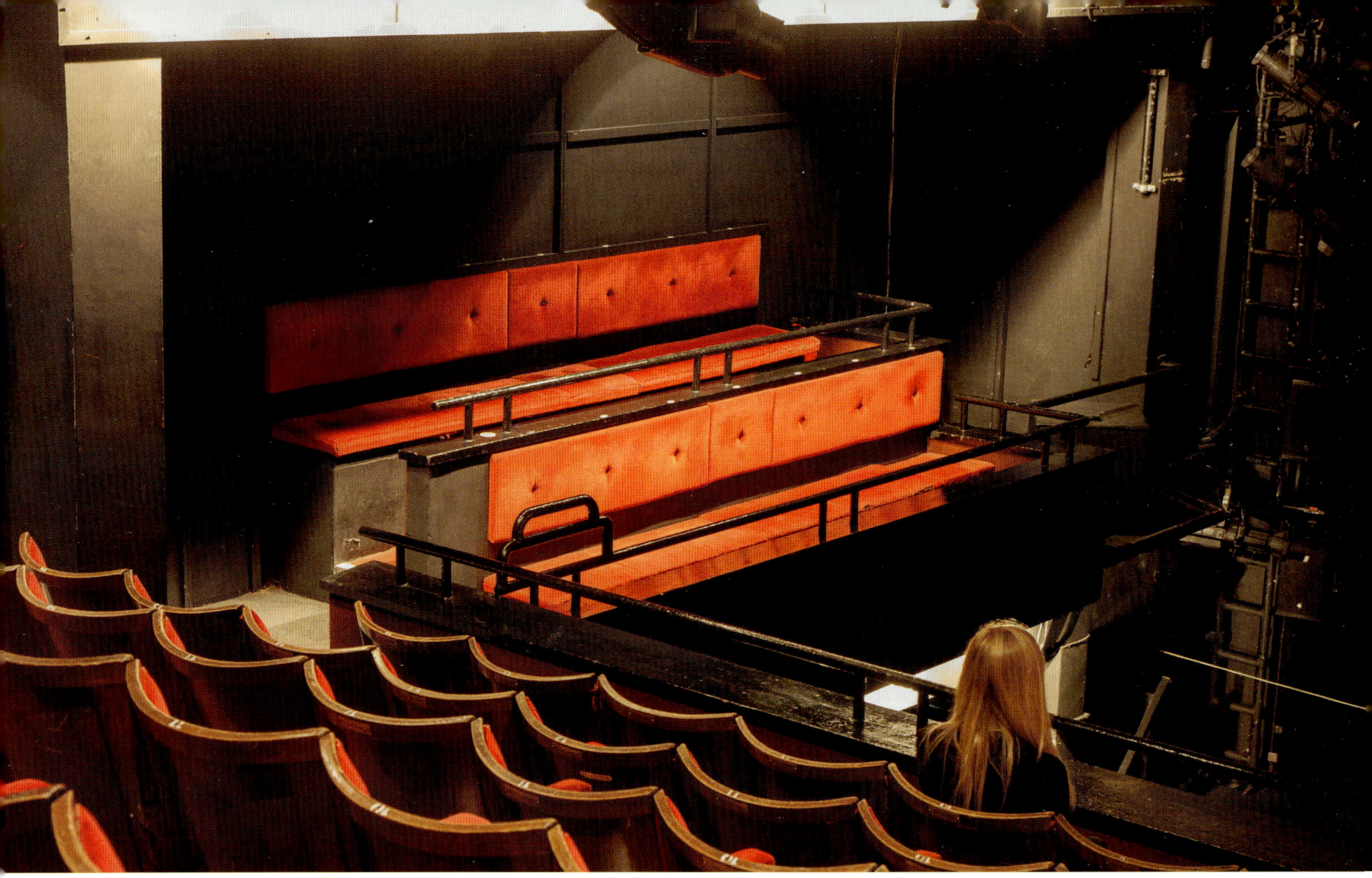

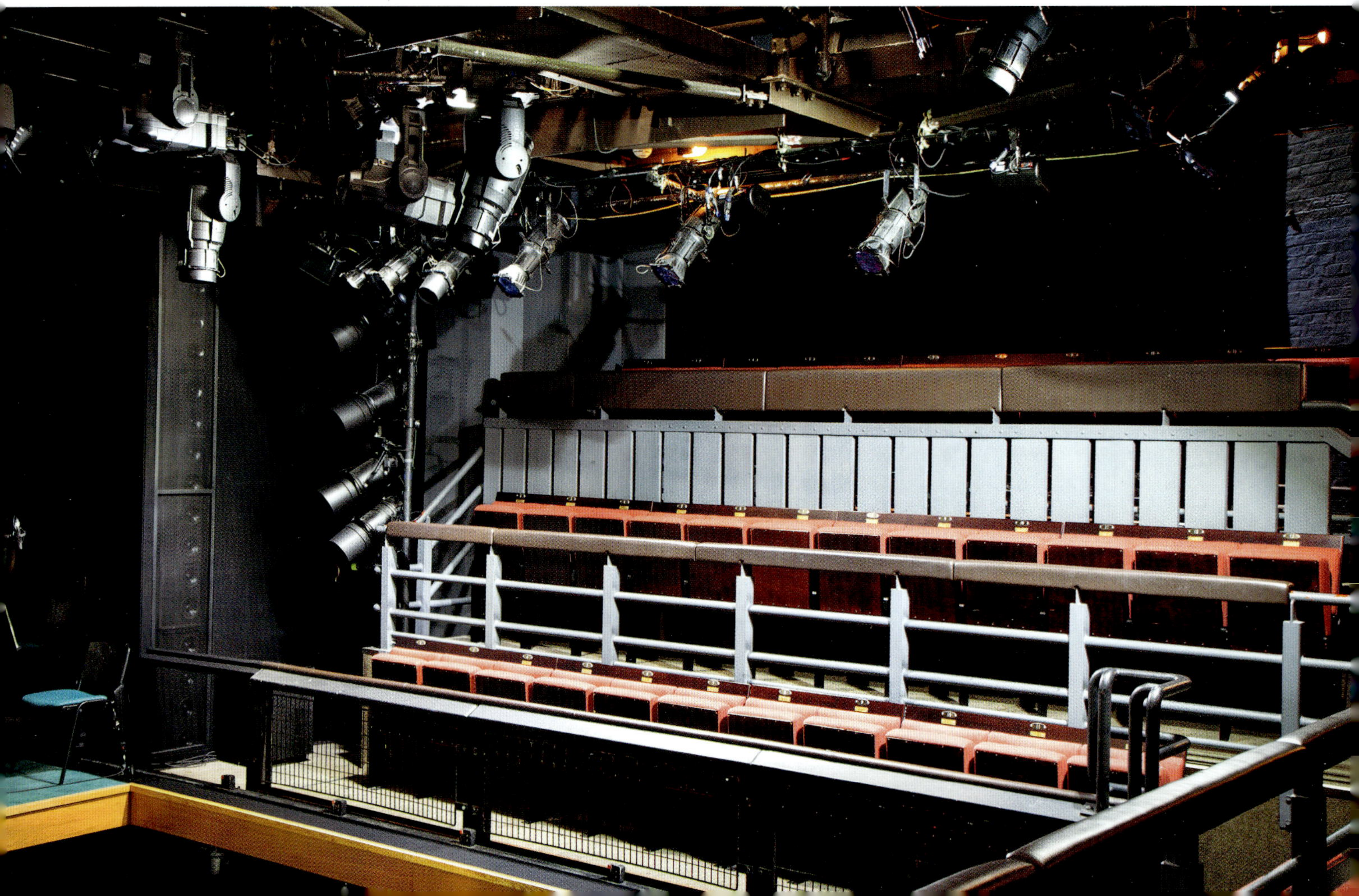

three and a half centuries. Our sequence is chronological, based on when the first theatre on the site was built; some of the great theatre sites have had as many as six playhouses erected on them.

In choosing the theatres we have not attempted to be comprehensive. What we have tried to do is to show the diversity and originality of London's playhouses; when two theatres are very similar in dimensions and character – Wyndham's and the Noël Coward, for example – we have chosen just one; and sometimes we have omitted a theatre because it is visually uninteresting. Into this category falls the tiny Arts Theatre near Leicester Square, whose extraordinary history includes the first English-language production of *Waiting for Godot*, the first male-on-male kiss on the English stage (*A View from the Bridge*), heroic seasons of Shakespeare and Shaw on its tiny stage, and, I may immodestly add, my own *A Christmas Carol*, revived over seven years. But nothing about the physical theatre has the slightest distinction; there is no gesture to it. That is something an audience can ignore, but not something a reader wishes to encounter in a book formed of photographs and descriptive text. We have similarly ignored the Barbican, the Donmar and the former New London, now Gillian Lynne, theatres; the Trafalgar Studios, enterprisingly converted into two auditoria from the old Whitehall Theatre and generating a great deal of new work, has slipped through our net, too. Perversely, perhaps, we have included a theatre that is not in central London at all, but which proved irresistible to write about and to photograph: the Richmond Theatre.

Nonetheless, I hope we have done justice to the range of playhouses in this city, which remain among its greatest glories both to the local population and to visitors. They have never been more popular, despite alarmingly and in some cases opportunistically inflated prices. There remains a constant grumbling groundswell of opinion that insists on their discomfort, their poor sightlines, their cramped foyers and their inadequate hygienic facilities, to say nothing of the lack of parking. Some people feel that they are inherently elitist, favouring the inhabitants of the most expensive seats; others that they impose a faux-genteel tone on what should be a much more easily interactive experience. Designers and directors are often frustrated by the cramped and creaky conditions backstage and indeed onstage. However, it seems that such factors do not outweigh the pleasure that audiences take in the largely nineteenth-century architecture of West End theatres, the promise they engender of something out of the ordinary, the delicious decorative elements scattered about the auditorium and, above all, perhaps, the individual atmosphere of each. This is a matter of design, but even more of history. Theatres, like churches, seem to be able to absorb the emotions uncorked within their purlieus into the very walls. There is a distinct sense, in most London theatres, of a continuing and dynamic residue of the actors and audiences who have filled these spaces over so many years, in fortune and in failure.

It is pleasant to report that London's playhouses are in better shape than they probably ever have been. When Raymond Mander and Joe Mitchenson wrote their classic book *The Theatres of London* in 1961, a strong thread of melancholy ran through it. Theatres were closing all over London, either being demolished or converted into cinemas. In their next volume, *The Lost Theatres of London* (1968), the melancholy had developed into a full-scale lament. The London County Council and later the Greater London Council seemed to be engaged in a vendetta against the theatre, which brought senior members of the profession tottering out onto the streets in protest alongside their younger colleagues. The GLC plan to wipe out the Covent Garden piazza and dozens of surrounding streets, including no fewer than six theatres, was the final outrage; after huge protests from restaurateurs, theatre people and the general public, the plan was shelved, and in the

OPPOSITE Top: The Arts Theatre. Bottom: The Donmar Warehouse. Both theatres are examples of the austerity of late twentieth-century theatrical auditoriums.

fullness of time formal legislation was enacted to protect endangered buildings; almost all West End theatres were immediately listed as either Grade I or Grade II. So they are safe. Many of them are in the hands of a small group of owners, all of whom have proved to be Maecenases, keen, of course, to make a decent living out of their theatres, but equally determined to revitalise them, to restore them if necessary, to make them more accessible and approachable. Nica Burns of Nimax, Cameron Mackintosh of Delfont Mackintosh and Andrew Lloyd Webber have poured vast sums of money into improving their theatres, with scrupulous attention to architectural and decorative authenticity, but without setting them in aspic.

What the theatres have survived is little short of miraculous – fire, crumbling architecture, property speculators, the London County Council. And they have emerged stronger. Each theatre, without exception, has layers of history, which is not an academic fact but a living reality. The builders and managers of these theatres, and the directors and designers and actors who presented the plays in them, were showmen and women, enticing audiences into fantastical grottoes of delight and fantasy where they would be magically connected to other people's lives. They provided spaces where you could leave your everyday concerns at the door, offering a transition from the real world into that other world of imagination, of exploration – of dreams and of nightmares, of the deeply, reassuringly familiar and the shockingly new. These theatres are not sacred spaces, temples; they are the antechambers of art. They prepare you to open yourself to inner worlds that the daily drudge dulls and suppresses. That is what this book celebrates: on the one hand, a huge commercial enterprise, on the other an open sesame to the part of us that is too rarely exercised but which is at our very core. It's an ancient phenomenon, but it has perhaps never in human history been more necessary.

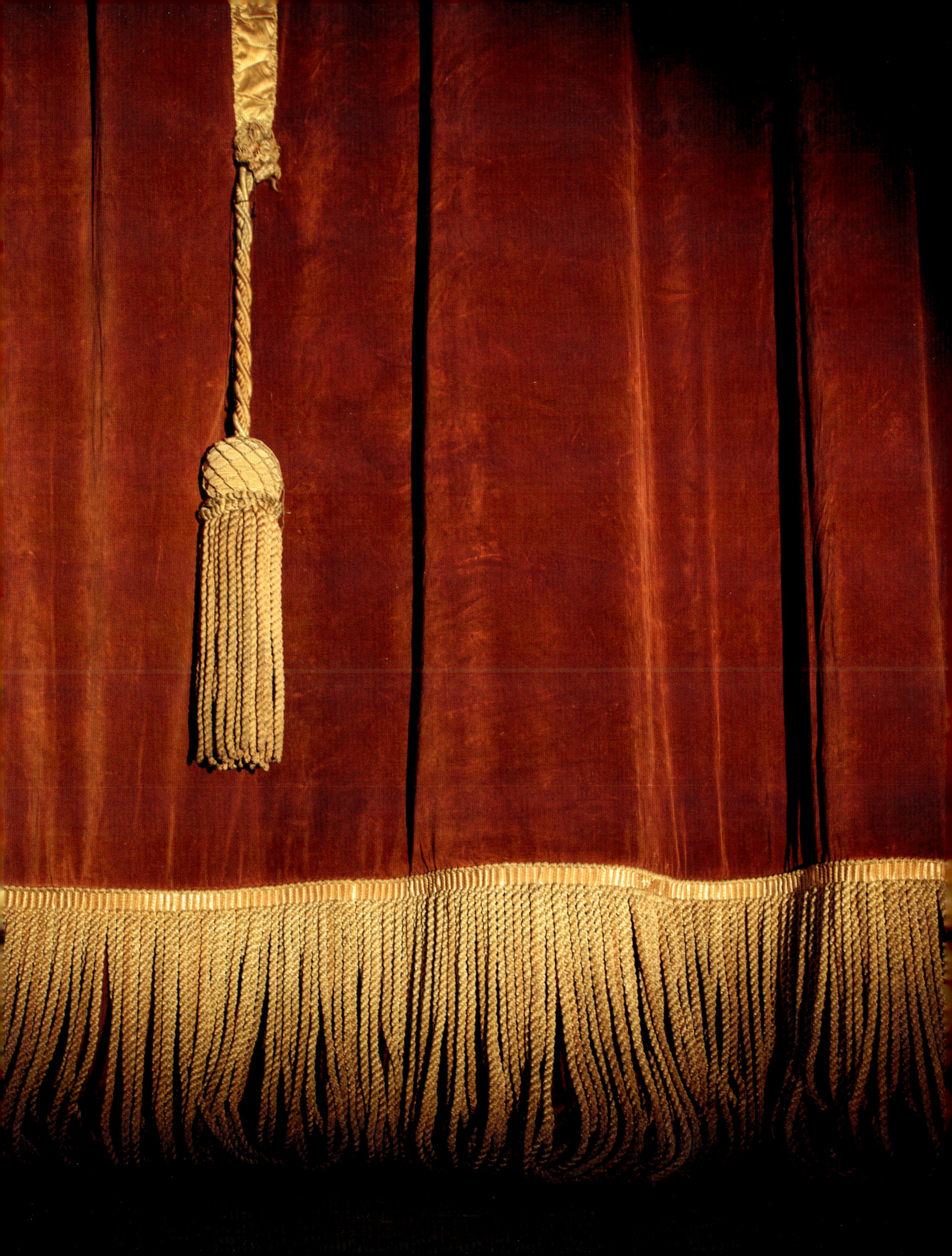

THEATRE ROYAL DRURY LANE

Un peu d'histoire. The Covent Garden area, for over two hundred years the very hub of London theatre, has a history of its own that stretches back to the seventh century and long precedes any theatrical associations. The Romans had departed the area by then, but they had had little regard for it anyway. It suited the Anglo-Saxon hordes very well, however, and they took up residence along the north embankment of the Thames. By the middle of the seventh century, the present Strand and Charing Cross areas had developed into busy trading districts; what we now call Covent Garden became, in the words of the Venerable Bede, 'a market for many peoples coming by land and sea'. This thriving little settlement was wiped out by the ferocious Great Heathen Army at the end of the ninth century when the Vikings descended on London. After their departure the land passed into the possession of Westminster Abbey, just a little downriver, and by the thirteenth century it had developed into the Abbey and Convent Garden, with arable land and orchards.

At the Reformation, the Covent Garden, as it had become known, was seized as part of Henry VIII's land grab of ecclesiastical property and awarded to the king's close associate John Russell. Not long after, Russell was made Earl of Bedford; the land stayed in the Bedfords' possession until the beginning of the twentieth century. They seem to have been somewhat negligent of their property, since Charles I severely upbraided the 3rd Earl for the filth and dangerousness of Long Acre at its north end; the Earl countered with the shrewd suggestion that His Majesty allow him to build on it, which, for the tidy sum of £2,000, he did. The great architect and theatre designer Inigo Jones was duly commissioned to create a piazza in the fashionable Italian manner, with houses and arcades on two sides and a church – St Paul's Covent Garden – on a third, but no sooner was the development completed than England was engulfed in the Civil War. The Puritan Commonwealth seized power in 1649; the king was beheaded. Theatres, which had been officially closed down in 1642, remained so for a further eleven years – until the return of the new king, Charles II, who, restored to his throne, restored the theatres too. The very first to be built was the playhouse that became the Theatre Royal Drury Lane.

'The Theatre Royal, Drury Lane', proclaims the magisterial *Survey of London*, 'is preeminent among all the theatres of London,' and on reflection it is hard to contest its judgement. Its nearly four-hundred-year history, at the centre of almost every development in British theatre before the Second World War, at any rate, would justify the claim. It is gratifying that the present building – the fourth on the site – itself lives up to the *Survey*'s claims. Not necessarily the most beautiful theatre in London, it is certainly the most imposing, its imperious portico with its six chunky columns a massive presence in modest Catherine Street, which at its lower end contains two other theatres, the Novello, on the corner with Aldwych, and the bijou Duchess, which gazes sideways and perhaps slightly nervously at its galumphing big brother up the road. The Novello is not a small theatre, but it is utterly dwarfed by

OPPOSITE The foyer, with statue of David Garrick.

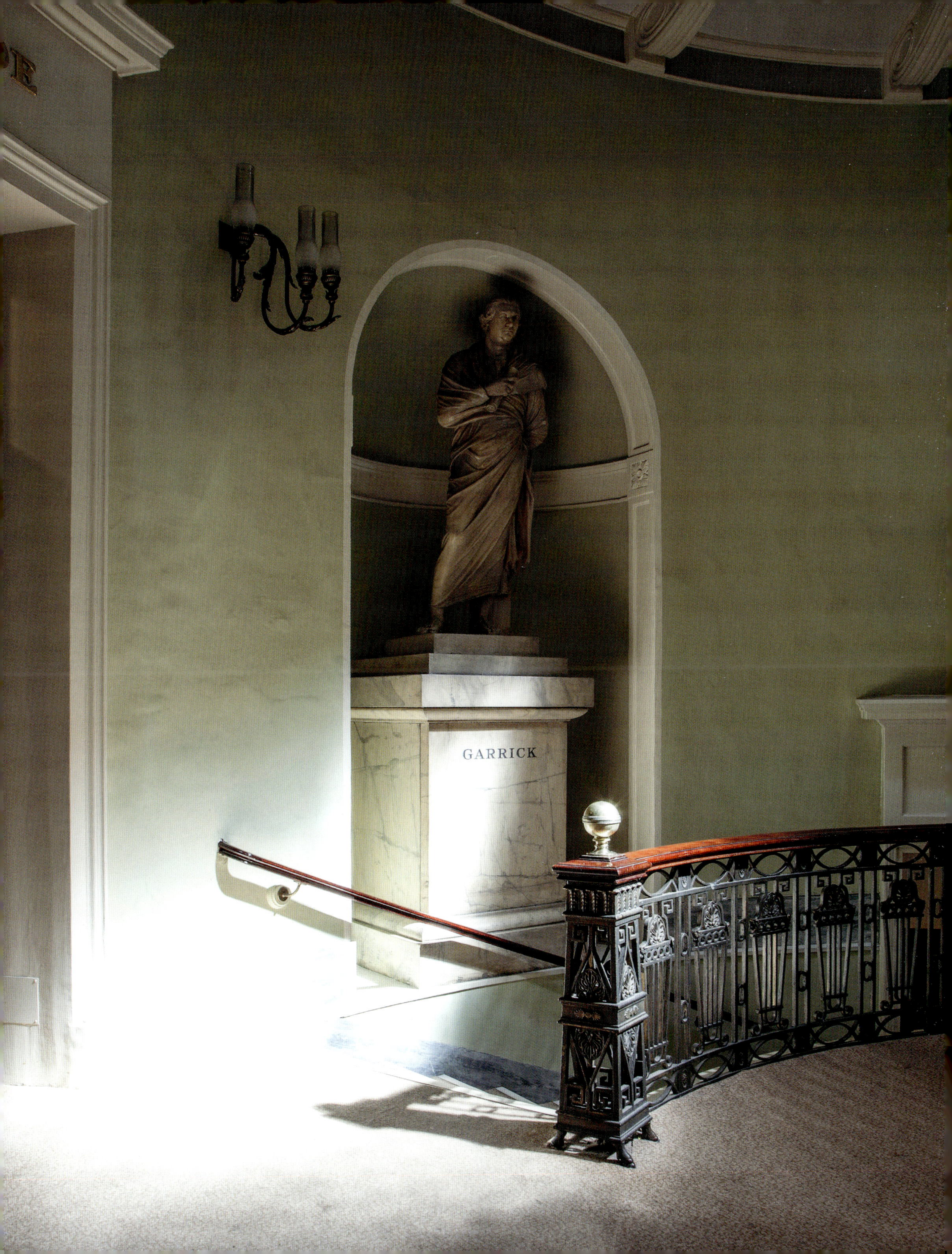
GARRICK

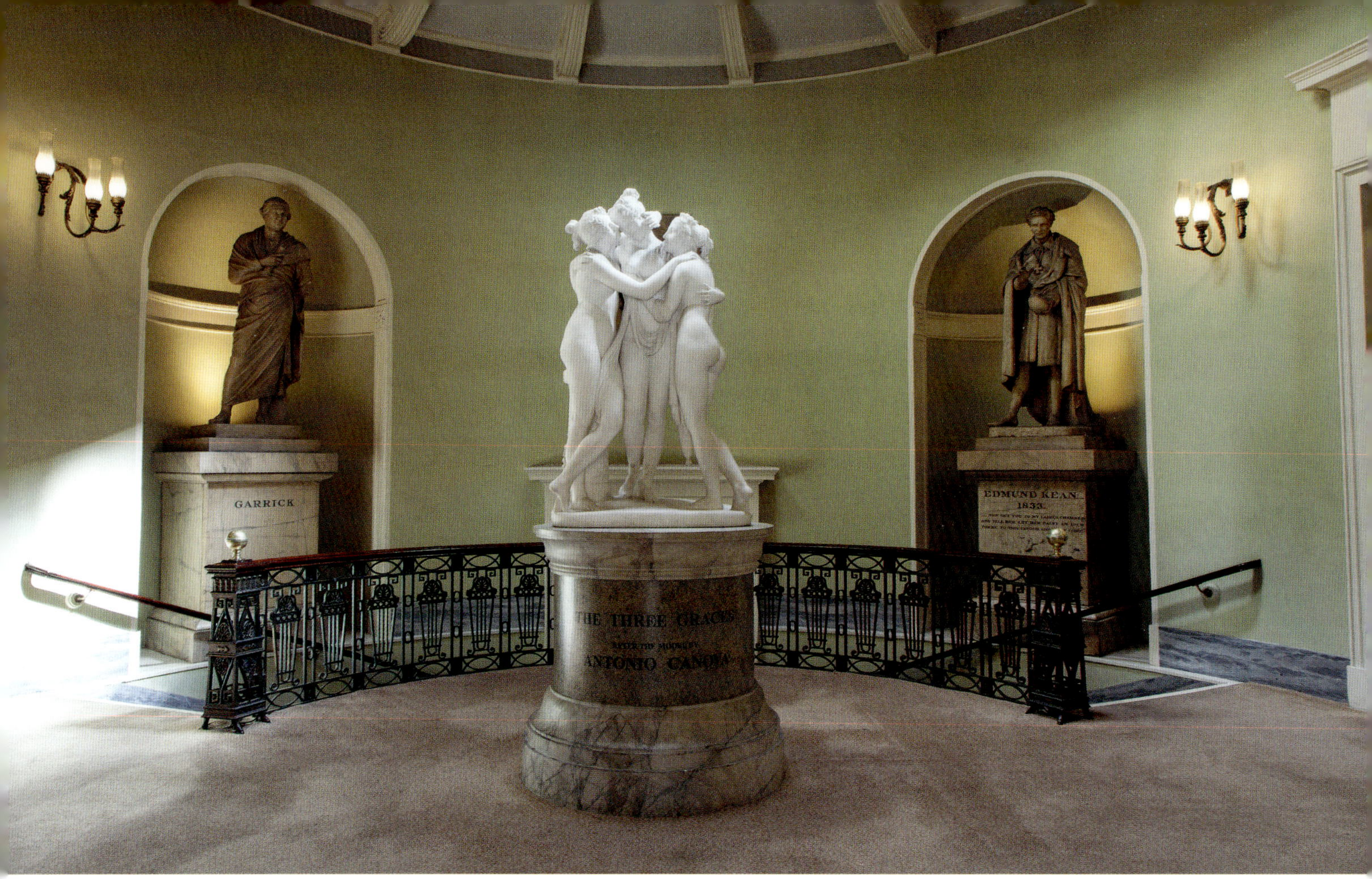

the Theatre Royal, which, stretching all the way back to Drury Lane, is a great warehouse of a building, a warren of extensive paint shops and prop docks and under-stage machinery, a superb and enormous auditorium, and a front of house of unparalleled spaciousness and splendour.

It is all a very far cry from the modest first playhouse on the site, which was built by the rakish Royalist Sir Thomas Killigrew. As a thirteen-year-old Killigrew had been page to Charles I, and later fled to France with Charles II, where he remained during the king's fourteen-year exile; stage-struck since childhood – when he had volunteered as an extra at the Red Bull Theatre in Clerkenwell – he spent his spare time writing plays. When the king was restored to the throne in 1660, theatres, banned under Cromwell's Commonwealth for over a decade, were reopened under royal licence. Killigrew was one of two men issued with letters patent to present plays; the other was Sir William Davenant (a former Poet Laureate and rumoured illegitimate son of Shakespeare). Killigrew was first out of the trap, re-forming the King's Men (Shakespeare's old company; later the King's Company) at Gibbon's Tennis Court in Clare Market and then at his old stamping ground, the Red Bull. Davenant, by contrast, established himself in the rather grander surroundings of Lincoln's Inn Fields, where with his compliant ensemble of young actors, the Duke's Players, he staged Baroque spectacles and operas, as if recreating the world of the old Stuart court. By contrast, Killigrew's company, led by Michael Mohun (according to Samuel Pepys 'the best actor in the world') and the witty comedian Charles Hart, was, as a group, opinionated, temperamental and insistent on proper pay and contracts.

ABOVE The foyer, with Canova's *Three Graces* flanked by statues of David Garrick and Edmund Kean.

It was for this pesky but brilliant crew that Killigrew built The King's Playhouse, in effect the first Theatre Royal, in what was then called Brydges Street (only the lower part of the street was then known as Catherine Street) on land leased from the 5th Earl, later Duke, of Bedford. Sensationally, the company included, for the first time in England, actresses: Elizabeth Boutell, Katherine Corey, Elizabeth Cox, Margaret Hughes, Elizabeth James, Mary Knep, Anne Marshall and, most famous of all, Nell Gwyn, plucked from the lowly ranks of the theatre's orange sellers. In order to train these young women, Killigrew and Hart created what was a drama school in all but name. The effect on the audience of seeing women on the stage for the first time was sensational, and dramatists like William Wycherley and John Dryden as well as Killigrew himself rushed to create roles for them; many of the plays – what we now call Restoration comedies – featured at their centre a 'gay couple': a witty man and woman. As often as not, the couple was played by Hart and Gwynn (by now Hart's mistress). The King's Playhouse, which opened on 7 May 1663, was where so many of these plays, now considered classics, were first performed. The playwrights had to work tirelessly to satisfy demand: a successful play might have a run of no more than three performances.

The theatre itself (which had only 706 seats) was a sort of hybrid between the old open-air theatres like the Red Bull and, before that, the Globe, and the later pre-Commonwealth theatres with scenery and lighting. It was a pop-up theatre, built in a stable-yard in the centre of the block of property bounded by Brydges Street on the west, Russell Street on the north, Drury Lane on the east and Little Brydges Street and Vinegar Yard on the south. Like the old Elizabethan theatres it was roofless, though higher-paying customers were more or less protected by a glass dome (Pepys and his wife once got caught in a heavy downpour, which drenched them). Performances, as in Shakespeare's day, were in the afternoon, at 3 p.m.

The Great Plague of 1665–6 shut the King's Playhouse for over a year, during which time Killigrew seized the opportunity to enlarge the stage; but in 1672 – having six years earlier escaped the Great Fire of London, which was largely confined to the City – the theatre, along with the adjoining houses, burned down. As often, however, this proved a spur to progress: within two years a new playhouse, altogether more sophisticated, was erected; the elegant facade was once thought to have been by Christopher Wren, but this has been discounted. The building was on a vastly bigger scale than its makeshift predecessor, occupying over 13,000 square feet (1,200 sq. m); this time it was bounded to the east by Drury Lane, to the west by Brydges Street, Great Russell Street on the north and Little Russell Street on the south. This huge building meant business, providing working areas for 120 performers, managers and technicians. No fewer than three rooms were allocated to scripts: a library for their storage, a room in which to copy the actors' parts and a second library for music scores, the theatre's account books and ledgers. Nothing like this had ever existed in Britain before, and very little has since; it was a de facto national theatre.

The management of this extraordinarily well-endowed facility was, for most of its existence, chaotic bordering on catastrophic. A succession of managers attempted to make the theatre efficient, alternately cost-cutting and expanding. Actors came and went in high dudgeon; the sons of both Killigrew and Davenant failed as managers, with the younger Davenant fleeing to the Canary Islands to escape being charged with embezzlement. Enter, in 1688, Christopher Rich, a lawyer and 'as sly a Tyrant as ever was at the Head of a Theatre', who caused the actors to decamp en masse: 'No fewer than sixteen (most of the old standing) went away; and with them the very beauty and vigour of the stage; they who were left being for the most part learners, boys and girls, a very unequal match for them that revolted.' Rich staggered on, going from bad to worse and often in defiance of the law, his regime

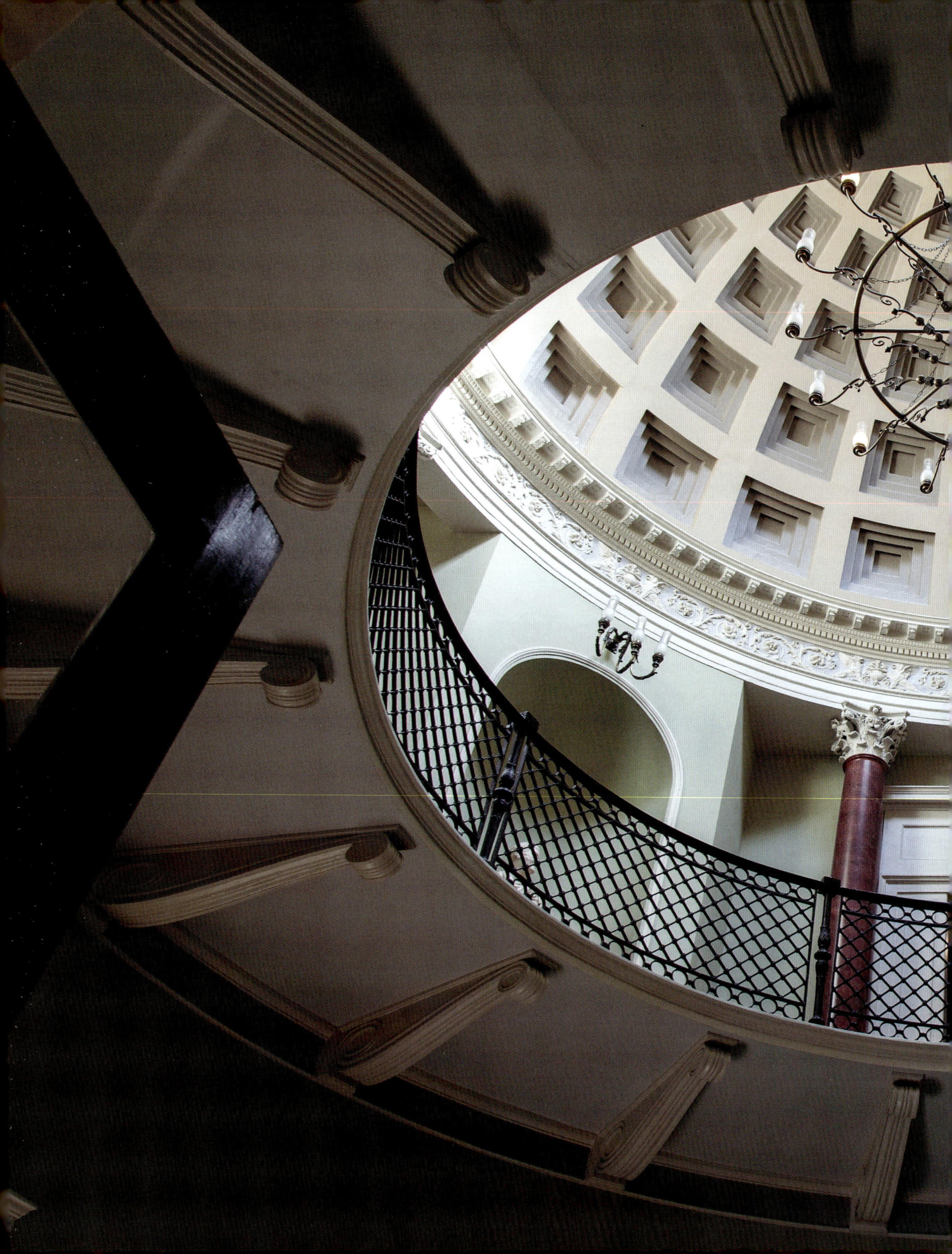

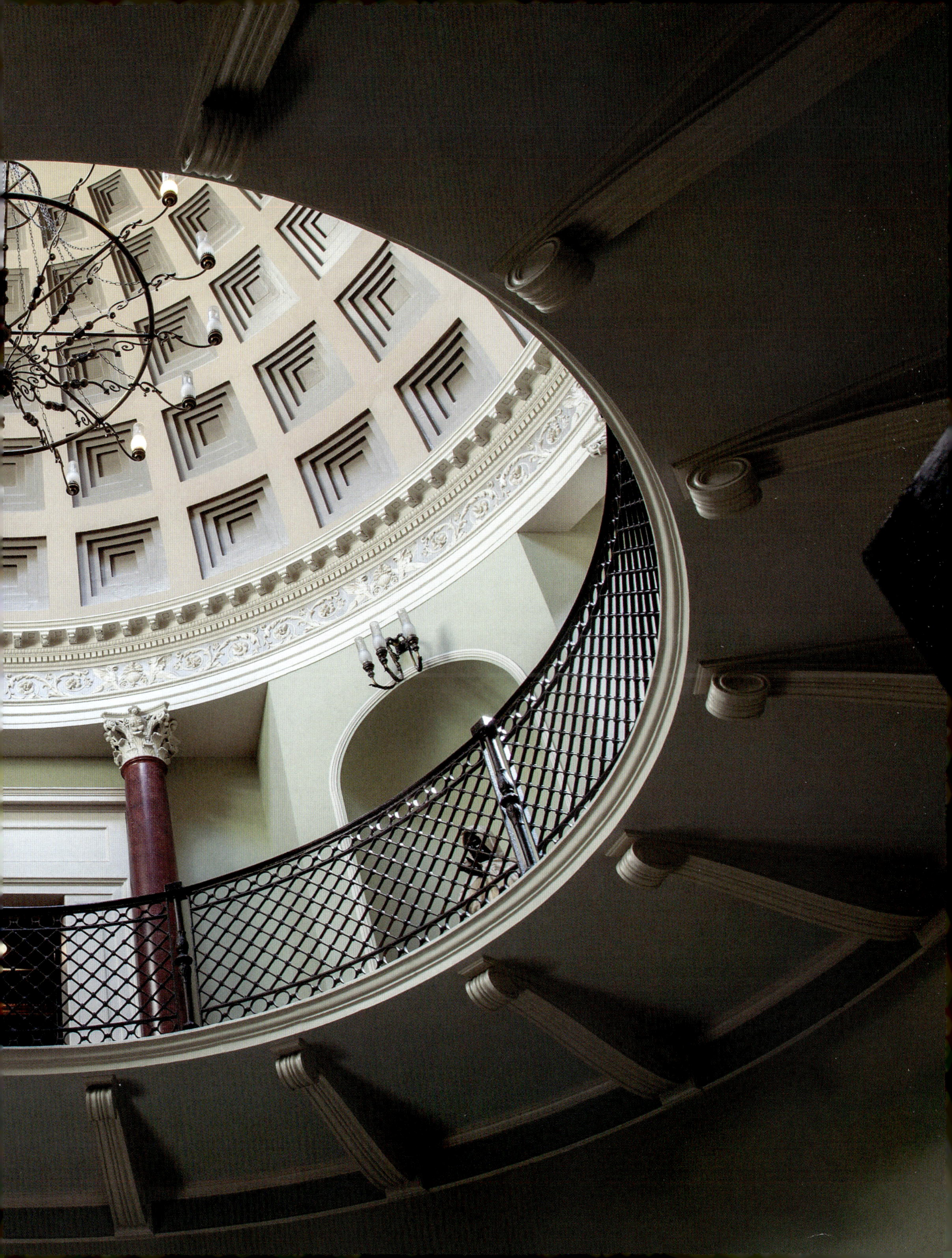

lasting for sixteen years, until an exasperated Lord Chamberlain transferred the licence to a certain William Collier, Tory MP for Truro and 'a lawyer of an enterprizing Head, and a jovial Heart'. Starting as he meant to go on, a day or so later Collier 'enterprizingly' showed up at the theatre 'with a Corporal and divers Soldiers armed with swords and Musquett[s and] in a riotous and violent manner broke open the Doors of the s[ai]d Theatre and turned out Mr Rich's servants . . . declareing that he took possession of the s[ai]d Theatre for himself'. Collier duly became manager, until the accession of the Whig-favouring Queen Anne made his leadership no longer helpful.

While all these managerial shenanigans were going on, plays somehow reached the stage and actors somehow acted in them. An early triumph, in 1696, was John Vanbrugh's *The Relapse*, in a genre somewhere between the outrageously uninhibited plays of the period immediately following the reopening of the theatres and the rather more sentimental ones of the early eighteenth century. Colley Cibber had his greatest triumph as Vanbrugh's Lord Foppington and for a while, in a triumvirate with two fellow actors, managed the theatre itself, until he lost the actors' confidence and was succeeded by the nobly-born Charles Fleetwood, who spent the last of his inheritance in buying the theatre's patent and then gambled away any profits that it might have made. Nonetheless, Fleetwood made some shrewd decisions, among them hiring the ferocious Ulster actor Charles Macklin, who in 1741 astounded the town with his portrait of Shylock, 'the Jew that Shakespeare drew'; that the actor's intensity was not feigned was conclusively proved when, during a backstage argument over a wig, he thrust a cane into a fellow actor's face, driving it through his eye and into his brain; the actor died. Astonishingly, Macklin was not imprisoned and continued to thrill and alarm audiences in Catherine Street for some years.

PREVIOUS The coffered dome over the foyer.

After the unprecedented outpouring of new plays in the last decades of the old century, the classics began to get a look in again. Apart from anything else, they did not require the Lord Chamberlain's approval; the draconian Licensing Act of 1737 curbed dramatists both politically and morally and drove many playwrights either to journalism or novel-writing. New drama went to sleep for over a hundred years; spectacle became the dominant mode, and Drury Lane was to be its principal forum. That and Shakespeare.

In 1747, after Fleetwood gambled his last, the thirty-year-old David Garrick – a protégé of Macklin's, though as different from him as both actor and man as could be imagined – took over Drury Lane, transforming standards there as well as astonishing the town with his own mercurial and startlingly lifelike performances. Tiny, unremarkable either facially or physically, but infinitely expressive, witty and inventive, he was famed across Europe, the first British actor to be taken seriously as an intellectual and as an arbiter of taste. He was, indeed, the inventor of modern acting, physically flexible and psychologically credible. It was Garrick as much as anyone who secured Shakespeare's reputation as the supreme genius of the English language (albeit in truncated and often rewritten versions of the plays); when he took over the theatre, he proclaimed it the House of Shakespeare. After his over a quarter of a century of management, he left it larger and more beautiful than he found it, transforming the auditorium by commissioning the brothers Robert and James Adam to renovate the interior in exquisite taste.

His farewell, in 1774, was a stupendous affair: not just *le tout théâtre* but *le tout Londres* was there – everybody of any account. For his last performance on that stage, Garrick did not reprise any of his great roles – many of which he had played during his last season – but revived a comedy, Susanna Centlivre's wildly popular *The Wonder! A Woman Keeps a Secret*, in which he played, for the umpteenth time, the jealous Don Felix. The play over, Garrick stepped forward. 'This is to me a very awful moment,' he

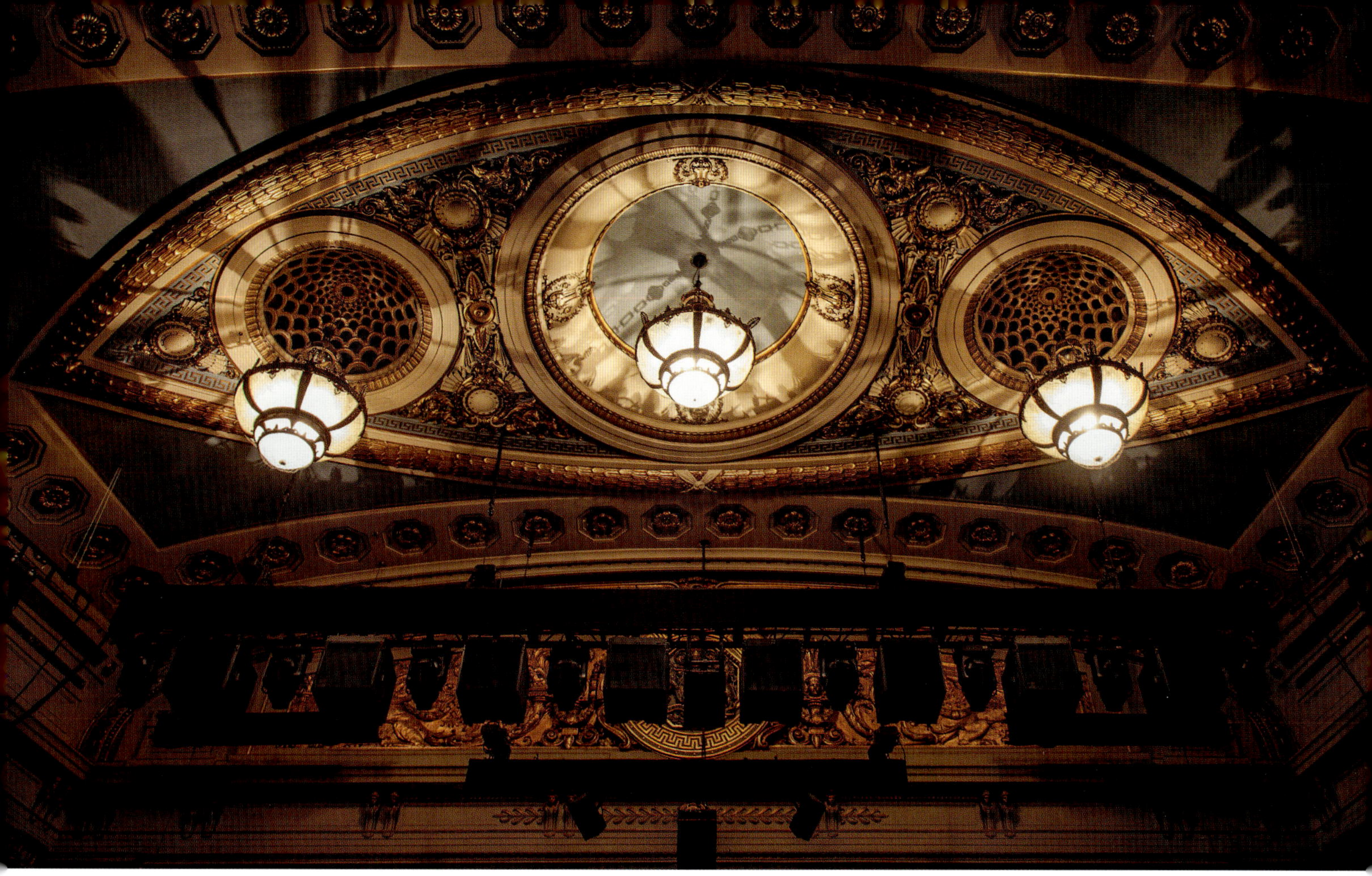

said. 'It is no less than a parting forever with those from whom I have received the greatest kindness, and upon the spot where that kindness and your favours were enjoyed.' As his friend and biographer Arthur Murphy wrote, 'Every face in the theatre was clouded with grief; tears gushed in various parts of the house, and all concurred in one general demonstration of sorrow. The word, farewell, resounded from every quarter amidst the loudest bursts of applause.'

When he left, Garrick sold his shares to Richard Brinsley Sheridan, another giant name in the history of the British theatre to be intimately associated with Drury Lane. Two of his greatest hits were first produced there, *The School for Scandal* and *The Critic*; and among the innumerable actors he employed was the eight-year-old Joey Grimaldi, who would later feature largely in the annals of the Lane, as it was commonly and affectionately known.

But the days of the old theatre were numbered, and in 1791 Sheridan supervised its demolition, commissioning the fashionable architect Henry Holland to design a stupendous new playhouse on an unexampled scale. The well-connected apostle of neoclassicism faithfully realised his client's grandiose aspirations for it. Opening in March 1794, it was, the theatre claimed, 'on a larger scale than any other theatre in Europe'; indeed, apart from churches, it was the tallest building in London.

The theatre proudly flourished its royal endorsement: the partitions of the stage box, occupied by the king and queen, were taken down and it was brought forward nearly two feet; a canopy was erected, superbly decorated with crimson velvet richly embroidered with gold, and adjoining the

ABOVE Detail of the ceiling above the proscenium arch in the auditorium – note the lamps and the ornate details.

royal couple sat their royal daughters. This box was unusually lined with light blue satin, 'fancifully festooned and elegantly decorated with silver fringe and rich tassels', very different from the rest of the auditorium. Its prominence and openness made it a perfect sitting target, and on the evening of 15 May 1800, someone in the audience took a pot shot at George III. Another member of the audience jostled the would-be assassin, causing him narrowly to miss his target; the king, apparently unfazed, ordered the show to continue.

The interior of the theatre was in horseshoe form and the prevailing colours of the boxes were blue and white, relieved with richly fancied embellishments. In the centre of the compartments into which the front of each tier was divided was a highly finished cameo, the ground of carnelian colour with exquisitely drawn figures from Ovid raised in white; the stage boxes had raised silver latticework of excellent taste and workmanship. Sixteen pillars in the Doric style, beautifully painted in imitation of porphyry, supported the back boxes, at each end of which a flight of stairs led to the foyer. It was all of the utmost splendour. But none of this was of the slightest consequence unless the theatre served its primary function of staging plays to the satisfaction of the audience, and here the theatre faltered. In commissioning the theatre, Sheridan and his fellow investors had been convinced of a very simple proposition: that the more people the theatre could hold, the greater the profit. This proposition was flawed in two important ways: first, was there audience enough to fill the theatre? And second, was the relationship between the audience and the stage satisfactory? The auditorium held 3,600 people, the vast majority of them seated a very long way away from the actors, who were not best pleased with the new theatre. 'A wilderness of a place', the great Sarah Siddons called it, and in 1803 she and her brother, the equally great John Philip Kemble, walked out.

As if it had irked the gods by its over-ambition, this stupendous monolith of a theatre burned to the ground on 24 February 1809, a mere fifteen years after its opening. One of its most vaunted features had been one of the first 'iron' or safety curtains, fitted with water tanks above; Drury Lane was, the builders boasted, 'A Fireproof Theatre'. More hubris: Sheridan lost everything as a result of the fire. Legend has it that he watched the conflagration from the street with a bottle in his hand. 'A man', he is said to have remarked, 'may surely be allowed to take a glass of wine by his own fireside', which *si non è vero, è molto ben trovato.* His personal wit, his genius as a playwright and his shrewdness as a statesman (as an MP he had been successively Chancellor of the Duchy of Cornwall and Treasurer of the Navy) were not matched by financial acumen: the building had cost twice the estimated £80,000 and Sheridan had personally to bear the cost of the overspend. It ruined him. His friend Samuel Whitbread, the brewer, headed a committee to rebuild the theatre. In his search for investors, Whitbread had only one condition: 'The Question asked before any Man or Woman will put down their Names', wrote Whitbread, 'is this: "Has Mr Sheridan anything to do with it?" A direct negative suffices.' Whitbread proved enormously effective as chairman, and the new theatre – substantially the one that today sits so massively in Catherine Street – opened in 1812 (the same year that poor Sheridan lost his parliamentary seat; he became ill and four years later died, debt-ridden and disappointed).

The magnificent new theatre was designed by Benjamin Dean Wyatt, a late starter at the age of 32, though descended from a family of architects. Before long he was at heart of the establishment as Surveyor of the Fabric of Westminster Abbey from 1813 to 1827; a few years later he was responsible for the Duke of York Column just off The Mall. Wyatt's design for the Theatre Royal preceded both of these, the result of a competition which he effortlessly won. It was his first important commission, and he was acutely mindful of the responsibility; he later wrote a book about it, which he called *Observations on the Design for the Theatre Royal, Drury Lane* (1813). Everything in his design was calculated to be as

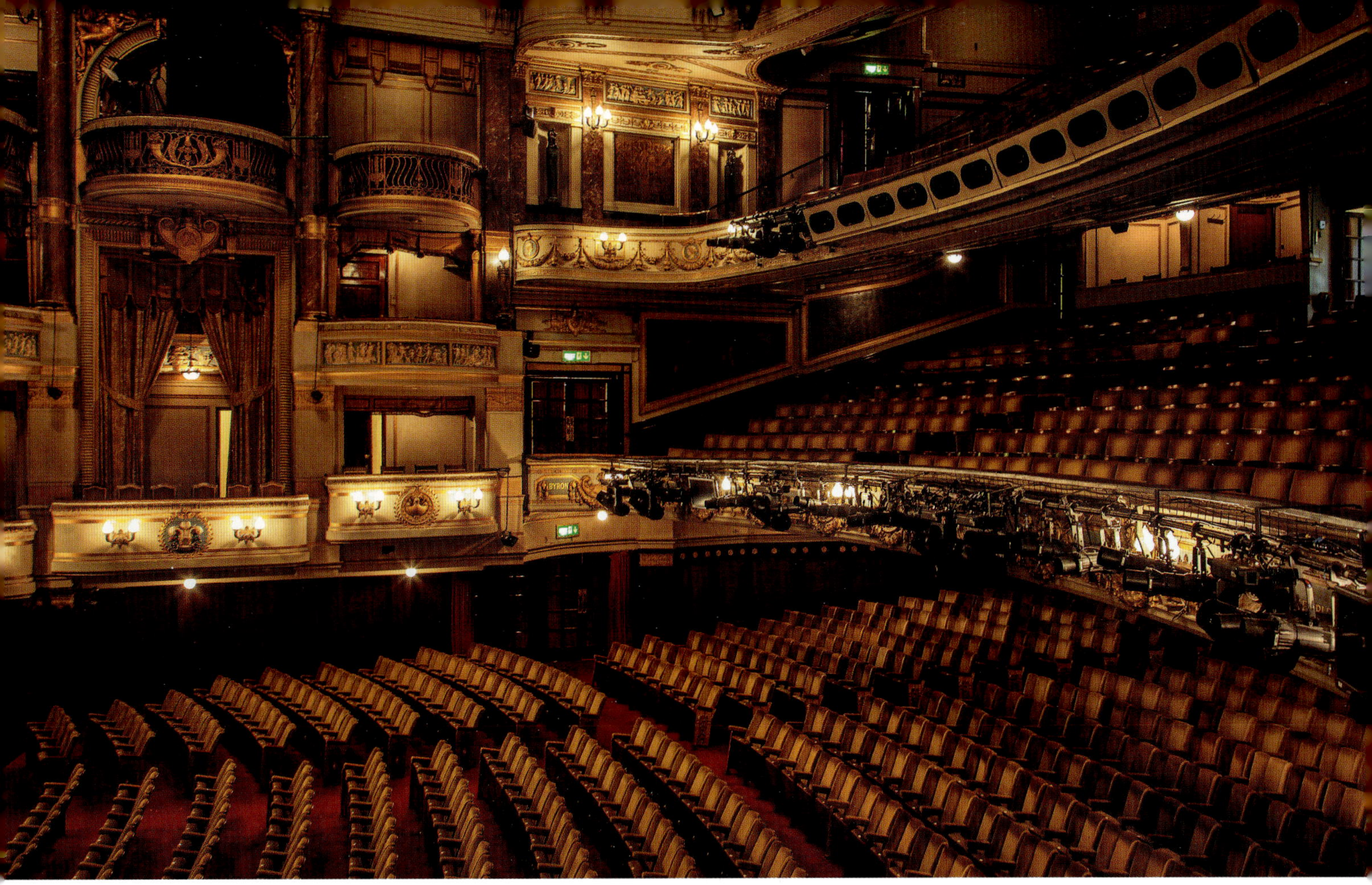

impressive as possible. Once past the majestic facade (not yet fitted with the distinctive portico, which was added in 1820) the audience moved into a foyer in high neoclassical style, suggesting a temple rather than a theatre; tripod altar lamps were artfully placed by the columns. There were three doorways, the middle one opening on to the rotunda, the north on to the king's staircase and the south on to the Prince of Wales's; a cast of Peter Scheemakers's then famous statue of Shakespeare reinforced the high seriousness of the proceedings. The auditorium itself – based partly on that of the theatre at Bordeaux, supposed to have the best acoustics in Europe – astonished contemporaries: 'It is indeed a magnificent object,' said Henry Crabb Robinson, 'The Proscenium is the most splendid scene I ever beheld.' It was decorated to within an inch of its life, but, observed Robinson, it would be absurd to reproach an architect with making a theatre too gorgeous: 'Let the prison be dry and rude so as to excite a sense of severity, let the temple and the hall of justice be majestically simple, but the public theatre should be pompous and profusely adorned.' Wyatt certainly obliged.

ABOVE The auditorium of the Theatre Royal Drury Lane.

The new theatre was smaller than its predecessor by some five hundred seats (this one seating a mere 3,060). The stage, too, was narrower and less deep, for reasons of economy – less decor and fewer performers would be required to fill it; this proved to be a misjudgement and was corrected. But acoustics and sightlines were better, despite the banishment of the galleryites to a far distant location very near the roof. This was not accidental. Wyatt had an agenda, which he spells out in his *Observations*: he wanted, he says, to 'spare the more rational and respectable class of Spectators from those nuisances to which they have long been

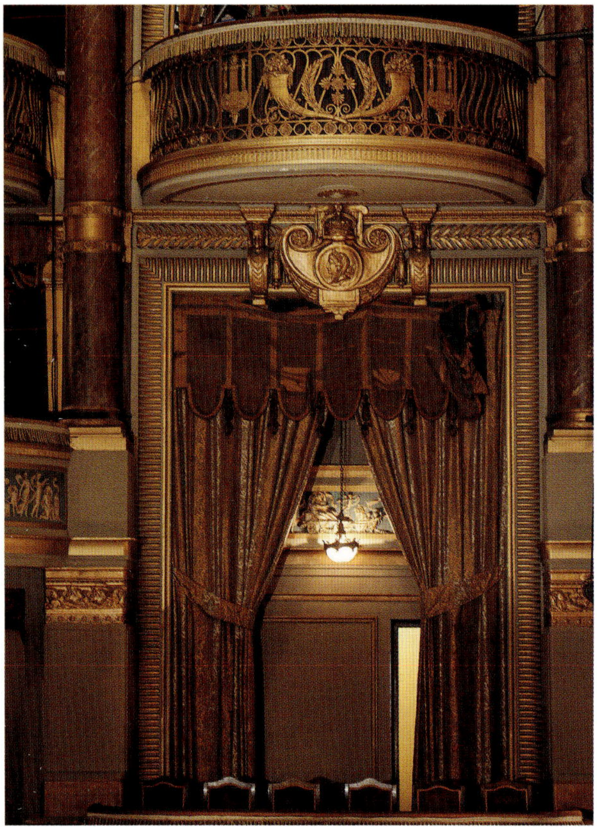

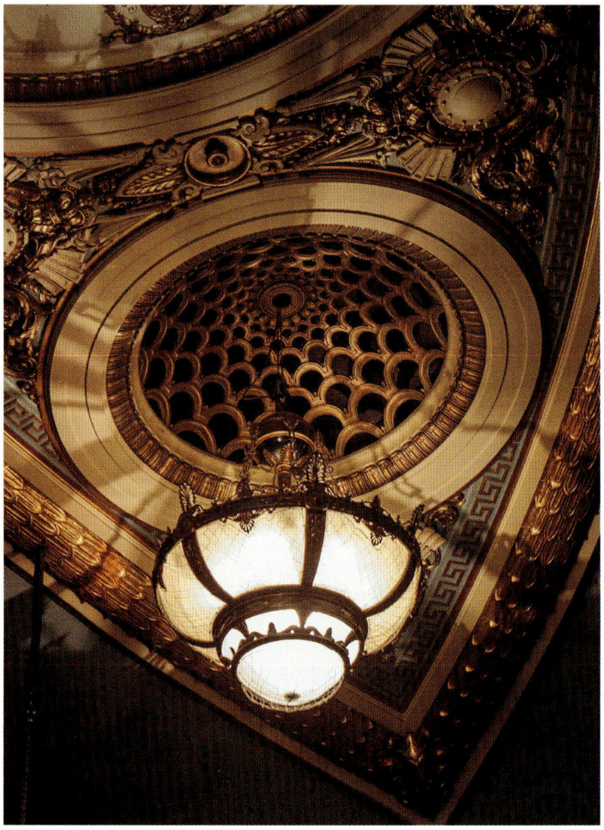

exposed, by being obliged to pass through Lobbies, Rooms, and Avenues, crowded with the most disreputable Members of the Community, and subject to scenes of the most disgusting indecency'. Knowing that it would be virtually impossible to keep the raffish element from mingling with the better class of theatregoer, he configured the entrances to the various parts of the house so as to exclude 'those whom it was desirable to exclude, without any declared intention of doing so'.

This little piece of social engineering was confirmed by the grandiose opening on 10 October 1812. It featured a poem by Byron that recollected in somewhat idealised terms the conflagration of the old theatre:

ABOVE LEFT The royal box.
ABOVE RIGHT Detail of one of the lamps in the auditorium.

> In one dread night our city saw, and sigh'd,
> Bow'd to the dust, the Drama's tower of pride;
> In one short hour beheld the blazing fane,
> Apollo sink, and Shakespeare cease to reign.

Would this 'new, nor less aspiring pile', Byron demanded, 'Know the same favour which the former knew / A shrine for Shakespeare – worthy him and *you*?' Byron thought it would:

> The curtain rises – may our stage unfold
> Scenes not unworthy Drury's days of old!
> Britons our judges, Nature for our guide,
> Still may we please – long, long may *you* preside.

This noble prologue was followed by a (severely cut) performance of *Hamlet*, in which Robert Elliston played the Danish prince, and the evening was rounded off with a merry ballad opera by the Irish playwright Charles Coffey, *The Devil to Pay; or, The Wives Metamorphosed*.

Almost immediately, it all started to go horribly wrong. On the verge of bankruptcy, the desperate amateur committee decided to take a gamble on a diminutive but astonishingly intense 27-year-old actor called Edmund Kean, into whose short life an extraordinary amount of experience had already been packed, all of which contributed to his unique performing personality and his alarmingly uncompromising manner. He made his debut at Drury Lane in January 1814 when his electrifying Shylock in *Merchant of Venice* astounded the audience, rapidly followed by equally shocking performances in *Richard III, Hamlet*, *Othello*, *Macbeth* and *King Lear*; their realism and force of emotion rendered the splendid classical interpretations of the reigning monarch of the stage, John Philip Kemble, hopelessly stylised and marmoreal. Among Kean's ecstatic audiences were Jane Austen, who had found it very hard to get tickets at all, and Byron, who, it was said, experienced convulsions during the actor's performance as Sir Giles Overreach in Philip Massinger's drama *A New Way to Pay Old Debts* (1625).

Despite these huge successes, the committee began making wayward decisions. A mere six years after the grand opening, dissatisfaction with Wyatt's magnificent auditorium led to its redecoration in the Prince of Wales's favoured chinoiserie, the first of many stages in the more or less continuous evolution of the building over the following hundred years. The nervous committee decided that it had better lease out the theatre: Kean put in a bid but was turned down because he proposed, according to the secretary of the committee, 'to exclude all the committee from interference or access to the Theatre, except through the money-taker – no Green room Loungers'. Jane Austen's favourite actor, Robert Elliston, was approved, largely, it seems, because he allowed the right of nightly free admission to 653 persons – nearly 25 per cent of the house. Elliston's reign was undistinguished, but he was responsible, in 1820, for erecting the present monumental and rather graceless portico, designed by Sir John Soane.

In the desperate quest for novelty, the theatre was in a state of regular rebuilding. In 1822, still under Elliston's management, Samuel Beazley entirely reconstructed the auditorium, banishing the chinoiserie and largely returning it to Wyatt's classical scheme; the original statues of the muses Melpomene (tragedy) and Thalia (comedy) were restored and panels of scenes from Shakespeare added. Light was provided by two tiers of fourteen candle-lit glass balls and, hanging from the centre of the ceiling, a very large gas-lit one in lotus form. At first the prevailing colours of the decorations were warm drab infused with dark red and highly enriched with gold, but three years later this was modified, the ground colour changed to white; the Shakespearean panels were replaced with others of inferior design, and the crimson furnishings of the boxes were replaced by green.

Elliston went bankrupt in 1826; his successor, an American, Stephen Price, ran the theatre from 1826 to 1830, but, as a member of the committee pithily observed, Price's 'want of Theatrical Knowledge soon brought him to a Stand Still'. The game of musical chairs continued through the rest of the century, as did the refurbishing of the theatre; interior decorators must have blessed the very name of Drury Lane. After Price's exit the theatre was given another facelift and an elegant colonnade was erected facing Russell Street; Alfred Bunn assumed proprietorship and in 1836–7 duly effected yet another transformation of the interior, this time modelled on Raphael's corridors in the Apostolic Palace of the Vatican – somewhat incongruously, because under Bunn the prevailing mixture of English opera and circus acts began heavily to favour the latter. Bunn, said a correspondent in a letter to the *Sunday Times*, 'had *disgraced* the boards of Drury Lane Theatre by converting it into a *bear-garden*' and had 'subsequently *dishonoured* it by causing it to be designated the shilling theatre'. A block of five

£100 shares, which would have entitled the owner to free admission for life, could fetch only 35 guineas at auction.

There were brief upturns in quality, including appearances by Dickens's favourite, William Macready, and by Samuel Phelps, the great Shakespeare reformer, but the theatre was rarely admired during this period. Nothing for it, then, but another refurbishment, which was effected in 1847 under instructions from Frederick Gye, more famously associated with the Royal Opera House. In this instance he was acting as manager for the rock-star hyper-conductor Louis-Antoine Jullien – or Louis George Maurice Adolphe Roch Albert Abel Antonio Alexandre Noé Jean Lucien Daniel Eugène Joseph-le-Brun Joseph-Barême Thomas Thomas Thomas-Thomas Pierre Arbon Pierre-Maurel Barthélémi Artus Alphonse Bertrand Dieudonné Emanuel Josué Vincent Luc Michel Jules-de-la-plane Jules-Bazin Julio César Jullien, to give him his full name. The bearer of all this nomenclature had great flair, purveying his own light classics as well as more substantial work, and he had the discrimination to invite Hector Berlioz to conduct his own music in the theatre; both men had a huge success.

Clearly, the redecoration had for once not been merely cosmetic. 'The theatre has been cleansed throughout,' said the *Illustrated London News*, 'a labour as requisite here as in the Augean stable of old.' The focus was on light: 'The inner circle of the ceiling . . . is painted to imitate a cloudless sky; around the circle are jets of gas, and, from an aperture in the centre, hangs a vast chandelier of cut glass; the aperture is wreathed, and around it are six winged boys, bearing festoons of flowers, in effect supporting the lustre. The main design of the latter is six flags, of drops, with the lines of the union-Jack marked on each by light. There is also a profusion of drops, in large tassels, festoons, and garlanded forms, too various to describe. The effect of the whole, when lighted, is remarkably brilliant. Around the dress and first circles, are also hung small lustres, with the gas lights in ground-glass shades.' All this was considered very state of the art: 'The whole of the ornaments – mouldings, fruit and flowers – are of papier-mâché, and were made, gilt, and fixed by Mr Bielefeld, in five weeks; the manufacture involving an extraordinary application of the steam-engine to decorative art.'

Alas, all this highly modern splendour was squandered on the circus. From 1851, Drury Lane became the home of noted equestrian acts; a despairing editorial in the *Illustrated London News* remarked that 'If the highest dramatic poetry be necessarily banished from the Drury Lane stage, owing to the fault of the proprietary . . . we see no reason why this equestrian spectacular poetry may not be substituted, until the requisite duty behind the scenes be performed by those who have this Temple of the Muses in trust, but neglect to discharge the obligation implied in their direction. If the intellect *cannot* be addressed, surely, if they can, the senses may, so that moral decorum be not violated.'

Things reached such a pass that the advisers of the Duke of Bedford proposed to demolish the theatre and build residential accommodation on the site. But the amiable and dilatory duke was disinclined to take such drastic action, and things tottered on. From time to time, inevitably, a hit or two slipped through the net. In the 1850s, '60s and '70s they were mostly written by the Dublin actor-playwright Dion Boucicault, culminating in 1875 in his sensational success with the melodrama *The Shaughraun*. On either side of his triumphs the theatre was twice converted into an opera house and then reconverted back. After the 1875 reconversion an enormous internal reconstruction was undertaken, reinforcing and restructuring the old building – just in time for its recovery of form. The actor, playwright and impresario Augustus Harris, already a West End star by the time he was 21, took over Drury Lane at the age of 27 and swiftly identified the theatre as the ideal venue for pantomime, preferably featuring a

OPPOSITE The old box office at the left end of the foyer.

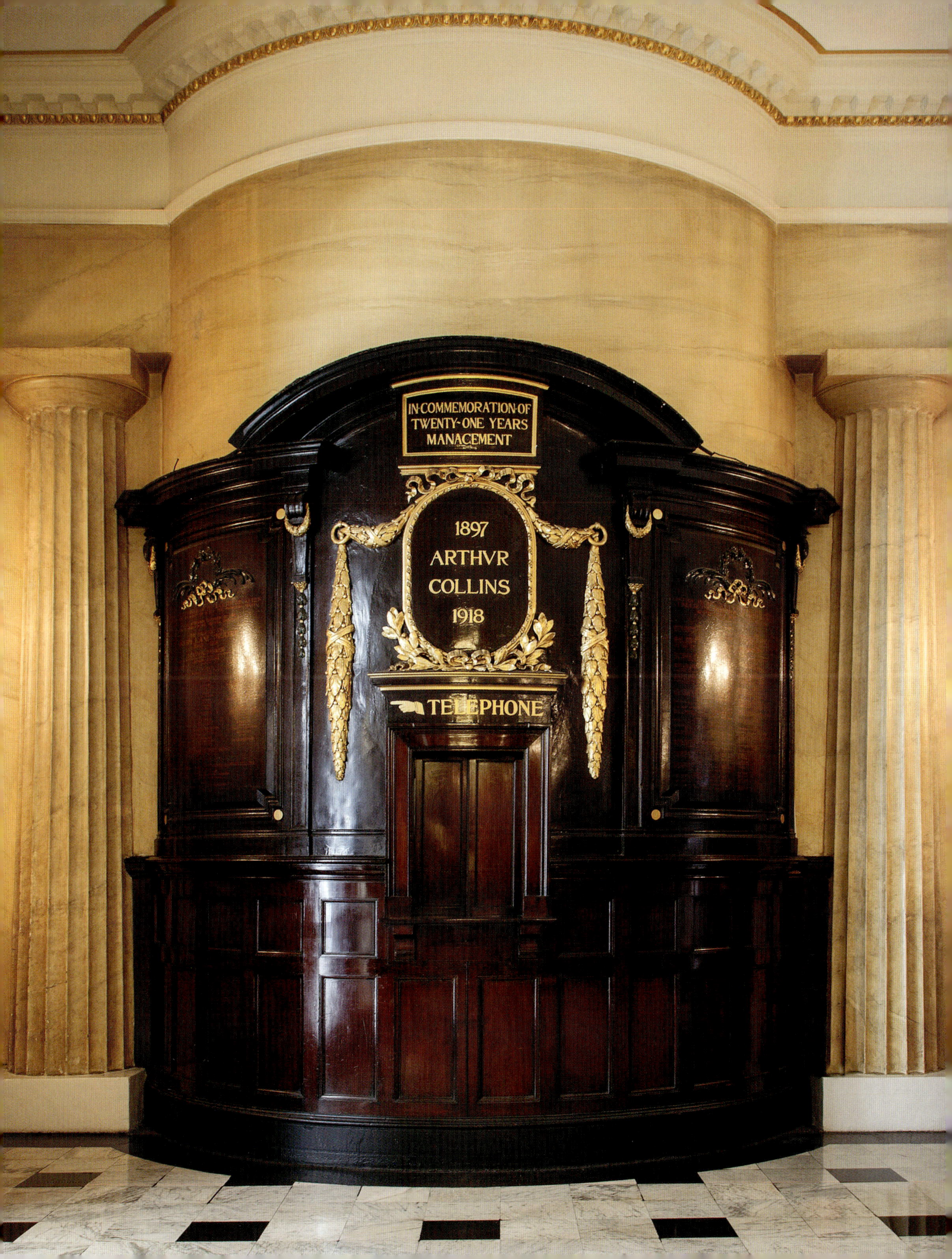
IN·COMMEMORATION·OF
TWENTY-ONE YEARS
MANAGEMENT
1897
ARTHVR
COLLINS
1918
TELEPHONE

great comic star like Dan Leno. Harris wrote over twenty of them, from *Babes in the Wood* to *Cinderella*, as well as notable comedies ranging from *Pluck: A Story of £50,000* to *The Derby Winner*. He radiated success, so much so that he was able to stave off both the Duke of Bedford's advisers and the newly convened London County Council (LCC) with its plan to expand the fruit and vegetable market at Covent Garden on the site of two theatres in the vicinity, in Drury Lane and Bow Street. But the new Duke of Bedford overruled them both, allowing Harris to renew the lease.

He was cut short in the midst of his triumphs, dead in 1896 at the age of 44, a genuinely loved and admired figure who had transformed the Drury Lane theatre's fortunes and brought it right up to the verge of the twentieth century in better shape than it had ever been – no longer the home of Shakespeare, as Byron had hoped, but prosperous, stylish and alive. Ironically enough, Harris was given an affectionately bestowed Bardic nickname, Augustus Druriolanus, which stuck. In the course of his short life he was knighted, made a sheriff and a deputy lieutenant of the City of London, and even, shrewdly, managed to get elected as a member of the LCC: another of those prodigious Victorians whose achievements are so frequently honoured in this book.

Harris's deputy Arthur Collins took the reins, pushing the spectacular element even further, notably in *The Whip* (1909) with its alarmingly recreated train crash and twelve real horses re-running the 2000 Guineas Stakes on an on-stage treadmill. But Drury Lane wouldn't have been Drury Lane without further expansion and refurbishment, and in 1899 the premises were further extended backstage; two years later the interior was again reconceived, or perhaps rationalised, with the circles brought further into the auditorium, the ground-floor boxes abolished, the stalls carved up for easier access and the seats upholstered in Russian leather ('cleaner and cooler than the material usually employed', reported *The Era*). The orchestra was partially sunk so the players' heads disappeared from view, and the whole theatre was fitted with electricity, including a backup system should the main circuit fail. Despite all these improvements, the LCC found the building wanting from the point of view of safety; the remedial work involved clearing away some balconies that had been there, astonishingly, since 1812. The stage itself was almost totally reconstructed and skylights were introduced to allow any smoke to escape in the event of a fire.

Almost inevitably, there was a fire, three years later, but the swift lowering of the safety curtain kept it from the auditorium, and the theatre reopened soon after the backstage reconstruction was complete with *The Marriages of Mayfair*, a fantasy about the theft of the Crown Jewels, at whose climax the villain rode off into the Alps, where he fell, spectacularly and in full view of the audience, to his death. One night it all got a little out of hand and the horse, ridden by the actor Lyn Harding, fell to its death. These alarming entertainments, the brainchildren of Arthur Collins, remained the staple fare of the Lane in the years of the First World War; while other houses were becoming nervous about the suddenly menacing infant art form of film, Drury Lane continued to present shows that offered more sumptuous escapism than the movies could yet provide. Just once, in 1916, the theatre hosted films – D. W. Griffith's two complementary masterpieces *The Birth of a Nation* and *Intolerance*.

Three years before, on the brink of the First World War, Drury Lane had an unaccustomed art attack – *avant-garde* art at that – when it submitted to the willpower and theatrical flair of Thomas Beecham, not only one of the greatest conductors ever produced by Britain but one of its greatest impresarios. In his quest to drag classical music in this country out of its comfortable rut, he invited Sergei Diaghilev's Ballets Russes to present their entire repertory of thirty pieces there; this included *Scheherazade*, *The Afternoon of a Faun* and *Petrushka*, all starring Vaslav Nijinsky, and – just six weeks after its scandalous premiere in Paris – *The Rite of Spring*.

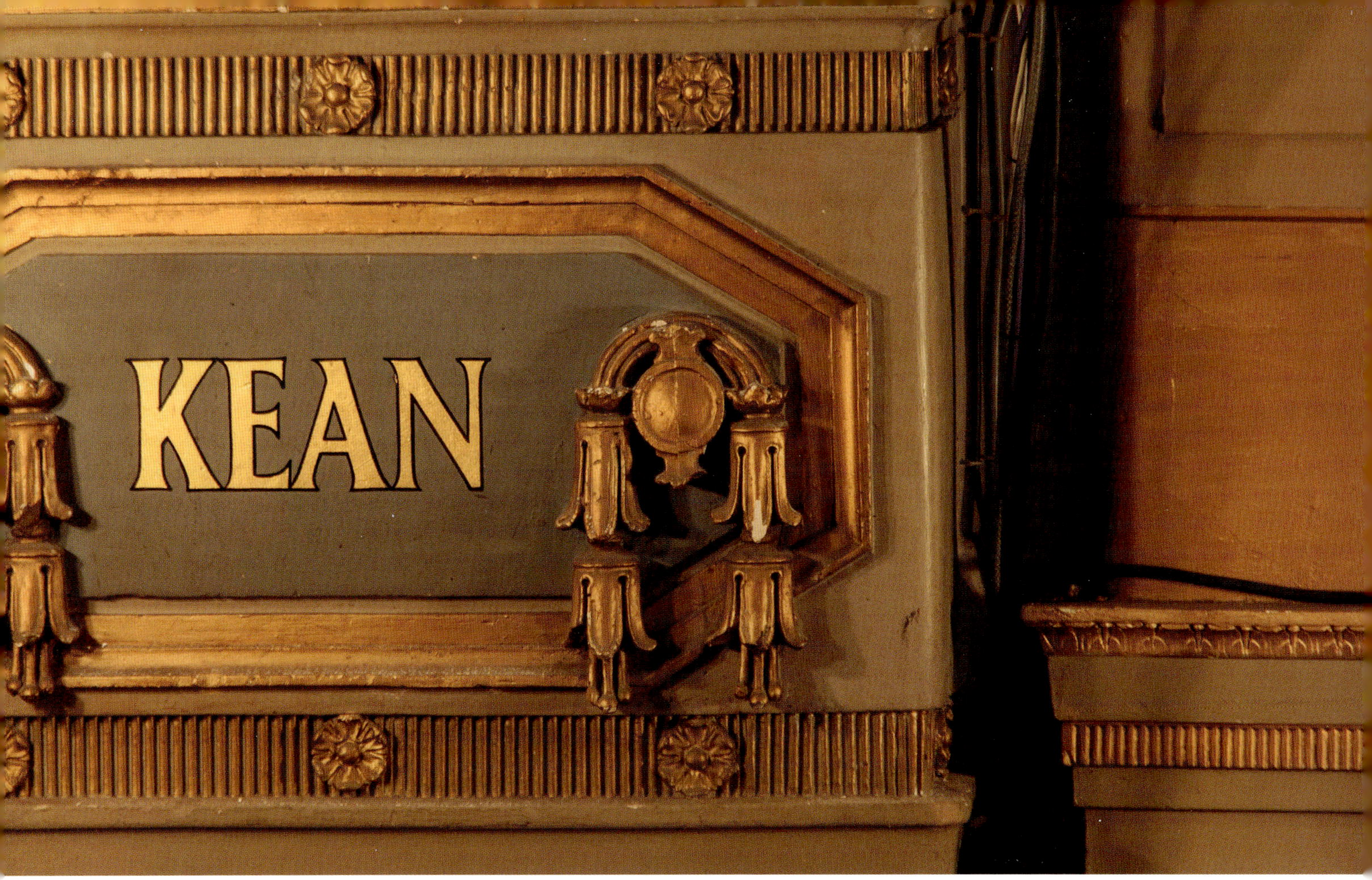

In addition, and no less sensationally, the season included Modest Mussorgsky's operas *Boris Godunov* and *Khovanshchina* and Nikolai Rimsky-Korsakov's *Ivan the Terrible*, all unknown in Britain and all starring the great actor-singer Feodor Chaliapin. The season, and the second one the following year – which introduced Alexander Borodin's *Prince Igor* and Rimsky-Korsakov's *Golden Cockerel* to Britain, to say nothing of revivals of *The Magic Flute* (little regarded at the time) and *Der Rosenkavalier*, which had only had its world premiere three years earlier – exposed the British public to a level of scenic artistry, musical exoticism, originality and astounding vocal and histrionic brilliance of which it had previously had no conception. The sophistication, cosmopolitanism and sheer colour of the work provided a huge and unprecedented firework display abruptly extinguished by the declaration of war in August. Theatres were abruptly closed.

Artistic life in Britain would never be the same again, though when the theatres reopened Drury Lane returned to more mainstream, if scarcely less exotic, fare. In 1920 it found a home-grown smash hit in *The Garden of Allah*, whose sumptuous and highly sexed Orientalism, derived from Robert Hichens's steamy 1904 novel, thrilled a war-weary London. It ran for two years; the moment it closed, the auditorium was, needless to say, yet again rebuilt – for the last time, as it happens. The changes that the architect J. Emblin Walker effected resulted in the theatre we now know: the horseshoe shape was abandoned; three cantilevered circles were installed (obviating the need for pillars); steel girders were installed in the proscenium; the orchestra well was enlarged, making the presentation of opera easier; new, larger

ABOVE Detail of the auditorium with Edmund Kean's name proudly displayed.

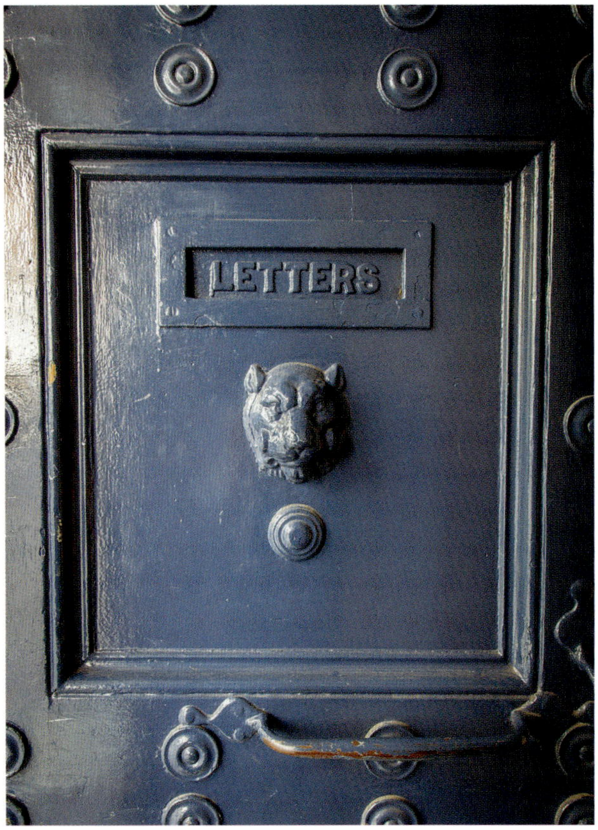

ABOVE The theatre's letterbox.

dressing rooms were installed; and the roof was, in every sense, raised. It was a monumental and challenging project; the rubble of the demolished auditorium had to be removed through holes in the wall and via small doorways. It took a year to complete the job and cost the astonishing sum of £150,000, but it was worth it: the new theatre was universally acclaimed. It had, said *The Stage*, been converted 'from an old, ugly building into a new, elegant, comfortable and commodious theatre'. It was, the paper continued, a 'transformation scene' to rival the greatest of the Drury Lane spectaculars. Most remarkably, it forms a harmonious whole with the Georgian foyers, still extant from the early years of the nineteenth century.

The new theatre opened with *Decameron Nights*, another exotic spectacular; though not quite as successful as *The Garden of Allah* it attracted large audiences. In 1925 the theatre came under the ownership of Sir Alfred Butt, a precociously young impresario and theatre-builder. He was a formidable operator who by the time he took on Drury Lane had been Lloyd George's Director of Rationing during the war (for which he was knighted); he was now a Tory MP and pursued a rigorously commercial policy at Drury Lane. But it was in 1931, under an outside management, that of the great impresario Charles B. Cochran, that the theatre could again claim to be at the centre of theatrical life. With *Cavalcade*, Noël Coward's extraordinarily ambitious account of the first thirty years of the twentieth century, charted the vicissitudes of an upper-middle-class family from the death of Queen Victoria to 1930. Though the piece constituted a sentimentally patriotic celebration of the stiff upper lip, it also engaged with the malaise of the century, from Boer War to First World War and from the sinking of the *Titanic* through post-war hedonism to existential crisis. Popular tunes of the period were used, but Coward himself contributed 'Twentieth Century Blues', perhaps the most personal and passionate of all his songs. There was a cast of four hundred, and the monumental scenic effects were in the tradition of the great Drury Lane spectaculars of the previous century. It ran for a year.

The Lane's next triumph, *Glamorous Night*, also commissioned specially for it, was as far from the twentieth century's blues as could be found: an operetta written by Coward's friend and rival Ivor Novello – another actor-dramatist-composer – who possessed a miraculous melodic gift that seemed, unlike Coward's, to spring less from technical skill than from deep inside a generous heart. Two more hugely successful shows followed, *Careless Rapture* and *The Crest of the Wave*, whose titles say it all. The shows themselves were, for the most part, absurd operetta fantasies, replete with skating scenes and gypsy weddings and fairgrounds, sumptuously set and clad. But in 1939 even the politically oblivious Novello became aware of the global threat posed by the Nazis and in response wrote *The Dancing Years*, which, *Cavalcade*-like, spanned the decades, in this case from 1919 to 1938, tracing the life of a young Jewish composer. The piece culminates in his confrontation with and then escape from the Nazis. Though censored until the outbreak of war in September 1939, its political position was unmistakable and unequivocal, if not exactly analytical. The show was wildly successful, and when the Theatre Royal, like all other West End theatres, was closed, it took to the road with equal success.

During the war, the Lane became the centre of the famous ENSA (Entertainments National Service Association), widely known as Every Night Something Awful, which sent out companies large and small across the country and to the Front; it somehow again became, in the words of its biographer Robert Whelan, 'the other National Theatre'. After the war the theatre reopened with a new Noël Coward show, *Pacific 1860*, but this was a sad, lifeless thing, despite – or perhaps because of – the hyperactivity of its star, Mary Martin. 'An orgy of good taste', *The Observer* called it. It was not so much the end of an era as a sad little postscript to it, as well as signalling the decline in the author's popularity and creativity very publicly; there is no such thing as a quiet little flop at Drury Lane.

The rest of the twentieth century at the Theatre Royal was dedicated, by and large, to hugely successful shows – almost all imports, and mostly from Broadway. One after another all the great Rodgers and Hammerstein shows played there, triumphantly, as did, most successfully of all, *My Fair Lady*, that apparently quintessentially English show written and directed by Americans, with a score by a Berliner. The important thing about all these shows was that they were done with a style and a confidence that nothing produced in Britain could match. Eventually, in the late 1960s, the native tradition reasserted itself (thanks largely to Andrew Lloyd Webber), but not at Drury Lane, and nor has it subsequently – American shows still rule, with the notable exception of *Charlie and the Chocolate Factory* and a revival of *Oliver!* By a delicious irony, Lloyd Webber, having become the most successful composer of musicals of all time, started in the 1980s to acquire theatres, and one of his first was the Theatre Royal Drury Lane. Over the twenty years of his ownership it has been slowly restored to its full glory, honouring its extraordinary history while remaining vitally alive to the new.

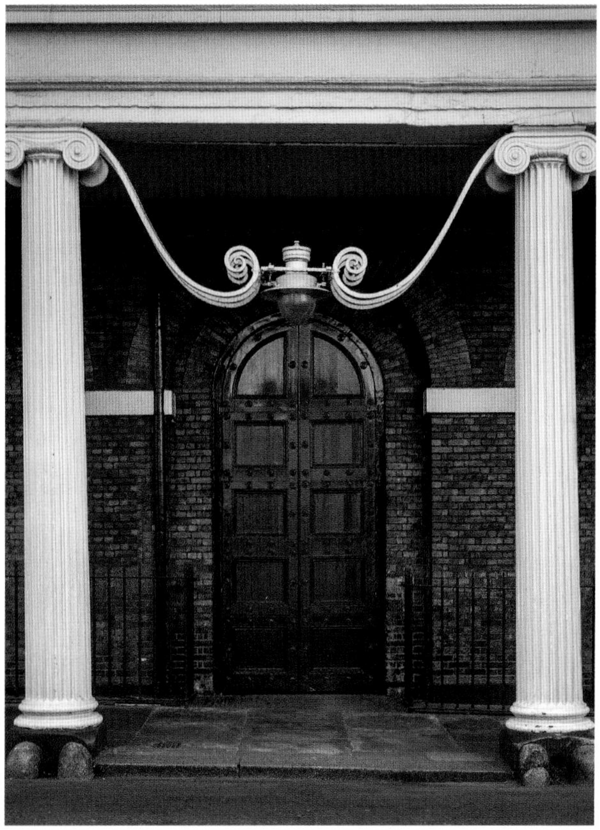

ABOVE Part of the colonnade on the exterior. Note the elegance of the lamp holders – fine examples of Regency style.

SADLER'S WELLS

The central London district of Finsbury, which is where, technically, Sadler's Wells Theatre belongs, was once a great fen, marshy peatland beyond the walls of the City of London. In the early seventeenth century, with the general expansion of London, trees were planted and gravel paths laid, turning the area into a pleasant area of recreation. In 1674 Edward Sadler (sometimes given as Richard Sadler), a vintner and later victualler who had acquired land and built property on the Outer Pond at New River Head in Clerkenwell, constructed a wooden Musick House in association with a dancing master, Francis Forcer; he thus effectively established a theatre, making Sadler's Wells second only in longevity to the Theatre Royal Drury Lane. Since then there have been five more theatres on the site. During the building of the music house, workmen happened upon a walled-up chalybeate spring. It was concluded that because the ground had once been part of the ancient Priory of Clerkenwell, this iron-rich spring, believed in medieval times to be possessed of miraculous powers, was the well after which the area had been named. Sadler was not slow to see the commercial potential of this. Promised that taking the waters would cure 'dropsy, jaundice, scurvy, green sickness and other distempers to which females are liable – ulcers, fits of the mother, virgin's fever and hypochondriacal distemper', people flocked to imbibe these 'excellent steel waters'. Having drunk their fill, they would then pass on to the music house, where a huge throng was entertained, we learn from Ned Ward's *A Walk to Islington* of 1699, by low-grade singers and fiddlers, and for a time an eleven-year-old sword dancer. There was in addition a slightly classier gallery where, says Ward, 'lovers o'er cheesecakes were Scraping and Humming' under a saucy painted overhang depicting Apollo, Europa and Neptune in sexually sportive mood. In time the wells seem either to have dried up or to have come to play second fiddle to the somewhat dubious entertainments on offer within.

Not, perhaps, the ideal breeding ground for the noble art of the theatre. Sadler died in 1699, to be succeeded by James Miles, who featured, among other turns, the spectacle of a man eating a live cockerel. Miles was succeeded by his son-in-law, who enlarged the building to include accommodation. With each successive change of manager Sadler's Wells seems to have sunk into ever further disrepute, causing its temporary closure by magistrates; it finally ended up in the hands of one John Warren, who took it to new depths, turning it into 'a nursery of debauchery', according to contemporary reports, the audience being 'vermin trained up to the gallows'. The whole area, indeed, was a byword for sleaze. At Christmas 1745, however, things started looking up when Thomas Rosoman, like Edward Sadler a vintner, but unlike him also an actor, took a 21-year lease on the premises with his friend Peter Hough, a tumbler. The asylum was now in the hands of the lunatics, which proved to be a very healthy development. In 1749 or thereabouts Rosoman built a new, smaller theatre, like the old Musick House largely from wood, and in 1753 he engaged a regular company of actors, who performed plays in tandem

OPPOSITE The exterior – architecture of a 'brave new world'. Note the early nineteenth-century houses in the background.

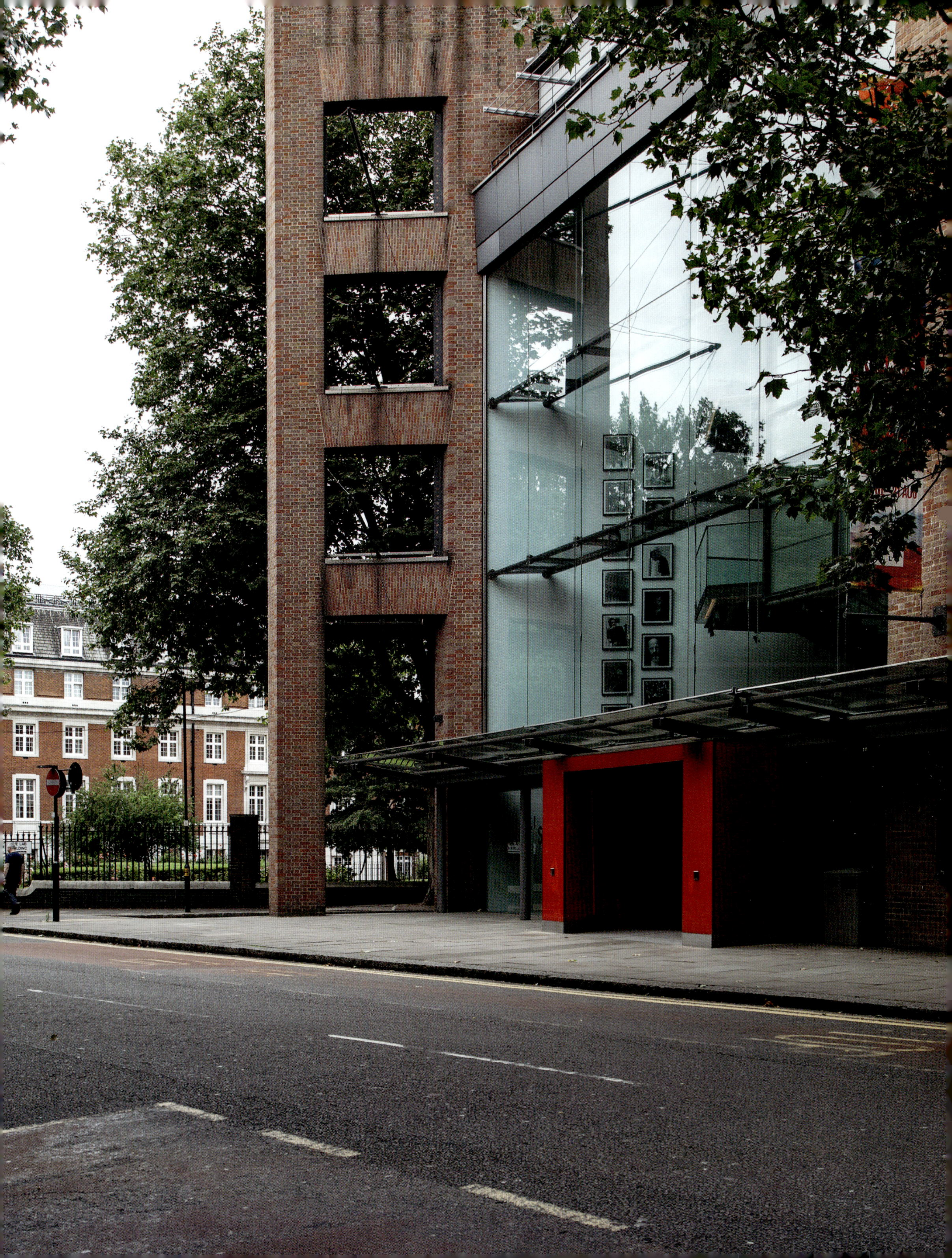

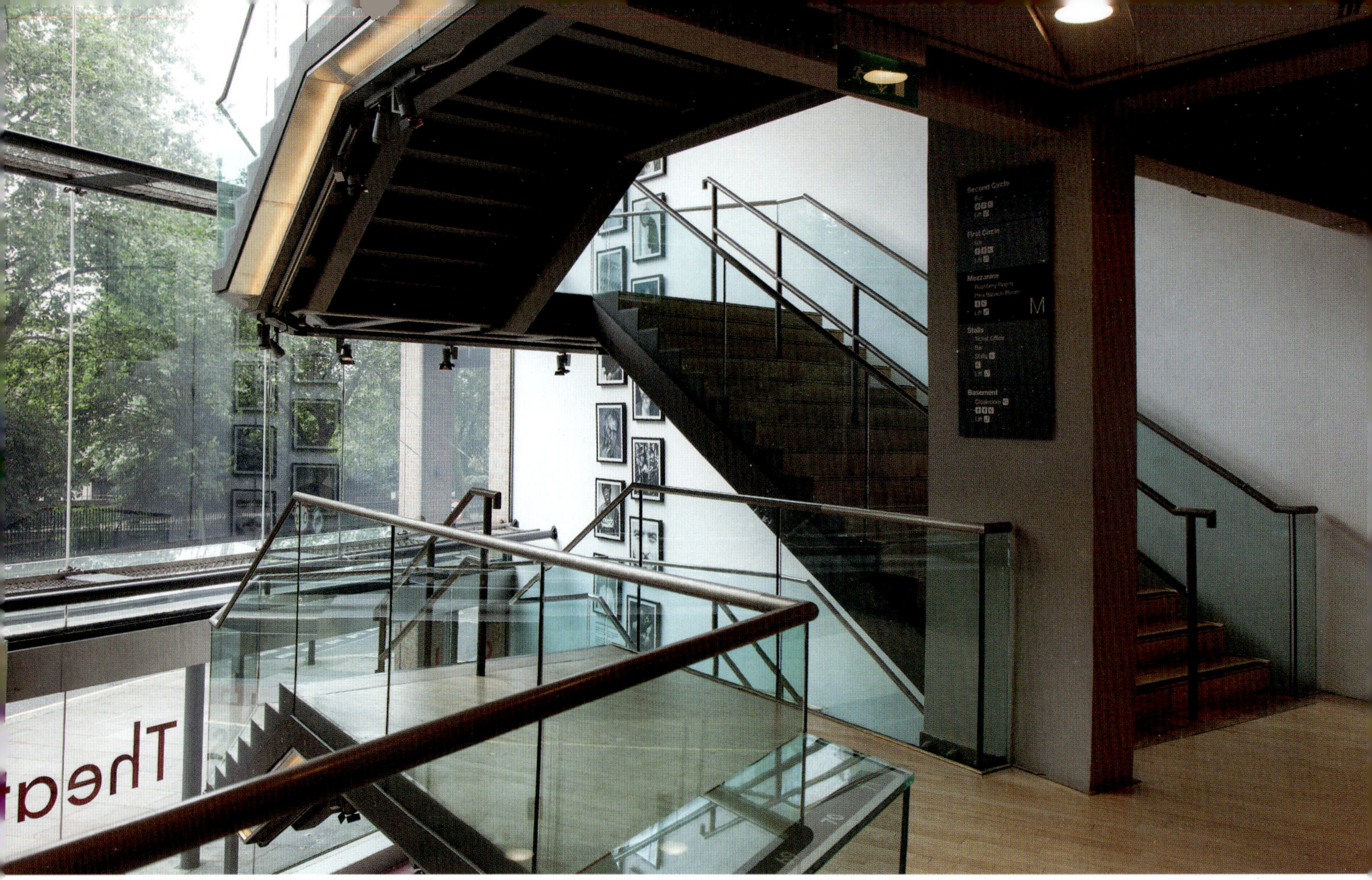

with variety performances: in 1762 Giuseppe Grimaldi, 'the Signor' and fearsome father of Dickens's hero Joseph Grimaldi, the king of clowns, first appeared there as chief dancer and ballet master. Fifteen years after building his first theatre Rosoman substantially rebuilt it, expanding it to nearly twice the size of the earlier building; a brick wall with iron railings, gates, chains and lamps was erected. Respectability was on its way.

Rosoman then retired, by now a rich man, and Thomas King, formerly the actor-manager of the Covent Garden Theatre and who had been involved in managing the Wells from 1769, took over the lease. The price of admission included a pint of port, but there was a distinct amelioration of tone, which drove ticket sales into rapid decline. King resorted to the familiar remedy, redecoration, and in 1778 and 1787 the interior was attractively made over. In 1792 a new leaseholder, Richard Hughes, appeared, who, in partnership with William Siddons, husband of the great actress Sarah Siddons, set about encouraging an altogether more toney clientele – 'a long et cetera of rank and fashion', as a contemporary commentator nicely put it. In 1799 Hughes and Siddons commissioned the prodigiously productive Charles Dibdin the Younger, late of Astley's Amphitheatre (from which he had walked out when his wife was dismissed for sewing during rehearsals), to write pantomimes and harlequinades for the theatre. They built many of these around the great clown Joey Grimaldi, who already had a long association with Sadler's Wells, having been brought onstage there at the age of two by his terrifying father; he made his formal debut there in a leading role in 1791 at the age of thirteen, acting alongside Grimaldi senior as Little Clown in the pantomime

ABOVE The staircase in the vestibule.

The Triumph of Mirth; or, Harlequin's Wedding. By the time he returned as a star in his own right, in 1800 in Dibdin's *Peter Wilkins; or, Harlequin in the Flying World*, he was married to Maria Hughes, daughter of the Wells' leaseholder. Despite this familial closeness, Grimaldi's relationship to the management was the usual early nineteenth-century business of furious disagreements, bitter recriminations, transfers of allegiance and forgings of new relationships, in an endlessly repeating pattern. Joey went from the Wells to the Theatre Royal Covent Garden, to Drury Lane and back again. In 1820, having returned to Sadler's Wells with a promise of shares in the theatre, he made a disastrous attempt to run it; *The Fates; or, Harlequin's Holy Day* was an abject flop. Joey sold his shares and withdrew from the Wells; three years later, his sprit broken and his body shattered, he retired altogether (at the age of 45) and slid into alcoholic depression; after spending time in debtors' jail he finally died, as the coroner put it, 'by the visitation of God', in 1837, not quite sixty.

The theatre, meanwhile, all through the Grimaldi years under Charles Dibdin's tenure, had enjoyed a remarkable reputation as a provider of spectacular entertainments. In 1802 he had introduced pony races; the horses were dramatically revealed to the audience by flinging open the large doors at the back of the theatre, and in order to accommodate his equine stars sheds and stables were erected in the fields beyond. This entertainment was wildly popular and continued at the theatre for more than 25 years. More spectacular yet was the transformation of the theatre into an aquadrome, requiring the installation, in 1804, of a vast metal tank under the stage. This mighty reservoir was 90 feet long, 24 feet across and 3 feet deep, originally filled directly from the New River just outside the theatre using an Archimedean screw, but later supplied direct from the mains. The appeal of even the most audacious feature was transient, however; ever newer novelties were required. Tirelessly inventive, Dibdin pioneered the genre of aqua-drama, creating over twenty years no fewer than 36 pieces, re-enacting great naval battles, floods and mythic encounters with sea monsters. In 1808 a further tank for waterfall effects was added in the flies. There were ships in full sail operated by small boys in duffle coats; the action was enhanced by fire effects counterfeiting explosions, volcanoes and burning castles, the colourful lights of the fireworks reflected in the water. 'Among the apparently perilous and appalling incidents exhibited', wrote William J. Pinks in his *History of Clerkenwell* (1881), 'were those of a female falling from the rocks into the water, and being rescued by her hero-lover; a naval battle, with sailors escaping by plunging into the sea from a vessel on fire; and a child thrown into the water by a nurse, who was bribed to drown it, but rescued by a Newfoundland dog.'

After a couple of decades of increasingly desperate invention, even this craze began to die out. Dibdin went, Grimaldi had retired; the theatre struggled to keep going. There were more pony races, with the added excitement that the animals actually entered the auditorium, thundering down planks, but even this palled. Curiously, during this period of decline the physical theatre was twice refurbished and expanded. Backstage facilities were improved: dressing rooms finally arrived at the Wells for the first time. When the London Wine Company took shares in the theatre they installed a wine room, a saloon and a coffee house, as well as giving the theatre its first official box office; a porch was added to prevent paying customers from getting drenched. During this period of dwindling returns there were frequent attempts to do away with the theatre and build tenement houses on what was a very attractive site, but it was invariably found that keeping the theatre going, even in its current decline, was more profitable than new building: audience capacity, after refurbishment, was well over two thousand. Proposals to turn the theatre into a riding school or a panorama were likewise rejected, but it was far from clear that things could continue as they were.

The Wells' survival was unwittingly ensured by Parliament. The Theatres Act 1843 rationalised the licensing of theatres, rescinding the exclusive right of Charles II's patent theatres to perform plays. At the same time it extended the Lord Chamberlain's powers of censorship, a deeply regressive move that had a disastrous effect on new writing in Britain, but by allowing any theatre to perform plays it also resulted in a huge upsurge in the performance of classics, which were not under the Lord Chamberlain's jurisdiction. The new lessees of the Wells, Samuel Phelps and his partner Mary Warner, were at the forefront of this classical revival: they had taken over the theatre, they said in their manifesto, 'in the hope of eventually rendering it what a theatre ought to be – a place for justly representing the works of our great dramatic poets'. Phelps was a fine actor who eschewed the grand theatrics of his predecessors David Garrick and Edmund Kean, but he was an even finer director; for the rest of his life he devoted himself to performing and staging Shakespeare's entire output (he managed to do 30 out of the 37 plays, including some that had not been performed since they were first seen). 'I never saw rehearsals more thorough,' said the dramatist Tom Taylor, 'more careful, or more business-like. Phelps was as able as he was indefatigable in stage-management.' This level of attention to detail became a hallmark of Phelps's regime, during which he gave between five and six thousand performances; the plays, performed more or less as Shakespeare wrote them – not, as hitherto, bowdlerised, sentimentalised, shorn of important subplots, their endings rewritten to send everyone home happy – were revealed to be the complex achievements of a master dramatist. And the town flocked to see them. Sadler's Wells had finally become legitimate, with all the pluses and minuses that that suggests. Phelps's King Lear was praised above all for its dignity: 'The majesty, as well as the paternal tenderness of Lear, is preserved throughout,' wrote *Bell's Weekly Messenger*; 'the grief, despair, and madness are kingly; and the business which the action inspires is heightened by the consciousness of the greatness of the mind that is suffering.' Even his Falstaff had dignity. During Phelps's time the theatre was renamed, somehow inevitably, the Theatre Royal, Sadler's Wells.

When his business partner retired in 1860 Phelps withdrew from the Wells; he continued as a freelance actor until the end, making his farewell with a notably dignified performance as Cardinal Wolsey in *Henry VIII* and leaving behind him a fine annotated edition of Shakespeare's works. Meanwhile, after a brief few years trying to follow in Phelps's footsteps, his old theatre reverted to its former rackety ways, becoming by turns a skating rink, a prize fight and then, humiliatingly, a pickle factory. Even this failed, and in 1876 the old place was abandoned after attempts to lure Phelps back came to nought; he died two years later. But theatrical ambition was not wholly extinguished, and three years later the lease was acquired by Mrs S. F. Bateman, lately Henry Irving's leading lady at the Lyceum until she was supplanted by Ellen Terry. Bateman hired the already renowned architect Charles J. Phipps (who would later design, among many other theatres, the Vaudeville, the Savoy and Her Majesty's). He entirely reshaped the interior, increasing the capacity and introducing gilded Corinthian columns and a tasteful celebration of the Muses; an act drop celebrated the Wells's glorious past: the signage outside the theatre celebrated it as Ye Olde Sadlers Wells Theatre. Bateman died in 1881, not living long enough to see it achieve any kind of success as a classical theatre. After a period of drift and dispute during which the theatre's very existence was again in doubt, the notoriously outrageous George E. Belmont (known as 'Barnum's Beauty') took over, running the theatre as to all intents and purposes a music hall, but interlarded with legitimate acts to avoid the necessity of securing a music hall license. This curious moonlighting existence was compounded, on and off from 1896, by the theatre's presentation of films; from 1900, Belmont formally installed

OPPOSITE Interior of the vestibule.

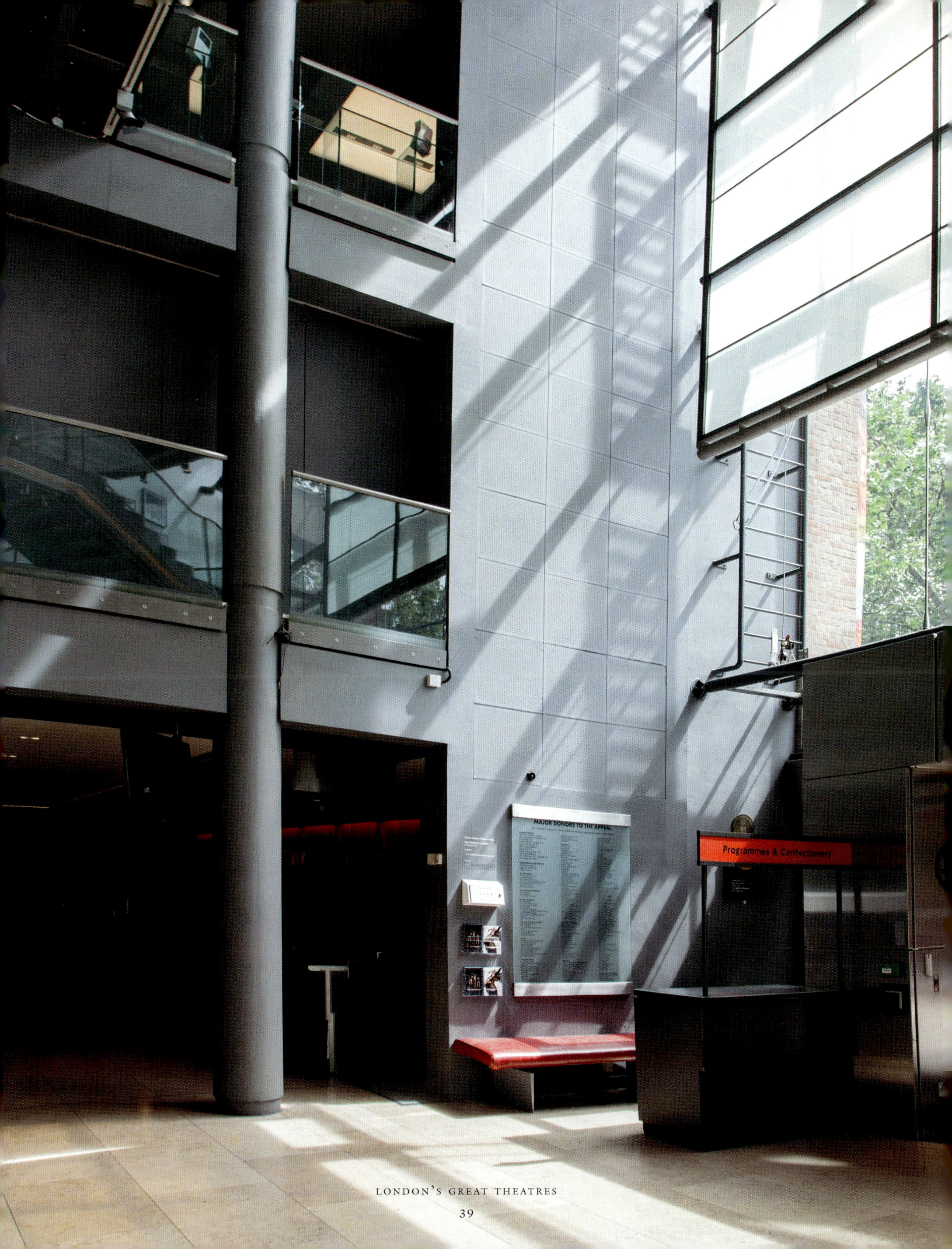
MAJOR DONORS TO THE APPEAL
Programmes & Confectionery

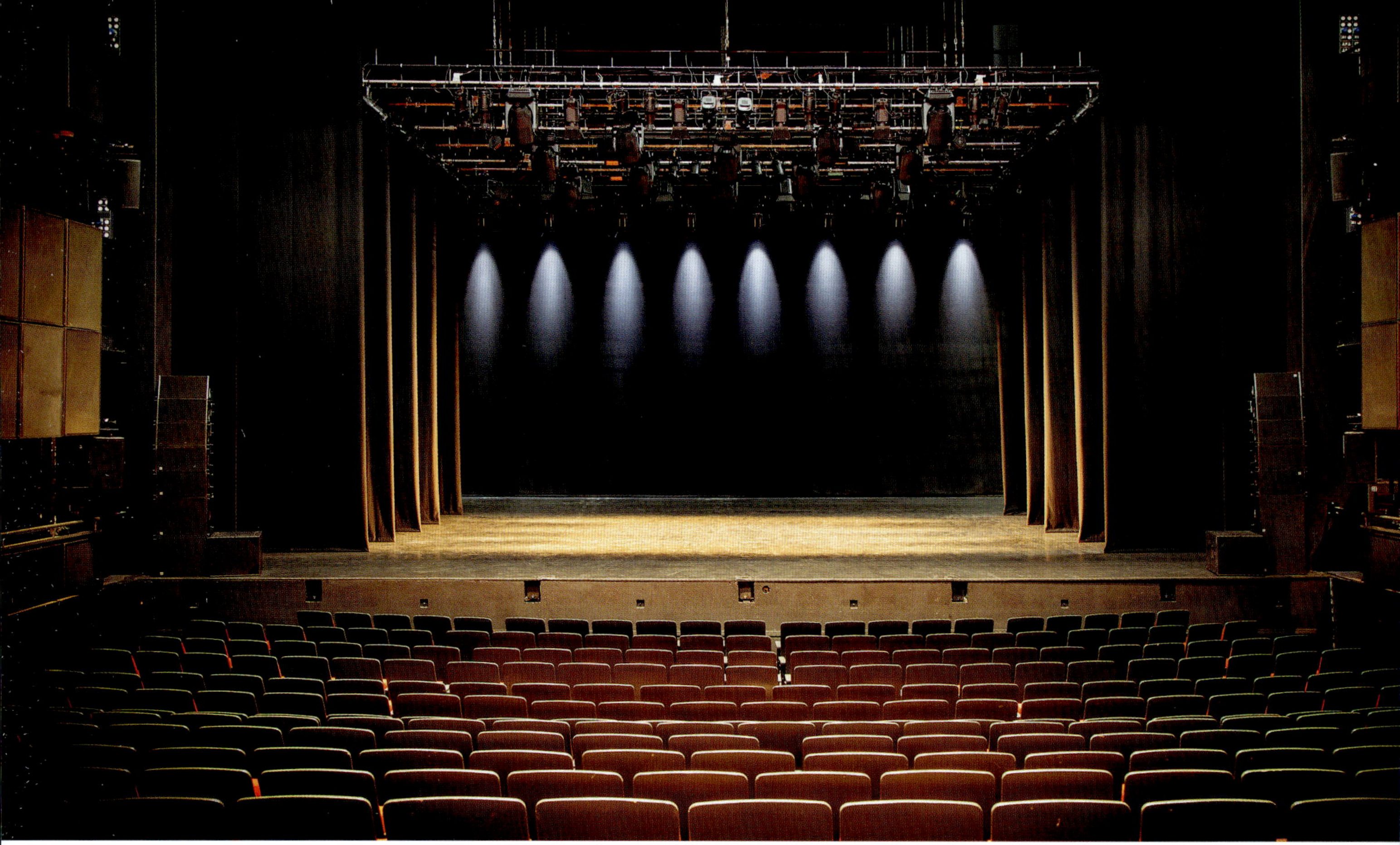

equipment (with the projectors initially operating from the gentlemen's lavatory). 'Poor wounded old playhouse!' cried a critic in the *Daily Chronicle* in 1914, 'shabby and disconsolate, its once familiar frontage half hidden with glaring posters . . . packed with pale eager-eyed little "flappers", whistling errand boys and chuckling old greybeards' enjoying the regular cowboy melodramas. A half-hearted attempt, supported by various theatrical luminaries, to reclaim the old place as a 'people's theatre' failed with the outbreak of the First World War; the building was formally closed in 1915.

After the war, serious damage was inflicted on it by intruders. A new potential saviour emerged in the highly dubious form of Ernest C. Rolls, owner of the Kennington Theatre and later a theatrical manager in Australia, noted for extravagant productions and a criminal record that encompassed bankruptcy, voyeurism and court tax evasion. Rolls purposed to rebuild the theatre, adding a restaurant and reviving the long-defunct well. In the event, he changed the facade and altered the foyer; this work was completed in 1921, but the refurbished theatre never opened, instead falling into ruin. At this point, as if on a white steed, Reginald Rowe enters. Poet, novelist and philanthropist, he was a governor of the Old Vic and had proved himself indispensable in managing its meagre resources. He had passed the wreckage of the Wells, which was up for sale as potential offices or a factory, and suggested that it might be the second auditorium that the Vic's Lilian Baylis had been looking for. The Vic was a cause with support in high places (though none from central government), and a successful appeal was launched under the leadership of the Duke of Devonshire.

ABOVE The auditorium, looking towards the stage. A rigorous effect, without frills.

The money came from many quarters, including several London boroughs and charitable foundations as well as private contributors who chipped in with individual bricks. A photograph of Baylis standing in the ruins of the crumbling playhouse alongside the ancient and monocled actor-manager Sir Squire Bancroft and a not much younger Sir Arthur Wing Pinero (whose 1898 play *Trelawny of the 'Wells'* had immortalised an earlier period of the theatre's history) confirmed the sense of destiny fulfilled that attached to the project.

The revived theatre was designed by F.G.M. Chancellor (of Frank Matcham's practice) to utilise as much of the old building as possible; aesthetics were a low prioity. It finally opened on 6 January 1931 – twelfth night – with *Twelfth Night* directed by Tyrone Guthrie, featuring John Gielgud as Malvolio and Ralph Richardson as Toby Belch, with the Russian ballerina Lydia Lopokova (Mrs Maynard Keynes) as a provocative Olivia. The production was well enough liked, but the new auditorium was not. It was deficient acoustically and in terms of physical comfort; above all it was charmless – more Malvolio than Belch, austerely virtuous, with no cakes or ale at all. The only concession to charm was a relief plaster 'tinted like old ivory', by the Yorkshire sculptor Joseph Hermon Cawthra of a scene from *A Midsummer Night's Dream*. At first the repertory encompassed plays, opera and ballet – the latter created by the former Diaghilev ballerina Ninette de Valois, the director of movement at the Vic – but it soon became apparent that the logistics of moving sets from the Old Vic in Waterloo to Islington and back were prohibitive, so the Wells was given over to the lyric arts (and renamed Sadler's Wells Opera and Ballet) while the actors retreated with relief to south London. Out of these operations, the Royal Opera and the Royal Ballet (and later the National Theatre and English National Opera) would eventually grow; the touring wing of the Royal Ballet continued to be known as Sadler's Wells Ballet and to perform at the Wells, until in 1990 it transferred to the Midlands under the name of Birmingham Royal Ballet, a mark of the immeasurable contribution made to British cultural life by that great if unlikely visionary Lilian Baylis.

The theatre, like all the theatres on the same site, was constantly refurbished and rebuilt, notably in 1959 when the acousticians moved in, installing various sound shields, one of which somehow symbolically blocked out the one concession to the decorative in Chancellor's 1931 theatre, Cawthra's *A Midsummer Night's Dream* relief; it was eventually put into storage. After the departure of, first, the opera company, in 1968, and then twenty years later the ballet, there was considerable uncertainty as to the building's purpose. In 1988 the usefully flexible Lilian Baylis Studio had been added, though it never quite shared itself with the community as planned. Everything changed with the creation of the National Lottery Fund. In 1994 the new chief executive, Ian Albery, pursued a visionary goal of a theatre that owed nothing to any other. In this, with its glass front, extended foyers and metal-dominated auditorium, Sadler's Wells has succeeded. The newest Wells is devoted almost exclusively to dance and is equipped with every technological feature that modern dance requires, which would surely have brought a smile of approval to the face of Charles Dibdin, with his state-of-the-art aqua-dramas and mechanically stunning pantomimes. And in direct line of descent from Samuel Phelps and Lilian Baylis, it has become a people's theatre, in this case of dance, always visibly teeming behind its glass facade, the heir to over three hundred years of theatrical history and innovation. Touchingly, Cawthra's *A Midsummer Night's Dream* relief has at last been prominently placed in the foyer, creating a link and an echo across the centuries.

HER MAJESTY'S THEATRE

It seems that with certain select London theatres, no matter how often they are closed down, or pulled down, or burned down, another theatre will pop up to replace them. Her Majesty's Theatre is one such – the present theatre is the fourth on the site, and it is impossible to write the history of British drama or opera in England without reference to them. But when the first theatre was built, in 1705, it was thought to be a considerable gamble. Until the end of the seventeenth century the Hay Market had been rural, with hedgerows on either side and not a dwelling to be seen until the hamlet of Charing, on the embankment below the Strand. The street itself was a highway on which carts carrying straw and hay were allowed to stand toll-free and ply their trade, until in 1692 the street was paved, and carts were charged according to the weight of their load. This now slightly less rustic outpost was colonised for theatrical purposes by Sir John Vanbrugh, speculator, architect, and author of two of the most enduring Restoration comedies, *The Relapse* and *The Provok'd Wife*. Queen Anne had given him and his business partner, who would manage the theatre, permission to form 'a company of comedians'. The business partner was another dramatist, or rather former dramatist: William Congreve, who, having produced five of the funniest plays in the language, culminating in *The Way of the World*, had given up writing for the stage, allegedly in disgust at the success of the excessively audience-pleasing plays of Susanna Centlivre, the current toast of the theatre.

Vanbrugh built his playhouse, which he respectfully named the Queen's Theatre, on land hitherto occupied by stables; it was of some magnificence, but it quickly became apparent that it was severely impractical, especially in the rather crucial area of audibility for the spoken word. The first production was, in fact, of an Italian opera, *The Loves of Ergasto*, the first such to be performed in London; for a great deal of its long history the theatres occupying this site have been involved with that uniquely undependable art form. Vanbrugh's first season was a failure; Congreve walked out, leaving his friend to manage it as best he could, which was not well at all. Vanbrugh was by now heavily involved in building Blenheim Palace, and mismanaged his own theatre so badly that he was forced to sell out to the unhappily named Owen Swiney (or MacSwiney), who in turn leased it out, in 1711, to the German composer George Frideric Handel, then aged 26 and at the height of his youthful fame. In that year, *Rinaldo* had its premiere, to be followed by an unbroken succession of 24 other new operas, one a year, among them three absolute masterpieces, *Giulio Cesare*, *Tamerlano* and *Rodelinda*. In 1734 Handel departed in a huff for the Covent Garden Theatre (now the Royal Opera House); the theatre continued with its Italian opera policy, often with great distinction.

Vanbrugh's playhouse had since the ascent to the throne of George I some twenty years earlier been known as the King's Theatre; maintaining the tradition of dramatist-owners, it was bought in 1778 by Richard Brinsley Sheridan, in partnership with the former stage manager of the Theatre Royal Drury

OPPOSITE The auditorium. The success of *The Phantom of the Opera*, which has run for over 30 years, has entailed a certain neglect.

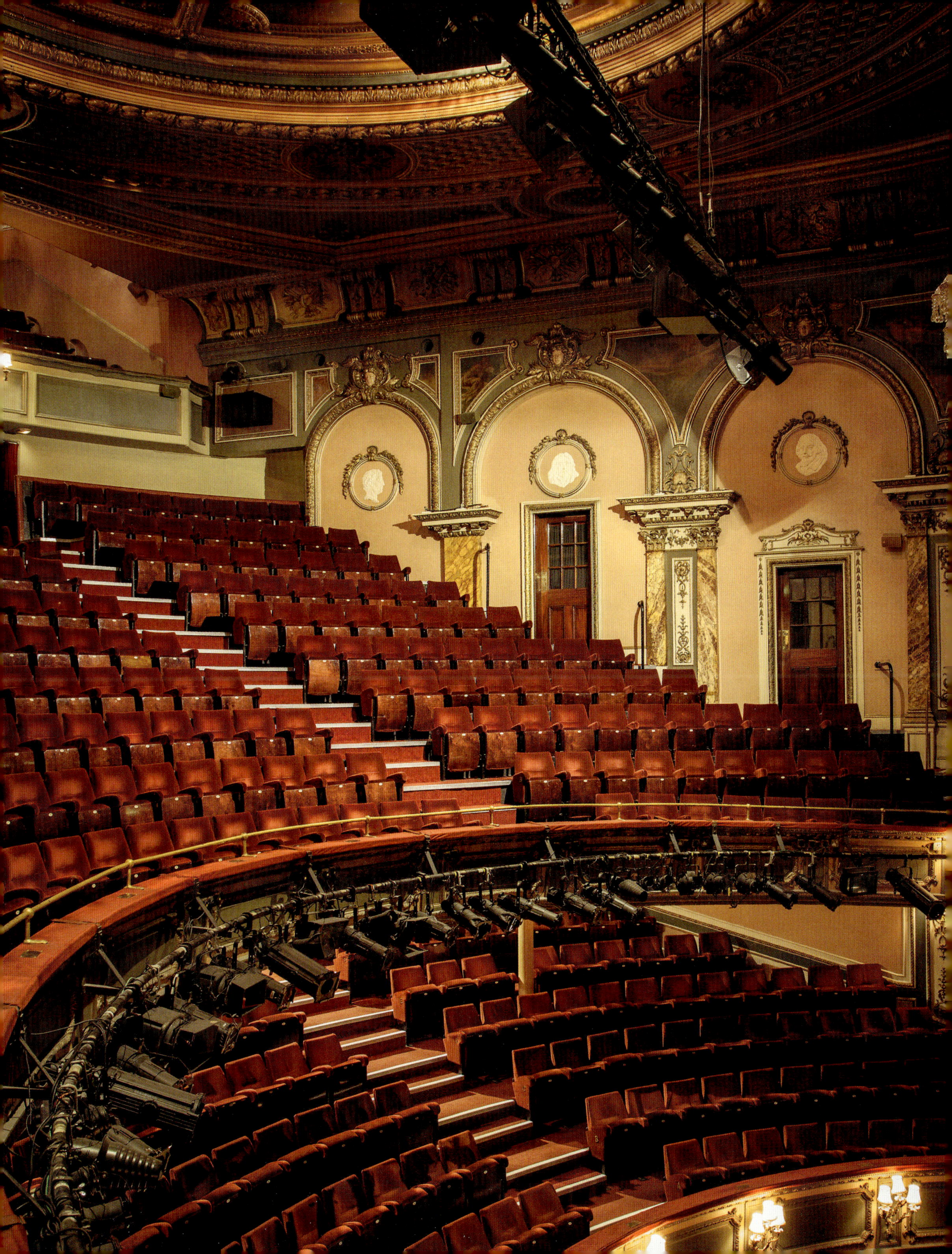

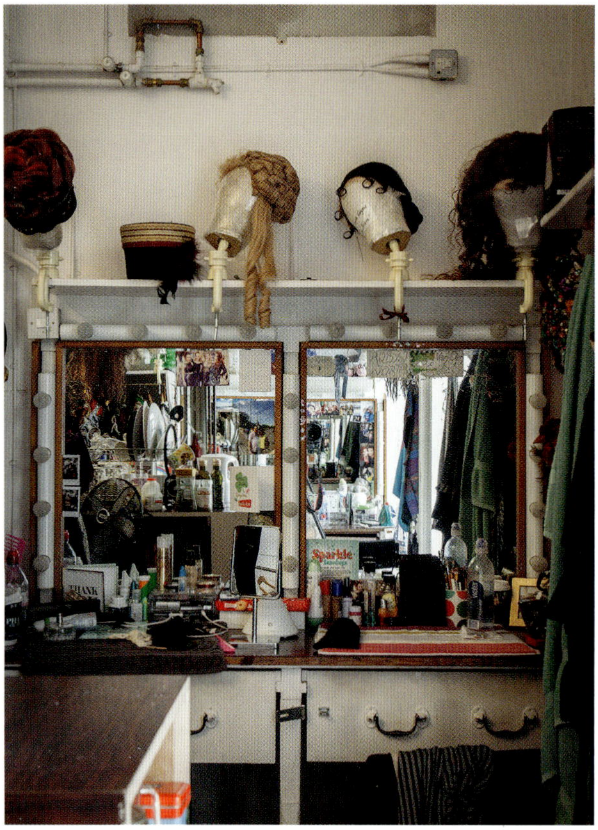

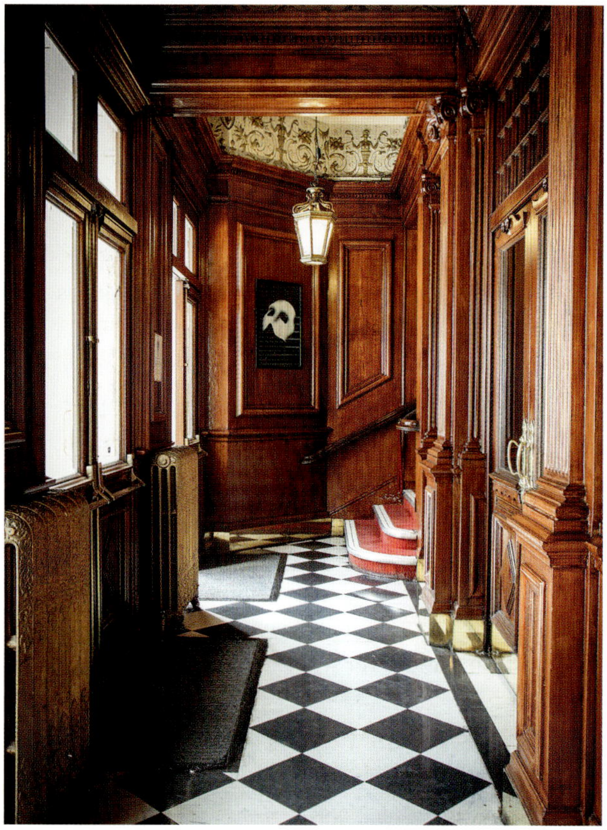

Lane, of which Sheridan was manager; he then hired the most famous (and expensive) architect of the day, Robert Adam, to remodel it, making the interior lighter and more appealing, removing the heavy columns and adorning the auditorium with two figures newly painted by Thomas Gainsborough. All this was judged a great success, but takings were never strong enough to recover the investment and the partnership broke up; Sheridan's debts grew ever deeper until finally, bankrupt, he sold the theatre to his own lawyer, who remodelled it yet again, ruining himself. This lawyer was arrested by his creditors, who sold the theatre to Sheridan's original partner, from whose grasp it was soon prised when the former dancing master Giovanni (later John) Gallini, who had always had his eye on it, became manager in 1785. Desperately short of funds, Gallini resorted to presenting amateur performances of lamentable quality: 'the dance,' one reviewer in *The World* lamented in February 1789, 'if such it can be called, was like the movements of heavy cavalry. It was hissed very abundantly.' Everyone was finally put out of their misery when the theatre burned down that June.

It was rebuilt even larger: it was now the biggest theatre in England, possibly the world. Four Mozart operas had their British premieres there: *La Clemenza di Tito* (1806), *Così fan tutte* and *Die Zauberflöte* (1811), and *Don Giovanni* (1816). Then the need for a bit of urgent remodelling was again felt, and – in keeping with its past – yet another distinguished architect, John Nash, was unleashed on it in 1816. He and his colleague George Repton lovingly lingered over it for two years, adding an arcade at the back of the building and a colonnade to its front; helpfully, they also increased the number of seats to

ABOVE LEFT A corner of a dressing room.
ABOVE RIGHT The narrow entrance.

2,500. Over the next six years, under the management of John Ebers, a music-loving bookseller, eleven operas by Rossini had their first English performances there; excited by so much interest and such splendid box office returns, the composer himself, accompanied by his wife, the great *soprano sfogato* Isabella Colbran, spent five months in London conducting his own work, this time under the management of Ebers's friend Benelli. Two more Rossini operas were brought to London for the first time, but Benelli had overestimated the limitless appetite of the British public for Rossini and, faced with ruin, decamped, leaving composer and performers unpaid. Under a new management, more and more Italian premieres ensued – more Rossini, Donizetti, Bellini – and the greatest singers vied to appear there.

When Victoria ascended to the throne in 1837 the theatre became Her Majesty's Italian Opera House. Now late Donizetti and early Verdi were on the bill. The then manager, Benjamin Lumley, was so impressed by the latter that he commissioned Verdi to write an opera for him; *I masnadieri* duly had its world premiere at Her Majesty's in 1847, conducted by the composer, and was a violent success – a success not unconnected with it being the first London appearance of the 'Swedish Nightingale', the soprano Jenny Lind. The audience included the Queen, Prince Albert, the Duke of Wellington and every one of the great and good who was able to secure a ticket. Lindmania possessed the theatre-going public; when she appeared in Giacomo Meyerbeer's *Robert le diable*, the audience 'arrived at last with dresses crushed and torn', said the *London Illustrated News*, 'and coats hanging in shreds, having suffered bruises and blows in the struggle'. But when the Nightingale was not singing, business was not good; shortly after, the brilliant conductor Michael Costa, who had built up the opera company to a level of high distinction, walked out, taking it with him to the Covent Garden Theatre. Despite the long overdue British premiere of Beethoven's *Fidelio*, the theatre went dark in 1852, only to reopen shortly after when – it's an ill wind that blows no good – the Covent Garden Theatre burned down. For five splendid years under the formidable impresario and sometime singer Colonel Mapleson there were more premieres of the latest operas by Verdi, Gounod, Cherubini and Nicolai, with the greatest singers alive; the romantic ballet, too, throve. And then, out of the blue, the curse of Prometheus struck yet again and it was Her Majesty's turn, in December 1867, to go up in flames.

Fortunately, the shell of the auditorium survived, and a new, formidably fireproofed theatre was rapidly constructed within it. It was ready by 1869, but alas there were no takers. Finally in 1875 the theatre was hired by Moody and Sankey, the American evangelists, for their hugely popular revivalist meetings; it was not until 1877 that Colonel Mapleson took it over again, providing yet more premieres – a curiously belated first English *Carmen*, followed by *The Ring of the Nibelung* in 1882. Sarah Bernhardt came touring, and there were pantos and a production of *Uncle Tom's Cabin*. But by 1891 theatre technology had advanced so rapidly that the barely twenty-year-old building seemed hopelessly out of date, and it was pulled down again with the intention of building an even more splendid, state-of-the-art new theatre.

And so it came to pass, under the aegis of one of the most formidable *hommes du théâtre* in British theatrical history, Herbert Beerbohm Tree, who invested a considerable sum in the new theatre. It was just a hop and a skip for him: he had up to that point been running the Theatre Royal Haymarket directly opposite. Tree cut an unusual figure in the theatre of his time, particularly in contrast to the dominant actor-manager of the late Victorian period, Henry Irving. Both men were passionately concerned with raising standards in the profession – for which, in 1895, Irving received a knighthood, the first actor to do so. Tall and slim, with a curiously cadaverous physiognomy, Irving excelled at the sinister and the inward, bringing to the stage a unique atmosphere that compensated for his poor voice and emaciated frame; in life, he comported himself with exceptional gravitas. By contrast, Tree was a massive, extrovert presence, splendid in carriage, generous in manner, scattered in focus. Mercurial, impulsive, bonny, fantastical, he was the last of what Micheál Mac Liammóir – who acted with him as a boy – called 'the baroque personalities'. He had three children with his wife and another six with his mistress. Where Irving was all darkness and containment, Tree was good cheer and constant adventurousness. The son of a prosperous German corn merchant who had settled in London, Tree completed his education at Schnepfenthal College in Thuringia, Germany. He then acted as an amateur for some years, until, defying parental disapproval, he started earning his living in that profession, with some success. After a provincial apprenticeship he had his first London triumph in 1884; three years later he was managing the Comedy Theatre, and that same year took over the Theatre Royal Haymarket, where he produced more than thirty plays over ten years. Splendid though his regime at the Haymarket was, it was clear that Tree's expansiveness needed a larger playground than the elegant confines of the Theatre Royal.

The new theatre, commissioned from Charles J. Phipps, the leading theatre architect of the day – this was his thirteenth in the capital – was more massive in its impact than its predecessors on the same site, incorporating as it did a large hotel, the Carlton; between them, they occupied the entire block. The impression was one of some splendour, having the aspect of a great French provincial *hôtel de ville*. The interior, in the manner of Louis XIV, was even grander, not unlike an opera house, and the stage machinery was the most advanced in the West End. The presence of footmen in the foyers and lining the sweeping staircases ensured a palatial atmosphere, which must have made George V feel very much at home when he graced the coronation gala held there for him in 1911. Invisible to the public though no doubt visited by royalty, Tree's private quarters, ensconced in the dome at the top of the theatre, continued the splendour. There, in addition to his living quarters, he installed a substantial banqueting hall where he entertained with Lucullan magnificence. This splendid hall became – to demonstrate another aspect of Tree's generosity – the location of the acting academy he founded, which rapidly evolved into the Royal Academy of Dramatic Art (RADA).

The productions at the new theatre were also of a magnificence that rivalled and even eclipsed those of Irving at the Lyceum. Tree specialised in adaptations of classics – Dickens, Thackeray, Tolstoy, Dumas – which offered him the sort of ripe roles at which he excelled, but he also commissioned new plays from provocative modern dramatists like Henry Arthur Jones and George Bernard Shaw, who wrote *Pygmalion* specifically for Tree and Mrs Patrick Campbell. Shakespeare, however, was Tree's absolute passion – his mission, in fact. He spared no effort and no expense to make Shakespeare appealing. For him, ultra-realism was the way forward: real rabbits in *A Midsummer Night's Dream*, live horses in *Richard II* – the latter in a scene not actually envisaged by Shakespeare, the arrival of the King in London, greeted by his cheering subjects. Tree dismissed as 'cant' the increasingly vocal Elizabethan revivalists: anything and everything that stimulated the imagination must be brought to bear on the task of bringing the Bard to life. It is little surprise that he became fascinated by the new medium of film, for which he recorded a number of Shakespearean scenes. Indeed he was filming in Los Angeles in 1915–16 when His Majesty's had the greatest hit of its young life, the musical *Chu Chin Chow*, written, produced, directed and acted by the Australian-Norwegian actor Oscar Asche; it provided wartime London with the exotic uplift it needed and ran for five years, into the 1920s, by which time Tree had been dead for some years.

So His Majesty's had thus reverted to the music fare – albeit somewhat less elevated than Handel, Mozart, Bellini and Wagner – upon which its success had always been built. And so it continued, though with occasional forays into plays. Among the musicals that settled in for long runs were Gershwin's *Oh, Kay!* in 1927; *Follow the Girls* and *Brigadoon*

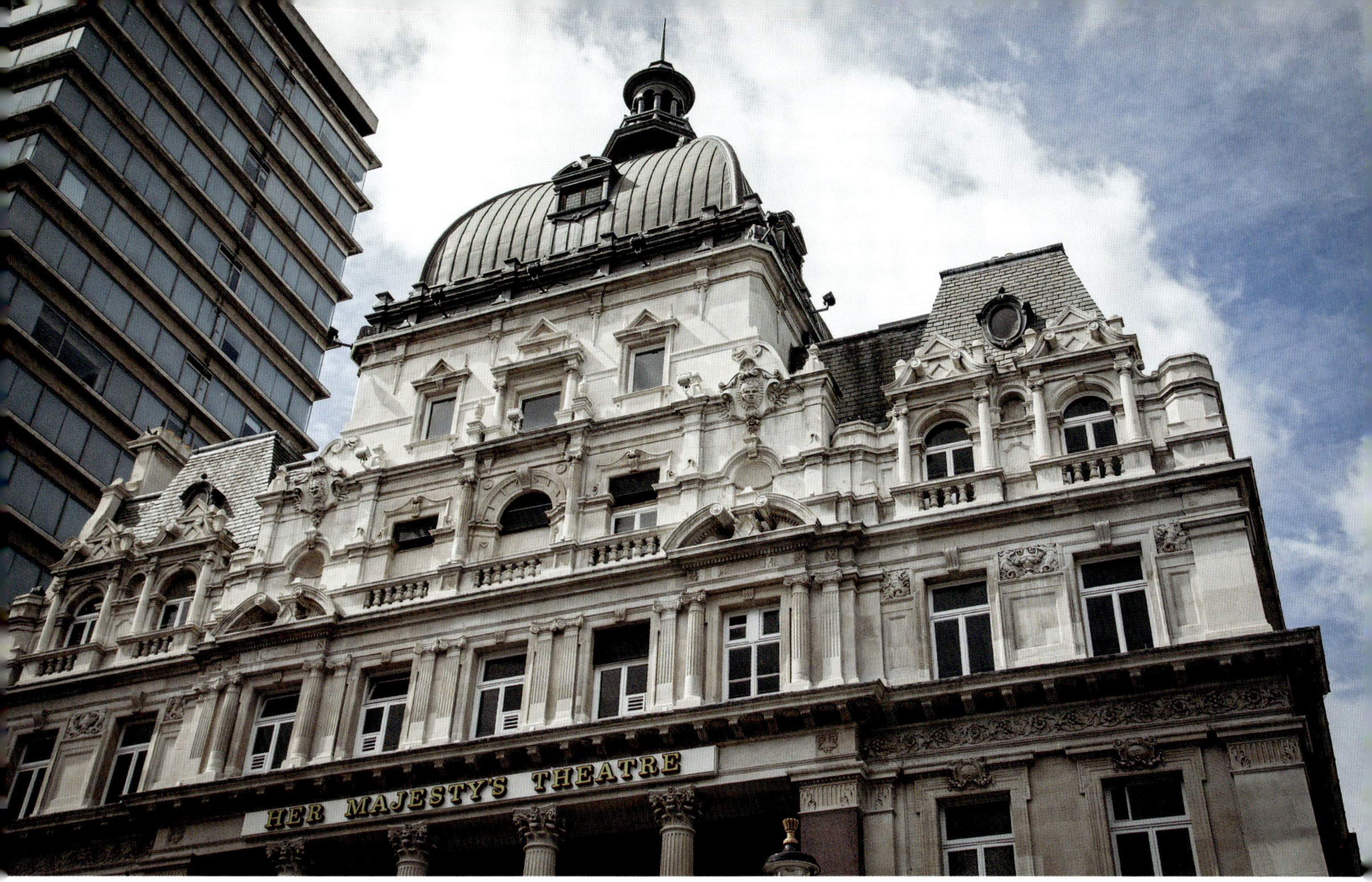

in the 1940s; *West Side Story* in 1958, with 1,039 performances; *Fiddler on the Roof* in 1967; and Stephen Sondheim's first great London hit, *Company*, in 1971. It saw its fair measure of flops, too, among them André Previn's *The Good Companions* and Alan Ayckbourn and Andrew Lloyd Webber's *Jeeves*. But the composer of that show returned with a world-beating triumph that must surely count as the apotheosis of Tree's wonderful theatre: *The Phantom of the Opera*, which opened in 1986 and which will presumably remain there as long as the building stands, is literally a part of the fabric of Her Majesty's, for the magnificent stage machinery installed in 1897 and still functioning has been incorporated into the set.

Curiously, despite this extraordinary succession of superb shows, led by a roll-call of the greatest performers in the musical theatre, it is the expansive spirit of Herbert Beerbohm Tree that seems still to preside over Her Majesty's. And perhaps the greatest show to have made its debut on that stage is Shaw's *Pygmalion*. On its notorious first night in April 1914, Tree had a very imperfect grasp of his lines; prompters were situated behind all the windows on the set. He also, as was his wont, completely forgot the plot of the play, so that when Mrs Pat as Eliza threw her slippers at him, he was struck dumb, thinking she had lost her mind. But he remained *radiant* through it all. 'A faint smile', wrote Madeleine Bingham in her biography *The Great Lover* (1978), 'can cross the faces of the theatrical establishment at the mention of the words Beerbohm Tree.' It still does.

ABOVE The exterior of Her Majesty's Theatre.

THEATRE ROYAL HAYMARKET

Rather cheekily, a certain John Potter decided in 1720 to build a theatre on the east side of the Hay Market, pretty well bang opposite the King's Theatre, on the site of an old inn. But in fact there was no rivalry between the playhouses: with the exception of Herbert Beerbohm Tree's relatively brief management of Her Majesty's Theatre, as it had by then become, the successive theatres on the west side of the road specialised in musical theatre – mostly opera – whereas the smaller house opposite largely confined itself to plays, even if it sometimes had to conceal the fact from the authorities. To begin with, Potter must have despaired of his investment because the modest new theatre, looking very much like a converted inn with a low canopy, stood empty for the first ten months of its life, while the vast edifice opposite – still unfinished – thrived. Eventually, the Francophile Duke of Marlborough took a lease on it and installed a troupe of French Comedians, as they were dubbed, in *La Fille à la Mode*. The theatre was known to the playgoing world as 'The New French Theatre' – despite the failure of the Duke's troupe to attract custom. The following year it was taken over by the versatile Aaron Hill – librettist, impresario, politician, economist, landscape gardener – but despite his many accomplishments he couldn't make a go of it either. It became a venue for tumblers, jugglers and dancers, which – notwithstanding the august presence of the King's across the road – was rather more in keeping with the area, which had become pretty rackety. It was, as a contemporary report had it, 'the resort of the loosest characters, after the closing of the theatres, who turned night into day' – so much so, in fact, that an Act of Parliament was passed, requiring taverns to close at midnight. A variety of amusements nonetheless flourished in the environs, often in a venue known as Mrs Midnight's Oratory, host to such irresistible acts as the Modern Colossus, the Female Samson, the Noted Ox with six legs and two bellies, the Beautiful Panther-mare, the five Dancing Bears, the much-applauded Stupendous Ostrich, and the Fire-eater, smoking out of red-hot tobacco pipes, champing lighted brimstone and swallowing his infernal mess of broth.

Tough competition. But in 1729 the theatre, now generally and affectionately referred to as The Little Theatre in the Haymarket, at last had a hit: an 'olio' – a ragbag, a medley – called *Hurlothrumbo; or, The Supernatural*, in which the author himself, one Samuel Johnson of Cheshire, performed – singing, dancing, playing the fiddle and walking on stilts. 'A more curious or a more insane production', writes one critic, enticingly, 'has seldom issued from human pen.' This Johnson was clearly a theatrical visionary, a pioneer surrealist, a dadaist, the Alfred Jarry of his day. There is a particularly vivid passage in which the stars are seen throwing down freezing daggers at the poor starving children in the streets, and another in which an aged woman wields a broom against spiders and all the young women who threaten to come near the narrator; as with Jarry, the play is replete with excremental humour. It ran for a year, drawing the admiration of the future novelist and head of the Bow Street Runners, Henry Fielding,

OPPOSITE The auditorium seen from the stage. One of the most beautiful theatres in London.

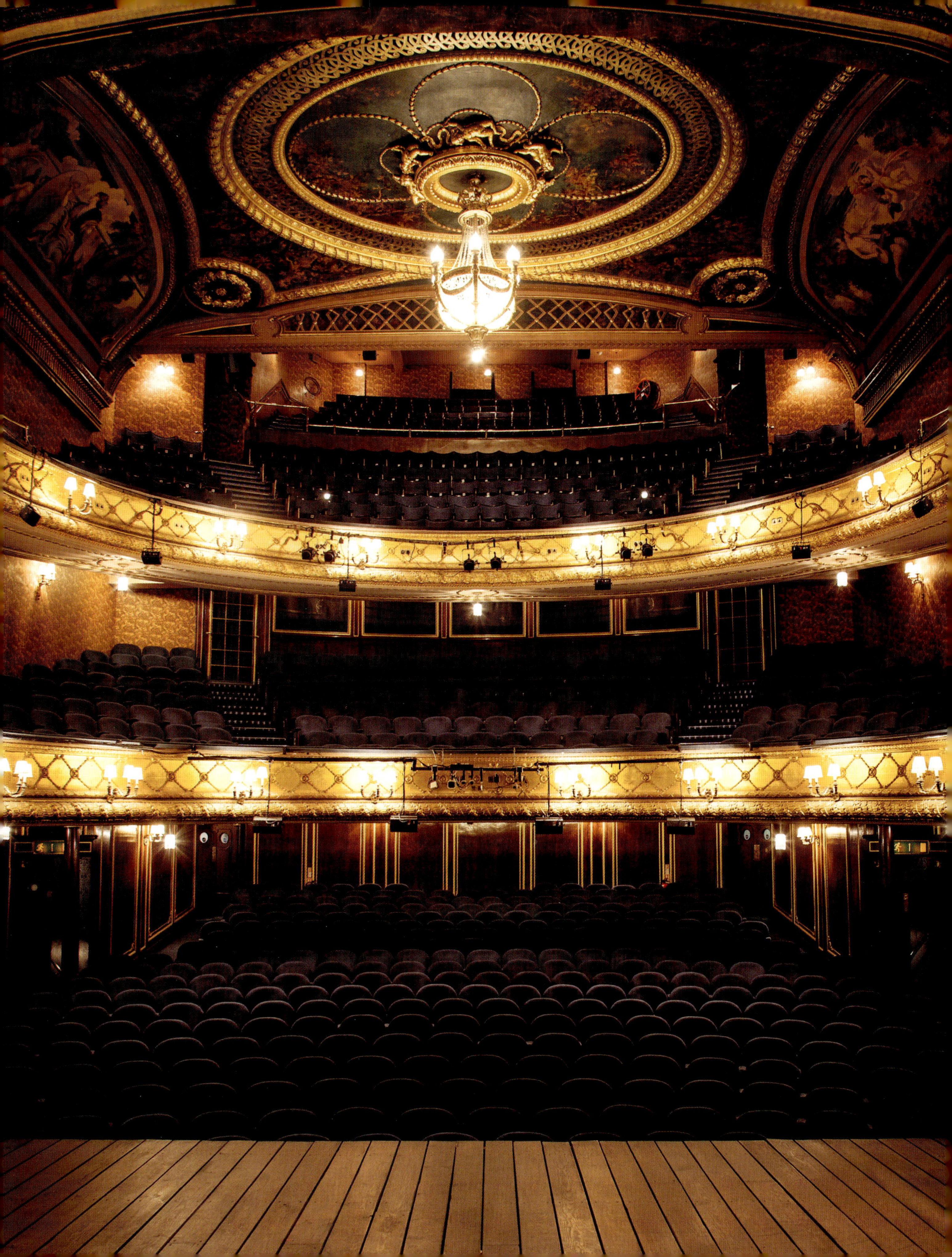

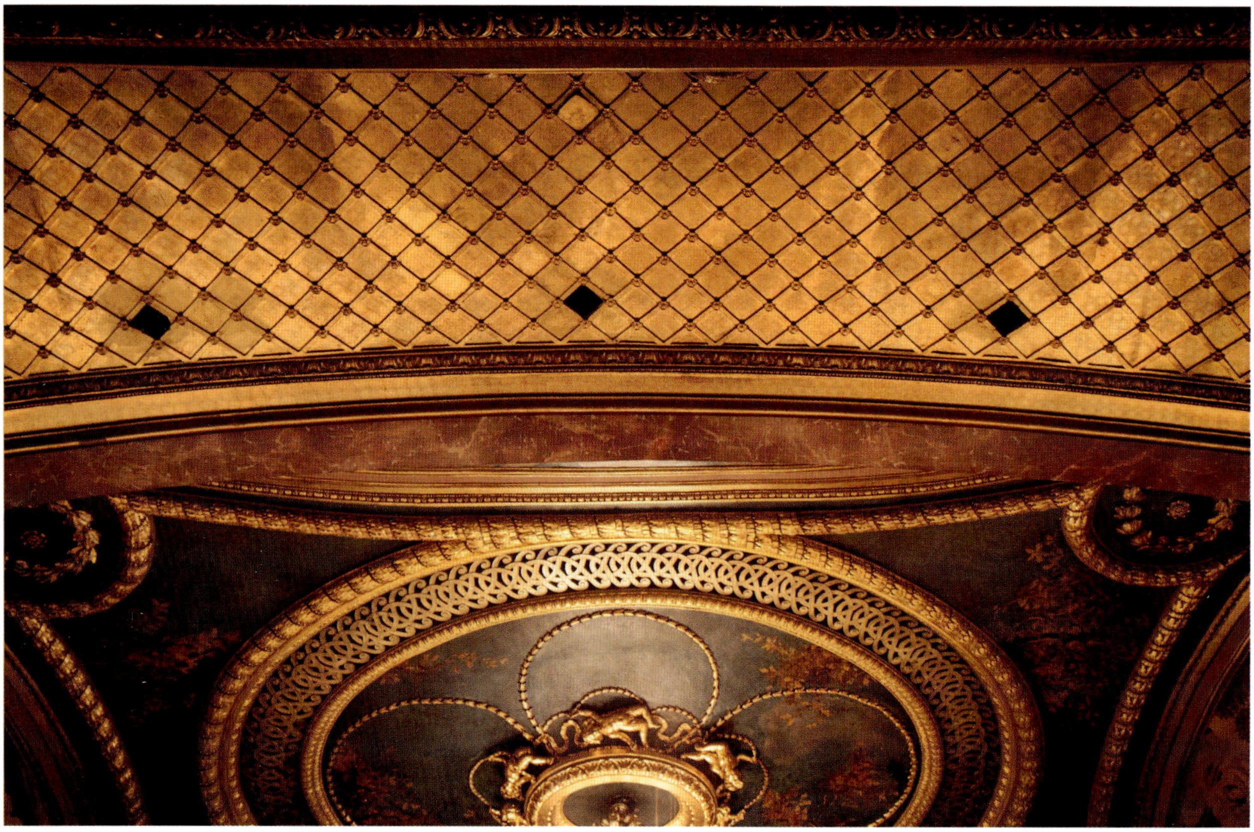

who was just getting into his savage stride as a satirist, set on a course that would culminate in the government, goaded beyond endurance, establishing the theatrical censorship that then prevailed for over two hundred years. In 1730, under the pseudonym Scriblerus Secundus, Fielding presented *Tom Thumb*, in which the satire, both literary and political, is quite explicit; it was riotously popular.

It was a period of extraordinary theatrical exuberance. In 1733 the actor-playwright Theophilus Cibber tried to introduce a little decorum with his distinguished Comedians of His Majesty's Revels, but it was not what people wanted: ever racier and more fantastical satire was what they craved. Fielding duly stepped up to the mark and installed his 'Great Mogul's Company of Comedians, recently dropped from the clouds'. Three years later these same comedians performed his play *The Historical Register for the Year 1736*, whose central character outrageously and obviously lampooned the prime minister, Sir Robert Walpole. This proved to be the straw that broke the camel's back, ushering in the Licensing Act of 1737, which forbade the production of plays (as opposed to musical entertainments) by theatres not holding letters patent and, more generally and ominously, the production of plays not authorised by the Lord Chamberlain. It marked a watershed in British theatre, a draconian law under which theatres squirmed and twisted from that time until the 1968 Theatres Act withdrew the Lord Chamberlain's censorial authority. Fielding gave up writing plays and turned instead to novels – literature's gain but the theatre's loss; there was to be no unbridled satire in British theatre again until the 1960s. The Hay-Market Theatre, as it was now more generally known, was the battlefield on which the great defeat had occurred.

ABOVE A detail of the auditorium. Note the fine workmanship.

Now that the theatre was policed by the Lord Chamberlain, presenting plays in theatres without letters patent – there were only two theatres with these, the Theatre Royal Drury Lane and the Covent Garden – required enormous ingenuity. It was only by happy accident, in the most literal sense, that in 1766 the Hay-Market Theatre became the third patent-holder. Until then it had a precarious existence, presenting plays under the pretence of holding concerts, with a rehearsal of the play thrown in *gratis* – a cunning ruse but not entirely satisfying to anyone. In 1747, ten years after Fielding's debacle, the utterly scurrilous and nakedly unscrupulous Samuel Foote, a brilliant mimic but an indifferent actor, took over, presenting crude satires purporting to be tea parties but which were mostly vehicles for *ad hominem* attacks on his fellow players. One of his noted productions was a cat opera, no less, performed entirely in mews and yowls and starring one 'Cat Harris'. Foote's success was, to put it mildly, variable, and he inspired deep and colourful contempt in his fellow authors. 'You *Samuel Fut* [*sic*] be pissed upon, with Scorn and Contempt, as a low Buffoon,' wrote Fielding, 'and I do, with the utmost Scorn and Contempt, piss on you accordingly.' Foote's tenure of the theatre was intermittent, but he happened to be running it when in 1766 his devil-may-care friend the Earl of Mexborough and various chums subjected him to a little practical joke: they gave him an unmanageable horse to ride, which promptly threw him; as a result of the accident he lost his left leg. Mortified, Mexborough used his influence to secure a letter patent for the theatre, which then became and ever after remained the Theatre Royal Haymarket. Foote bought the theatre outright, remodelling the interior. This latest incarnation of Foote's theatre had only moderate success, totally eclipsed in 1770 by a funambulist called Maddox, by far the most commercially successful performer ever to appear at the theatre. Thereafter Foote continued on his erratic way until he was engulfed in scandal, accused by his own coachman of sexual assault; he was eventually acquitted, but not before the appearance of a pamphlet entitled *Sodom and Onan*, 'A Satire Inscrib'd to [—] Esqr, alias the Devil upon Two Sticks'; for disambiguation, the blank between the brackets was filled by an engraving of a foot. He died a year later, but had a characteristically disruptive afterlife: when in 1805 his satirical play *The Tailors* was revived at the theatre, the eponymous craftsmen rioted.

The altogether more sober George Colman took over in 1776, renovating the theatre and slowly rebuilding its reputation, to such an extent that when Drury Lane was closed for renovations in 1793–4 the Haymarket played under the older theatre's patent. In February 1794 the Haymarket was honoured by a visit from the king himself, but this went horribly wrong when the crowd surged forward to see him at close quarters: twenty people died, with many others 'dreadfully bruised'. This unfortunate incident did nothing to diminish the theatre's ever-rising stock, any more than Colman's son and heir George Jr running the theatre from his cell in the King's Bench Prison in Southwark for a while, where he had been incarcerated for debt. Despite Colman Jr's personal extravagance, the theatre continued to be profitable. Its ascent to glory was confirmed when John Nash, industriously introducing his neoclassical Regency elegance to London, was commissioned to rebuild it. He caused the site to be shifted southwards so that patrons, beautifully framed by his superb portico, were afforded an unbroken view down Charles II Street to St James's Square as they left the theatre. Nash did little of note to the auditorium, which was found to be chilly and unwelcoming: 'petrified', according to one querulous contemporary report. The new theatre opened successfully enough in July 1821 with a revival of *The Rivals* and thereafter was host to a number of companies. Among the most successful, and the sensation of the 1833 season, was the Irish actress Julia Glover, who trumped her admired Hamlet at the Lyceum some years earlier with her account of Sir John Falstaff in *The Merry Wives of Windsor*; in the seventeen years since she had donned Hamlet's inky cloak her waistline had expanded

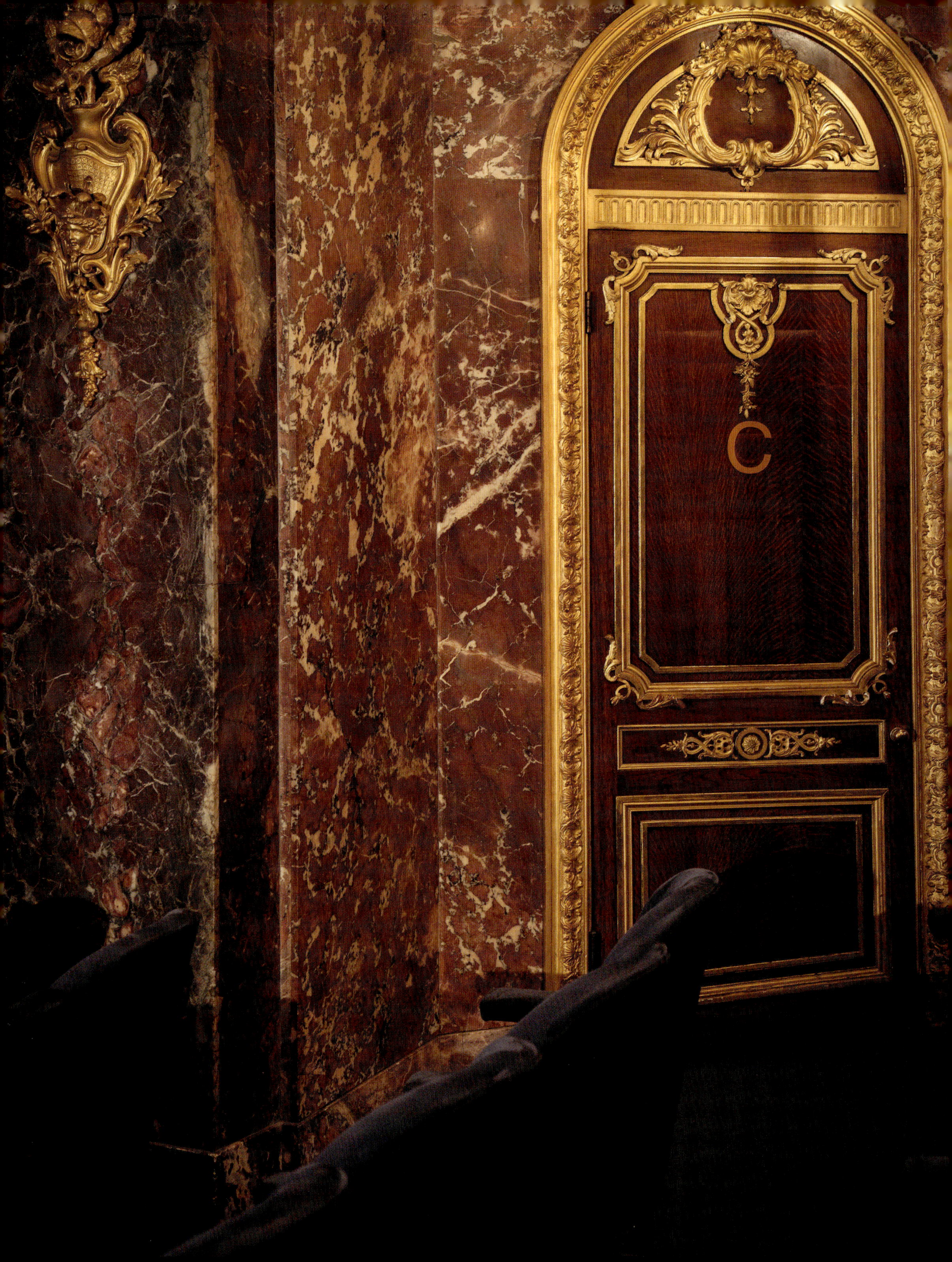
C

considerably, provoking one ungallant critic to observe that she required little make-up to play the Fat Knight.

In 1837, the unstintingly generous Benjamin Webster became the Haymarket's manager, presenting many of the greatest actors of his time: among the first was Samuel Phelps, an early pioneer of authentic Shakespearean texts, in his debut as Shylock. Under Webster, the theatre's reputation was consolidated. The 1843 revision of the Theatres Act, though a disaster in terms of censorship (it brought ever more theatres under the Lord Chamberlain's authority), had one beneficial effect: it allowed many more playhouses to present plays without subterfuge; despite, or perhaps because of, the competition, the three patent houses (Drury Lane, Covent Garden and the Theatre Royal Haymarket) now stood out as the leaders of the profession. Webster rebuilt the interior of the theatre, installing a resplendent chandelier and orchestra stalls, but eventually his financial reserves ran out and he moved on to another theatre, the Adelphi, handing over to John Baldwin Buckstone, who instituted something of a golden age at the Haymarket, establishing it as a house of comedy. Though at first he presented classics like *The Rivals* and *The School for Scandal*, more and more new plays received their premieres here, including no fewer than seven by W. S. Gilbert (before Richard D'Oyly Carte brought him and Arthur Sullivan together). W. H. and Madge Kendal – 'Mr and Mrs Kendal', as they were invariably styled – were the leading players, always acting opposite each other; Madge's gifts were perhaps greater than those of her husband. Buckstone himself generally appeared – to riotous effect – in afterpieces which he himself also wrote. 'Few men,' wrote *The Times*, 'have possessed to a greater extent the power of communicating the spirit of mirth to an audience.' He was helped too in his vocation by remarkable physical attributes and a peculiar, hilarious voice. Charles Dickens had admired Buckstone since he was a boy, going home, he said, 'to dream of his comicalities'.

OPPOSITE A door in the auditorium. How well the red marble complements the gold.

Buckstone died in 1878, secure in the love of his public and the profitability of his theatre. It is said that he haunts the theatre still: Patrick Stewart caught a glimpse of him when he was appearing there in *Waiting for Godot* in 2009. It's a wonder that the poor ghost can find its way around: the building has changed so often since Buckstone's day; interestingly, it only ever appears during hits. It must have been well pleased with Buckstone's immediate successors, the Bancrofts, another husband-and-wife team: Squire, monocled, moustached and nobly profiled, and Marie, known a Effie, feisty and characterful. They took on the lease after an epoch-making few years at the Prince of Wales Royal Theatre in Soho, where their great successes were in the socially realistic plays of Tom Robertson with their strikingly monosyllabic titles: *Ours*, *Caste*, *Play*, *School*. One of the Bancrofts' great innovations was to hand the play over to the writer to direct, which Robertson duly did, aiming to achieve a naturalness and ease in both staging and playing, and encouraging a detailed realism in the design, which rejected the still dominant melodramatic tradition. The plays were quickly dubbed 'cup-and-saucer dramas', establishing the genre of drawing-room comedy, which held sway in the West End – notably at the Theatre Royal Haymarket – for fully 75 years.

The theatre in general was becoming polite, intelligent and respectable – even though the plays themselves often conveyed sharp social criticism – and standards both onstage and in the auditorium began to rise; the Bancrofts, pioneers of enlightened actor-managerial conduct, awarded Robertson an emolument for each performance of his plays, establishing the notion of royalties. They also set to work on the building, enclosing the playing area within the proscenium on all four sides to give the West End its first picture-frame stage, introducing box sets, with their increased sense of illusion. They raised the ceiling, added a stone staircase and

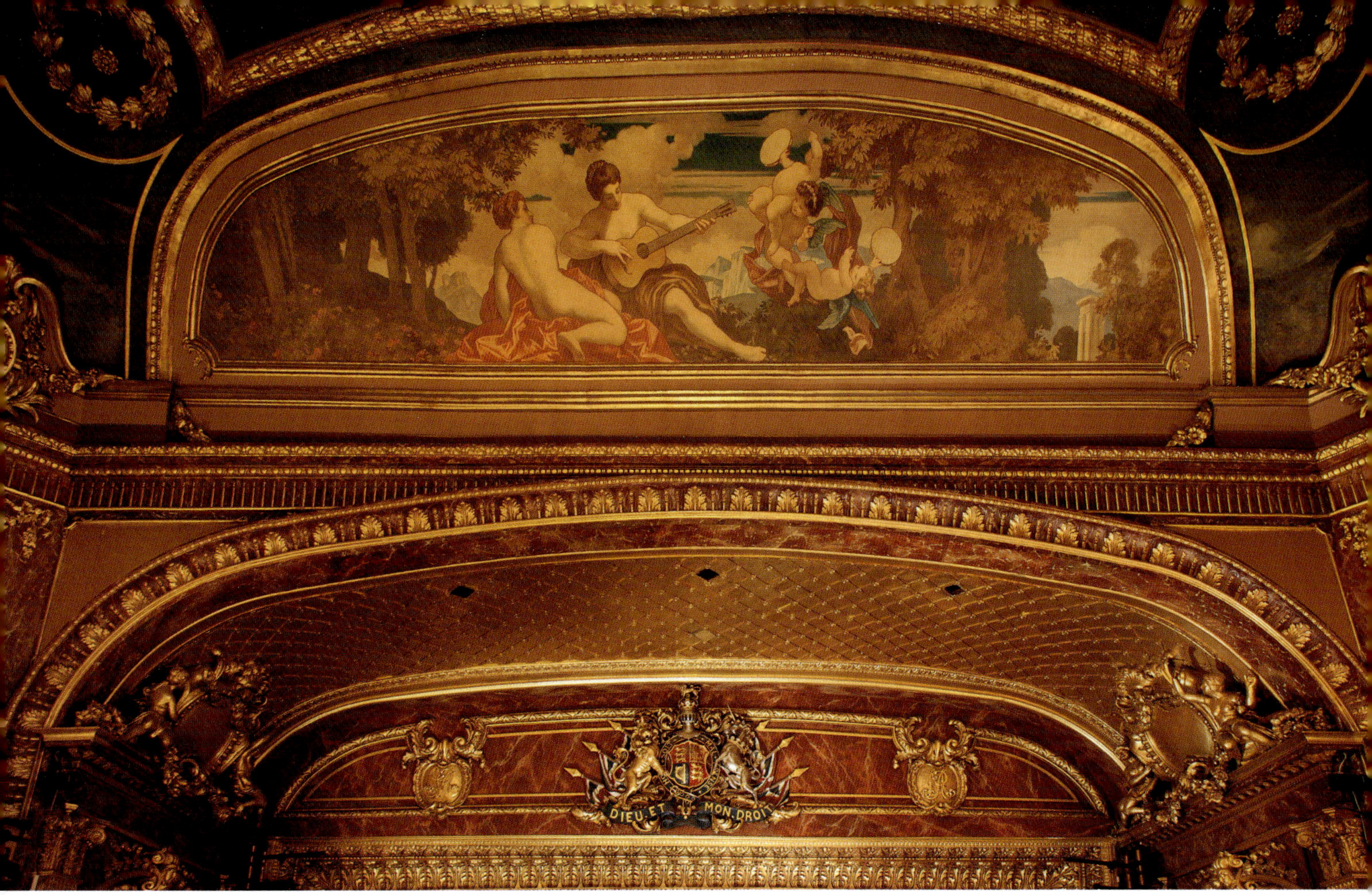

a refreshment room and removed all obstacles to give a clear view of the stage. They also abolished the pit, filling it with seats and calling the resulting area the 'orchestra stalls'. The former pittites were banished to an upper circle. They did not take this banishment lying down and caused a small riot on the opening night of the newly reconstructed theatre, which took place in January 1880 in the midst of the densest, cruellest fog London had ever known. Having struggled through the peasouper, they made their presence felt: for its first twenty minutes, the performance – a revival of Edward Bulwer-Lytton's comedy *Money*, first produced at the same theatre forty years earlier – proceeded to the accompaniment of a screaming, roaring protest, which only subsided when Effie Bancroft made her entrance; by the end, the whole house joined in the applause. It is the last recorded riot in a London playhouse, a grand old tradition that kept the theatre in touch with its origins in the marketplaces and in the courtyards of inns. Theatre was upwardly mobile now, not always to its advantage.

The Bancrofts had five exceptionally successful years in the Haymarket and then retired, making only occasional professional appearances thereafter. Bancroft was knighted in 1897, only two years after Henry Irving, the first theatrical knight – a measure of his impact not so much as an actor but as a pioneer and ambassador for the theatre. The Theatre Royal Haymarket was similarly haloed with distinction, a quality confirmed by the stupendous and dynamic figure who, two years after the Bancrofts' departure, took it by storm. Herbert Beerbohm Tree had been acting professionally for only six years when he had his first London success; three years

ABOVE The auditorium, above the proscenium arch. Note the fine carving of the details and the mural.

later he took over the Comedy Theatre, where his triumph as the Russian Demetrius in *The Red Lamp* by W. Outram Tristram emboldened him to install himself at the Theatre Royal Haymarket; on arrival he immediately made the place brighter by installing electric lighting. And enlightened was his policy, too, rather different to the Bancrofts': a striking blend of literary adaptations, melodrama, Shakespeare and radical, modern plays. He supported new playwrights by producing special cheap 'Monday night' performances of their work. Ever conscious of the box office, he did the classical plays – *The Merry Wives of Windsor*, *Henry IV*, *Hamlet* – at matinees, and popular successes at night. Tree's Falstaff was one of his great achievements; his Hamlet less impressive. 'I never saw anything so funny in my life,' purred W. S. Gilbert, 'and yet it was not in the least vulgar.' Tree played Dr Stockman in Ibsen's *An Enemy of the People*, which had nearly caused a riot when he did it in Chicago: he played the role in a humorous fashion, said his biographer Hesketh Pearson, 'that would have surprised the author', but the play was judged a huge success.

Among the radical new plays Tree commissioned from British authors was Oscar Wilde's *A Woman of No Importance*, which premiered in 1893. Wilde was doubtful whether Tree would be able to play the witty, amiable Lord Illingworth, but he relished the part, seeming to carry the role into private life. 'Every day', said Wilde, 'dear Herbert becomes *de plus en plus Oscarisé*.' He told Tree that he would always regard him as the best critic of his plays. 'But I have never criticised your plays,' replied an astonished Tree. 'That's why,' rejoined Oscar. Two years earlier, Wilde's dramatic masterpiece *An Ideal Husband* had had its first outing at the Haymarket, during one of Tree's absences when he was touring America; the theatre and the author were a perfect fit, as has been demonstrated over and again in the subsequent 125 years.

Tree's smash hit at the Haymarket, the play that made him enough money to be able to invest significantly in the newly built and much larger Her Majesty's Theatre across the road, was cut of coarser cloth. *Trilby*, in which Tree played the role of Svengali in 1895, was an adaptation from the novel by George du Maurier. The part of the charismatic and terrifying music teacher was considerably beefed up to suit the actor, who donned extravagant curls and a set of false teeth to give what was as much his defining role as Matthias, the murderous burgomaster in *The Bells*, had been for Henry Irving. It gave free rein to Tree's sense of fantasy, his embrace of the exotic and his physical inventiveness; audiences were spellbound. He continued to play the part until he died, some twenty years later. By then the Theatre Royal Haymarket had passed from Tree to the actor-manager Cyril Maude, who, after a successful decade, closed the theatre for five months, remaking it from top to bottom: the interior was entirely reconstructed by C. Stanley Peach in steel, brick and mortar, restoring the pit 'so long absent from this theatre'. It reopened in 1905 with a transfer of *Beauty and the Barge*, 'a farce in three acts'. There was the occasional daring production, like Maurice Maeterlinck's *The Blue Bird*, and the first licensed production of Henrik Ibsen's still fiercely controversial *Ghosts*; otherwise it was host to solid West End fare, culminating startlingly in 1939, just before the Second World War, with Noël Coward's sexually ambiguous *Design for Living*, the quintessential 1930s play, which at its first London production, only five years after Coward wrote it, already seemed to belong to a vanished world.

The theatre closed again for refurbishment, a major reconstruction this time under the supervision of the architect John Murray, introducing some of theatre's most distinctive features, including the large lounge bar under the stalls floor decorated in Louis XIV manner and its uncommonly large cloakroom. No sooner was it done than war broke out, and there was a brief cessation in performances; when they resumed it was with difficulty because of the call-up, which resulted in a shortage of actors, stagehands and box office workers. The Blitz, arriving in September 1940, stopped almost all West

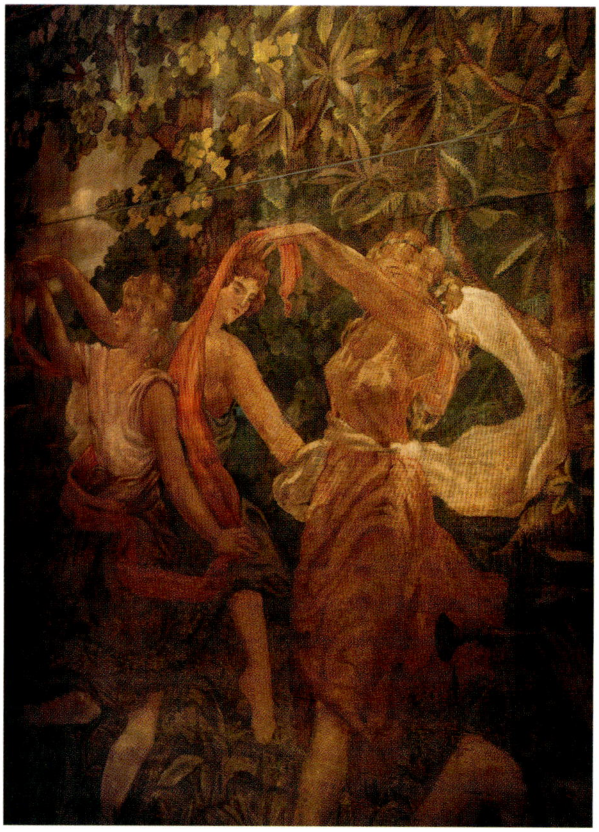

End performances. During this terrifying period, with bombs falling nightly across the city and hitting theatre after theatre, John Gielgud – by then in his mid-thirties and established as the very embodiment of classical theatre both as an actor and a director – stayed in an apartment in the Theatre Royal Haymarket, where he had recently directed and appeared in Congreve's Restoration comedy *Love for Love*. Having been turned down for active service, Gielgud flung himself, like his fellow actors, into the job of keeping up the spirits of the embattled population, either touring to war zones or back at home at in the West End. Noël Coward, having failed to secure employment at a high level in the Foreign Office as he had confidently expected, returned somewhat huffily to the Haymarket in 1942 with two plays, both of which had been written and scheduled to open three years earlier. He played the wildly contrasted leading parts in both – the mercurial and flamboyant Garry Essendine in *Present Laughter* and the cockney paterfamilias Frank Gibbons in *This Happy Breed*, of which the *Daily Express* wrote: 'Mr Coward . . . in his own part occasionally permits himself to speak for an England which, though tired, is still possessed of an invincible stamina.' The year 1942 was as grim as any Britain had ever known, and the world of the theatre, at home and at the front, helped to keep the darkness at bay. And the Haymarket, with its incomparable classical portico and its evocation of a long-vanished era of elegance, was a particularly visible manifestation of that spirit.

In 1944, when victory was at last in sight, John Gielgud masterminded an extraordinary affirmation of the power of theatre to divert, to delight and to illuminate. The repertory included Somerset Maugham's *The Circle* as well as *Love for Love*, *A Midsummer Night's Dream*, *The Duchess of Malfi* and *Hamlet*, this latter being the fourth and final time Gielgud played the part; the company included Peggy Ashcroft, Max Adrian, Miles Malleson and Leon Quartermaine. The season was managed by Hugh 'Binkie' Beaumont, the greatest impresario of his time, under the banner of HM Tennent Ltd, an organisation that became almost synonymous with the Theatre Royal Haymarket for a quarter of a century. It was a feast of superlatively staged, exquisitely designed and matchlessly performed theatre, elegant and witty, stimulating to mind and senses and much more polished than the rougher and readier but often more viscerally exciting fare on offer at the Old Vic, then in exile at the New Theatre under Laurence Olivier and Ralph Richardson. Gielgud and Olivier, at the head of their

ABOVE Detail of a mural in the auditorium.

OPPOSITE The royal box. Note the extravagant combination of marble (in particular the little marble balustrade), gilt and the silk curtains.

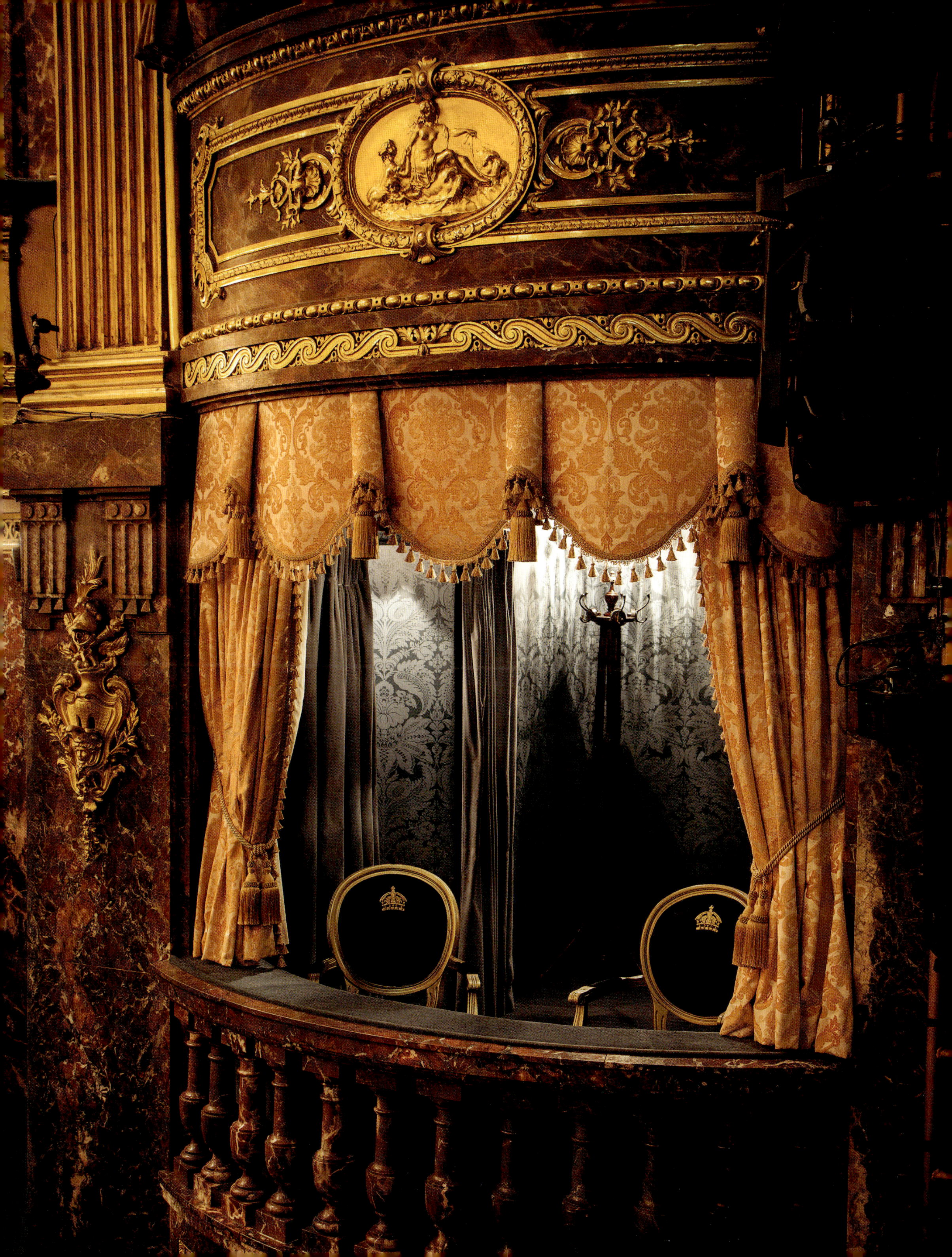

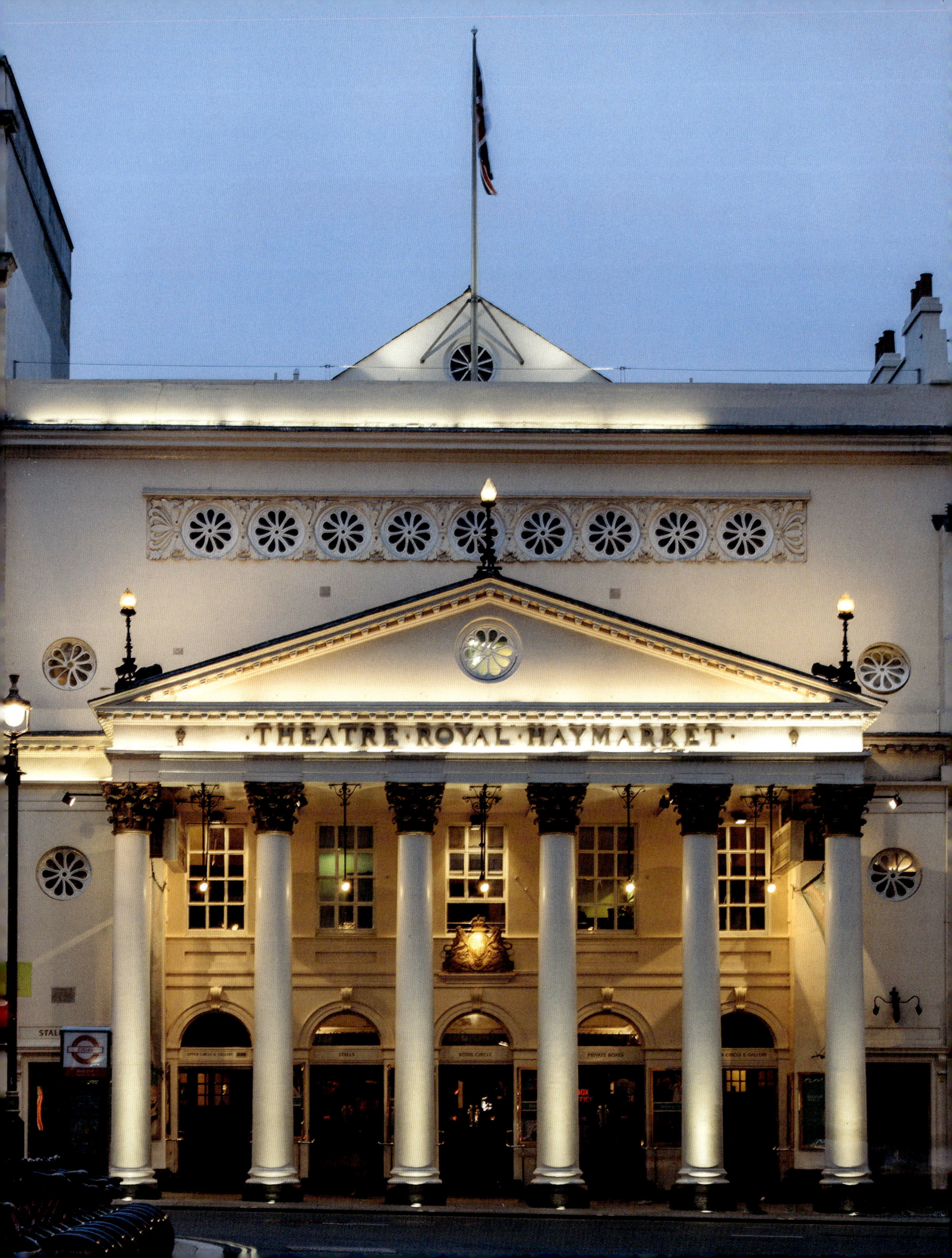
THEATRE·ROYAL·HAYMARKET

respective companies, seemed to embody opposite but complementary qualities, encompassing almost everything that was meant then by British acting: Gielgud's subtlety, all oboes and cellos and thinking at the speed of light; Olivier's animal instinct, false noses and beards and pratfalls and terrible howls of pain welling up from deep in the unconscious. Gielgud's Hamlet and Olivier's Richard III were the twin peaks of classical acting in their day and cast long shadows over subsequent generations.

That season at the Theatre Royal Haymarket set the bar for British theatre for some quarter of a century. Binkie Beaumont, with his silky diplomacy and ruthless maintenance of standards, turned the Haymarket into a sort of national theatre *avant la lettre* with a loose grouping of highly distinguished actors – Gielgud, Richardson, Ashcroft, Evans, Wendy Hiller, Sybil Thorndike – in permanent rotation; designers like Cecil Beaton and Rex Whistler; and shrewd, tasteful directors of the ilk of Glen Byam Shaw, Frith Banbury and Gielgud himself. There were plentiful revivals – *Lady Windermere's Fan* and *The Importance of Being Earnest* in 1948 – and exciting imports from France and America: Gielgud directed Tennessee Williams's *The Glass Menagerie* with Helen Hayes, and *The Heiress*, an adaptation of Henry James's *Washington Square*, with Richardson and Ashcroft. In the coronation year, 1953, Coward gave a rare performance in a play not written by him, *The Apple Cart* by George Bernard Shaw, with Margaret Leighton as his co-star. This was rather a risqué choice: the play concerns a king who, crossed by his prime minister and cabinet, threatens to abdicate and stand for parliament. But nothing else that appeared at the Haymarket throughout the 1950s could be classed as risqué. The house dramatist was N. C. Hunter, whose gently elegiac plays offered splendid roles for the regular actors; the plays of Enid Bagnold, Lady Jones in real life, were more bracing, but the characters and their dilemmas seemed very distant from the lives of most citizens of post-war Britain, whose anxieties and indeed whose appetite for challenge and change were increasingly supplied away from the West End; with the foundation of the Royal Shakespeare Company and the National Theatre, managers were increasingly obliged to compete with their larger budgets and superior cutting edge.

The Theatre Royal Haymarket continued to offer polished productions of classics, but it seemed increasingly to cater to an audience seeking relief from the harsher, more challenging world of the modern theatre. In 1971 Louis Michaels took over and continued this comfortable policy: the productions were still star-led but a little less classy, with exceptions like Trevor Nunn's richly detailed production of Shaw's *Heartbreak House* with Paul Scofield, Vanessa Redgrave and Felicity Kendal; there were many transfers from Chichester. The loss of the enlivening touch of Beaumont's vanished hand was keenly felt. Significantly, a number of former directors of the National and the RSC theatres were to be found at the Theatre Royal, most notably in the three seasons of the Peter Hall Company presented by Bill Kenwright from 1995 to 1997. The theatre has not lacked for successful productions, nor daring ones: Ian McKellen and Patrick Stewart had a triumph with *Waiting for Godot* in 2009. The problem is a tricky one: the loveliest auditorium and some of the most elegant front-of-house facilities in the West End create a climate not obviously conducive to cutting-edge work, which in its day, and in its way, John Gielgud's work with Binkie Beaumont was. Gielgud and his colleagues were playing to the strengths of the building; too many of his successors are compelled to fight against it.

In 2018 the theatre was bought by the Anglo-Russian billionaire and philanthropist Sir Len Blavatnik for the unprecedented sum of £40 million. The profession and audiences await with fascination the new era, both for the Haymarket and for the theatre at large. We live in interesting times.

OPPOSITE Perhaps the most elegant entrance to a theatre.

ROYAL OPERA HOUSE

One of the two possessors of the precious letters patent issued by Charles II on his return to the throne was William Davenant; it was bought after his death by the famously despotic lawyer-impresario Christopher Rich, who, having been driven out of the Theatre Royal Drury Lane, defiantly began building a new theatre on the site previously occupied by Davenant's company at Lincoln's Inn Fields. The job was completed by Rich's far more genial son John, a brilliant showman, dazzling mime, creator of the English Harlequin – and shrewd businessman. His great triumph there was John Gay's burlesque *The Beggar's Opera* (1728) with its proliferation of wittily orchestrated folk tunes and politically provocative action: the show, said the wags of the day, made Gay rich, and Rich gay. Actually, it made Rich rich; in 1732 he ploughed some of his immense profits from the show into building a new theatre on the edge of Inigo Jones's Covent Garden piazza. This was the first Covent Garden Theatre. The opening production was a revival of William Congreve's mordant comedy of sexual manners *The Way of the World*, but Rich's personal taste ran rather more to spectacle, and inevitably he turned to opera, the great fashionable art form of the day. In 1734, in a brilliant managerial coup, he persuaded the hugely successful 48-year-old George Frideric Handel, with a long run of operatic triumphs at the King's Theatre in Haymarket behind him, to become, in effect, composer-in-residence of the new theatre.

This first Covent Garden Theatre was of some splendour. Designed by Edward Shepherd and with an auditorium lavishly decorated by the Venetian painter Giacomo Amiconi, it held nearly two thousand people; Amiconi was a specialist in mythological scenes, which admirably suited Handel's subject matter. In his first three and half years there he produced an astonishing sequence of masterpieces: *Ariodante*, *Alcina*, *Atalanta*, *Arminio* and the ode *Alexander's Feast*, as well as (perhaps just to show that he could write a piece whose title didn't begin with A) *Giustino* and *Berenice*. When opera began to lose its audience he turned to the newly popular form of oratorio, returning to Covent Garden and again inexhaustibly producing masterpiece after masterpiece, all first performed in the theatre over five years: *Samson*, *Semele*, *Belshazzar*, *Judas Maccabaeus*, *Solomon*, *Theodora*, *Jephtha*. This triumphant succession ended, after a short gap, in 1757, with the resonantly named *The Triumph of Time and Truth*, on which Handel had worked over the course of fifty years; he died, frail and blind, two years after its first performance.

Rich died in 1761. Under his successors the theatre's fare became less musical and more dramatic; Oliver Goldsmith's *She Stoops to Conquer* and Richard Brinsley Sheridan's *The Rivals* had their first performances there as part of the final surge of the wave of dramatic energy liberated by the Restoration. Thereafter, softened by the more sentimental taste of the new era and reined in by the Theatres Act 1743, which invested the Lord Chamberlain with the duty of censorship, playwriting went into steep decline until near the

OPPOSITE Looking across the auditorium. Note the rich velvet curtain and the spun gold designs.

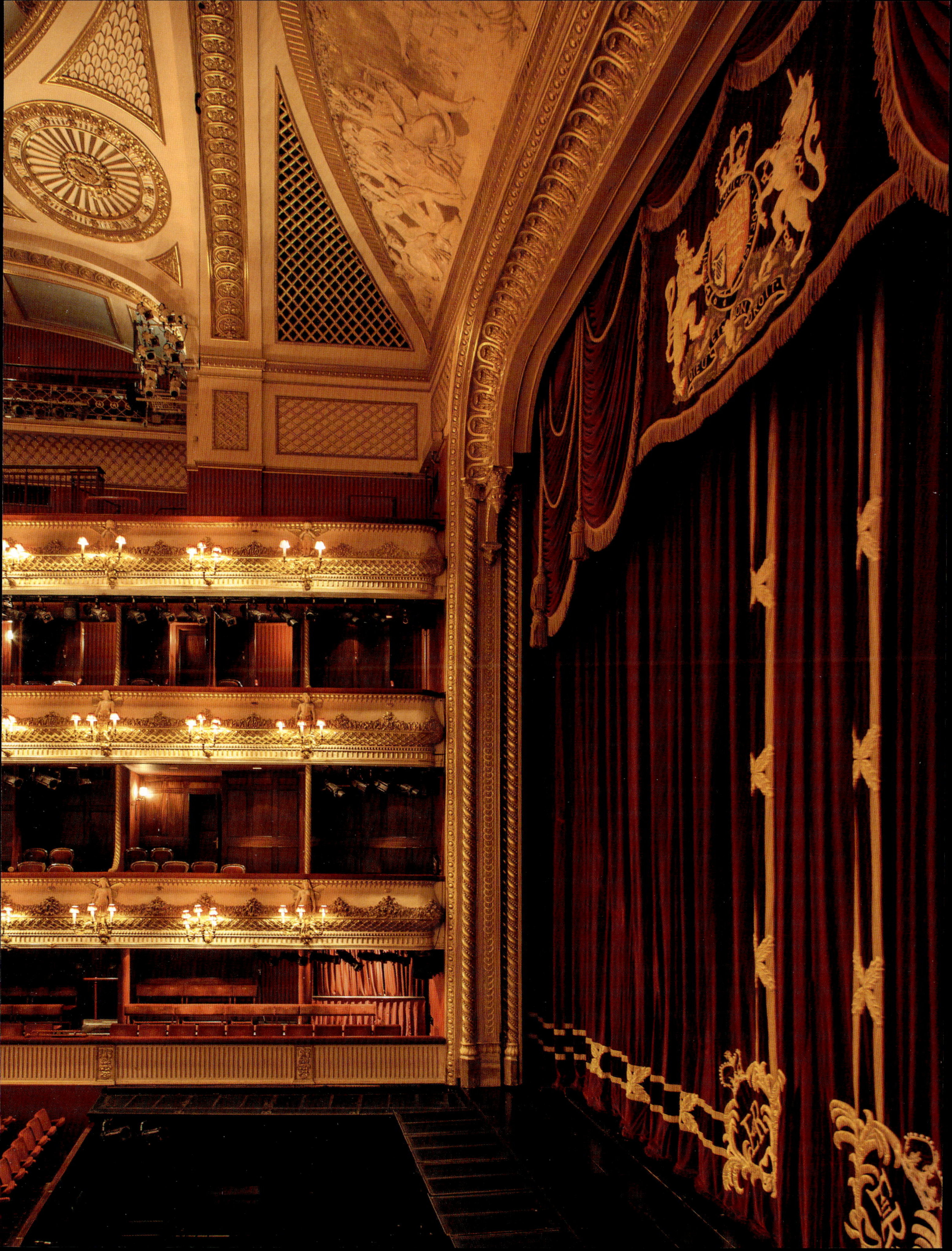
DIEU ET MON DROIT

end of the nineteenth century. In future, both at Covent Garden and at Drury Lane, the other great patent theatre, the work inclined ever more towards spectacle, which, though it would have warmed Rich's heart, dismayed connoisseurs of the drama. Meanwhile, the area around the theatre, notably in Bow Street where its entrance was, had become considerably less salubrious so that Shepherd's splendid and nobly conceived building was surrounded by the sort of low life with which, from its beginnings in Shoreditch, the theatre in Britain had always been associated. The quality who emerged from the opera, the ballet or the play ran the gauntlet of pubs, gaming houses, porn shops and brothels in the street where once Oliver Cromwell – and later the woodcarver Grinling Gibbons, the dramatist William Wycherley and the star actors David Garrick and Charles Macklin – had lived. The situation was only aggravated by the development, initiated by the Earls of Bedford, of a vegetable market in the centre of the piazza. This market quickly sprawled across the whole area, which progressively fell into disrepute, attracting pickpockets, pimps and prostitutes. As early as 1740, only six years after the construction of the first theatre, a magistrates' court was established at 4 Bow Street, slap in front of it; here the great novelist and savage critic of government Henry Fielding, appointed Chief Magistrate of London, meted out justice and with his half-brother John created the first modern police force, the Bow Street Runners.

Perhaps in an attempt to improve the tone of the area, the theatre was elegantly remodelled in 1782. Only ten years later it was again refashioned at huge expense, and then – the fate of so many theatres in the eighteenth and nineteenth centuries – in September 1808 it burned down; Handel's organ and a large number of his manuscripts were lost in the conflagration. It is a mark of the esteem in which the Covent Garden theatre was held that a public subscription for a new theatre was launched under the patronage of King George III and two of his sons, the dukes of York and Northumberland.

A mere three months after its predecessor had gone up in flames, the foundation stone for the new building was laid by no less a personage than the Prince of Wales (later George IV). By September 1809 the monumental new theatre opened, designed by the distinguished architect Robert Smirke, whose other public buildings include the British Museum, the east wing of Somerset House and what is now Canada House; the new theatre was modelled on the temple of Minerva in Vei, outside Rome, adorned with four large, fluted Doric columns, enclosed by iron rails and decorated by bas-relief figures representing the Drama ancient and modern. The side of the building was even more impressively endowed with classical figures and the greatest Greek and Roman writers; at the centre of them sat what *Illustrations of the Public Buildings of London* (1825) called 'OUR immortal Bard', surrounded by the emblems of dramatic poetry and his own characters: Prospero, Miranda, Caliban, Ariel, the Macbeths and Hecate. The interior of the theatre was of unexampled splendour, with huge staircases and porphyry columns; the auditorium, horseshoe in shape, had three tiers of boxes. From the central circular part of the ceiling, which was painted sky blue, hung a magnificent chandelier, outshining the other fourteen that were scattered throughout the auditorium. Around the dress circle were wreaths in burnished gold surrounding the rose of England; the first circle fielded the thistle of Scotland, and the second the shamrock of Ireland, a configuration repeated throughout the house. The reflection of the lights on the gold, thought the anonymous author of the *Illustrations*, 'gratifies the prevalent taste for splendour with one blaze of refulgence'.

The opening production – rather tempting fate, one might have thought – was of *Macbeth*. No supernatural disasters occurred, but the new management, led by the distinguished tragedian John Philip Kemble, had invited trouble with their decision to raise prices in order to recoup the cost of building the stupendous new theatre. On the opening night the audience members in the cheaper

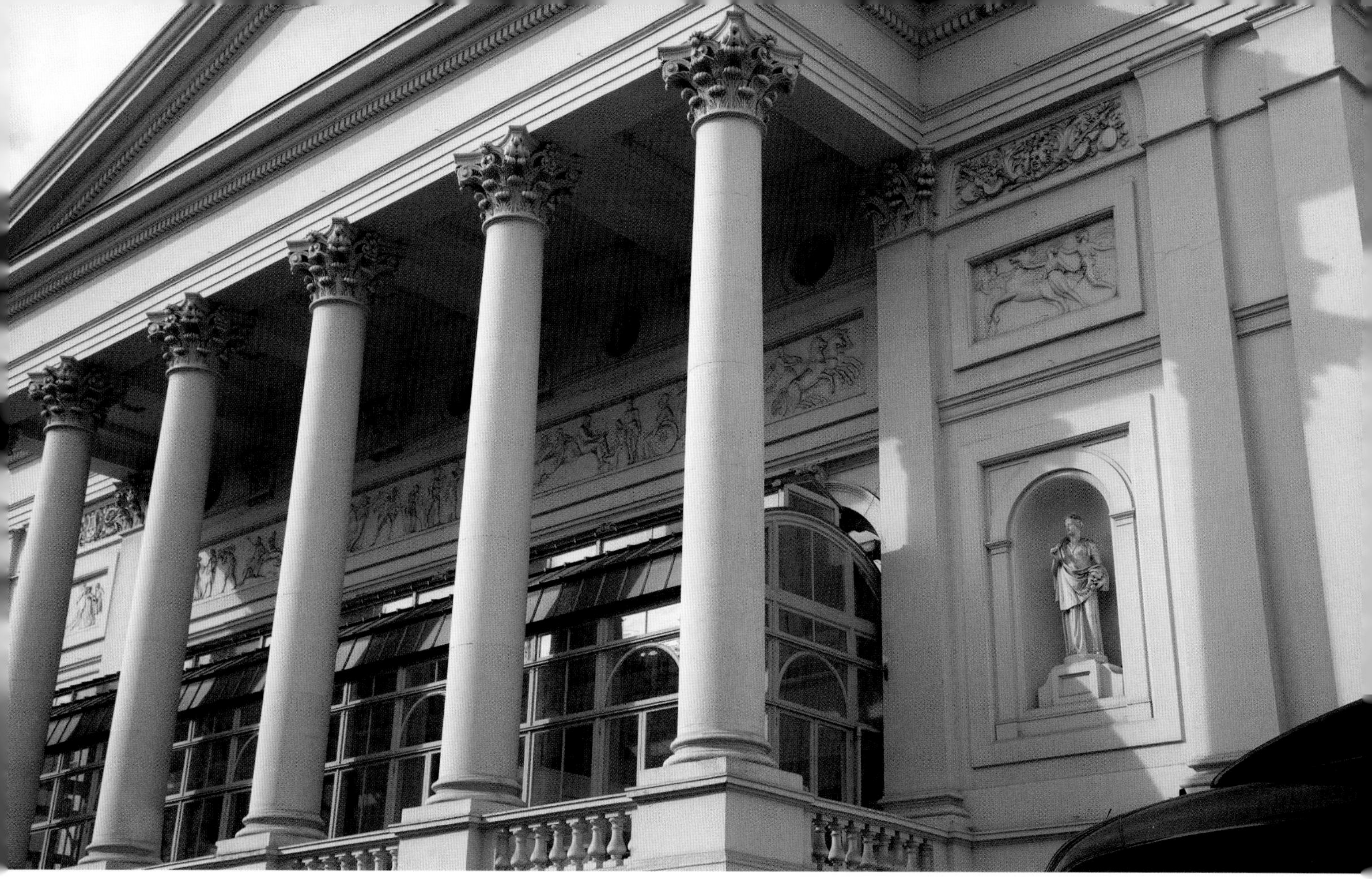

seats, incensed by the increase in prices, were in hostile mood and barracked the stage unremittingly. No appeal from the stage would quell them; finally Kemble had to send to the courtroom opposite for help from the Bow Street Runners. This only increased the rioters' determination; they finally left the theatre at 2 a.m., returning the following day, and every subsequent day, to renew their demands. It became a kind of sport. At the end of the first week, the rioters solemnly brought in a coffin with the message 'Here lies the body of the new price, which died of the whooping cough on 23 September 1809, aged 6 days.' It hadn't quite: Kemble held out for three months, at one point bringing in a champion boxer to quell the protesters before ignominiously caving in; the Old Price Riots became a proverbial reminder to theatre managers of who needed whom. The following season Kemble tried to raise prices again, but he was once more slapped down and business as usual was resumed. The audience was king – as it demonstrated again in 1812 when Kemble's sister Sarah Siddons, perhaps the greatest actress of the eighteenth and early nineteenth century, gave her farewell performance. She chose to take her leave of the stage in what was universally acknowledged to be her finest role, Lady Macbeth, in which her majestic physique and supreme command of pathos had made an unforgettable impression. Such was the enthusiasm of the public that the play could not continue after her final scene. Eventually the curtain was brought down while the cheers and foot stamping from the pit continued; when it was brought up again, she

ABOVE The portico above the entrance. Such is its situation, squashed into Bow Street, that a decent view of the whole front is hard to obtain. Note the bas-relief and two statues from Smirke's 1809 building.

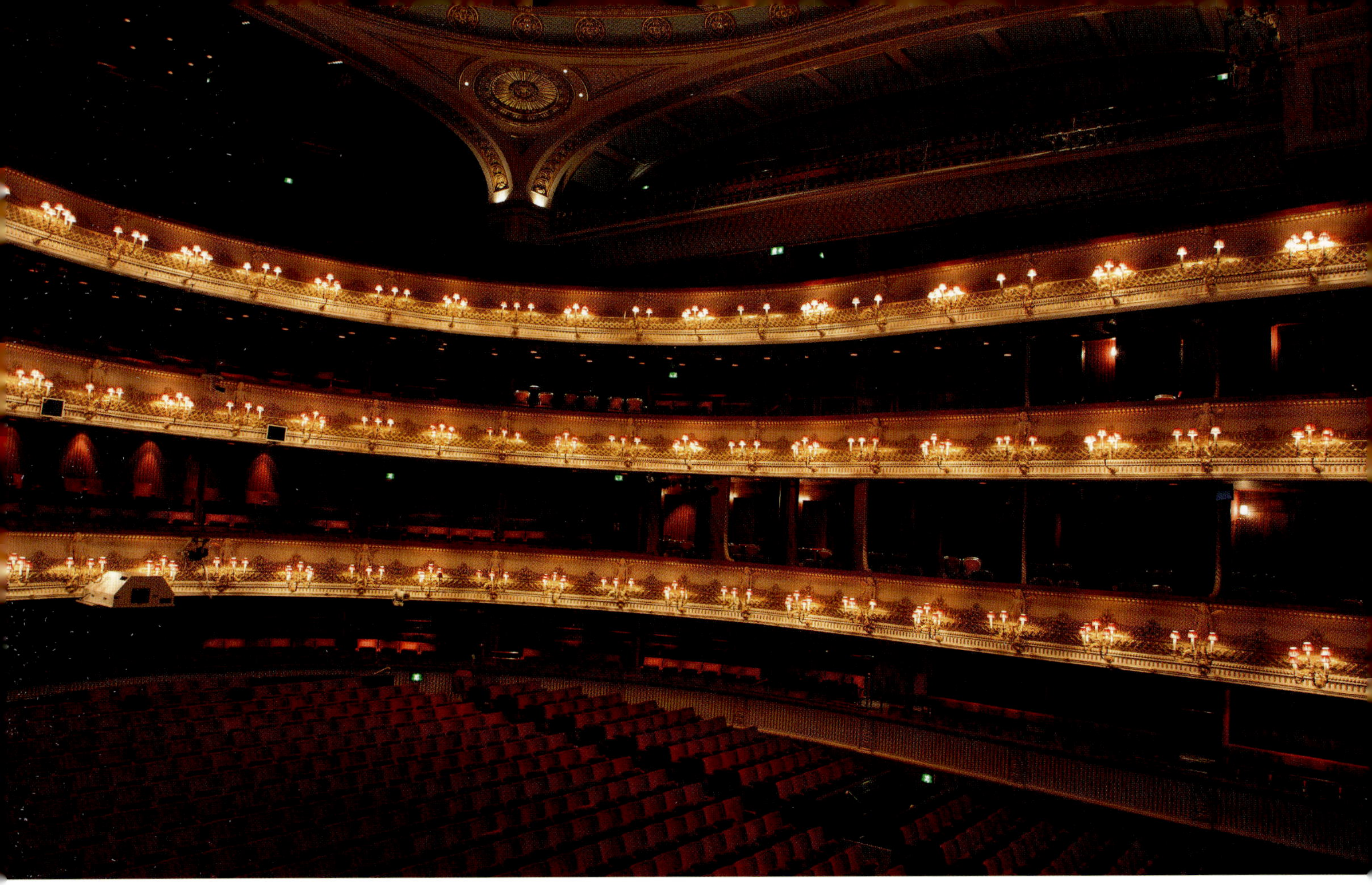

was discovered in her own clothes and out of character. Still they roared. Only after she made a powerfully emotional speech would they depart.

Another, more sombre, farewell was that of Carl Maria von Weber, who having composed and triumphantly conducted his fairy opera *Oberon* for the theatre in 1826 died suddenly at the end of the run; his remains were not returned to Germany until eighteen years later, under the aegis of Richard Wagner. In 1833, Edmund Kean made his departure from the stage at Covent Garden: he had what seems to have been a heart attack while playing Othello. Collapsing into the arms of his son, who was playing Iago, he uttered the words 'Oh God, I am dying. Speak to them, Charles!' – his last, on any stage. He lingered a little after that, but it was the end of the most startling career of the epoch; the end, in a sense, of that epoch.

The greatest successes, perhaps, that the Covent Garden Theatre ever had were the pantomimes of the great clown Joseph Grimaldi. He was so irresistibly comic 'as to put dullness to flight and make a saint laugh', said one admirer. 'His acting and manner . . . leaves all competition at a very humble distance.' The appeal was across the board: the famously severe Lord Eldon, the British Lord Chancellor, remarked that 'never, never, did I see a leg of mutton stolen with such superhumanly sublime impudence as by that man' – impressive expert evidence. Grimaldi's first great pantomime triumph was *Mother Goose*, for Christmas in 1806. It was a non-stop variety show of surreal brilliance in which live ducks flew out of pies, chairs and tables hovered eight feet in the air, huge balconies suddenly

ABOVE The auditorium, showing the three tiers of balconies.
OVERLEAF Surely the grandest opera house auditorium in the world – the quality of the details are in perfect harmony, as is the curtain, the design of which relates to the rest of the auditorium.

disappeared, hats turned into bells that started to chime, and bottles became buzzing beehives. In one climactic sequence the Vauxhall pleasure gardens were created onstage in all their opulent beauty, only for this vision of loveliness to be rudely disrupted by Joey starting a serenade on a tin fish-kettle. 'He gets all the gentlefolk up on their feet to dance a crude sort of hoe-down, whips off the tablecloths and juggles the crockery. Waiters charge frantically from side to side', writes Andrew McConnell Stott in *The Pantomime Life of Joseph Grimaldi* (2009), 'as plates smash and live birds splutter skywards from beneath the dinner platters, confusion that increases its speed and intensity until it reaches a crescendo of pandemonium', whereupon a cheesemonger steps forward and explains that he's the set designer; he is duly – and rightly – applauded to the rafters. It was clearly an early nineteenth-century *Hellzapoppin*'. Grimaldi returned again and again to Covent Garden over the next triumphant fifteen years; his long, slow decline, as his health and spirits failed, was mostly elsewhere.

In its attempts to woo audiences, Covent Garden embraced up-to-the minute innovations: Sir Goldworthy Gurney's invention of limelight, combining incandescence and candoluminescence, was pioneered here; the great actor William Macready discovered how to narrow the limelight down so that it could spotlight one individual onstage (usually him). But the theatre's fortunes declined; the drama had lost its hold on the audience. Fortunately, in 1846 the conductor Michael Costa, who had established Her Majesty's Theatre in the Haymarket as the main centre of ballet and opera, fell out with his management and transferred his allegiance to Covent Garden, on condition that the auditorium was reconstructed. Bellini and Donizetti, the staples of the Italian repertory, called, he said, for a different atmosphere. The theatre duly closed at the end of 1846, reopening four short months later, with an entirely and elaborately redesigned interior by the Italian civil engineer Benedict Albano, as the Royal Italian Opera. It is heartbreaking to read the detailed and enthusiastic accounts of the new building, particularly those sections that remark on the wonderful protection it afforded against fire, since after only nine years of successful life, on the night of 5 March 1858, the theatre burned to the ground. Urgently summoned back from Paris, the horror-struck manager Frederick Gye was joined at the site by Queen Victoria, who accompanied him into the ruined remains. 'The Queen leaned on my arm,' reported Gye in his diary, 'asked me many questions & showed great sympathy.'

This royal endorsement gives some sense of the degree to which the opera house was now seen as a national institution: it had to be rebuilt. At first there was a plan to find a new site – there was talk of building a new theatre in Leicester Square, or perhaps of converting the National Gallery – but it was finally resolved to allow a new opera house to rise, phoenix-like, on the site of the old. Edward Barry, the 27-year-old son of Charles Barry, who was one of the architects of the Houses of Parliament, designed the building, which in its essentials is the one that stands today. The grand Renaissance style facade, which incorporates the bas-relief and two of the statues from Smirke's razed building, is always a surprise as one enters Bow Street, lacking as it does any space from which to contemplate it. It rears up majestically, but without the dignity of the square or boulevard enjoyed by most Continental opera houses. Instead it abruptly faces what was, until very recently, a magistrate's court, one from which in 1895 Oscar Wilde was sent down to trial, and where 82-year-old Bertrand Russell (scion of the Bedford family) was committed to a month in jail for his part in the 'Ban the Bomb' protests of the 1960s. The Royal Opera House has never been an ivory tower; it was always part of noisy, smelly life, and entering it, right up until the 1970s and the departure of the market, necessitated negotiating cabbage leaves and rotting fruit.

The foyers, too, despite a fine staircase leading to the dress circle, feel foreshortened, but perhaps the somewhat cramped feel of these areas was part of Barry's cunning plan, ensuring that entering the

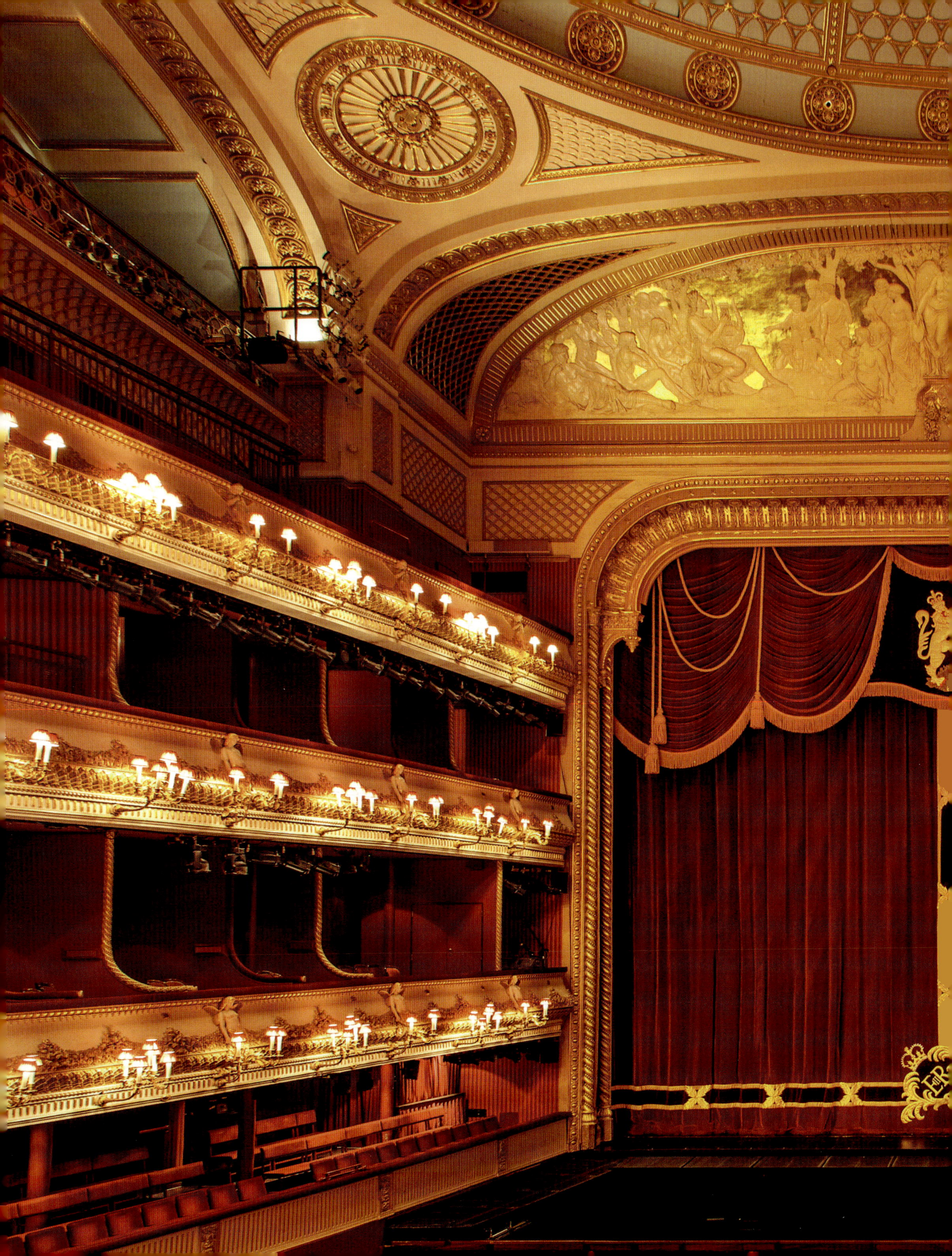

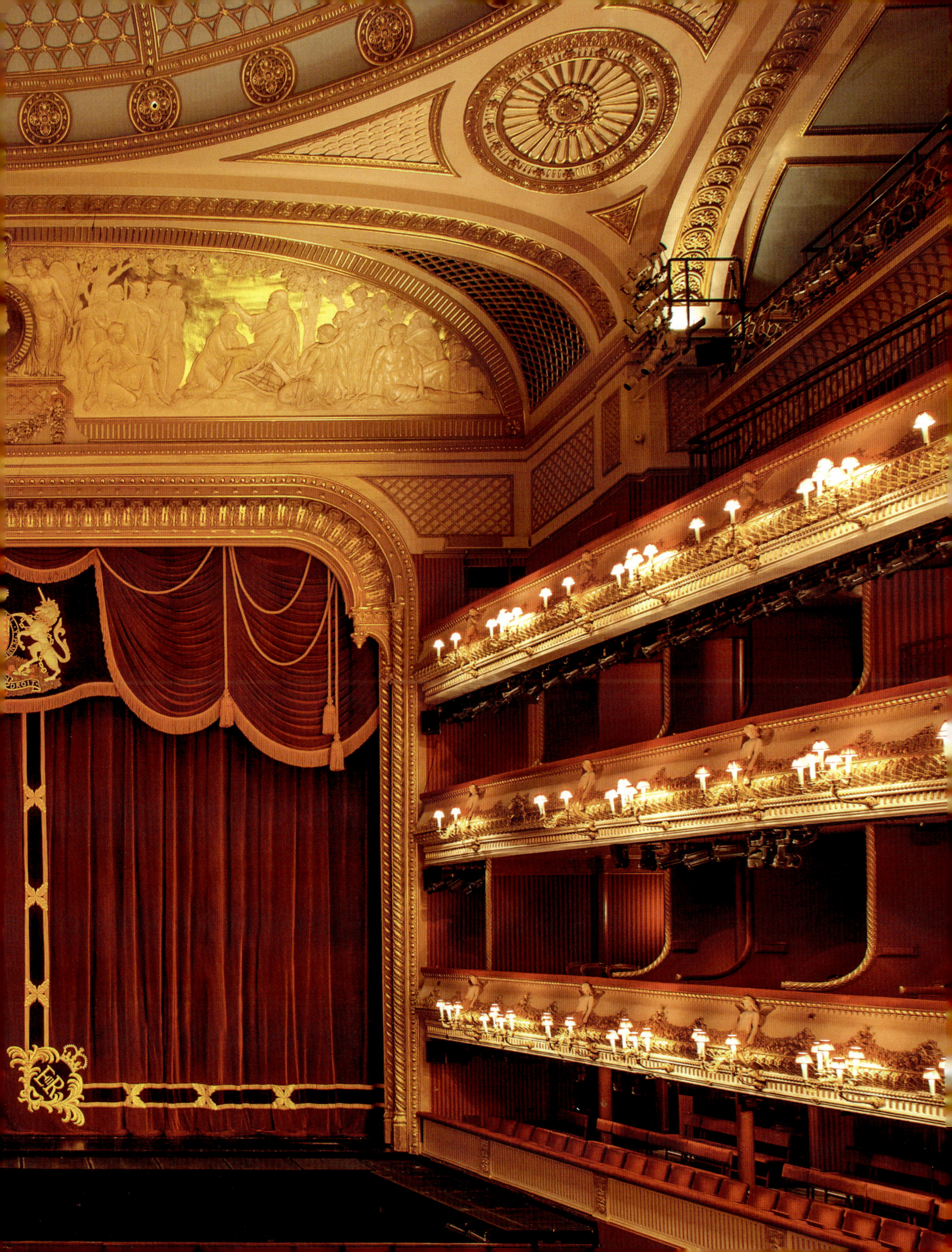

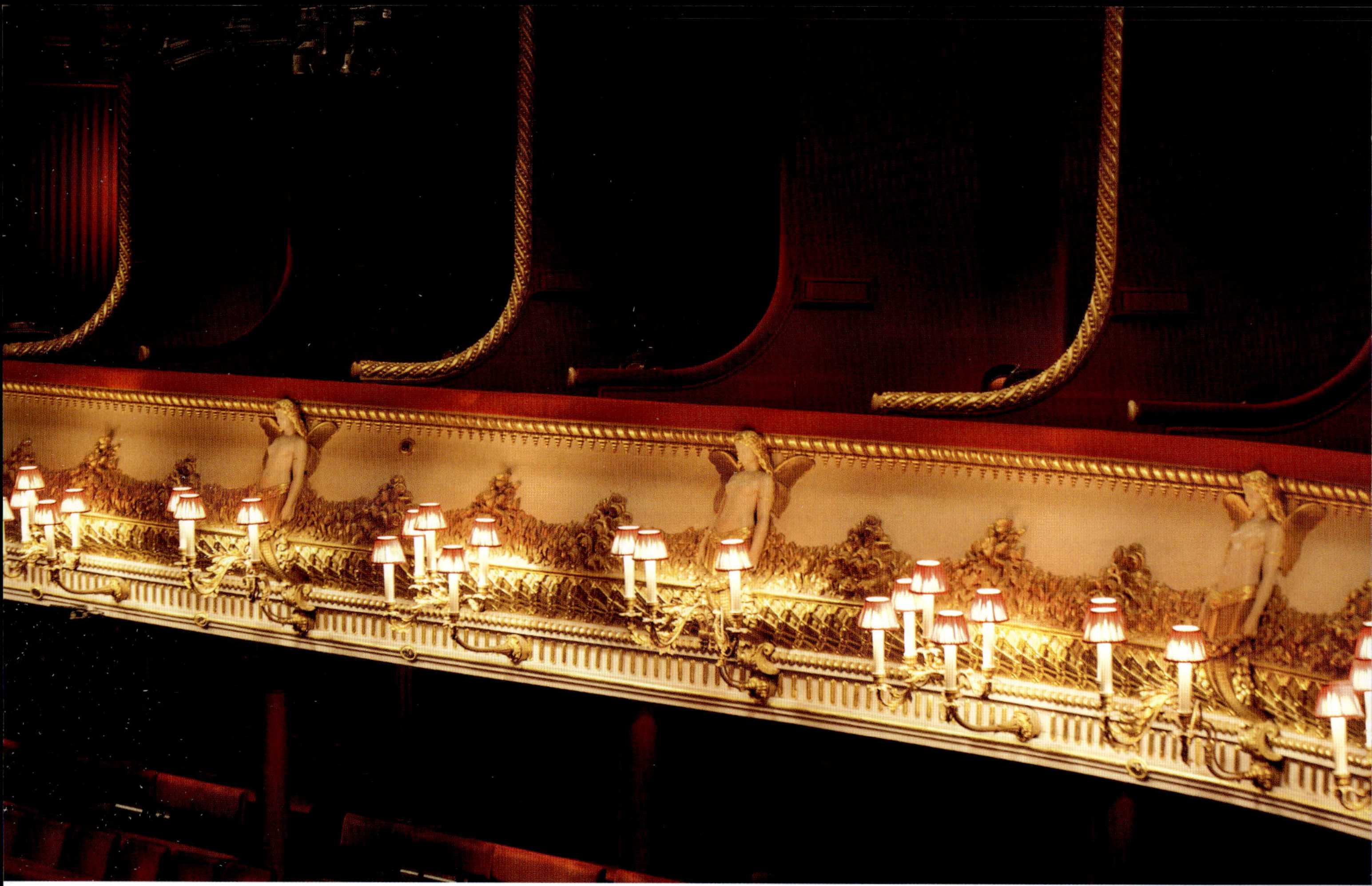

ravishing auditorium always comes as a delicious shock. It is certainly the most beautiful auditorium in Britain, and has a fair claim to being the most beautiful opera auditorium in the world. The pale blue, cream and gold of the walls and decorations is in deeply pleasing contrast to the profound burgundy reds of the magnificent curtain and the seats. The horseshoe shape, with its six tiers of boxes, ensures a direct connection between stage and audience; standing on the stage, one feels in touch with the back row of the upper circle. The acoustics are remarkable, even for the spoken word. Many a time the house manager has had to appear unamplified before the curtain with an announcement about indisposition; there has never been any problem hearing him, and the groan from the very top of the house is as loud and clear as the announcement itself. Despite various alterations, especially to the stage, the backstage area and the front of house, the auditorium itself is essentially as Barry designed it; among his notable achievements are the reworking of the interior of the National Gallery and the Birmingham and Midland Institute, but the Royal Opera House, with the adjacent Floral Hall, also designed by him, is his claim to glory.

Frederick Gye opened the new house with Meyerbeer's *Les Huguenots*, and the course was set: opera in the original language, with the biggest stars available. It was a largely successful policy and not unadventurous: all the latest operas appeared there, including, by the mid-1870s, even Wagner's (albeit, and inexplicably, in Italian translation). Gye's stewardship was suddenly and shockingly terminated in 1878 when he was accidentally shot while hunting.

ABOVE Some of the boxes, showing the candelabra, which shed a soft light through the auditorium. Note the gilded rope-like bands between the boxes.

His incomparable managerial skills were missed; his son and successor did not inherit them. By 1884 William Holland had taken over the theatre and commissioned Frank Matcham – one of his very earliest undertakings – to convert it into a circus, which involved creating a ring at stage level. To avoid dust flying into the faces of the audience, the ring was fitted with four-inch-thick coconut matting weighing over two tonnes. 'Raised seats, constructed from the ring to the dress circle, comprised the pit (with upholstered seats) and five rows of luxurious stalls,' enthused *The Era*, 'all having a clear and uninterrupted view of the ring.' There was stabling for 38 horses and ponies at the rear of the stage. The opening performance was on a stupendous scale, beginning with a trick equestrian act from Jacques Tourniare (the present writer's great-great-grandfather, as it happens), continuing with elephants and clowns and, indeed, an elephant clown, after which Madame Oceana performed sleight-of-hand tricks; the climax was provided by The Princess Lilian, an equestrian monkey. All a rather far cry from *Lucia di Lammermoor* and *La vascella fantasma* (as *The Flying Dutchman* had been known at this address).

After the passing of the circus, various managers took the theatre for short, undistinguished seasons. Finally, a consortium of highly placed figures approached Augustus Harris, the brilliantly effective manager of the Theatre Royal Drury Lane, to restore the theatre's fortunes. They would guarantee to take half of the boxes for the whole season, which not only made the thing financially feasible, it ensured aristocratic patronage – always good for the box office. Harris immediately set about securing the greatest voices of the age. 'I have had stars in all my pieces. I do not think the public want experiments,' he baldly stated in an interview in *Strand* magazine. But he was not averse to taking risks. In the 1892 season he gave the first full *Ring* cycle at Covent Garden, conducted by a 32-year-old Gustav Mahler. So successful was it, not least owing to Mahler's conducting – 'I had to take a curtain call after each act,' he said, 'and the entire hall shouted *Mahler* until I reappeared' – that a second cycle was given at Drury Lane. As if this were not enough, he threw in a performance of *Fidelio*, equally triumphant. The Royal Opera House, as it became known that year, was now established as one of the great opera houses of the world.

Harris died in 1896 and Covent Garden was administered more or less in his spirit by an entity called the Grand Opera Syndicate. And then, in 1911, the antic spirit of Thomas Beecham danced onto the scene and was never far away for almost the next thirty years. Generally considered to be the greatest of all British conductors, though entirely self-taught, he was also by far the richest, having behind him the vast fortune generated by his grandfather, inventor of Beecham's Powders and Beecham's Laxative Pills. He and his father, Sir Joseph, were equally obsessed by opera and seemingly undismayed by making vast losses: 'I spend my money on opera', said Sir Joseph, 'the way other men do on the turf.' Nor did his passion stop at merely subsidising opera: in 1910, in a sensational and initially secret deal with the Duke of Bedford, he bought a considerable portion of the Covent Garden freehold, including the Opera House. Thomas Beecham duly took a place on the board and brought with him to Covent Garden the legendary impresario Sergei Diaghilev and his sensational Ballets Russes, whom he had already hired at Drury Lane. Beecham's conducting of these difficult scores was a marvel in itself. In 1912 he conducted the British premiere of Richard Strauss's *Der Rosenkavalier*, only a year after its first performance in Dresden. 'There is an insatiable taste in the British public for music-drama,' he said in his autobiography, *A Mingled Chime* (1943); whether it was true or not, he behaved as if it were. Like Weber in Dresden and Mahler in Vienna before him, he took responsibility for everything, manifesting a keen interest in acting, staging, even diction; rehearsals were arduous, the singers and orchestra challenged to their limits. The music, he believed, must grow out of the drama, and the drama out of the music.

Just at this highly promising moment in the history of the Royal Opera House, war broke out, and all odds were off. During the war the building became a furniture depository. As it happens, the last play in that final London season before the war was *Pygmalion*: on its first night, at Her Majesty's Theatre on 11 April 1914, the curtain came up on the piazza in Covent Garden, where a number of opera-goers and a rather lippy flower girl were taking refuge from the rain.

While the Zeppelins hovered over London and the opera house had become a furniture store, Beecham was out on the road with the newly formed Beecham Opera Company, bringing British opera and British singers to new levels. In 1916, Sir Joseph Beecham died suddenly, leaving huge debts: the war had prevented him from selling the land adjacent to the opera house, and Thomas Beecham was now in an extremely precarious position financially. Nonetheless, at the end of the war, when the house reopened, he rejoined the still extant Grand Opera Syndicate, becoming Artistic Director of the Opera House – a new title. There was a resident company as in European opera houses, largely drawn from the singers of the Beecham Opera Company. But the world was no longer what it had been: the days of a large and enormously wealthy upper class had gone. Finally, in 1920, with no one to bail him out, Beecham joined the long procession of opera bankrupts. He was unable to pay the Ballets Russes for their services so Diaghilev withdrew the company, leaving the Royal Opera House in disarray. At this Beecham himself withdrew from opera, and indeed from musical life, for two years to regroup financially, having lost a staggering £104,000 on his operatic ventures, the equivalent today of £2.5 million. His place was taken by the British National Opera Company, dedicated to the cause of English opera and opera in English: it failed.

Despite unceasing financial problems, benefactors were found, often at the last moment; the fabric giant Courtaulds, for example, underwrote the Royal Opera House for three years. In 1925 a vigorous new administrator arrived in the form of Colonel Eustace Blois, who published figures which for the first time revealed the impossible economics of opera: the quixotic nature of the venture was underlined by the revelation that seasons of Wagner or presentations of, say, *Der Rosenkavalier* would still make a loss even if sold out. But *Rosenkavalier* was exactly what the great German conductor Bruno Walter brought to London again and again between the years 1924 and 1933, during which time he was unofficial chief conductor of the house, bringing with him the cream of singers from the Vienna State Opera – Lotte Lehmann, Richard Tauber, Elisabeth Schumann, Richard Mayr – to offer supreme performances of the Austro-German repertory, including *Don Giovanni*, *Fidelio* and *Die Walküre*. In 1926, in contrast to all this German high art, the final, final farewell of Dame Nellie Melba took place in Covent Garden, summoning up another world of opera – another world, full stop. She was 68 and had sung opposite Caruso and de Reszke; her debut had taken place in 1886.

Sir Thomas Beecham, meanwhile, newly solvent, was hovering in the wings. Out of the wreck of his father's affairs he had created Covent Garden Properties, which owned the estate that included the Royal Opera House, and was thus well placed to pounce – which he finally did in 1934, installing his newly founded London Philharmonic Orchestra in the pit and resuming the title of Artistic Director; Bruno Walter was barely notified of the change. Here Beecham reigned until 1939, witty, charming, generous, implacable and ruthlessly untrustworthy. The repertory was enormous: French, Italian, German, Czech, Russian and of course British opera. Musically, it was a period of almost unimaginable splendour: for those involved, according to Beecham's assistant Geoffrey Toye, 'it was the greatest musical experience of their lives'. Among the singers were the sopranos Conchita Supervia and Rosa Ponselle, the bass Ezio Pinza, the baritone Mariano Stabile and, perhaps most golden of all golden voices, the tenor Beniamino Gigli. Serenely confident in his own abilities, Beecham invited the greatest conductors of the day to share

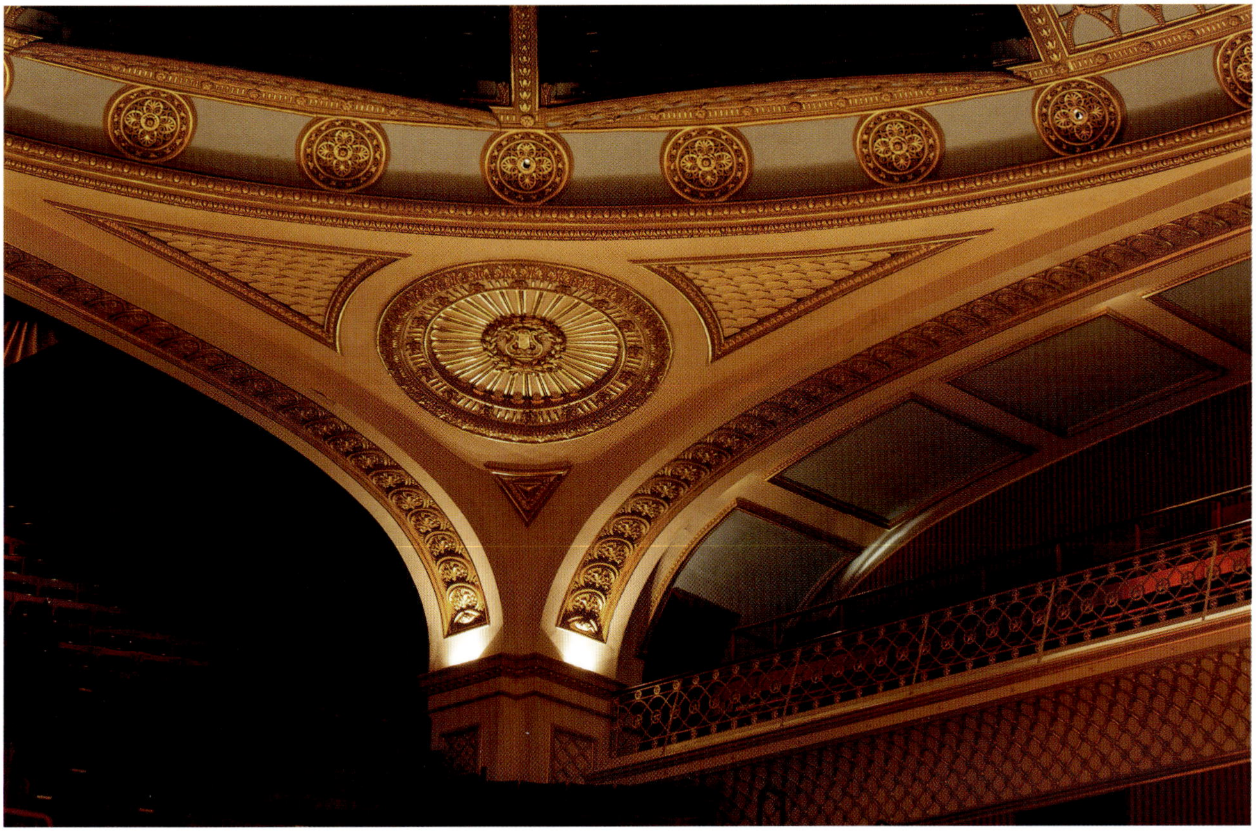

his pit: Wilhelm Furtwängler, Fritz Reiner, Vittorio Gui, Felix Weingartner, Erich Kleiber and Hans Knappertsbusch (but not Bruno Walter, or indeed Toscanini, that 'second-rate Italian bandmaster', as Beecham dubbed him). He transformed the old place from the dramatic perspective, too: where under Walter singers had simply fitted into the existing old sets, Beecham imported a certain Dr Erhardt to supervise new settings and direct the singers. He even gave the audience lessons in manners: if they talked or arrived late and noisily, he simply laid down his baton and then started all over again.

This glorious epoch was, like Beecham's former period of operatic glory, stopped dead in its tracks by the outbreak of war; he upped and went to Australia and America for the duration, and the Royal Opera House, stalls boarded over and glitter ball installed, became a Mecca ballroom. After a brief period of closure, theatres, concert halls and art galleries opened again: the government realised that the arts would be central in maintaining morale. While Londoners waltzed and cha-cha-cha'd around Barry's auditorium, the artistic life of Britain underwent a remarkable change. Tours of Britain, and later of actual war zones, were arranged, the companies received with enthusiasm everywhere: the Sadler's Wells Ballet in particular behaved heroically under fire. The Council for the Encouragement of Music and the Arts was established under the chairmanship of the great economist John Maynard Keynes, and plans for a new relationship between government and arts were laid. Among the most visible of the projects proposed by the Arts Council (as it became known) would be the establishment of a centrally funded Royal Opera House – a radical

ABOVE A corner of the ceiling, showing the exquisite craftsmanship of the design as well as its invention and harmony.

step, a final acknowledgement of the seriousness and importance of opera and its indispensability as an essential feature of a great capital city. 'It is the Arts Council's business', Keynes told the BBC in 1945, 'to make London a great artistic metropolis, a place to visit and to wonder at.'

At the heart of the new Royal Opera House would be ballet. Ninette de Valois, initially Lilian Baylis's ballet mistress at the Old Vic, had created a world-class ensemble at Sadler's Wells, breeding star dancers and choreographers – Robert Helpmann, Frederick Ashton, Alicia Markova, Anton Dolin and Margot Fonteyn – and incidentally encouraging a whole generation of great stage designers; this would become the Covent Garden Ballet Company, which would provide the matrix for the new opera company the Arts Council planned, but which did not yet exist. It thus fell to the ballet to reopen the opera house, which they chose to do by performing Tchaikovsky's masterpiece *The Sleeping Beauty*; the symbolism was lost on nobody. On 20 February 1946, in the presence of King George VI, the Queen, the Princesses Elizabeth and Margaret and the entire social, artistic and political establishment, the Royal Opera House awoke from its six-year slumber. De Valois had judged it perfectly: the war-weary, rationed and artistically undernourished audience were enchanted by the physical production – Oliver Messel's gauzily romantic costumes and sets; the music, under the baton of Constant Lambert; and the glorious dancing of the company, above all perhaps that of the 27-year-old Margot Fonteyn as Aurora.

So the Royal Opera House was alive again, a phoenix risen out of the ashes of post-war London – but without any opera. Having established the Covent Garden Ballet company, it now fell to David Webster, the general manager of the Opera House, to create an opera company from nothing. He was a surprising candidate. Former general manager of Lewis's Department Store in Liverpool, he had never run an opera house; though he had helped to keep classical music going in Liverpool during the war and was a well-informed and well-connected dilettante, he had much to learn. He could expect little guidance from the chairman of his board, Lord Waverley, who had never seen an opera at the time of his appointment; indeed the whole of the revival of the opera house was dogged by ignorance and compromise. At no point was Sir Thomas Beecham, who had devoted years of his life and several fortunes to the house, approached. 'They never came near me!' he said, and though he returned occasionally to conduct, he nursed bitter resentment for the rest of his life, sniping at the organisation at the slightest opportunity. It is hard, however, to imagine Beecham – by then in his late sixties – having the appetite or patience for the sort of careful wheeling and dealing that the new post-war world of arts administration called for; and in 1949 the building itself was bought from his Covent Garden Properties by compulsory purchase order, so he longer had any say in the matter.

Webster, a kind of bourgeois mandarin, proceeded largely on a basis of masterly inactivity; though to begin with he made a number of crucial mistakes, including the appointment as music director of a worthy but dull German conductor, Karl Rankl, Eugene Goossens and Bruno Walter having turned the job down. He was also saddled with a highly problematic central policy: the operas would be performed in English. This noble but misplaced ideal meant that he was dependent on English singers, or those very few international singers who were prepared to learn the repertory in that language. Among those who did were the superb German singers Elisabeth Schwarzkopf, Ljuba Welitsch and Rudolf Schock, which was acceptable when they were singing from the German canon but often risible when they stepped outside it. There was a catastrophic *Carmen* and an only moderate *Fairy Queen*. With poor singing and dull conducting, production values dominated; designers like Oliver Messel and Edward Burra often saved the day, but only just. Webster, in an uncharacteristically radical move, appointed the 22-year-old Peter Brook

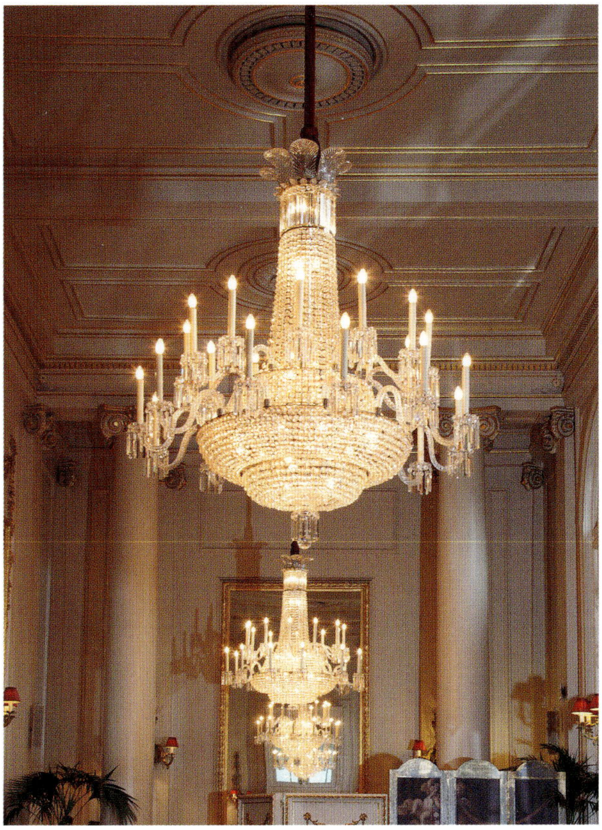

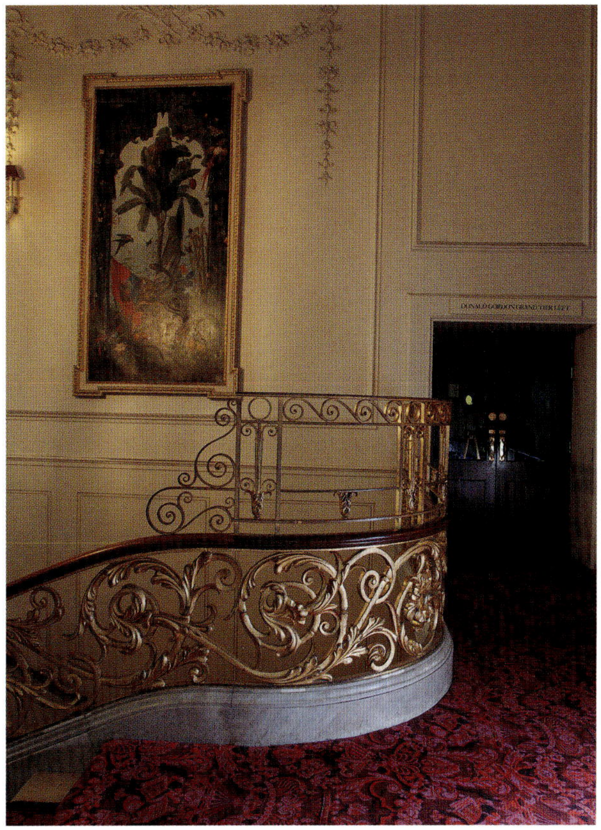

as head of productions. A dazzlingly precocious talent, Brook was appalled by the conditions and after doing a number of respectable productions (one of which, *Boris Godunov*, was still in the repertory thirty years later) decided in 1949 to blow the lid off things with a production of Richard Strauss's *Salome*, with nakedly sexual designs by Salvador Dalí.

In the wake of the scandal this created – reviews predictably described the production as 'puerile' – Brook resigned. In the same year, 1950, Webster decided not to renew Karl Rankl's contract. Neither Brook nor Rankl was formally replaced, but the great Austrian conductor Erich Kleiber was a very regular visitor in the pit and orchestral standards picked up almost immediately; John Barbirolli made frequent electrifying appearances. In 1952 Maria Callas, already legendary for her performances at La Scala in *bel canto* and *verismo* repertory, made her first sensational appearance at the Royal Opera House in Bellini's *Norma*. Webster was beginning to get into his stride at last, and he was now to be much fortified by the arrival first of Charles Moore, the Earl of Drogheda, as chairman of the trust, and second George Lascelles, the Earl of Harewood and cousin to the Queen, as his assistant, a young man deeply versed in opera and its production. The house was changing. English-speaking policy had been amended to include 'special' performances in the original language, for which it was much easier to attract stars; these were accordingly much more popular. *Norma* had, of course, been sung in Italian. There were nonetheless important commissions from English composers: in 1951, Benjamin Britten's *Billy Budd* made a powerful impact, although his subtle and complex contribution to the Coronation celebrations,

ABOVE LEFT Chandeliers in the Crush Bar.
ABOVE RIGHT Detail of the main staircase.

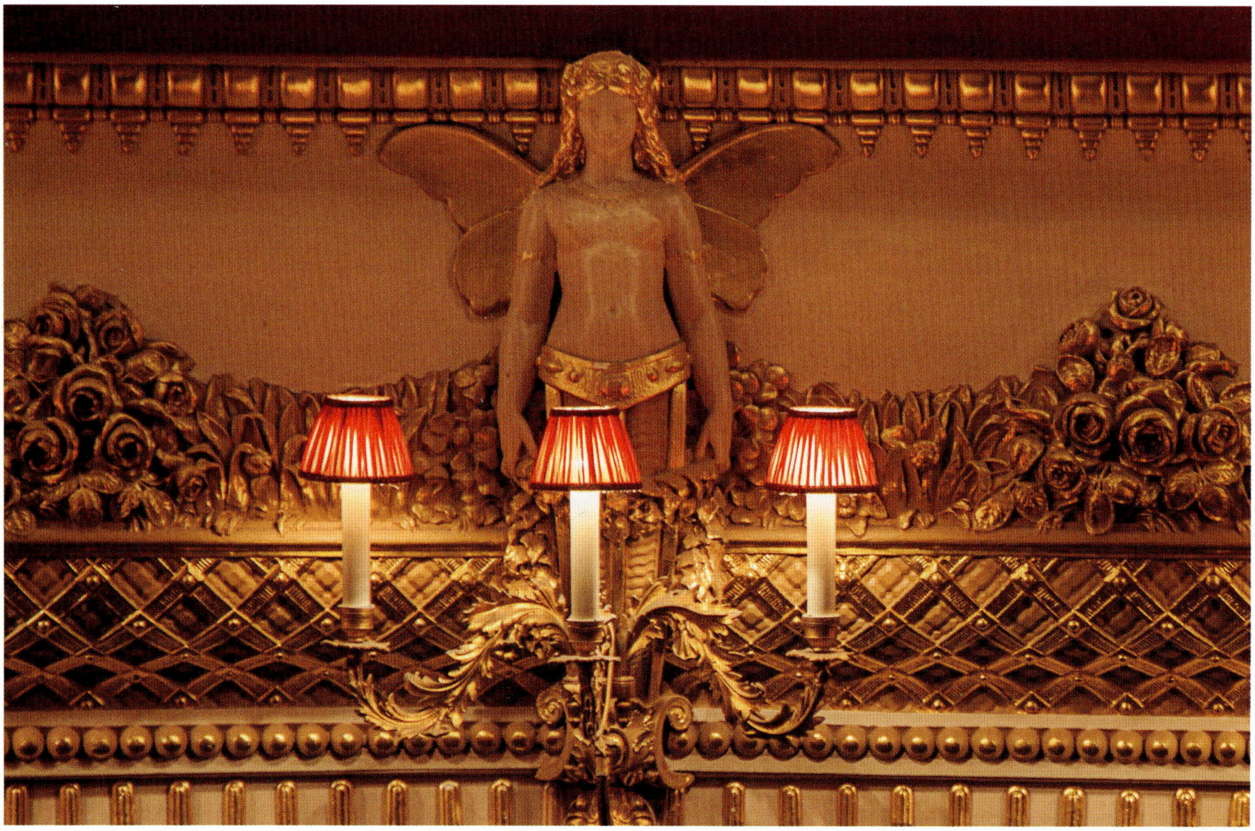

Gloriana, about the ageing Queen Elizabeth I, was thought to be a tactless way of welcoming the young Elizabeth II. The year 1954 saw both Michael Tippett's difficult *A Midsummer Marriage*, featuring the young Australian soprano Joan Sutherland, and William Walton's much more accessible though less durable *Troilus and Cressida*, in which Elisabeth Schwarzkopf and Peter Pears appeared.

It is nonetheless true that, despite these important achievements – and the immense improvement in musical standards that followed the appointment of the Czech conductor-composer Rafael Kubelik as music director – the opera company's first ten years were patchy, a fact rather underlined by the Royal Ballet's acclaimed celebration of the centenary of the building in 1957. Frederick Ashton, the resident choreographer, continued to create masterpiece after masterpiece; the training, grounded in Russian practice, ensured continuity of tradition; new choreographers from within the ranks and from abroad were constantly encouraged. The company's annual visits to New York were high points of the dance calendar and – newly ennobled as the Royal Ballet – it was regarded as at least on a par with the Bolshoi and George Balanchine's New York City Ballet. The Covent Garden Opera Company rather paled in comparison.

And yet in 1958, the productions of Berlioz's *Les Troyens* by John Gielgud starring Jon Vickers, and Verdi's *Don Carlo* directed by Luchino Visconti, with a cast that included Tito Gobbi, Carlo Bergonzi and Boris Christoff and conducted by Carlo Maria Giulini, were unmistakably the work of a great company functioning at its peak: even Kubelik's

ABOVE A candelabrum dominated by a female figure whose wings suggest a fairy from *A Midsummer Night's Dream*, albeit somewhat more serene.

angry resignation that year, provoked by a typical British press persecution (and stoked by a rather xenophobic Thomas Beecham), failed to damage the company's new confidence. The British music press was internationally notorious for its brutality and a number of distinguished artists, both singers and conductors, declined to appear there. Elisabeth Schwarzkopf, at the height of her powers and the veteran of many Covent Garden productions, was so shocked by the vituperative press's reception of her Marschallin in *Der Rosenkavalier* (one of her most renowned roles) that she refused ever to sing at Covent Garden again, and she never did, though she was by this time a British citizen. Despite this ugly atmosphere there followed a sequence of extraordinary triumphs: Callas in *La Traviata*, a *Fidelio* conducted and staged by Otto Klemperer, and a dazzling production of Poulenc's *Dialogues des Carmélites*.

Perhaps the most astonishing event of all was the production in 1959 of Donizetti's *Lucia di Lammermoor* by Franco Zeffirelli, with Joan Sutherland, who under the patient tutelage of her husband, Richard Bonynge, had discovered a matchless upper register and a profound instinct for coloratura. A world-class singer suddenly appeared before an astounded public, singing a role for which few others were now equipped: both the opera and the singer were cheered and cheered to the echo; Zeffirelli's achievement, too, was exceptional, bringing to life a vanished world of romantic theatre. And the Royal Opera House basked in the glory which it had done so much to make possible.

The appointment in 1961 of the Hungarian conductor Georg Solti, abrasive and passionate, as music director was a definitive turning point. Throughout the Solti years, both the opera and ballet companies, despite the usual operational difficulties, remained brilliantly effective and productive and widely admired, and in 1968 it too was ennobled, becoming the Royal Opera Company. By 1970 the philosopher Isaiah Berlin remarked that Covent Garden had become 'an absolutely central part of London, as much part of the experience of being English as the BBC'. But the question of money began to loom more and more ominously over the heads of both ballet and opera companies. In 1966 an internal Royal Opera House report had stated that a minimum of eight new productions a year was necessary to keep the house alive artistically and indeed commercially: the opera-going public needed to be kept diverted. By comparison with the rest of Europe the companies received very low subsidies from central government, and the opera company was now facing a great deal of vigorous competition from the former Sadler's Wells company, which in 1968 had moved to the London Coliseum in the West End. There, under the new name English National Opera, it was becoming increasingly ambitious, mounting a complete *Ring* cycle, for example, and becoming extremely adventurous in the staging of operas. Indeed, by the mid-1970s it had become very much the home of directors' opera: ENO was arguably more radical and exploratory in its staging than any theatre company in Britain, dramatic or lyric. This made the resignation of Peter Hall even before he took up the job of head of productions – a job that had not existed since the resignation of Peter Brook twenty years earlier – a serious blow for the Royal Opera House. He and the conductor Colin Davis had been appointed, at Davis's insistence, as joint artistic directors in 1969; but for reasons that were never entirely clear Hall withdrew, leaving Davis feeling very lonely as he took up the formidable challenge of succeeding Georg Solti, who had stood down surrounded by glory after a historic directorship.

As it happens, Davis, depressed or not, inaugurated his regime with a glorious *Marriage of Figaro*, which made an immediate star of the young New Zealand soprano Kiri te Kanawa, and a superb new production of the Cinderella among Mozart's operas, his late masterpiece *La clemenza di Tito*, which did a great deal towards restoring the piece to the centre of the international repertory. Other triumphs very close to Davis's heart were new productions of *Les Troyens* and of *Peter Grimes* with a visionary Jon Vickers in the title role (he had also repeated his superbly driven Aeneas in *Les Troyens*). The *Grimes* was a very clear testimony to the straitened times: the set was ingeniously constructed of wood salvaged from the previous production, a triumph both of art and thrift. Money was an ever-oppressive subject in the late 1970s, with inflation running at an all-time high. By a cruel irony, so was the Royal Opera House's popularity, with both opera and ballet playing to an average of 94 per cent of the total capacity. Clive Priestley's report into the financial affairs of the Opera House (and the Royal Shakespeare Company) had given the house a clean bill of financial health; indeed Priestley had been surprised by the value for money that the organisation represented. The Royal Opera's first international tour was a huge success, but there was no question about it: more money was needed, and the embattled government was in no position to give it.

Under great financial pressure, Davis had appointed the distinguished German director Götz Friedrich as his head of productions, and together they were responsible for a series of outstanding productions, including Allen Berg's opera *Lulu*, newly completed by Friedrich Cerha, and a striking *Ring* cycle. The report underlined what everyone knew: it was not economies that were needed but further expenditure, above all on the fabric of the building, which had scarcely received any attention since its reopening after the war. An extension at the back of the building was planned. In order to raise money for it, the house's royal patrons – Prince Charles of the opera, his aunt Princess Margaret of the ballet – went into action with a vengeance, touring the world to raise funds – which they did, to the tune of £10 million. The Prince of Wales opened the extension in 1982, which helped the work enormously, but the early 1980s were a dispiriting time. Productions were abandoned or cancelled; as often as not they were borrowed from other houses rather than initiated at Covent Garden. Overall there was a sense of being directionless, despite the occasional reminiscence of the old glory days, as when Plácido Domingo made his debut as Verdi's Otello conducted by the legendary Carlos Kleiber, son of the conductor who had begun the slow transformation of musical standards at the house nearly forty years earlier.

Economic circumstances could scarcely have been less propitious. Ingenuity, flexibility and imagination were needed if the Royal Opera House was to survive. This was the Thatcher period, and government commitment to the arts was half-hearted; ideas of accessibility and outreach were already in the air, and the house was clearly perceived as a bastion of the Establishment, a playground of the very rich – despite the fact that 30 per cent of all seats were priced at below £10. The inspired sponsorship of the socialist publisher Paul Hamlyn enabled the house to create performances where on certain designated nights all seats in the house were available at between £1 and £3. In a brilliantly successful attempt to integrate itself with the area – now transformed since the removal of the market in 1974 into a large pedestrianised shopping district – a huge screen was erected in the piazza for transmission to passers-by, while the ballet had a sensational success with its big tent in Battersea Park. The educational wing expanded: a typical event sponsored by the department was a hugely popular production of *Carmen* in which all but the lead roles were sung by local people.

But the actual work of the house must be central to any of these schemes and promotions: people paying £1 a ticket must still see the very best that opera can provide. Claus Moser, now chairman, and John Tooley, general director, made a superb appointment as music director: the great Dutch conductor Bernard Haitink, fresh from a decade as music director of Glyndebourne Festival Opera. He immediately consolidated and revitalised the orchestral playing and ensured that the revival of the standard repertory was not routine but instead

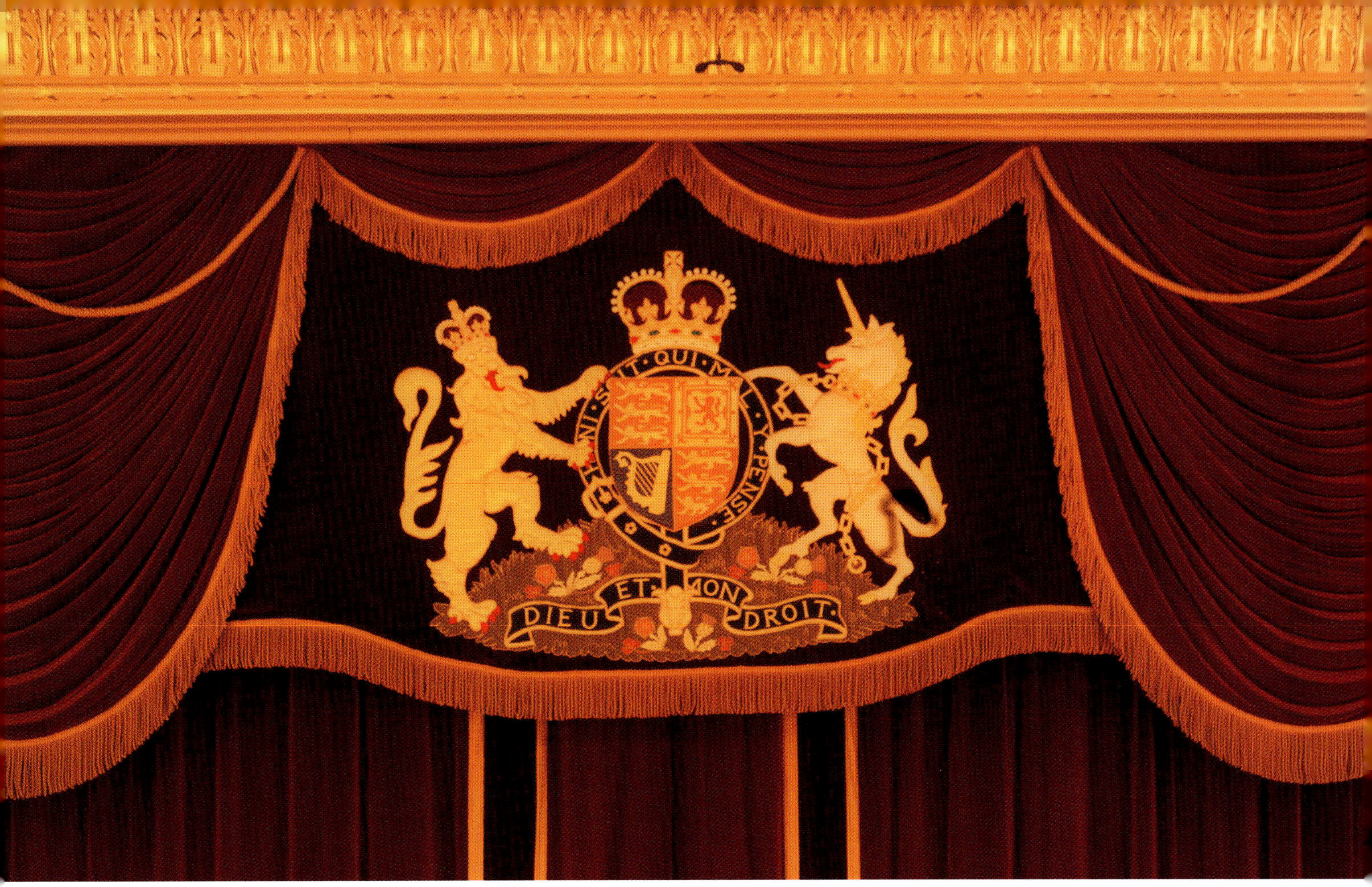

a constant illumination of these great works; for the most part he allowed his younger colleagues to lead the new commissions and occasional pieces. A series of dazzling new operas were seen: Harrison Birtwistle's epic *Gawain* (1991) and Nicholas Maw's *Sophie's Choice* (2002). Perhaps the climax of Haitink's regime was a new *Ring*, wildly controversial as a staging but musically peerless. From his arrival at the Royal Opera House in 1987 it had been known that another, much more radical reconstruction of the building would be necessary and that the Royal Opera would have to decamp for a while. The whole process was traumatising for the company, but the remodelling of the theatre – brilliantly achieved by a team under Jeremy Dixon – transformed the backstage area as well as expanding the front of house to incorporate the adjacent Floral Hall; the auditorium remains exactly as it was, in all its mid-nineteenth-century glory.

There have been further transformations, further streamlinings of the building; foyers and bars have been enlarged and made easily accessible; the Linbury has been rebuilt. One can perhaps feel a certain nostalgia for the days when the magnificently Dickensian commissionaire Sergeant Martin, round as a barrel and magnificently moustached, welcomed guests at the front entrance, but Barry's wonderful auditorium remains a thing of glory and the world-beating level of music drama and ballet it hosts belongs to an organisation at its zenith.

ABOVE The royal coat of arms in the curtain. Note the superb embroidery of the gold thread.

ADELPHI

It is only since 1993, when Andrew Lloyd Webber bought the theatre, that the Adelphi's severely Art Deco facade has been visible from the street, a sight previously denied whole generations of theatregoers. It had been covered by signage. No doubt it was considered irredeemably old-fashioned; now it is one of the glories of London theatre architecture, its auditorium a thing of supremely elegant beauty and its front of house – somewhat expanded and reconstructed – one of the most attractive foyers in town, all sconces and statuettes in black, mirror and chrome. The architect of this marvel was the Swiss-born, London-trained Ernest Schaufelberg, who was also responsible for the earlier, dinkily bijou Fortune Theatre in Russell Street. The Royal Adelphi, as it briefly was, was built for the legendary showman Charles B. Cochran, and it aimed to be as 'now' as possible, opening in December 1930 with the extremely racy backstage musical *Ever Green* by Rodgers and Hart, with dialogue by the English writer Benn Levy. The stars were Jessie Matthews and Sonnie Hale, who at the time were conducting a very public love affair; night after night they raised the roof with 'Dancing on the Ceiling', which sensationally featured London's first revolving stage, then topping it with that quintessential thirties number 'Je M'en Fiche du Sex Appeal!' Throughout its 85-year existence this 1,500-seat theatre has for the most part housed musicals, and the arch panache of the place suits them down to the ground. With its facade now revealed, the Adelphi dominates the north side of the Strand.

It is conjoined – a little oddly, it seems at first sight – to a rather splendid building to its left, which was originally part of the theatre it superseded – also called Adelphi. In fact there have been no fewer than four theatres on the site. From the beginning of the nineteenth century, the Strand, home at one time to the Gaiety, the Savoy, Terry's and the Vaudeville as well as the Adelphi, was the centre of theatrical life, the Shaftesbury Avenue of its day – so much so that by the end of the century the Piccadilly Line was extended down to Aldwych in order to cater to the theatre crowd. Nor was it merely legitimate theatres: across the road from the Adelphi was the original Coal Hole tavern, where the impresario Renton Nicholson arranged song-and-supper evenings featuring his satirical 'Judge and Jury' shows as well as risqué *poses plastiques*, in which naked women formed *tableaux vivants*, ostensibly in imitation of notable works of art. It was here too that the Wolf Club – founded, it was said, for oppressed husbands forbidden to sing in the bath – had their meetings; Edmund Kean, who dangerously stalks his way through this book, eyes glinting madly, was among its co-founders. At a later stage the much more sedate Gilbert and Sullivan would repair there to sing over new songs for their shows.

The Strand's first theatre, the Sans Pareil, was built in 1806 on the site of today's Adelphi. Without compare it certainly was, but not in a flattering way: matchlessly sloppy, shabby, overcrowded and unsanitary, it was the brainchild of John Scott, a prosperous manufacturer of colours, famous for a hugely successful washing blue known as True Blue. A loving father, Scott built the theatre for his

OPPOSITE The auditorium with a veritable army of spotlights.

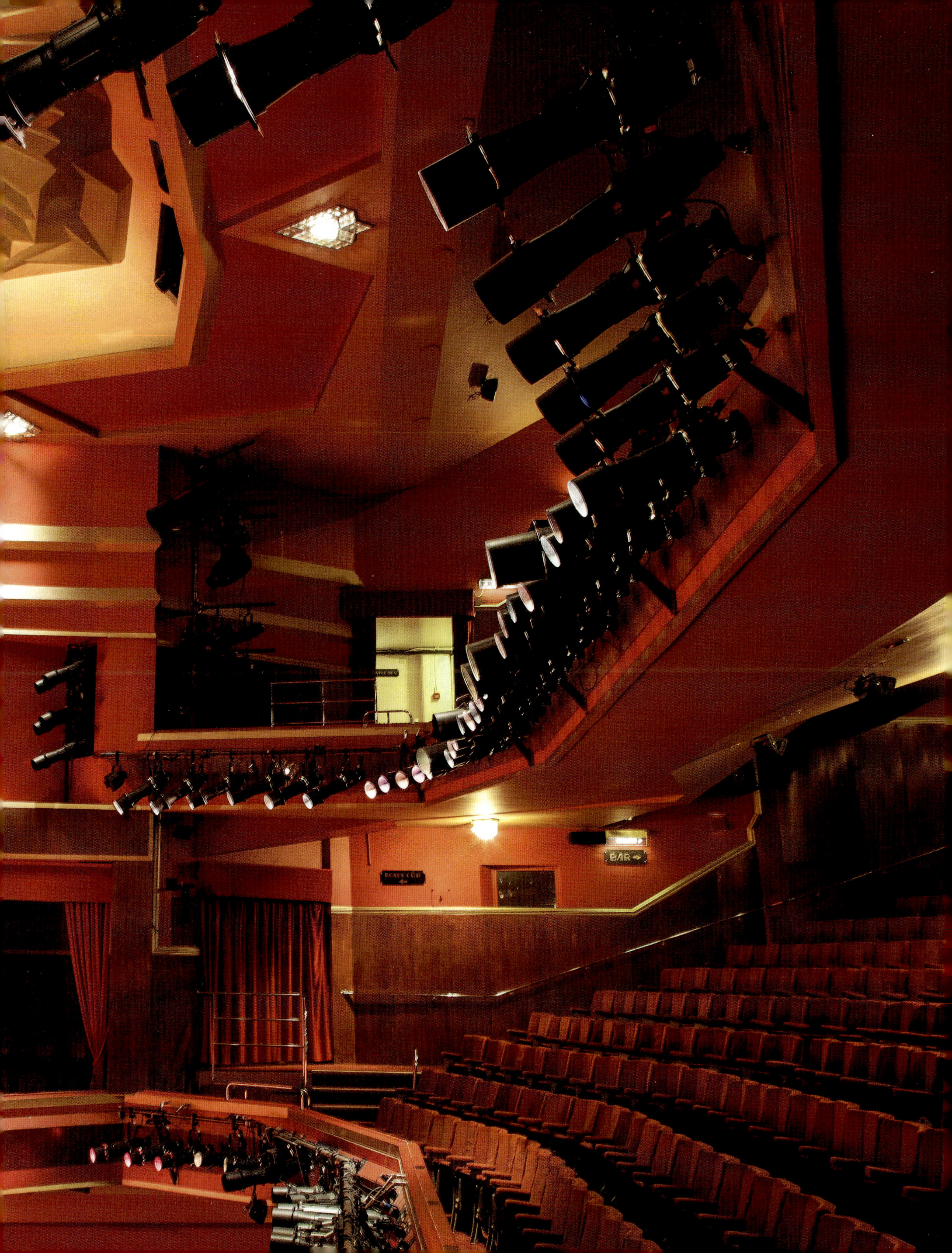
BAR

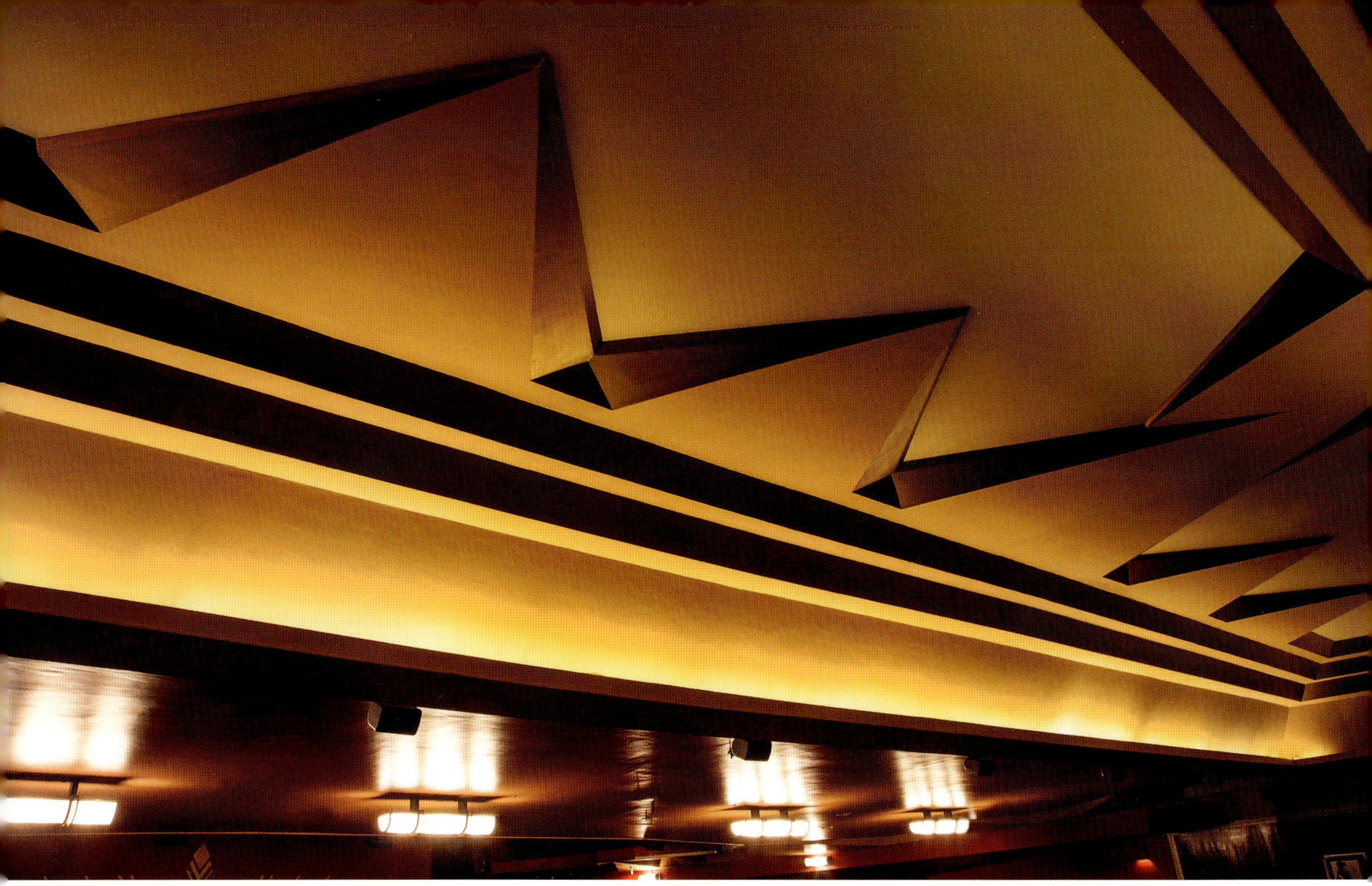

daughter, a sort of aged Infant Phenomenon. Jane performed in all the pieces and wrote most of them too; her name, printed in very large capitals, always had a line to itself on the poster and in the programme. Paternal pride could do no more. She had a following – but of the same sort as Florence Foster Jenkins; later Jane became famous for creating the title role in the hugely successful melodrama *Black Eyed Susan*, but that was in another theatre. After that triumph she retired, in 1819 – the same year, as it happens, that the old Sans Pareil was completely rebuilt and opened under the name of the Adelphi, a nod to the famous neoclassical complex on the other side of the Strand built by the siblings John, Robert, William and James Adam, the name being derived from the Greek word for 'brother'. A mere two years later the new theatre was felt to need further alterations, notably the addition of huge gas chandelier, but it was still far from satisfactory. 'It was of such structure and proportions that you might have imagined an Assembly Rooms at an old inn converted into a theatre, and permanently kept in its provisional state,' wrote the *Illustrated Times*. 'The straightness of the sides, the lowness of the penthouse that ran off the back of the pit, the cramped condition of the basket-boxes behind the dress-circle, were personal inconveniences to every sense of bodily comfort, sight, and breathing.' Nonetheless, it had a roaring success almost immediately with *Tom and Jerry*, chronicling the adventures of two feckless Londoners, the first long run in theatre history: it played for over a hundred consecutive performances. After that a series of melodramas, popularly known as 'Adelphi screamers', followed, as well as burlettas – straight plays into

ABOVE Detail of a corner of the theatre showing the Art Deco ceiling.

which musical numbers had been inserted simply in order to circumvent the monopoly of the two, later three, patent theatres which had the exclusive right to present 'spoken drama', a right that was not finally revoked until the passing of the Theatres Act of 1843.

The first Adelphi Theatre's claim to immortality lies in the period just before that date, with the long series of theatrical adaptations – almost all burlettas – from the works of Charles Dickens, including what appears to be the very first, John Baldwin Buckstone's *The Christening* of 1834, based on Dickens's story 'The Bloomsbury Christening'. This was rather convenient for Dickens, who was at the time living just across the road in Buckingham Street. The area was very much part of Dickensland: the blacking warehouse in which he spent two formative and terrible early years was just a little further on, by the river. The Adelphi itself is mentioned in *The Pickwick Papers* (1837), where a theatre-crazed youth such as Dickens himself had been is described as 'repairing three times a week to the Adelphi'. Theatrical adaptations of his novels followed as quickly as Dickens could write the books – *The Pickwick Papers* appeared as *The Peregrinations of Pickwick; or, Boz-i-a-na*; *Nicholas Nickleby* as *Doings at Do-the-Boys Hall*; and *The Old Curiosity Shop* as *One Hour from Humphrey's Clock*; indeed sometimes they arrived onstage even before Dickens had written the final instalments. When in 1844 Madame Celeste and the comedian Benjamin Webster took the theatre over, Buckstone was appointed resident dramatist, which ensured even more Dickens, notably the Christmas books: *A Christmas Carol, or Past, Present, and Future*; *The Chimes: A Goblin Story of Some Bells that Rang an Old Year Out and a New One In*; and *The Haunted Man and the Ghost's Bargain*.

The continuing success of the theatre led to its being rebuilt yet again. The second Adelphi, now nobly retitled the Royal Adelphi, opened in 1858 with an immeasurably superior auditorium based on a great circle that encompassed both seats and stage, ensuring, for the first time at this address, an unbroken view of the latter. The remade theatre, designed by the hugely prolific T. H. Wyatt, was favourably received, particularly in comparison with its predecessor: 'Most Londoners have been inside the Adelphi, and will remember it for the most inconvenient theatre that ever was entered,' snarled the *Illustrated Times*. Webster garnered high praise for the shrewdness and originality of his policy: 'Mr Webster sees that theatres must draw the great average of their revenue from the middle-class, and his regulations have, for the first time perhaps, placed the middle-class within the theatre on a footing of complete equality with the highest and wealthiest in the land.' These same middle classes were, it seems, led as much by their stomachs as by any aesthetic imperative: 'At most theatres, the refreshments are either of a very inferior kind, repulsive in their look, and poisonous in their tendencies; or they are doled out at enormous prices' (*plus ça change, plus c'est la même chose*). Webster, it appears, took this department firmly into his own hands: 'he has scoured refreshments by those purveyors who have a character at stake, and who will supply viands of the best quality. Drinks, for example, will come from Sainsbury's, whose lemonade', said the *Illustrated Times* tartly, 'is made of lemons.'

Webster's efforts were rewarded with great success, notably in the plays of the Irish actor-dramatist Dion Boucicault, newly returned from America. His *The Colleen Bawn* (1860), one of the great successes of the Victorian era, ran at the Adelphi for a then astounding 231 performances. The Dickens connection then came full circle with his last work for the stage, written in collaboration with Wilkie Collins. *No Thoroughfare* (1867) is a raging melodrama that culminates in a villain-destroying avalanche, and it was a tub-thumping triumph both with critics and public, particularly for its star, Dickens's friend the flamboyant Anglo-French actor Charles Fechter, as Obenreizer, the aforementioned villain. 'It is a hit in every sense of the word!' cried the theatre journal *The Mask*.

Dickens was rather sniffy about it, feeling that he could have staged it better himself. But it is pleasant that he, theatre-obsessed to the last, should have had a copper-bottomed success in the playhouse, and especially in the haunt of his youth, the Adelphi, before taking his own final bow three years later.

Webster retired, and in 1878 the brothers Agostino and Stefano Gatti, Swiss restaurateurs who had opened a brilliantly successful restaurant in Charing Cross, secured the freehold of the theatre. This led, inevitably perhaps, to a further refurbishment, including the provision of an adjacent restaurant that occupied almost the whole of the front part of the building and which was 'magnificently furnished', according to the ever-vigilant *Illustrated Times*, 'being replete with every thing that constitutes a first-class London restaurant'. This establishment, sadly demoted, has become the Crystal Rooms, a gaming venue, but you can still glimpse the splendour of the rooms themselves. The by now vastly expanded theatre had immediate success with what quickly became known as the 'Adelphi dramas': stirring, manly pieces in which heroes were heroes and heroines loved them, deeply, desperately. Among the greatest stars of these pieces were Jessie Millward and William Terriss, lovers in life as onstage. Terriss in particular was idolised, not only by audiences but by his fellow players. Preposterously handsome and of splendid physique, he brought truth, depth and a matchless insouciance to the cardboard figures he played; he was the same man offstage, every schoolboy's dream of the captain of cricket – affable, funny, courteous, dashing. Only one person in his life ever disliked Terriss; alas for him, this man was a former extra in the Adelphi company who was becoming increasingly embittered at his failure to advance in his career. As he met with ever more rejection, Richard Archer Prince focused all his ire, all his sense of outraged justice, on Terriss, and finally, dressed in a cape and wide-brimmed hat, accosted him one December night in Maiden Lane behind the Adelphi, and stabbed him to death. When Henry Irving heard that his friend and sometime colleague Terriss had been murdered, he said: 'Terriss was an actor, so his murderer will not be executed.'

And indeed, Prince was found guilty of murder but was judged to be of unsound mind and sent to Broadmoor, where he died forty years later, in 1937. But Terriss's fans did him proud at the funeral: there were some 50,000 of them in attendance. There were flowers from everyone in the theatre of the slightest note, and from the Prince of Wales. 'He died', said Ellen Terry, 'as a beautiful youth, a kind of Adonis, although he was fifty years old.' Terriss's death seemed, as the great scholar of the Victorian theatre George Rowell has noted, to sound the death knell for an entire innocent world of theatre – the melodramas and silly comedies in which he excelled. Only three years later, in a somewhat subdued atmosphere, as if the events of that December night three years earlier were still in the air, the Adelphi underwent yet another transformation, reopening in 1901 in elegant new form as the Century Theatre in honour of the widely anticipated brave new world ahead. But the audience would have none of it, and after three years it became the Adelphi again, which made sense on several levels, since the design by Ernest Runtz was a restrained *hommage* to the Brothers Adam. 'Delicate lilac and yellow tones prevail,' reported *Building News*. 'Marble is in evidence, but not aggressively so. Gold there is, but not in such quantities as to suggest that the one idea of decorative art is dependent upon the coveted metal.' In 1908 the celebrated impresario George Edwardes, manager both of Daly's and the wildly successful Gaiety Theatre at the other end of the Strand, took the theatre over from the Gattis. In the early part of the twentieth century, under his unerring guidance, the Adelphi was home to a sequence of smash-hit musical comedies, including *The Earl and the Girl* (1904) and ending, triumphantly, with Vivian Ellis's *Mr Cinders* (1929), which ran for over five hundred performances.

Despite all this success, it was deemed by the hugely powerful and canny Charles B. Cochran, by now the manager, that the building needed to be

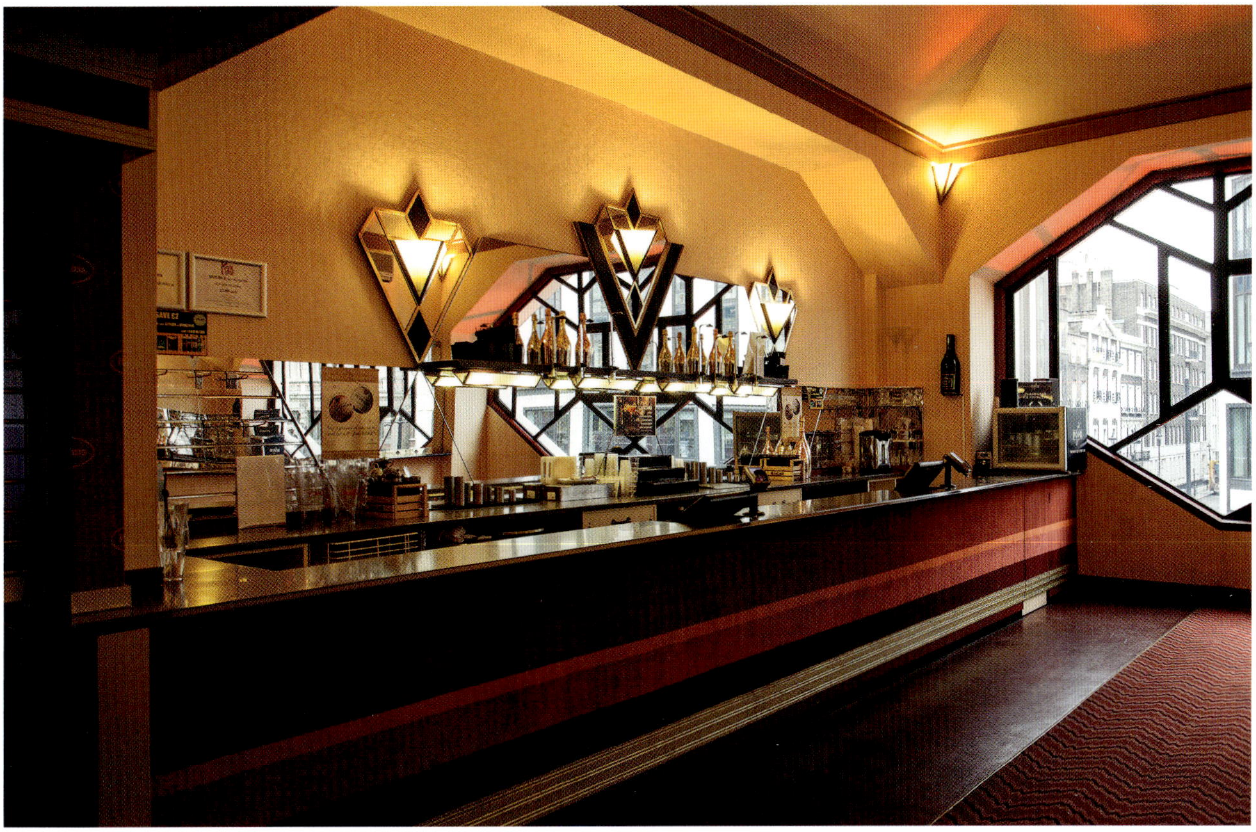

brought up to the minute. Schaufelberg was brought in, with the splendid result we now see, which opened in a blaze of flashlight in December 1930 as the Royal Adelphi – one last attempt at ennoblement before its regal pretensions were finally abandoned in 1940. But in the mid-1950s, despite over two decades of hit shows, the theatre was threatened with demolition when Woolworths, then an all-powerful force in the high street, bought the entire block in which the theatre sits and proposed to build one of its own stores in its place. It failed, and while the much-loved Woolies has since disappeared from British streets, the Adelphi is still standing. That this is so is thanks to the London County Council, which vetoed Woolworths' plans; fifteen years later, however, now engorged into the Greater London Council, it forfeited all its kudos by proposing to demolish the entire street, including the Adelphi, Vaudeville, Duchess and Lyceum theatres, as well as the nearby Garrick. The fight-back started in Rules restaurant, which stands in Maiden Lane opposite the stage doors of both the Vaudeville and Adelphi; four beautiful and historically resonant playhouses were saved and Covent Garden was redeveloped into its present, very engaging form. Sometimes, just occasionally, the theatre can be in the vanguard – even if its purpose, as in this case, is conservation. I like to think that Dickens would have approved.

ABOVE The bar at the Adelphi Theatre.

THE OLD VIC

The Old Vic means two things: a theatre with an extraordinary two-hundred-year history, and an idea – an idea that changed the whole of British theatrical culture. The two are of course inseparable, but the idea of the Old Vic as we understand it began in 1880 with Emma Cons, social reformer, first female alderman to be appointed to the London County Council and passionate evangelist of temperance in the form of the coffee tavern movement, and it came to fruition under her niece Lilian Baylis, who took on Cons's mantle after her death in 1912 and laid the foundations for a great deal of what we now take for granted in theatre, dance and opera. Not that that was what she intended – not in the least. It's a remarkable, inspiring and very British story, but it is by no means the whole story, which starts over two hundred years ago, in 1818.

The original theatre on the site, the Royal Coburg, had no nobler purpose than the perfectly honourable one of making a great deal of money from providing entertainment. The initial funding was raised by subscription, and one of its organisers – who had connections at court – had secured the patronage of Princess Charlotte of Wales and her consort, Prince Leopold of Saxe-Coburg; the theatre was named after her. This was canny: Charlotte was the Prince Regent's daughter and was as popular as her father was not; she and her husband were the Kate and Wills *de ses jours*, in reverse – the princess was next in line to the throne should her father and her grandfather, George III, predecease her. The golden couple laid the foundation stone of the new theatre, which was near Waterloo Bridge, in May 1816. Work proceeded slowly; meanwhile Princess Charlotte fell pregnant. In November 1817 she gave birth, but the child was stillborn; she herself died hours later. Her obstetrician Richard Croft, devastated, shot himself the following February while officiating at another confinement. The nation, genuinely dismayed at the loss of the one member of the royal family whom they actually admired, plunged into mourning, as did her adoring husband.

Building work on the theatre was slow; at the time Prince Leopold declared it open, in May 1818, it was still incomplete. The first night was less than a triumph; *Trial by Battle* was the principal item on the bill. Backstage, life was imitating art: the harlequin insisted that he had to appear first because of a prior engagement at another theatre, but the manager refused; the confrontation soon degenerated into fisticuffs, with the other acts plunging in and mayhem ensuing.

Pity about the show, then, but the theatre itself – designed by the German architect Rudolph Cabanel, and handsomely furnished – was a great success. The facade, essentially the same as the current theatre's, was plain but striking, and the exterior brick walls untreated. The lighting arrangements were much commented on: 'a superb central lustre . . . will shed a beautiful and brilliant light over the whole house,' announced a handbill issued for the opening. Wear and tear were obviously considerable, because the theatre was refurbished as soon as 1824, at which

OPPOSITE The auditorium at the Old Vic.
OVERLEAF The auditorium, showing the safety curtain. The ornamentation of the column's capital may not be appreciated by the occupant of the seat behind it.

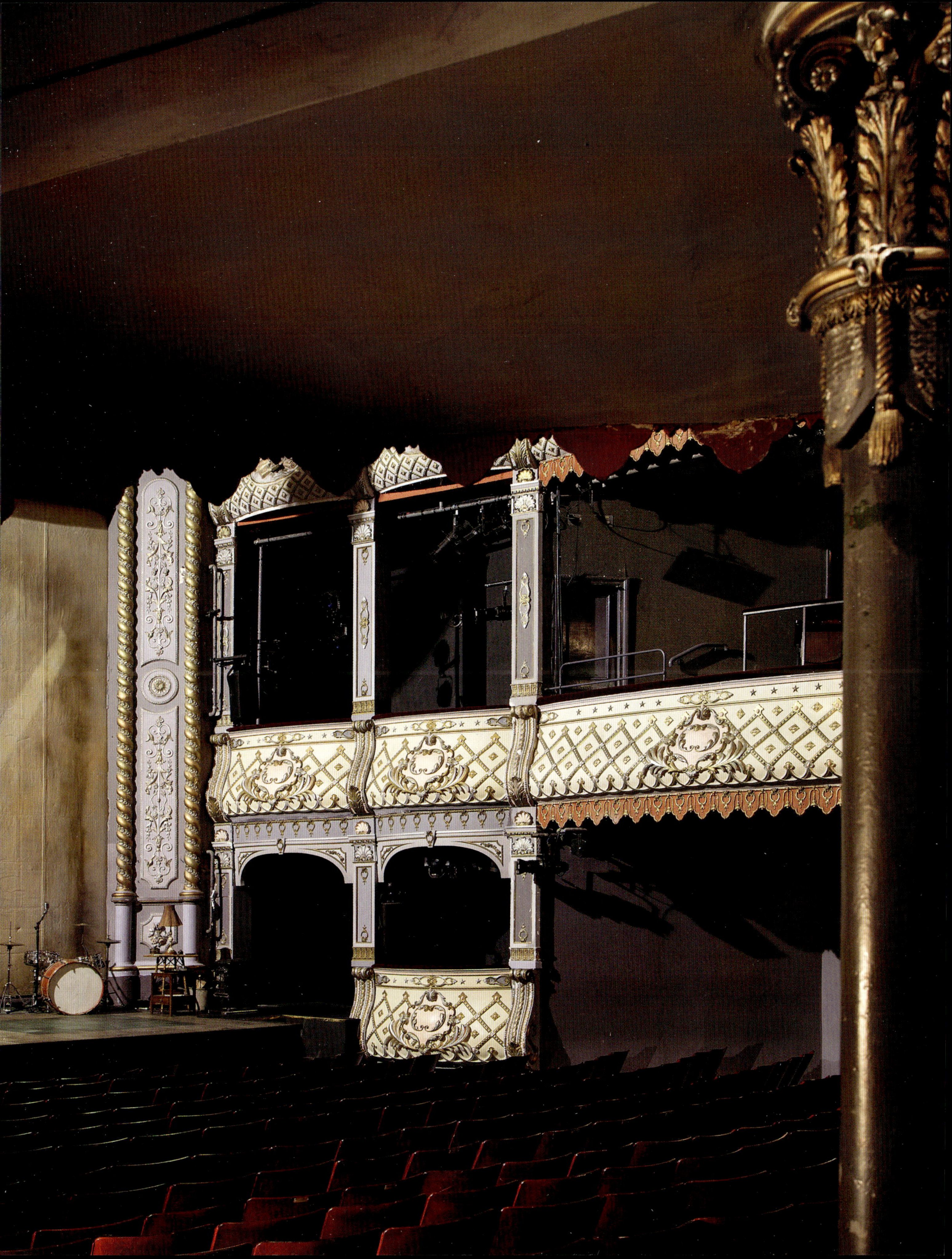

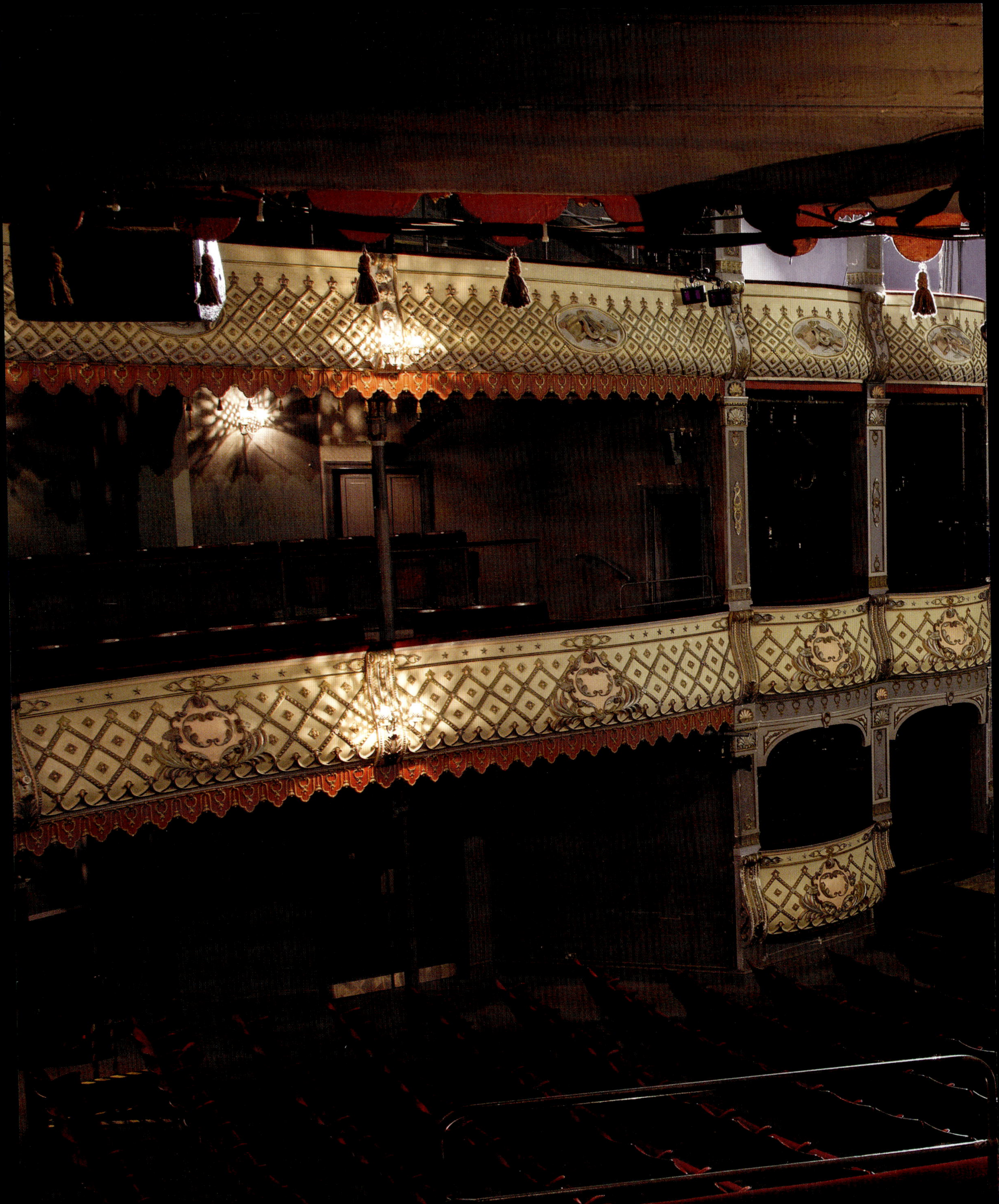

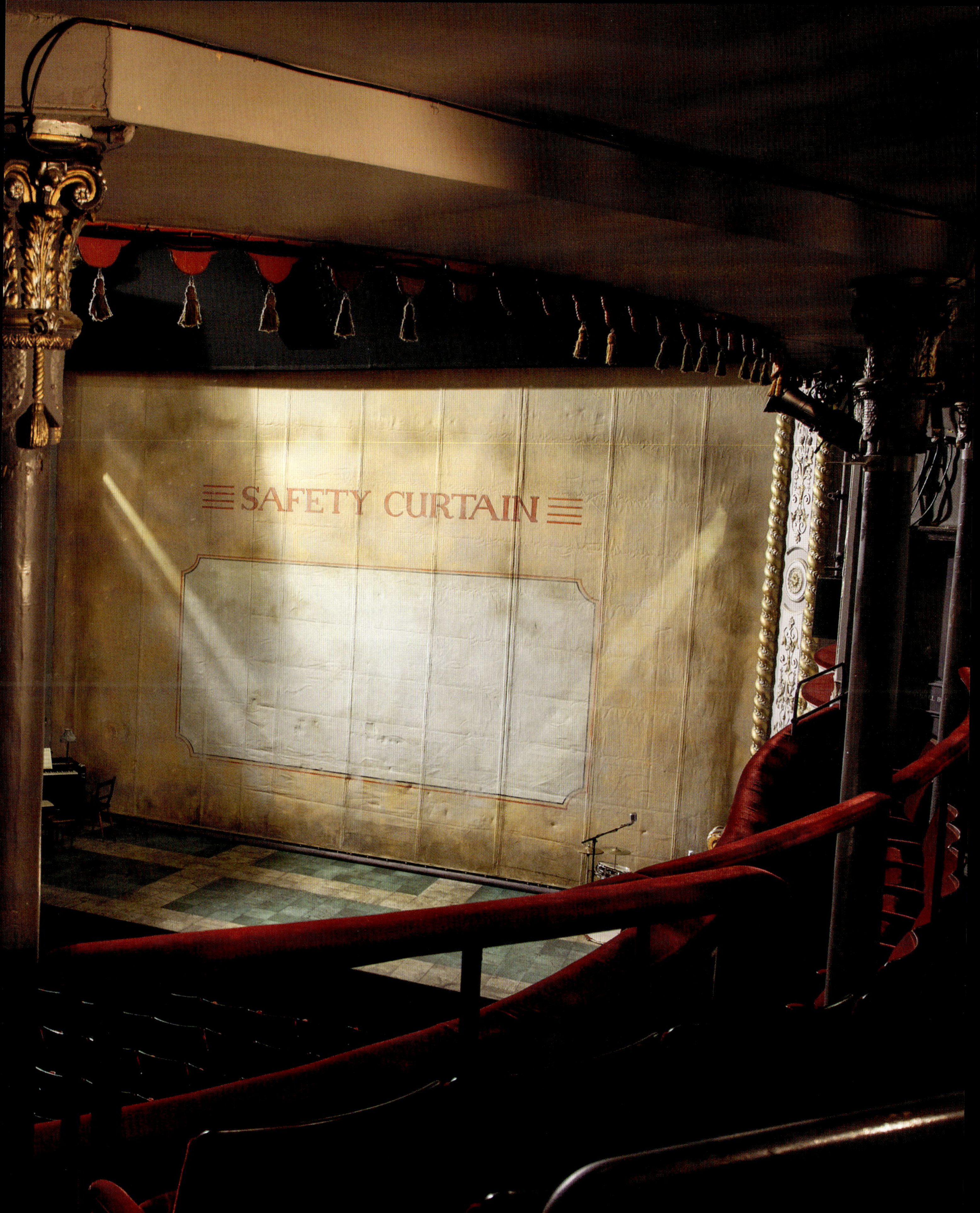
SAFETY CURTAIN

time the manager persuaded the great Edmund Kean to come and perform there. He was not impressed. 'I have never acted', he told the over-lively audience, 'to such a set of ignorant, unmitigated brutes as I see before me.' The usual fare was odd: blood-curdling melodrama, generally with a temperance theme. But perhaps its professed worthiness encouraged Victoria, Duchess of Kent (mother of the fourteen-year-old Princess Victoria, heir to the throne since the untimely death of Princess Charlotte) to lend her name to the theatre, which, handsomely redecorated, now became the Royal Victoria. The theatre, still pursuing its policy of moralising melodrama, was popularly known as the Vic, but a further rechristening was about to come when in 1871, under the management of J. A. Cave, it closed down for a total revamp, reopening with a resplendent new interior designed by Jethro Thomas Robinson, the leading theatre architect of his time; among his colleagues was a young Frank Matcham, who in time married Robinson's daughter and would himself become perhaps the greatest of all theatre architects.

Robinson's design of the interior of the theatre (the facade was essentially untouched) was greatly admired. The magnificent stage was described in the *Building News and Engineering Journal* that year as having 'traps, slides, and bridges throughout the whole extent behind the curtain, with ample depth and height for all possible apparitions from aerial or subterranean regions, as the "effects" of the scene may require', and it was set some fifteen feet further back to enlarge the auditorium. The domed ceiling, horseshoe balconies, moulded gold decorations and blazing proscenium were topped with flags and other patriotic emblems – as befitted the theatre's newest name, the Royal Victoria Palace of Amusements. The capacity was hugely increased with a massive gallery in which a thousand people could be seated, bringing the total potential audience to three thousand. Four large bars catered to this multitude, offering the delicacies of the season 'upon scales of tariff adapted to the patrons of the respective departments'. It was now, proclaimed *Building News*, an ascertained fact that 'food for the mind, whether at museums, International Exhibitions, or theatres, cannot be received and appreciated without the addition of an abundant supply of creature comforts for the inner man.'

This was essentially the theatre as it stands today, although over the subsequent century it was to experience many further transformations until Robinson's auditorium was at last lovingly and authentically restored. Robinson was one of the first architects to specialise in theatre; he was, indeed, architectural adviser to the Lord Chamberlain. When he died suddenly in 1878, at the age of 49, he was widely mourned; Matcham took over the practice, so the succession was guaranteed. All the great architect's skill, taste and engineering expertise, however, were not enough to restore the theatre's fortunes, and after a couple of years' struggle the manager Cave finally threw in the towel. The theatre's reputation tumbled as it rapidly turned into a den of vice, bawdiness and alcohol, onstage and off. Or so Emma Cons – feminist, suffragist, Christian socialist and evangelical proponent of decent, affordable and clean housing for the working class – saw it. She lived nearby on the facility she had created, the Surrey Lodge, and was prepared to get up in her dressing gown and slippers in the middle of the night to stop the Vic's drunken male clientele from beating their wives and lovers. As much to put an end to the theatre's baleful activities as to offer an alternative, Cons took a lease on it in 1878, spending a considerable sum of money on cleaning the place up and reopening it in 1880 as the Royal Victoria Hall and Coffee Tavern, 'a cheap and decent place, run on strict temperance lines'. Miss Cons never secured a full theatrical licence and was therefore unable to present complete plays, instead offering bills that consisted of variety turns, sketches, concerts and lectures, all vetted to ensure that they were squeaky-clean and devoid of any unchristian sentiments.

The transformation of Emma Cons's worthy community centre into the Old Vic that provided such fertile soil for artistic growth was the work of her no less remarkable niece Lilian Baylis, who joined her aunt in the work in 1898 and assumed control on her death in 1912. Before committing herself to eleemosynary works, Cons had been an engraver and glass-worker, but Baylis was a performer – a dab hand at the violin and the mandolin who had done shows with her family in the Gypsy Revellers troupe in South Africa, where they had all emigrated. Although she shared her aunt's evangelical Christian views, she believed in the transforming power of art, especially the art of opera, and determined to establish a performing tradition at the Vic. To facilitate this, Baylis boldly embraced the newfangled medium of cinema, showing films there. Acquiring a performance licence for the theatre when she took over the lease, she also put on the occasional opera, and in 1914 took the even bolder decision to present all of Shakespeare's plays, including many that had rarely been seen since they were written. Throughout the First World War, as bombs fell from the ever-looming Zeppelins, and for some years after under the supervision of her sorely tested artistic director Ben Greet, Shakespeare's plays held the stage at the Vic, until, by 1923, the theatre had performed the entire First Folio, the first such cycle ever.

Money was always tight. Actors were paid a pittance and the design budgets were risible. But under a succession of ambitious artistic directors, standards rose. Young actors like John Gielgud, Peggy Ashcroft and Edith Evans were irresistibly drawn by the chance of exploring the classical repertory; up-and-coming stars like Laurence Olivier joined their ranks, as did film stars like Charles Laughton. The Vic became synonymous with Shakespeare, although it branched out into the work of his contemporaries, notably Ben Jonson; Baylis also developed a small team of dancers under the leadership of the Irish choreographer Ninette de Valois, a former member of the Ballets Russes. Around the same time she started a public appeal for funds to resurrect the abandoned Sadler's Wells theatre in north London. With its opening in 1931 her dance team grew into a separate company, the Vic-Wells Ballet – the foundation of what would in time become the Royal Ballet; it was soon joined by the Sadler's Wells Opera, which developed over the years into the English National Opera. Thus the Wells and the Vic now both housed dance, opera and drama companies, but the actors soon retreated to the Vic, where the work grew in accomplishment and audacity, while the ballet and opera companies ploughed their own furrow in Islington.

In 1937, garlanded with honours and utterly worn out by more than forty years of unceasing uphill effort, Baylis died. She was an eccentric, erratic figure, given to taking direct advice from the Almighty (who generally advised her against acceding to requests for salary increases) and taking up her familiar position every night in her box at the side of the stage, where she cooked her evening meal

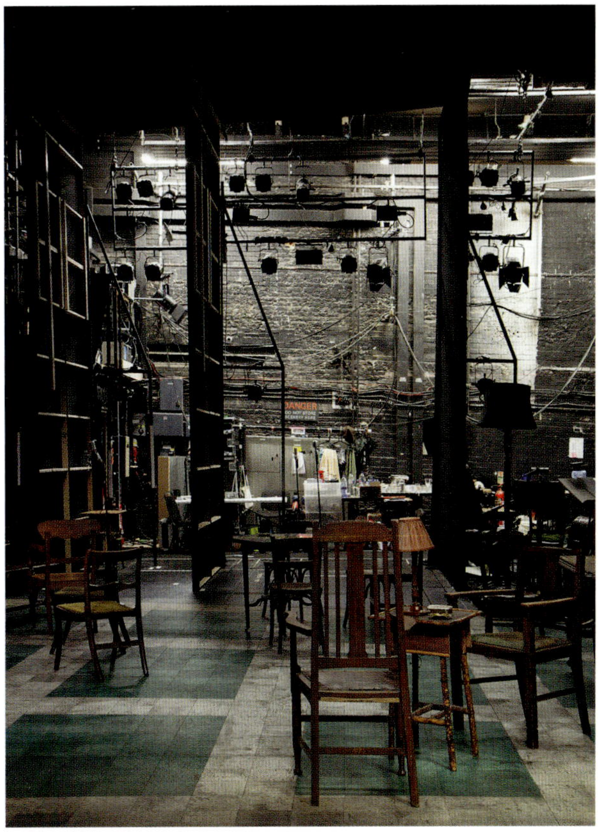

ABOVE Backstage at the Old Vic.

of sausages and onions on a small portable gas ring, most often dressed in her robes of honorary doctor of the University of Oxford. She was no scholar; she knew little of acting or of staging. But despite this apparent lack of qualification she remains perhaps the single most indispensable figure in the British theatre of the twentieth century.

The Vic continued its work until a bomb ripped through the building, nearly obliterating it, during the German aerial invasion in 1940. The Old Vic company moved to the New Theatre (now the Noël Coward) for a number of seasons, as well as constantly touring the British Isles, which gave it a truly national identity – to the extent that it was widely assumed that after the war it would receive official endorsement as the long dreamed of National Theatre.

But it was not to be. The theatre itself was reopened in 1950, considerably reconstructed, and the company continued its work there for another thirteen years, by which time Parliament had finally passed the National Theatre Act: its leader was to be Laurence Olivier, and it was to be housed in a magnificent new custom-built theatre of its own. While that was being built, it would take up temporary residence at the Old Vic. This makeshift arrangement ushered in the astonishing thirteen years of Olivier's regime, during which time it was known as the National Theatre at the Old Vic. It represents one of the great golden periods of British theatre history, not of course without its lows, but with an almost unparalleled series of highs in terms of acting, directing, design and writing – a company working together at full stretch, covering the world's repertory as well as commissioning new plays, rediscovering old ones, testing new acting and directing talent, bringing established actors to new heights. The Vic was altogether too small for such a venture, but the combination of its history and the gallant spirit in which the new enterprise was launched made it feel like the apotheosis of everything Lilian Baylis had envisioned, despite the brisk bar trade during the interval.

There was nothing either cosy or predictable about it. It was, apart from anything else, a tremendous and passionate triumph over physical circumstances. Olivier ran the operation from a couple of Nissen huts in the back streets of Waterloo station; he would cap a hard day's administration or rehearsal (either as actor or director) with a towering performance onstage at night. It destroyed his health and robbed him of the prize of leading the company into the new building which he had so long dreamed of and planned. The last night of the National at the Old Vic, on 28 February 1976, was a show called *A Tribute to The Lady* – Lilian Baylis – given by Gielgud and Ralph Richardson alongside Albert Finney and other members of the National Theatre company, with Peggy Ashcroft incomparably brilliant as Miss Baylis herself. In the audience, swathed in white cotton, were Sybil Thorndike, who had first appeared on that stage in 1914, and Michael Redgrave, who had given many highly original performances there in the 1930s. Laurence Olivier, heartbroken and very angry, was nowhere to be seen.

After the National departed to its concrete behemoth on the Thames there followed a number of experiments in management at the Vic that foundered, for one reason or another, though there were fine things along the way – not least Derek Jacobi's famous Hamlet (but also Peter O'Toole's hilariously blood-drenched Macbeth, famous in a different way). In 1985, the Canadian entrepreneur Edwin 'Honest Ed' Mirvish astonished everyone by buying the theatre. At first there was general dread that its glorious tradition would be destroyed. Instead, Mirvish and his son David spent nearly £2 million on handsomely restoring J. T. Robinson's original auditorium. In so doing, of course, they banished the ghosts from the intervening years – which included the Baylis years, during which the theatre was frequently altered, suffering, as the Theatres Trust somewhat tartly remarks, 'a series of radical attacks in the name of production fashion'. The Olivier period saw the most radical of all these attacks: under the supervision of the great Irish

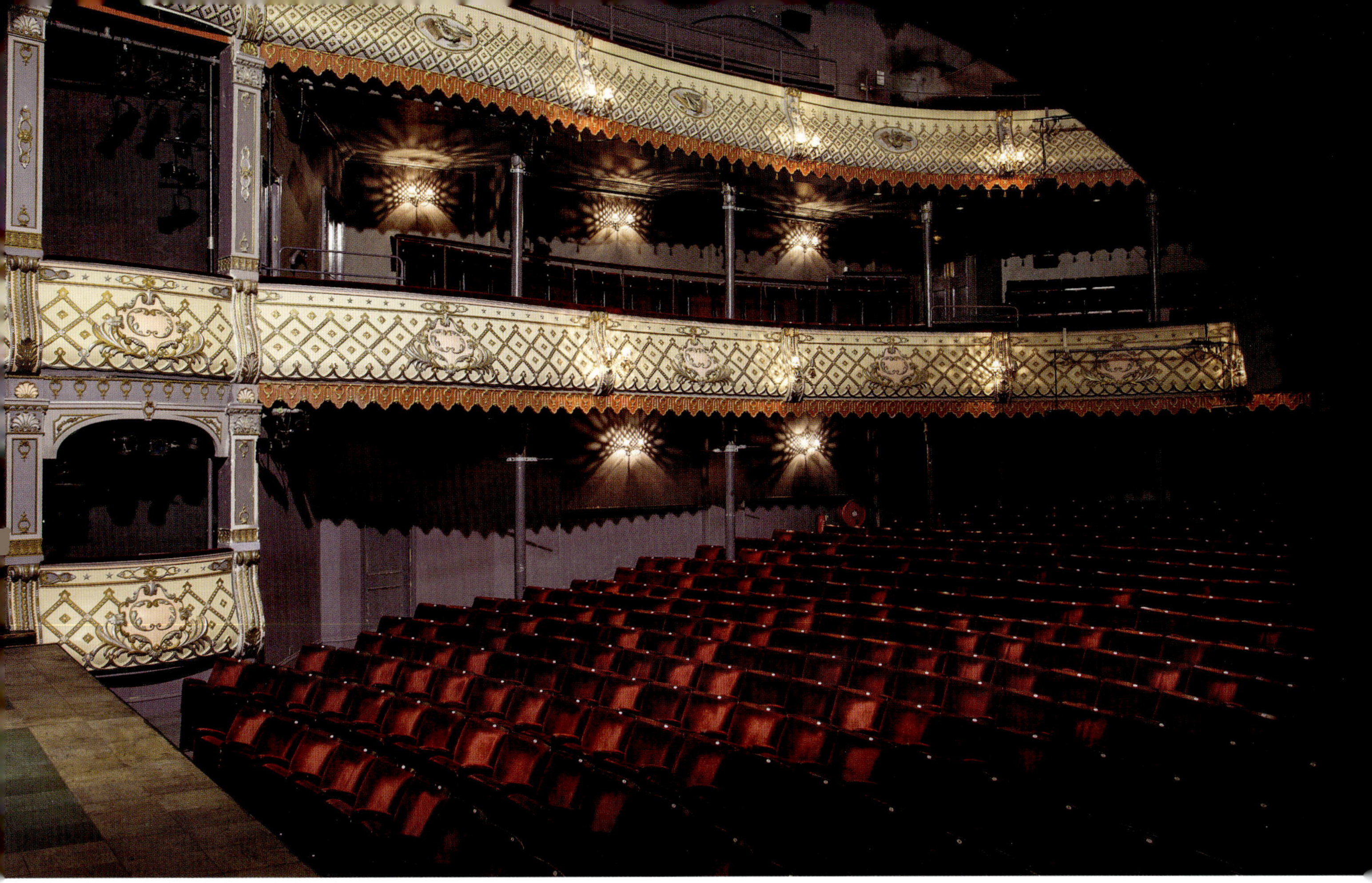

designer Sean Kenny, the stage was thrust out into the auditorium, the proscenium replaced with grey wood, the boxes taken over for light and sound equipment, and the decor rendered sober and functional. There was a purpose behind these changes, however. It was not, as might have at first appeared, any kind of modernism or puritanism. On the contrary: the auditorium was dulled down in order to heighten the brilliance of what appeared on the stage.

Most theatres are always in evolution, and restoring them to their original architectural condition is a risky business. It is deeply satisfying to sense that the walls of a theatre have absorbed the blood, the sweat, the toil and the tears of actors and audiences past.

ABOVE The auditorium. The fine fronts of the balconies are the only ornate feature of the auditorium. Elsewhere a spartan simplicity reigns, except for the seats.

Today's Old Vic is oddly antiseptic, despite its gorgeous fabric. But give it time. The Mirvishes installed first Jonathan Miller and then Peter Hall as artistic directors; neither could balance the books. Ed, honest to a fault, finally admitted that he couldn't make it work and threw in the towel. He took care to sell the theatre on to a trust, which appointed two remarkable artistic directors in a row: the actor Kevin Spacey, followed by the director Matthew Warchus, who have not only made the theatre prosper but have given it a role that, since the departure of the National Theatre, it had seemed to lack, doing fearless, high-definition work. Unsurprisingly, actors are queuing up to perform there. The ghosts, so rudely ejected, are quietly coming back.

VICTORIA PALACE

The Victoria Palace occupies the site on which once stood a now almost wholly forgotten theatre, the Royal Standard Music Hall, which at the time of its demolition in 1910 could proudly boast the longest record of uninterrupted music hall and variety performances of any theatre in London. That theatre was itself the second on the site, in an area not noted for theatre. Its story follows a familiar pattern: in 1832 a small hostelry called the Royal Standard was established in Stockdale Terrace, at the top of what is now Victoria Street. The proprietor, John Moy, following a growing trend, created a room for musical entertainment – or 'harmonic meetings' as they were somewhat euphemistically called. Demand was good: between the Standard and Westminster Abbey lay an area dominated by the massive Watney brewery; all around it was accommodation for its employees, fringed by the infamous slum which Dickens dubbed the Devil's Acre. Between them, the slums and the brewery provided a busy clientele, eager to be entertained as well as refreshed. In 1840, Moy duly secured a licence for singing and dancing on the premises. Such was its success that he enlarged the building, formally naming it Moy's Music Hall; this was later upgraded to the more impressive-sounding Royal Standard Concert Rooms.

By now the area had changed radically. A good part of the slums had been wiped out during the construction, in 1851, of Victoria Street and replaced with imposing blocks, often with shops on the ground floor, but also by pioneering mansion blocks; it was here that the first purpose-built flats so common on the Continent and in Scotland were introduced to London. Meanwhile the great railway age was hitting its stride, and in 1860 a long-needed station serving the south of England was opened and named Victoria (after the street, not the queen). Huge numbers of visitors now filled the area, which became increasingly prosperous; many companies established their headquarters there, and the mansion blocks became more and more splendid. The theatre naturally partook of this prosperity. In 1863, Alfred Brown took it over and refurbished it. Henceforth it was to be the Royal Standard Music Hall; the stage was in fact part of an adjoining room, while the customers sat at tables.

Twenty more years of splendid business in the ever expanding and ever more genteel neighbourhood emboldened a new proprietor, Richard Wake, to pull the whole thing down and start again, now *sans* hotel. The splendid new Royal Standard was, said *The Era*, purring its enthusiasm, 'the most comfortable Hall of entertainment in London', no mean boast in the theatre-mad metropolis of the period. 'The refreshment department has always been the careful study of the Proprietor,' noted the paper. 'There is a large and handsome Grill Room, open from 12 a.m. to 12 p.m.; Billiard Room, with two tables by Burroughes [and] Watts; large Public Bars on the ground floor.' Contemporary prints seem to confirm the splendours of Wake's refreshment department, and the greatest artists of the day were happy to appear there. Nonetheless,

OPPOSITE Detail of the auditorium. A good example of 'Matcham's Baroque'.

OVERLEAF The domed roof of the auditorium gives an almost kaleidoscopic effect.

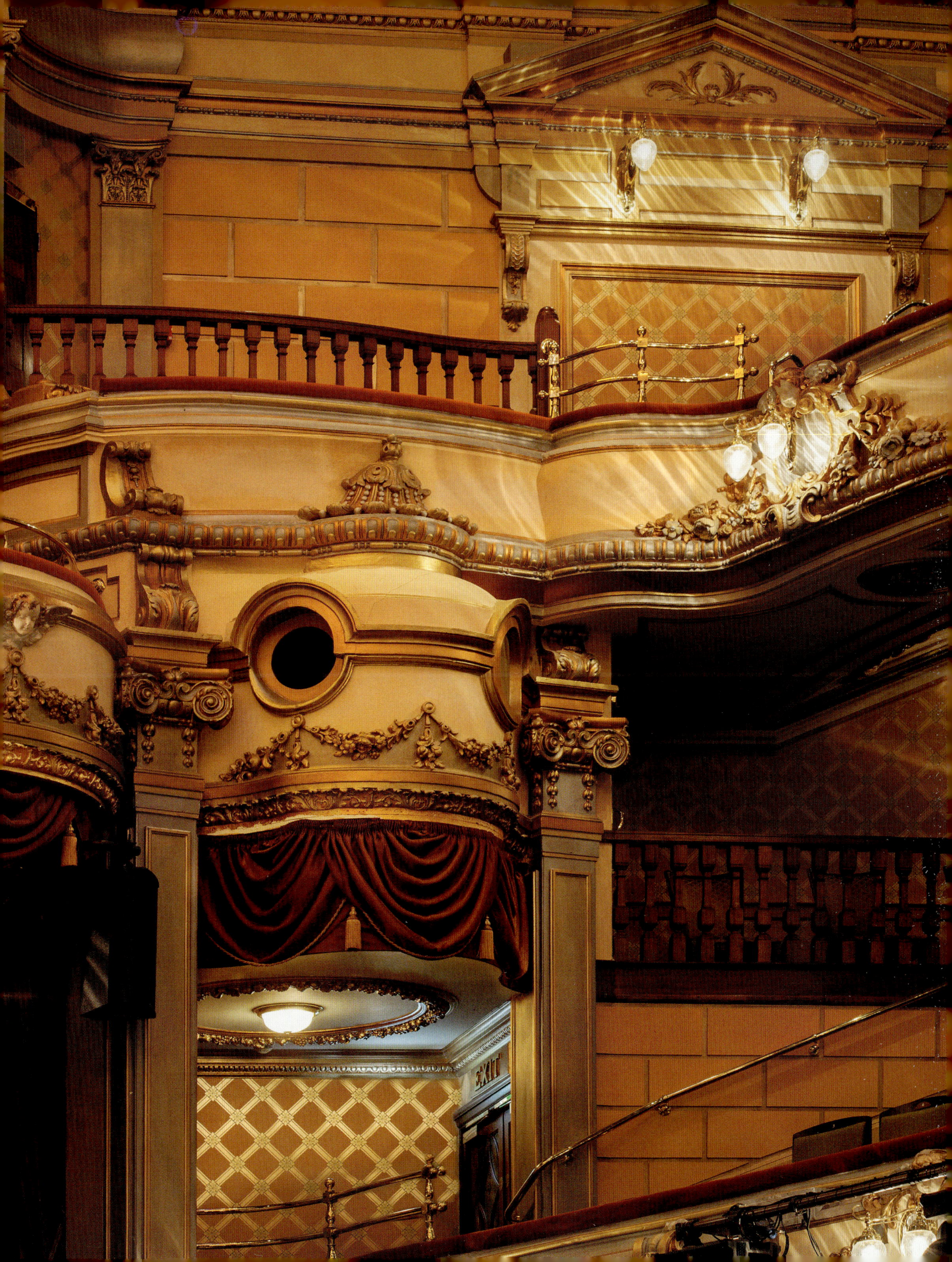

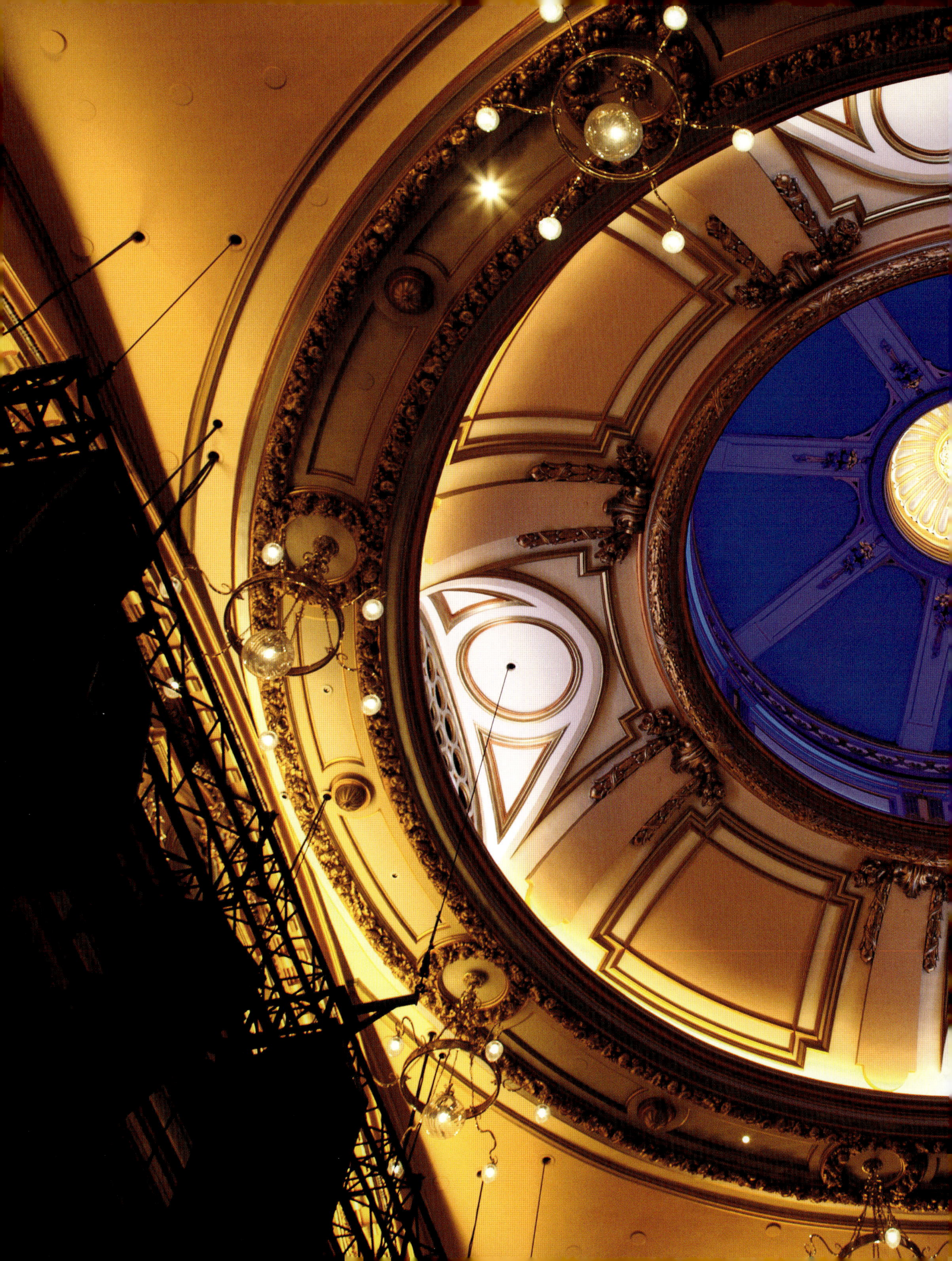

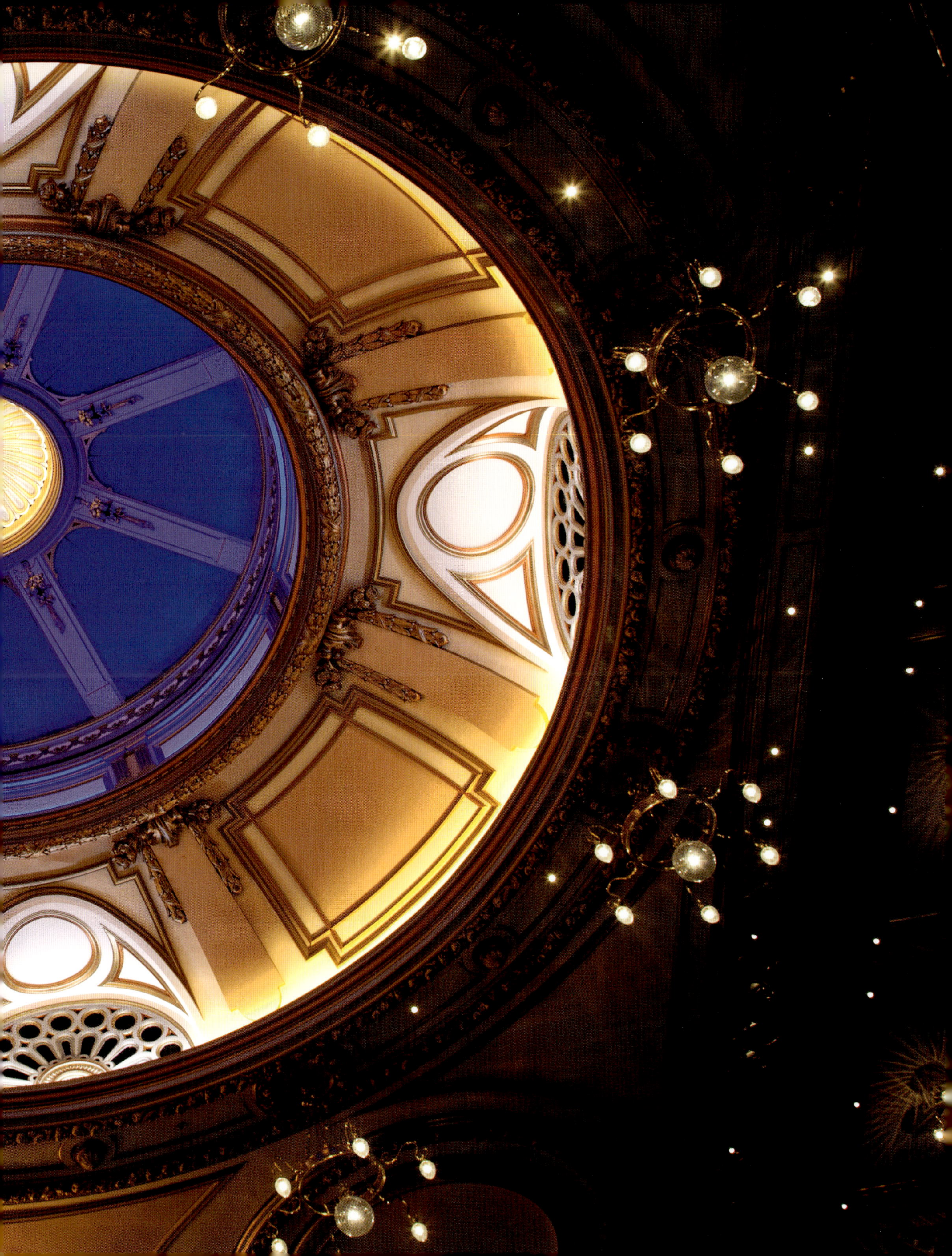

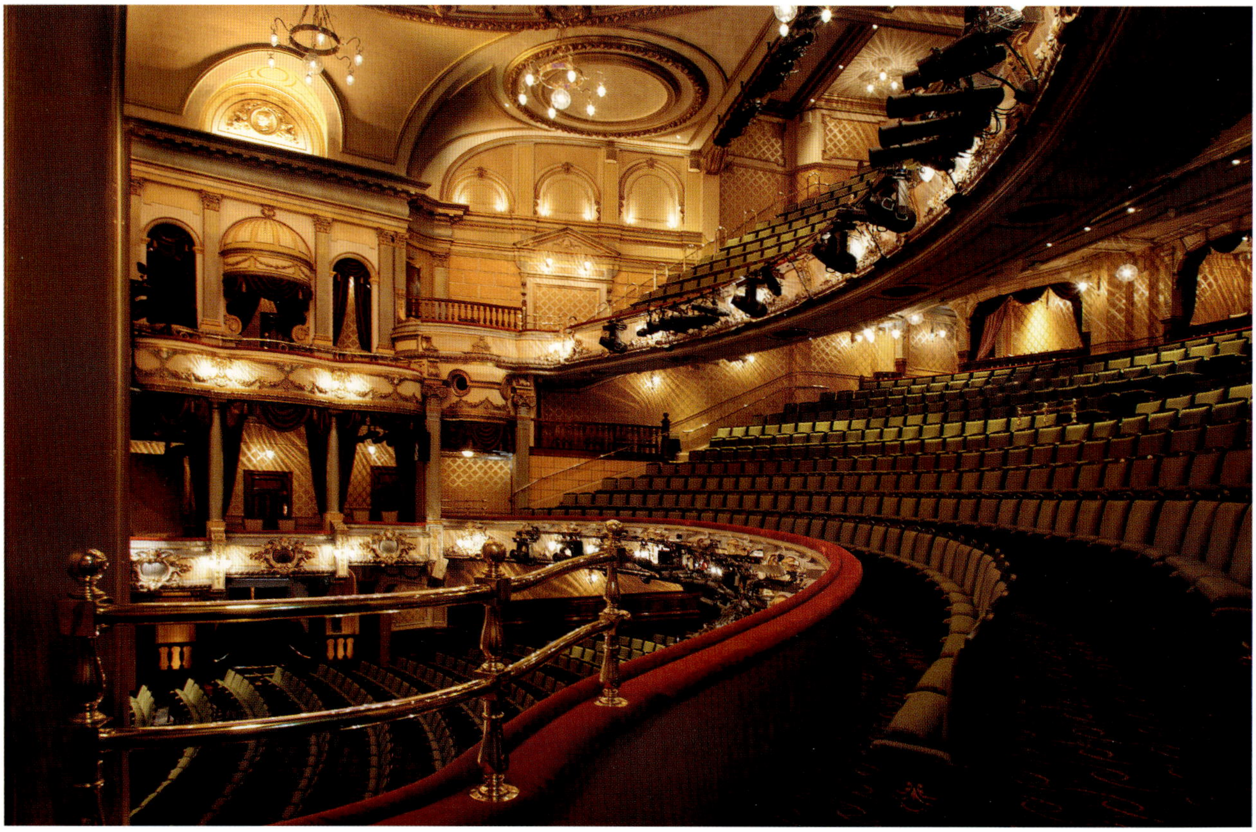

when Thomas Dickie bought it he immediately had it thoroughly overhauled, papered and painted, to general approval; it reopened in 1898, the same year in which the old 1860 Victoria station was demolished and replaced by the present magnificent edifice, directly in the Royal Standard's eyeline.

The station is still there, but the Standard's days were numbered. It had caught the eye of Alfred Butt, a brilliant and dashing figure who had rapidly risen from the counting-house of Harrods to become company secretary of the Palace Theatre at the age of nineteen; six years later he was its manager, and in 1906, at the age of 27, he was appointed managing director. Ever-expanding, in 1910 he created a federation of theatres that was second only in size to the Moss Empires chain of music halls. That same year he snapped up the Royal Standard, immediately demolishing it and commissioning Frank Matcham, prince of theatre architects, to create a new theatre, which, as a nod to Butt's first theatre, would be called the Victoria Palace. Matcham was nearing the end of his career, but he certainly went out in a blaze of glory. The London Palladium opened in 1910, the Victoria Palace in 1911 and the Bristol Hippodrome (designed in tandem with Bertie Crewe) the following year. The Victoria Palace shows him at the very height of his powers, in full command of the style described by John Earl as 'Matcham's Baroque'. There is always something of the seaside about Matcham's designs: they bespeak good humour, fun and fantasy; they promise a good time. The facade of the Victoria Palace has a strong Italian feeling, emphasised by the loggia above the canopy; the dome, bringing a Roman touch to the whole, is incongruously topped by a gold statue of the legendary Russian ballerina Anna Pavlova,

ABOVE The auditorium from the royal circle balcony.

whom Butt had sensationally introduced to London audiences just a year before at his other Palace, in Cambridge Circus.

The interior of the Victoria Palace is astonishing, not so much in any single aspect but in the harmonious coexistence of so many contrasting styles, from Berninian floridity in the auditorium to a set of bars and lounge areas each in a different style – Tudor, neoclassical, Art Nouveau. It is a part of Matcham's extraordinary personal manner, this unique combination of generosity and exuberance, allied to serene confidence in his technical skill. It was not intended for those who see theatre as a sacred art. The Victoria Palace is, like so many of his other theatres, a perfect setting for a day out, a lovely classy junket: a People's Palace, in fact.

And so it was from the very beginning, when it opened in 1911 with a bill featuring Harry Lauder, Little Tich and Vesta Tilley, among the greatest music hall entertainers of their, or any other, day; it was virtually the climax of that particular form of raw and racy entertainment. Variety, ever more family-oriented, replaced it, to be supplanted in turn by television; meanwhile, in the wake of the end of the First World War, revue – fast, funny, fleet-footed – was all the rage at the VP (as it was widely known). The most successful of these, right at the end of the 1920s, was *The Show's the Thing*, written by Archie Pitt and starring Gracie Fields, all-singing, all-dancing diva of the North. The songs featured sum up the whole: 'Clap Your Hands', 'We're Not as Bad as We're Painted' and 'Dance Away Your Blues'. By 1934 the blues had not entirely departed, and presumably somebody somewhere felt that in the wake of the Great Crash, and amid the lowering political climate of the time, such frivolity was no longer what audiences wanted and that the 88-year-old Rev. Walter Reynolds's stirringly patriotic pageant *Young England* – 'an avowed effort', said the *Melbourne Argus*, 'to revive the Victorian interest in drama which had a courageous hero, a chaste heroine, and an utterly worthless villain' – was just the ticket.

It turned out that frivolity was exactly what audiences wanted, and they were thrilled to discover that the play lent itself to infinite mockery. In this the actors happily encouraged them. On one typical night, the villain, when led away by the police, paused to say 'Foiled!' The crowd shouted not only 'Foiled!' but 'Baffled!' 'Beaten!' 'Frustrated!' 'Outwitted!' 'Trapped!' 'Flummoxed!' The villain waited until the wits were through, then hissed back: 'Stymied!' One of the show's sets included a Salvation Army 'citadel' with doors marked 'Men' and 'Women'. Every time an actor started for one, the crowd shouted: 'Wrong door, wrong door!' Sometimes the actors were pelted with coins ('quite painful', one elderly actor reported). Finally, to the uncontained delirium of the entire audience, the curtain fell on the baronial hall, whose back wall had miraculously changed into Loch Lomond in springtime. Britannia, flanked by Brownies, Wolf Cubs, Scouts, Guides and the complete company, stood superb against an erratically lowered Union Jack. The play ran for a year and was seen by 250,000 people, many of them returning again and again. The entire episode is one of the most delectable anomalies of recent theatre history.

In 1937, the theatre had a bona fide hit, *Me and My Girl*, which starred the diminutive, bug-eyed Lupino Lane, Teddie St Denis and George Graves. The story, concerning a cheeky cockney who unexpectedly inherits an earldom, was scarcely an example of searing social realism, but its very English zaniness and lovely, tuneful, tender score by Noel Gay made it an enduring success, though its triumph was not immediate. It made little impact when it opened, but a matinee performance was broadcast on BBC radio shortly after, as a substitute for a major sporting event that had been cancelled; a little later it was televised, which did ticket sales no harm either. The musical's hit song, 'The Lambeth Walk', became a universal dance craze that helped to boost morale during the war years – on both sides, despite being officially described by a Nazi spokesman as 'Jewish mischief and animalistic hopping'. Russ

Morgan and Duke Ellington recorded it with great success; and it was the subject of a pioneering instance of what we would now call a meme, when the Ministry of Information made a short propaganda film, *Lambeth Walk – Nazi Style*, which edited footage from Leni Riefenstahl's *Triumph of the Will* to make it appear as if the leaders were dancing to 'The Lambeth Walk'. Joseph Goebbels, it was said, put the editor of the film on a Gestapo list for elimination when Britain was defeated. *Me and My Girl*, meanwhile, was revived three times during and immediately after the war, as well as being filmed (under the title of its hit song).

The Victoria Palace again became associated with a national institution when the great comedy troupe The Crazy Gang – three double-acts (Flanagan and Allen, Nervo and Knox, Naughton and Gold) and a loose cannon (the monstrously moustached 'Monsewer' Eddie Gray) – moved in in 1947 for *Together Again*, and never really went away again until their last show there in 1962. They were a sort of British Marx Brothers – early Marx Brothers, with Flanagan and Allen supplying the equivalent of Zeppo's sentimental songs – but more importantly they provided a link with the great tradition of the music hall; they would not have been out of place in the Royal Standard a hundred years earlier. When they were in residence they provided a link with another, nearly adjacent palace, whose royal inhabitants could – and did – consider the theatre as their local. King George VI particularly loved the Crazy Gang, and his daughter – now Queen Elizabeth II – has happy memories of seeing them. It is touching to think of those early generations of Windsors, whose reluctance to enter a theatre – especially one where the plays of William Shakespeare or (God forbid!) Anton Chekhov were being performed – was well known, should have been drawn to the Victoria Palace like moths to the flame whenever the Crazy Gang were in town.

Next to be installed in the Victoria for any length of time was, alas, *The Black and White Minstrel Show* – featuring white actors in blackface – which stayed until the early 1970s, when everyone really should have known better. Thereafter, with very rare exceptions, it's been musicals, musicals all the way, especially, for some reason, shows about great performers of the past (Buddy Holly, Al Jolson). *Annie* stayed for years, as did *Billy Elliot* – two shows with juvenile heroes. In 2016 the theatre was sold to the impresario Cameron Mackintosh and, in a great tradition, closed for major refurbishment; it would reopen in December 2017 with a transfer of the world-beating Broadway mega-hit *Hamilton*. The refurbishment, lovingly and lengthily (and very expensively) carried out at Mackintosh's behest by Clare Ferraby, the doyenne of theatre restorers, provided the theatre with a new flytower at the back of the existing building and completed, in Ferraby's words, what Matcham had started, restoring the brighter colours that had been so commented on when the building originally opened, endowing the whole theatre with a sense of luminosity. How wonderful that the sharpest, most innovative musical theatre show of the early twenty-first century should punch out its fierce and challenging rap in this voluptuous Edwardian environment, sensuously celebrating textures and shapes, immersing its audiences in grace and beauty and charm. The theatre lives.

OPPOSITE TOP Details of the ceiling in the auditorium.
OPPOSITE BOTTOM Stalls seats, beautifully restored.

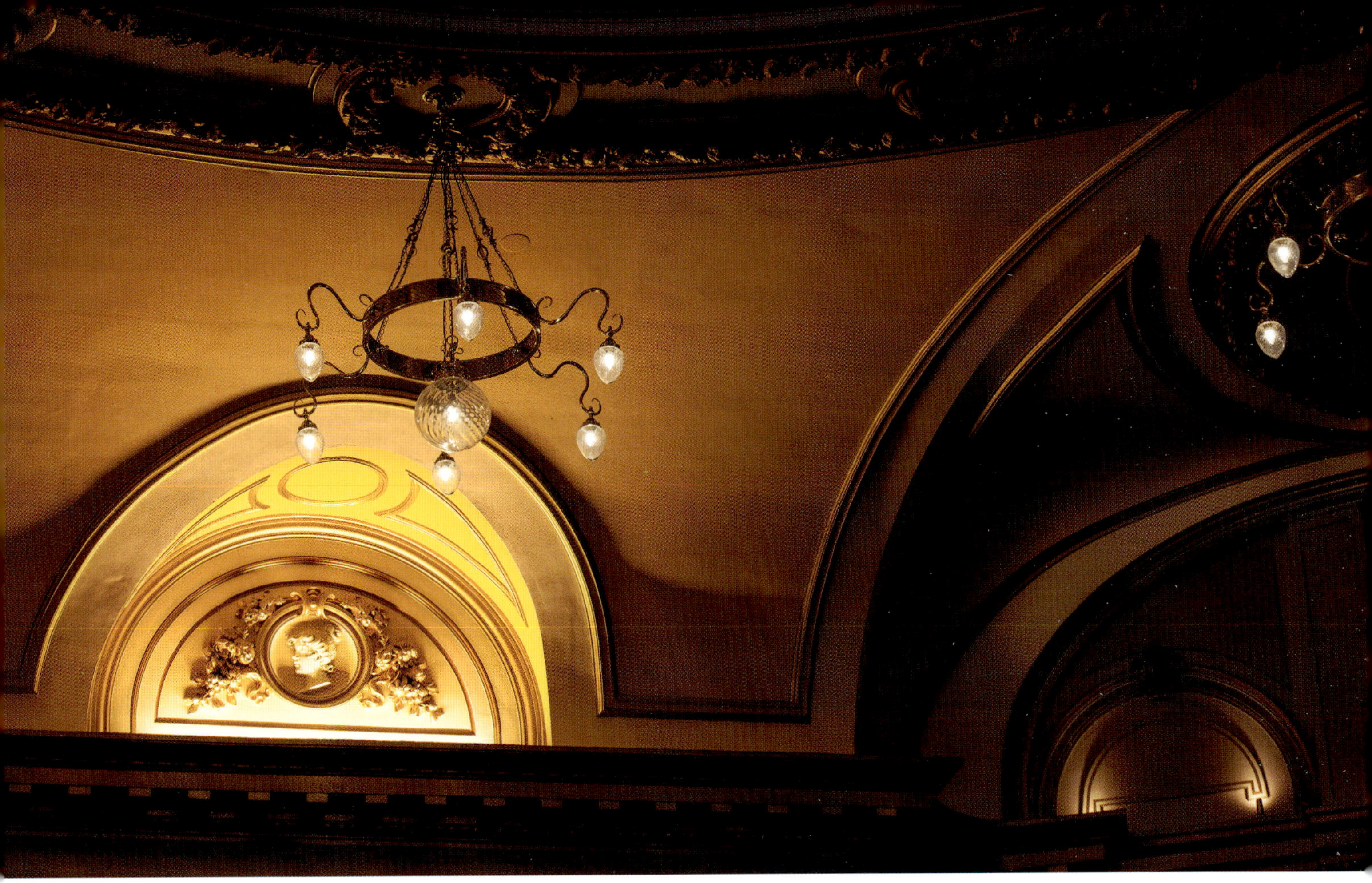

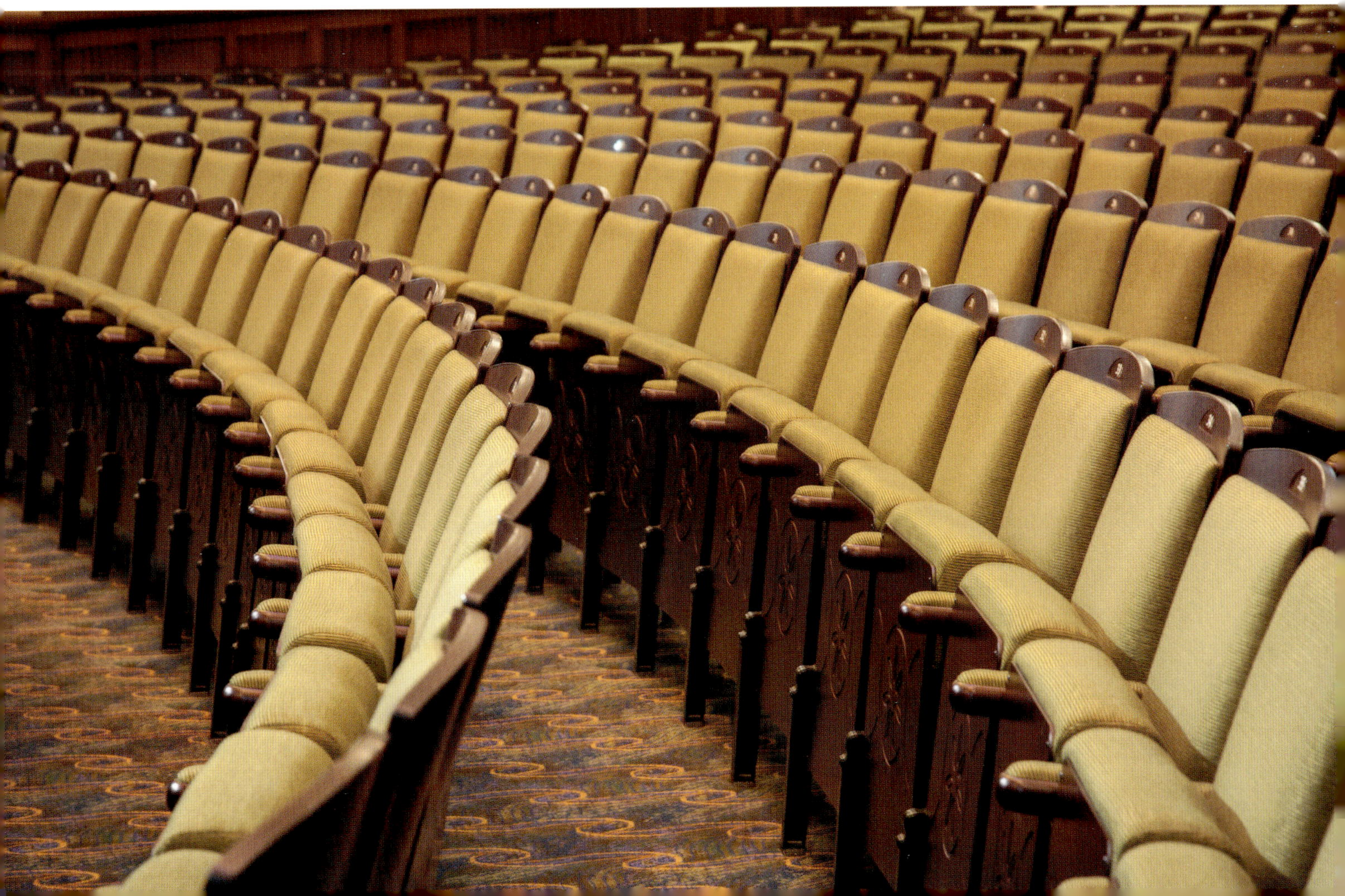

WILTON'S MUSIC HALL

The sweetly named Graces Alley in Tower Hamlets, where Wilton's Music Hall is to be found, is a modest little street that looks on to the equally amiably named Wellclose Square, but both lie at the centre of a district heavy with history, much of it of a distinctly rackety variety. It was only in the fourteenth century that the swampy land itself was reclaimed by that great speculator the medieval Church, which, after draining it, developed wharfs, docks and market gardens and built an abbey on the reclaimed land. The Church profited from all this enterprise only briefly; with the Tudor Reformation, the abbey was burned to the ground and the land accrued to the Crown. The Wellclose area, however, was designated a liberty under the local jurisdiction of the Tower of London, which afforded some protection; indeed the governor of the Tower had the authority to license plays within his bailiwick. By the early eighteenth century, nearby Goodman's Fields in Whitechapel was a highly successful theatrical venue: there were premieres of plays by George Farquhar and Henry Fielding, and it was there in 1737 that a young wine merchant from Lichfield called David Garrick made his sensational debut as Richard III.

Mostly, though, the area was noted for its factories and its churches: by the eighteenth century a theologically diverse assemblage of places of worship had been erected, catering to Anglicans, Danes, German Lutherans, Roman Catholics and Jews; the new sugar-refining industry introduced unhealthy factories, manned by a largely German workforce that happily integrated with the indigenous community. It was the building of the London and St Katharine docks in the late 1820s that fundamentally changed the area: the sailors had their needs, and Whitechapel did its best to supply them. Brothels and taverns flourished. A pub called the Prince of Denmark, named in honour of the nearby Danish embassy, opened at 1–4 Graces Alley; when the German Allrich Eden took it over he promoted it to the King of Denmark, but by 1839 it had been demoted again; locally it was known as the Mahogany Bar, in honour of the splendid wooden counter of imported Caribbean wood that always remained in place throughout the tavern's many transformations. Whatever its name, its destiny was about to change. In common with other taverns, it saw the possibilities of providing properly structured entertainment, and a couple of back rooms were converted into a concert room; before long the pub became a playhouse, putting on plays in the patriotically named Albion Saloon Theatre. Alas, the building collapsed – so comprehensively that the original freeholder rebuilt it again from scratch, returning it yet again to its original identity as the Prince of Denmark, a simple pub, or rather one of the newly popular gin palaces.

The building's somewhat up-and-down career took a historic turn in 1846 when it was purchased by a sometime solicitor's clerk from Bath called John Wilton, who fulfilled a long-held dream by opening

OPPOSITE The faded quality of the paint and plasterwork creates a misleading sense of neglect, which lends a feeling of discovery, as if entering some forgotten theatre.
OVERLEAF Note the floorboards, the faded blue on the walls and the paintings of figures from an Indian saga, as well as the barrel-like shape of the roof and the barley-sugar columns.

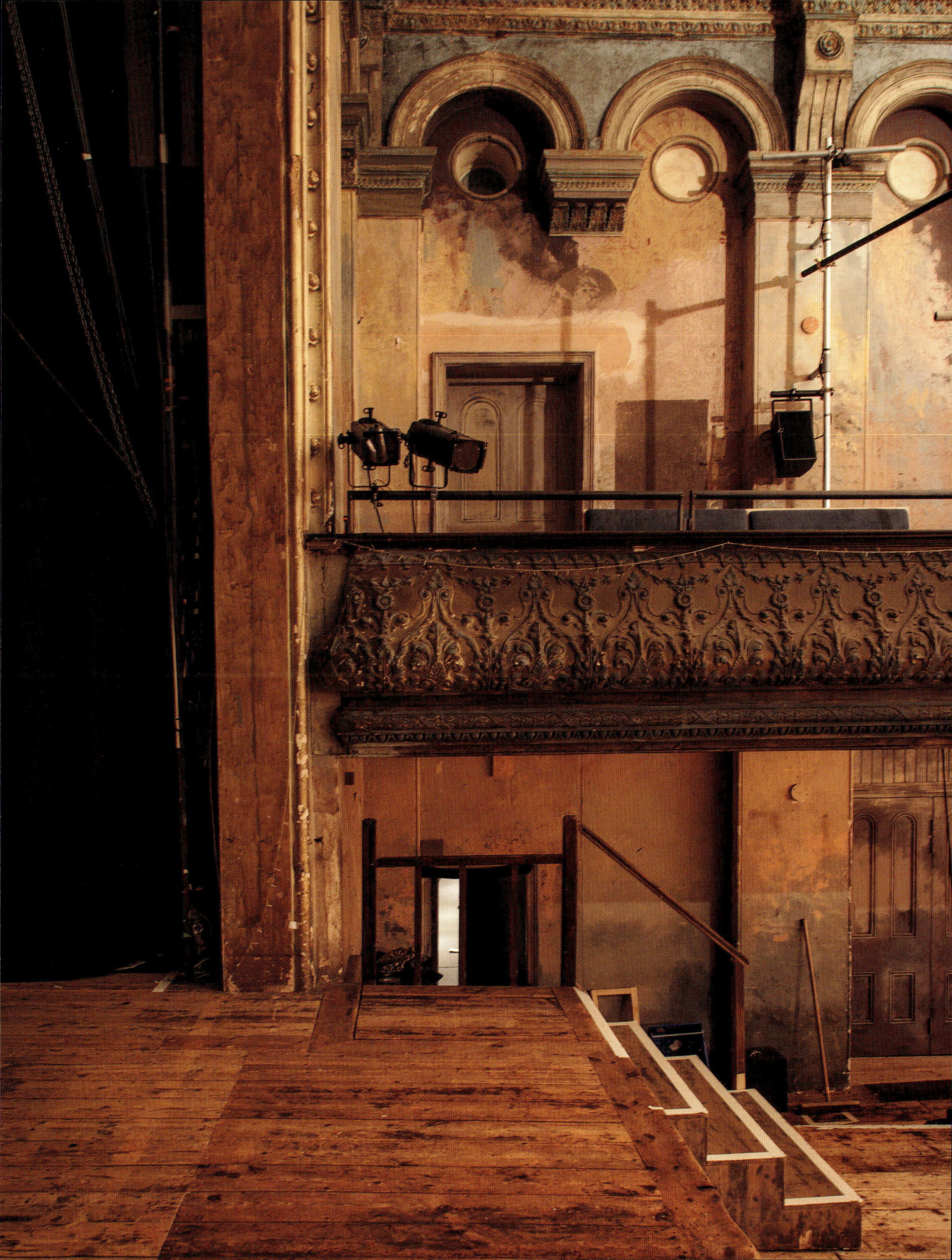

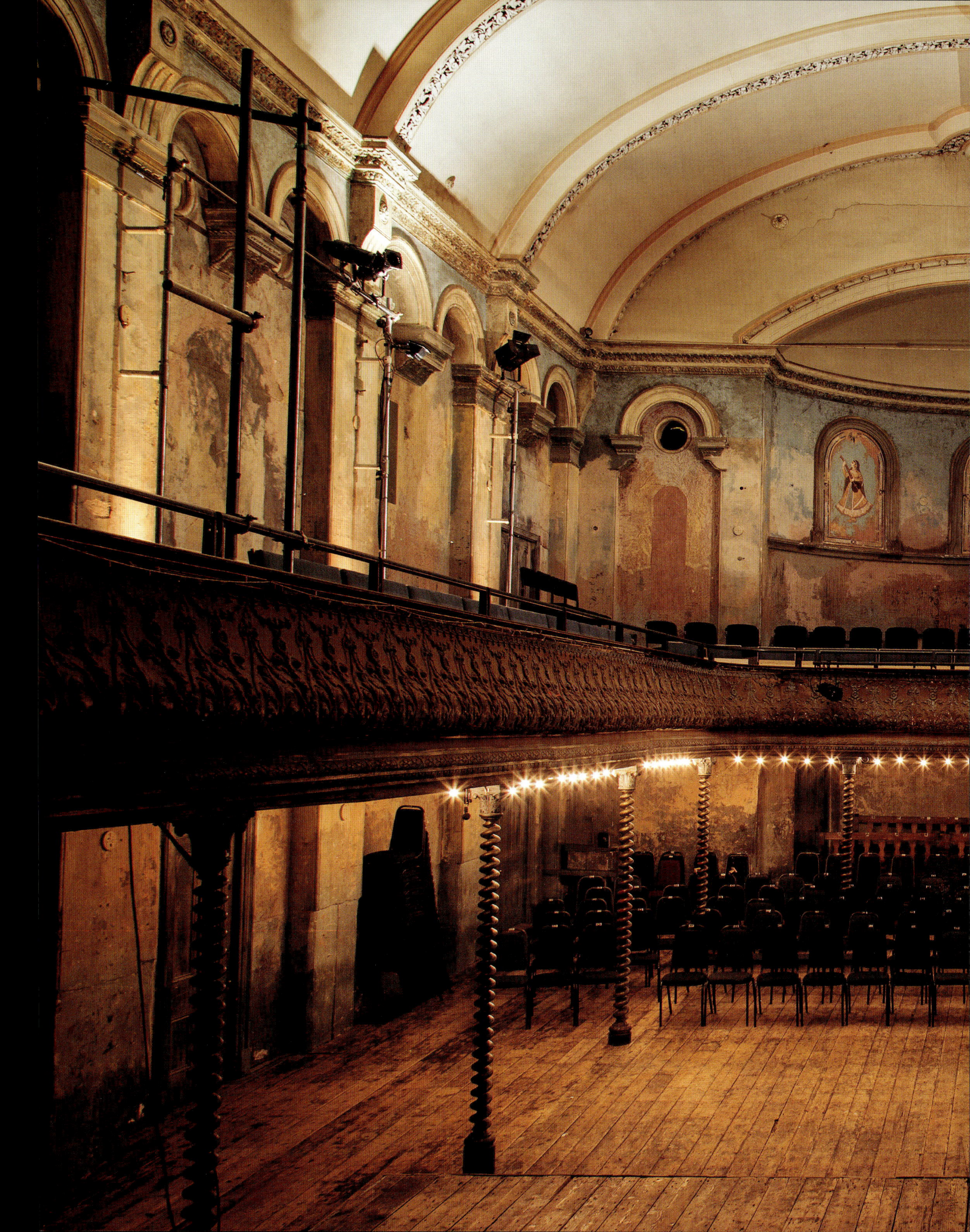

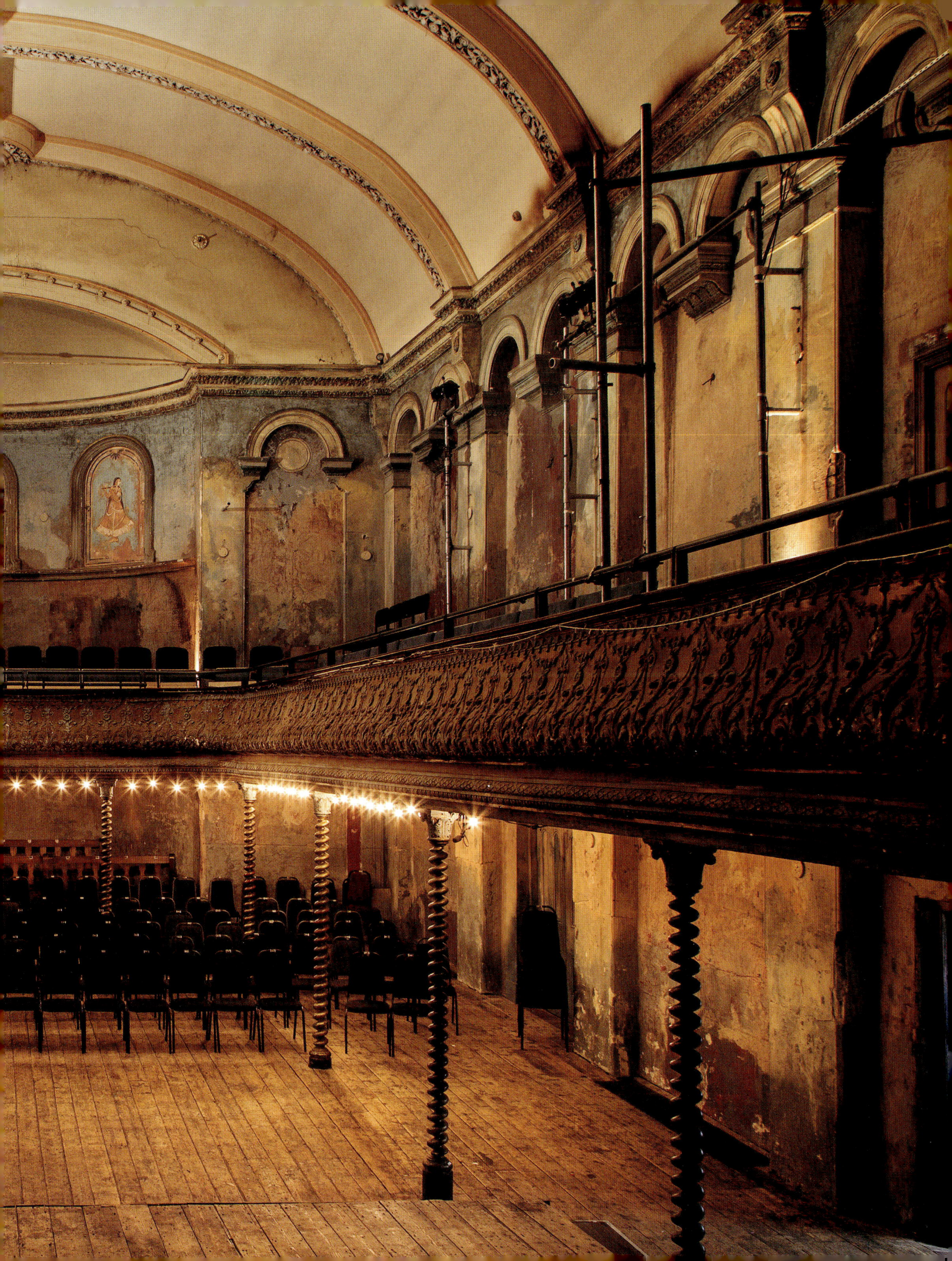

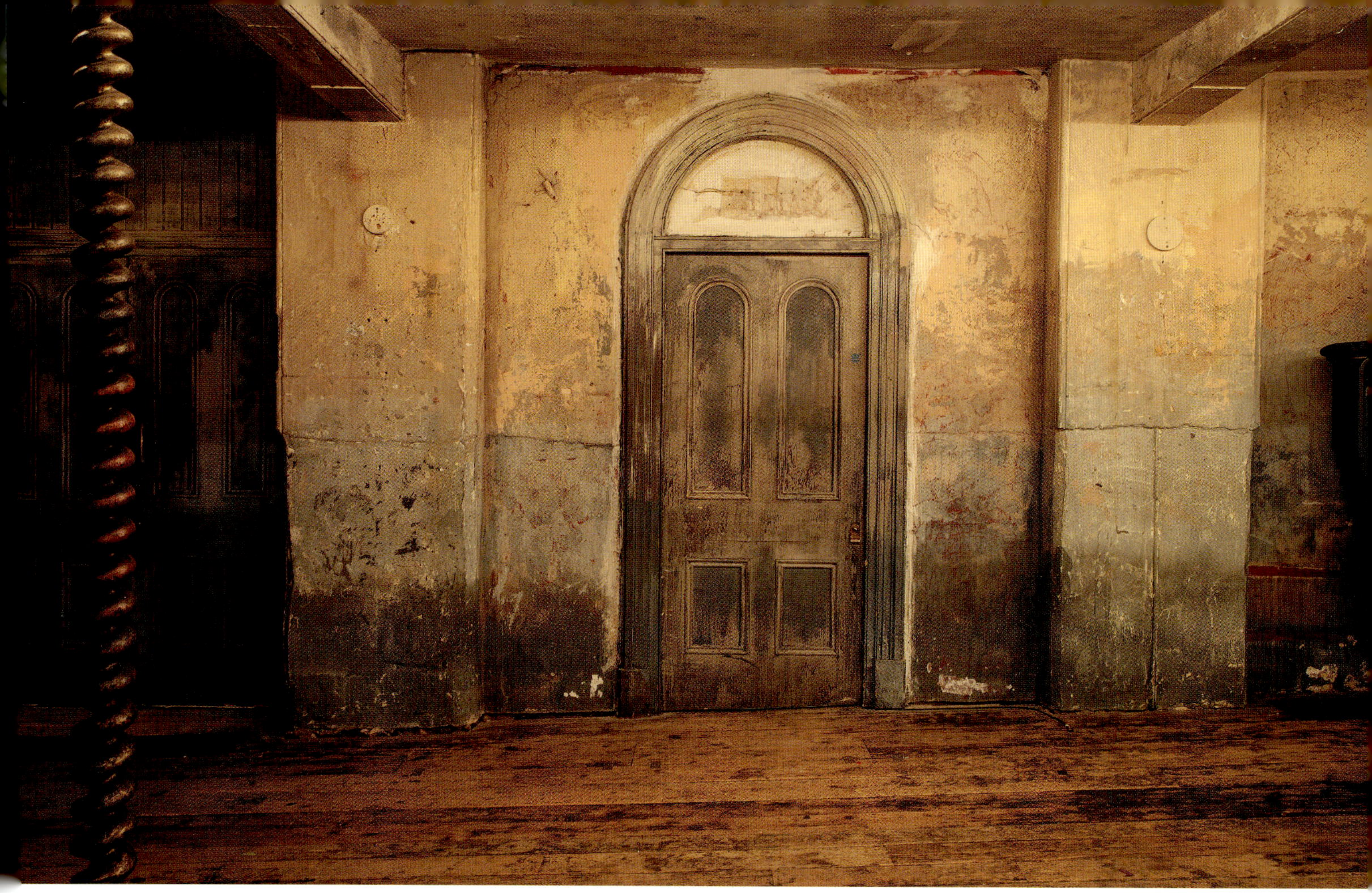

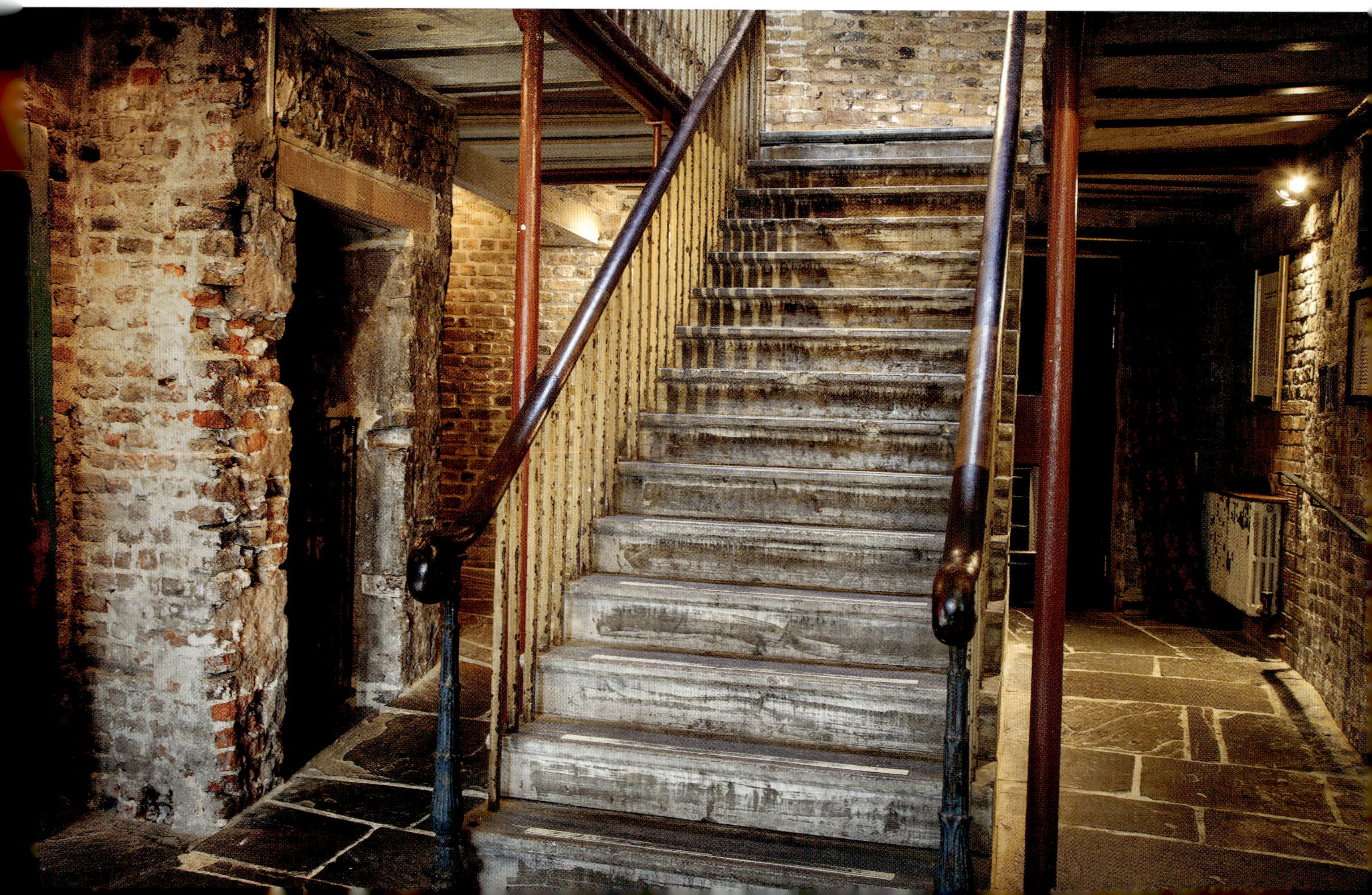

a small music hall behind the pub; its success was such that in 1859 he decided to convert the tavern into a music hall of unparalleled splendour. Naturally, and quite properly, he named it after himself. And there it stands today – not Wilton's actual building, but one identically rebuilt after a devastating fire in 1877, after Wilton himself had retired. As an exact replica of the original, it is the only surviving example of a music hall from that golden epoch when there was still a certain intimacy between performers and public, and before Oswald Stoll and the other music hall magnates built their massive behemoths of mass entertainment. The miraculously preserved little theatre on Graces Alley is entirely human in scale.

For anyone involved in the theatre in any way – actors, directors, composers, designers, audiences – walking into Wilton's is an emotional business. It catches at the throat; it gets the pulse racing. In ways hard at first to define, it seems to embody the particular excitement of theatre. It is something, perhaps, to do with its proportions: the place seems to throb with possibility and anticipation; the small stage aches to be populated. There seems to be a sense about the place of audiences past and audiences to come. Seeing a play or a show there confirms this: the place vibrates with communication, a playful energy surges through it. Why this should be so is one of the mysteries of architecture. The physical properties of Wilton's are not hard to describe – a rectangular room with a vaulted ceiling, a balcony supported by so-called barley-sugar columns made of twisted iron, with, at the opposite end of the theatre to the stage, a semicircular recess topped with a vault; another vault, this one gold-leafed, surmounts the stage. If this were a church, one would be talking about its apses and exedra. There is, in fact, something slightly ecclesiastical about this most secular of venues, more Nonconformist than Catholic or even Anglican, but still somehow charged with strange energies.

OPPOSITE TOP A detail of the auditorium.
OPPOSITE BOTTOM The staircase from the entrance – note the rough brickwork.

John Wilton was no Puritan, but it was his life's work to reform the music hall, which was still emerging from its stone age period. He was a founder member of the Music Hall Protection Society (as well as the Mutual Anti-Agency Society, committed to preventing what he called 'incompetent vocalists etc.' from being forced upon proprietors by their unscrupulous representatives). He was dedicated to establishing standards, moral, artistic and culinary. His method was simple: offer the best. He refused to foist inferior or lewd work on his customers, and nor would he pander to the local yobs, of whom there were many: the area around Wellclose Square was awash with riff-raff, more often than not of a nautical persuasion, 'a very rough, stormy class of sea-faring customers'. Bouncers – 'two policemen-looking men' – hovered in the auditorium. Wilton was eager to lure respectable people to his 'Magnificent New Music Hall' with what he called 'harmless and humanising enjoyment'. He was equally passionate about beautifying the auditorium, lavishing money and skill on it: the distinguished painter-decorator Jacob Maggs from Wilton's home town of Bath was hired to design the theatre, which was constructed by local builders; the whole thing cost a staggering £2,000 – the equivalent of some £800,000 in the early twenty-first century.

There were mirrors throughout, chandeliers hung from the ceiling and the walls were richly ornamented. For heat and more light, five hundred gas burners were installed, their glow richly reflected in the burnished vault above the stage. The sun-burner, as it was called, was a technological wonder: 'a solid mass', marvelled *The Era*, 'of richly cut glass in prismatic feathers, spangles, and spires, brilliantly illuminated by 300 burners, besides the new sunlight of 100 jets which, we believe, is the largest ever made . . . the glass covering contains 27,000 pieces of cut glass, the dazzling effect of which is unequalled'. The modestly proportioned auditorium held no fewer than 1,500 people, who must have been crammed in very tight indeed, especially since many of them were seated at tables, where the

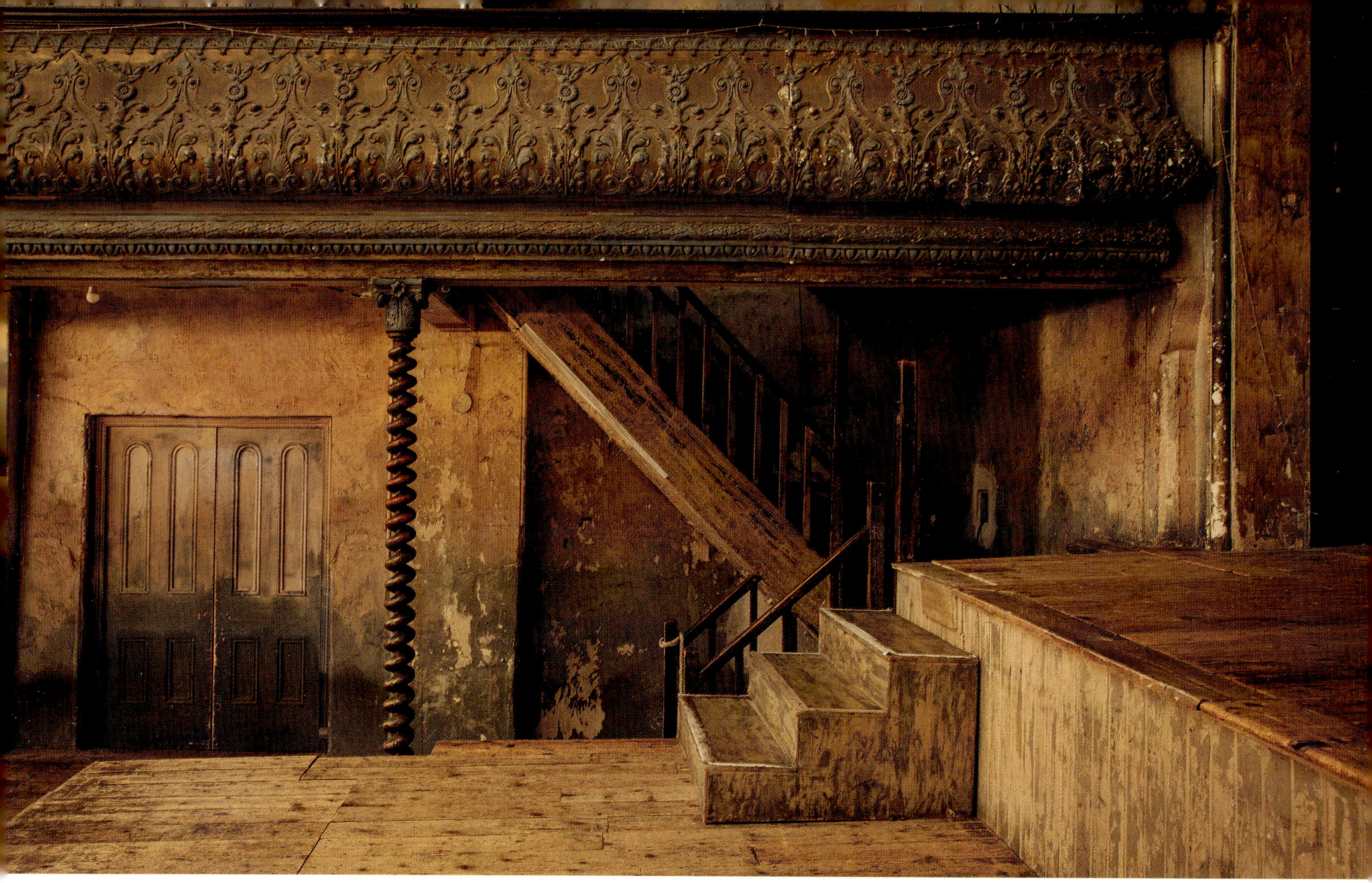

waiters zipped about taking orders. Fortunately, the nonpareil sun-burner had an outer shaft which, according to *The Era*, carried off all the heat of the room, 'so that however crowded [it] may be, as it was on the opening night, not the least inconvenience is felt from the heat, although there are nearly 500 lights in the room. This is a great thing for concert-rooms, and cannot be too publicly known.'

The entertainment was – at least to begin with – of an improving nature: operatic excerpts were heard, as well as the occasional madrigal and glee. Wilton had a fanatical passion for acoustics and was proud of the audibility in his new building: 'hearing throughout', he boasted, 'is perfect.' Later, the repertory broadened to include ballet and circus; while on the opening night, 28 March 1859, the customers were regaled with the talents of the great Sam Collins, 'The Inimitable Irish Gem' (born in Marylebone and with not a drop of Irish blood in him); Mr and Mrs Randall, 'the best Duoloquists Before the Public'; and Mr Charles Sloman, 'The Only English Improvisatore', who would compose elaborate verses to order; a week later the bill was dominated by black entertainers, though these may have been white performers in blackface. Wilton succeeded in his mission: his music hall was successful, orderly and attracted some of the best artists of the day. He retired in 1868, garlanded by the admiration of his peers and the approval of the local community; he had raised the tone by many notches. The new management kept the standards he had established and managed to snare, for a prodigious ten-week run, one of the greatest stars of the day: George Leybourne, commonly known

ABOVE Detail of the auditorium. The barley-sugar column adds an interesting accent to this scene.

by the name of his greatest hit, 'Champagne Charlie', one of the new *lions comiques*, guying the fashionable dashing young men about town. Alas, the limitless supply of champagne from vintners wanting him to promote their product did for him: he was dead at the age of 48.

The golden age of Wilton's came to an end with the great fire of 1877; the rebuilt theatre never attracted the audiences it had known before. The shipping trade had gone into a temporary period of decline, and with it went a substantial proportion of the venue's regular clientele. No matter with what delights the successive managers regaled their audiences – even bullfighting – revenues fell catastrophically, and in 1881 Wilton's closed its doors. Its life span as a music hall had been just over twenty years. During its last period, in the world beyond the theatre, late nineteenth-century evangelism had been taking hold; appalled by what they had heard about the goings-on inside, a fearless group of Methodists had entered Wilton's and, falling on their knees, had prayed in the midst of all the singing and dancing and laughter that 'God would break the power of the Devil in that place'. And lo, it came to pass: seven years after Wilton's closed, the Methodist East End Mission was firmly established in this former den of iniquity, under the name of The Mahogany Bar Mission (Moggy's Bar, to its regulars); it was of course a teetotal organisation, dispensing tea and buns and performing good works to the benefit of the ever-changing and often sore-pressed local community. During the Great Dock Strike of 1889, in which a staggering 100,000 dockworkers took part, Moggy's dispensed soup to their often starving families; in October 1936 it provided refuge for the anti-Mosley protesters in Cable Street, just up the road, and a few years later accommodated the frightened victims of the Blitz. In later years, very occasionally, the mission gave a nod in the direction of theatre, or at any rate entertainment, by hanging a white sheet from the balcony to present magic lantern shows.

But, as Feste so pertinently remarks in *Twelfth Night*, the whirligig of time brings in his revenges, and despite the mission's noble eleemosynary activities, by the 1950s Methodism had gone the way of the old music hall and somehow lost its audience. In 1956 the premises were taken over by the Coppermill Rag Sorting Warehouse, whose trade was recycling dressmakers' offcuts into cloths for wiping ships' engines. Coppermill treated the old building with respect, but the hyperactive London County Council of the early 1960s suddenly descended, determined to cut a swathe through the old neighbourhoods as it had done in the West End; John Betjeman valiantly rode up to the defence, and – with support from the Goons Spike Milligan and Peter Sellers, both of whom had their roots in variety entertainment – it was reprieved. In 1973 the building was awarded Grade II listing status, and from then on it was safe – if not secure. A long-running fundraising campaign was mounted and the building, cleared out but not yet restored, was hired out to film companies, including, touchingly, for Richard Attenborough's *Chaplin* (1992), though Wilton's active life had already ended before the great clown was born.

Finally, in 1997, Fiona Shaw performed T. S. Eliot's *The Waste Land* there, and the great auditorium was restored to its proper destiny as a peerless live theatre. Since then, and thanks to tireless fundraising by the passionate Frances Mayhew, Wilton's has been rediscovered and restored, but not Disneyfied: 'retaining genuine historic fabric and avoiding misleading restoration', as the official manifesto has it, is the aim, 'so that future generations can interpret the significance for themselves in their own way based on the physical evidence'. As sensible an approach to the revival of historic theatres as can be hoped for.

LONDON PALLADIUM

The London Palladium in Argyll Street is sometimes described as Britain's best-known, sometimes its best-loved, theatre, yet it stands apart from the mainstream of London theatres, partly because of its distinctive fare, partly because of its striking facade and partly by dint of its location: it is the only theatre in the immediate vicinity. In the seventeenth century Oxford Street was a rough highway, leading symbolically as it did direct from St Giles's notorious den of thieves between Great Russell Street and Seven Dials to the gallows at Tyburn (now Marble Arch). The gallows were removed in 1783, but the street was lined with pubs and bear pits and lowlife theatres: a dangerous place to be after nightfall. The area was transformed in the early nineteenth century by John Nash's creation of Regents (now Piccadilly) Circus, Regent Street and then Oxford Circus. Among the many grand properties in the newly gentrified area was the ramshackle Argyll House on Argyll Street, the residence of Archibald Campbell, 3rd Duke of Argyll – an unsavoury fellow, 'slovenly in his person', his contemporary Hugh Walpole wrote, 'slow, steady where suppleness did not better answer his purpose, revengeful, and if artful, at least not ingratiating'. After the unlamented death of the duke, the house was purchased by another Scottish nobleman, George Hamilton-Gordon, 4th Earl of Aberdeen, who remained there until his death in 1860. Aberdeen had the misfortune to be prime minister from 1852 to 1855, presiding over the shambles that was the Crimean War. His politics had outlived their time, as had the house in which he died; the moment he was gone it was demolished, and a firm of vintners bought the site, installing extensive underground cellars. Above, they built a large covered market which they named the Corinthian Bazaar, after the prevailing architectural style of the street, commissioning Owen Lewis to design a splendid classical facade, the grand pediment supported by eight magnificent acanthus-topped columns.

Perhaps it was too splendid for a mere market, because despite its aviary and swish refreshment room it never took off, and the proprietors started to think of alternative uses for the space. Hippodromes featuring indoor horse racing were all the rage, and the Argyll Street site was duly converted to that purpose; feeling the need for more than purely equine entertainment, the proprietor of what was now grandly called the Palais Royal entered into partnership with the circus impresario Frederick Charles Hengler, who had established a number of provincial circuses; such was the success of the London venture that it was redubbed Hengler's Grand Cirque and the distinguished theatre architect Charles Phipps commissioned to redesign the interior, which now held seven hundred customers. For a while after Hengler's death in 1887 the venue continued to present circus performances, but in 1895 another novelty claimed it, and for four years it became the National Skating Palace. Seasonal circus fare returned with the new century under the guise of the Royal Italian Circus, as well as a remarkable cyclorama depicting Jerusalem and the Crucifixion; neither triumphed. Finally, the whole site, which was by now structurally unsound, was sold on to a highly

OPPOSITE The safety curtain, bearing a picture of the theatre's facade at the time of Charles Hengler.

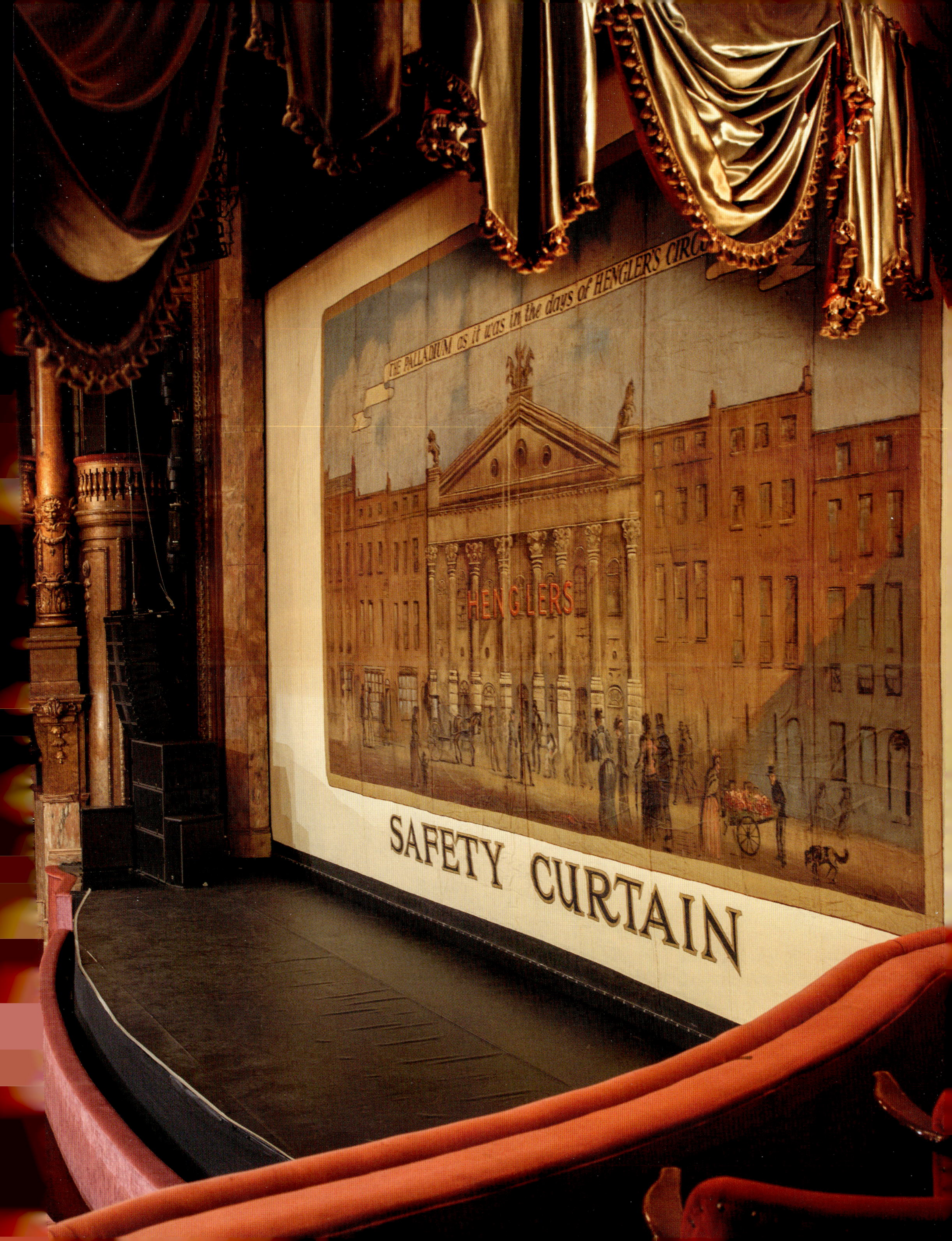
THE PALLADIUM as it was in the days of HENGLER'S CIRC
HENGLERS
SAFETY CURTAIN

ambitious impresario by the name of Walter Gibbons, who now found himself in possession of land that had covered a huge spectrum of entertainments (if the Crucifixion can be so described), to say nothing of its sitting on top of wine cellars; Dionysus, god both of wine and of theatre, was unquestionably the resident deity.

Gibbons was a formidable personality: the remarkable trajectory of his career had taken him from toiling in a nail factory in Wolverhampton to singing first in opera and then on the halls; he next pioneered newfangled cinematic Bioscope presentations, which often featured short films of music hall artists but sometimes went as far afield as South Africa for the last stages of the Boer War. Gibbons was no pussycat: he and Oswald Stoll were the employers' representatives in the very ugly Music Hall Strike of 1907. The managers fought a tough fight but in the end the strikers prevailed, largely because the stars supported their less-well-paid colleagues. Despite their common front against the strikers, Gibbons and Stoll were rivals, and the former's purchase of Argyll Street in the name of his London Syndicate Halls was with a view to creating a variety theatre that would rival and indeed outdo Stoll's Coliseum, as well as Edward Moss's smaller but equally flamboyant Hippodrome. Somewhat provocatively, Gibbons hired the architect of both of those flagship venues, Frank Matcham, who, in a somewhat slow year for him (he earlier effected some changes in the Hammersmith Palace of Varieties), was charged with knocking the competition out of the water. The contemporary press had no doubt that he'd succeeded: 'one of the most magnificent places of entertainment in the world', gasped one correspondent. 'The only modest things about it are the prices of admission. All else is on a scale of Gargantuan grandeur.'

Matcham and Gibbons made the bold decision to preserve Owen Lewis's splendid facade. The Corinthian Bazaar's temple-like entrance was deftly converted by the addition of steps, an entrance in the middle and an awning into an instantly inviting theatre. Matcham also added statues representing Art, Science and Literature, which dignitaries he clearly felt were big fans of music hall, for they are invariably present in his theatres; masks of comedy and tragedy feature too, though the latter has been rather underused over the theatre's hundred-year existence. They named the new theatre the Palladium, an original coinage, it would appear, on the doubtful assumption that the Bazaar's facade is Palladian; if it is, it is in markedly modified form. But the splendour of the new theatre's exterior was a mere prelude to the wonders within. The foyers of the new theatre were in the French Rococo manner and unusually accommodating, in particular the huge Palm Court that extended across the entire width of the ground floor of the theatre. 'It is to be a colossal rendezvous,' predicted Gibbons. He understated. Like Stoll, he saw the theatre as no mere venue for performance but as a place – 'in the continental fashion' – where people would come together to share their news, their business, their hopes and their dreams. The Palm Court, made of delicately mottled Norwegian rose granite, was scattered about with small tables, each with its own shaded light. 'The number of twists and turns, the alcoves and retreats', rhapsodised Gibbons, 'will ensure privacy for those who want to discuss their business or their pleasures.' The Palm Court accommodated a thousand people; a ladies' orchestra played between acts. Upstairs, in the Imperial Grand Circle, the Louis XV salon was similarly splendidly appointed. The auditorium, like all of Matcham's auditoriums, was immediately welcoming – a blaze of light coming from all directions, not least the two pendant fittings, each with fifty lamps in it. The decor, like the foyers in French Rococo style, was light, too: the upholstery and decorations in warm shades of *rose du Barry*, the walls of brightly coloured marble and the panels in white, pink and gold. Remarkably, the experience of being in the

OPPOSITE Detail of columns adorned with masks. The carving is not of the highest quality.

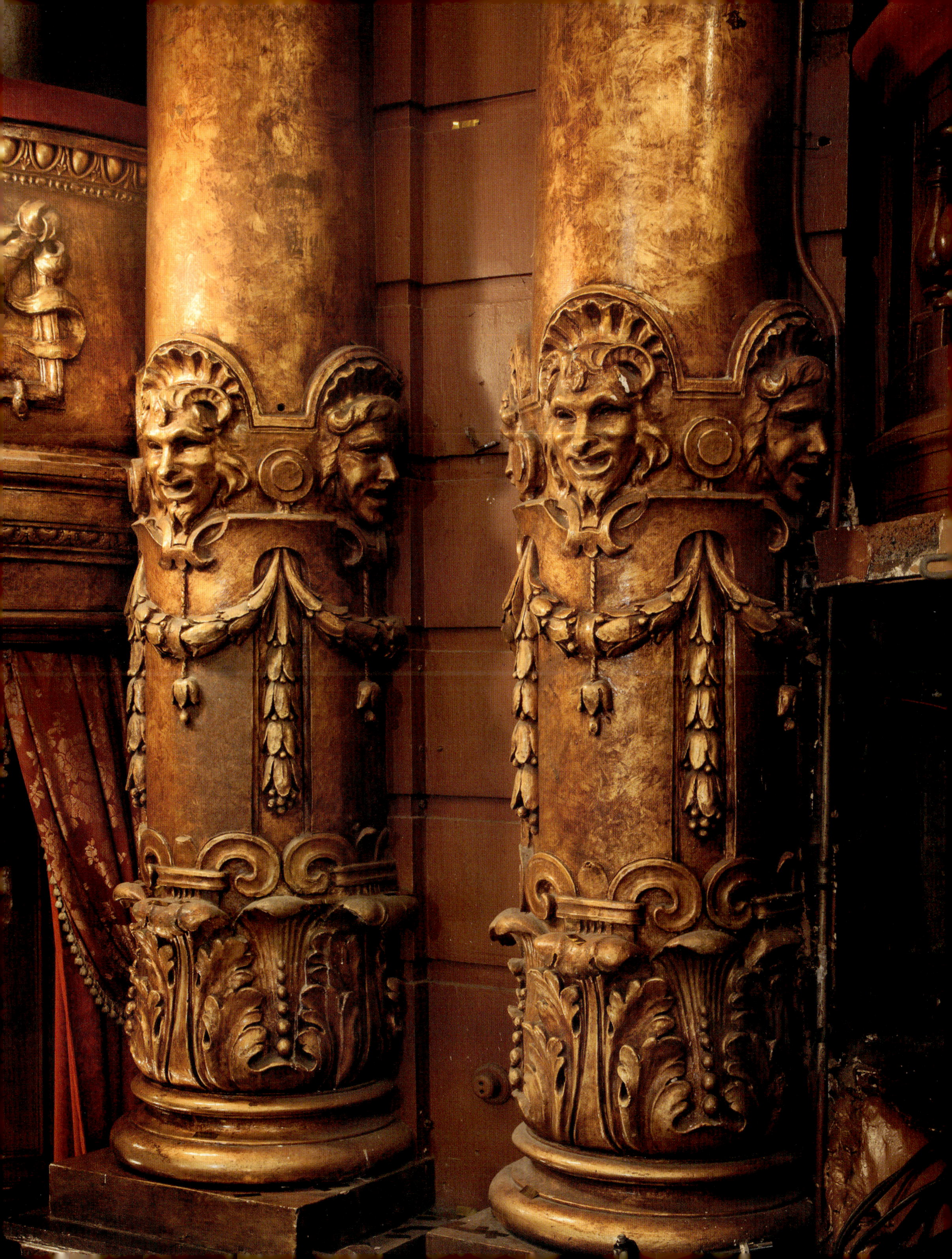

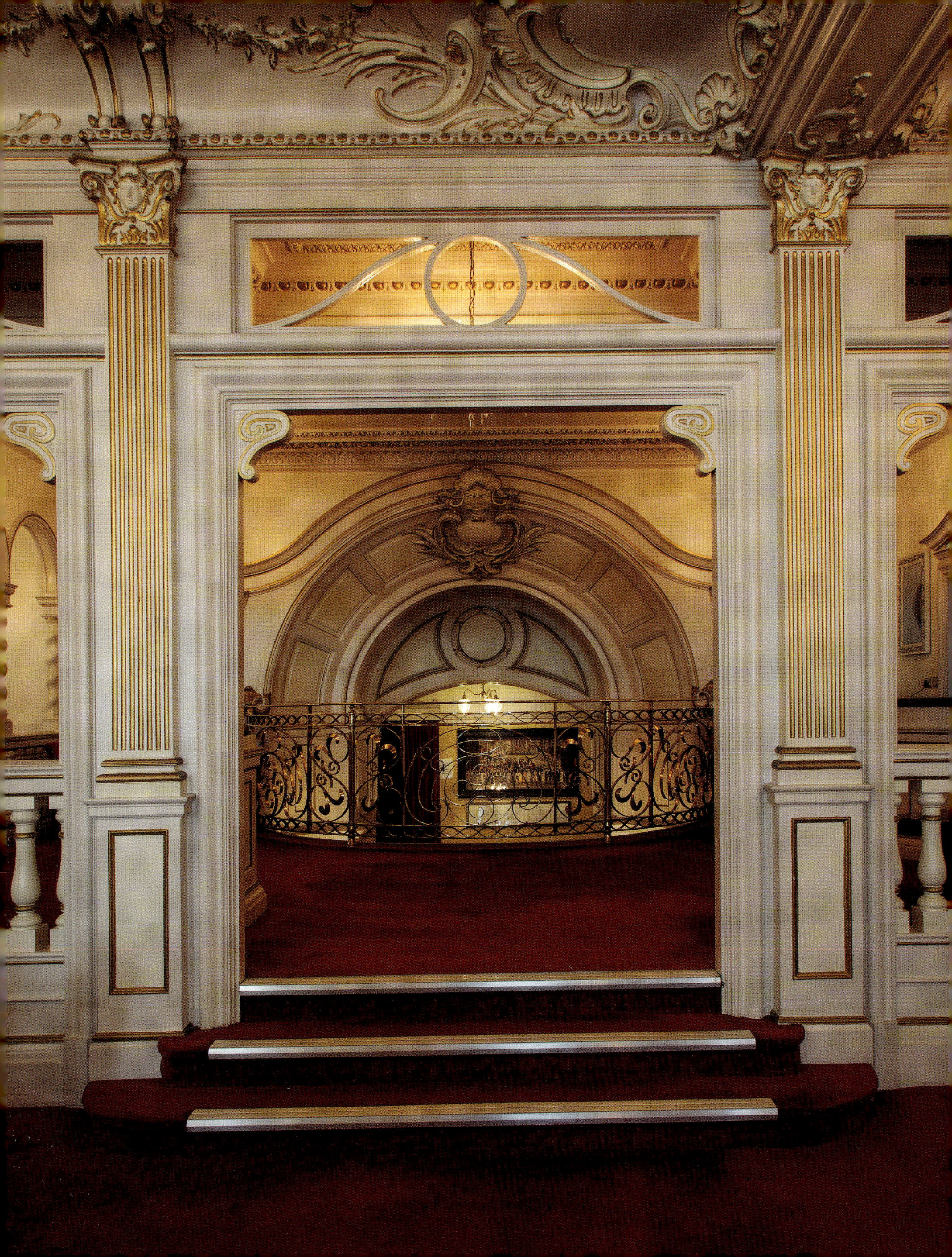

auditorium is not overwhelming; it is almost intimate, despite holding 2,328 people – a mere 200 shy of the Coliseum's 2,558. But where Stoll's theatre is epic in feeling, Gibbons's audience seems in much more direct communication with the stage. Matcham's two great sweeping circles, cantilevered as in St Martin's Lane, are and feel closer to the stage; looking out into the auditorium one feels no sense of the immensity of the building. Occupants of the boxes might feel even more intimately connected to each other on account of the telephones connecting them – a baleful anticipation of mobile phones and not, one can only hope, a facility frequently indulged in.

There is nothing intimate about the stage, though, which is incontrovertibly vast – 90 by 50 feet, made up of adjacent electric lifts for rapidly changing sets. 'We can produce anything,' said Gibbons. And they did. The opening programme, on Boxing Day 1910, gives a hint of what variety meant at this end of the market: the orchestra first struck up the 'Palladium March' composed specially for the occasion and dedicated – what a surprise! – to Walter Gibbons, Esq.; a series of novelty acts followed, including Gladys 'the greatest juvenile xylophonist'; the world's greatest acrobats and hoop manipulators; the March Hares in 'merry vaudeville variations'; the great comedienne Nellie Wallace; and finally a full one-act play, presented by and starring Martin Harvey, one of the great theatre personalities of the day and late of Sir Henry Irving's company. The second act brought Yuletide Revels, with 'a beautiful ballet divertissement' featuring Miss Topsy Sinden singing and dancing, 'supported by a corps de ballet of fifty charming girls' in a show 'replete with sparkling music, dainty costumes and magnificent scenery'. All in all, the programme opined, 'a feast of colour and art'. The second half ended with a series of great performers: Ella Shields, famous for her song 'Burlington Bertie from Bow'; Decima Moore, former Gilbert and Sullivan star and now very much a legitimate actress and singer; and, top of the bill, Ella Retford, the greatest panto principal boy of her time. Even more indicative of the scope of the new theatre's programming is an announcement for a Sunday concert given a month later by the London Symphony Orchestra, in which Fritz Kreisler – perhaps the greatest of all violinists – gave a performance of the expansively beautiful concerto Sir Edward Elgar had just written for him. During the 1920s Sir Thomas Beecham frequently gave concerts there, too.

The life of the music hall artist (despite their recent victory over managements) was not easy: twice nightly and three matinees a week was the rule at the Palladium. Gibbons, well enough pleased with his new theatre, sold it in order to pursue other ventures; a series of loosely strung together entertainments followed, all highly successful.

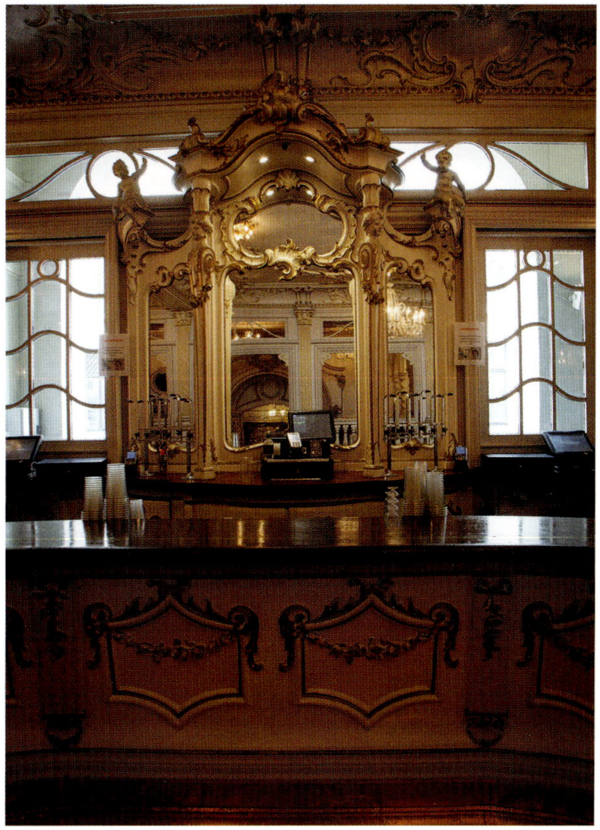

OPPOSITE Part of the upstairs foyer.
ABOVE RIGHT One of the bars at the London Palladium.

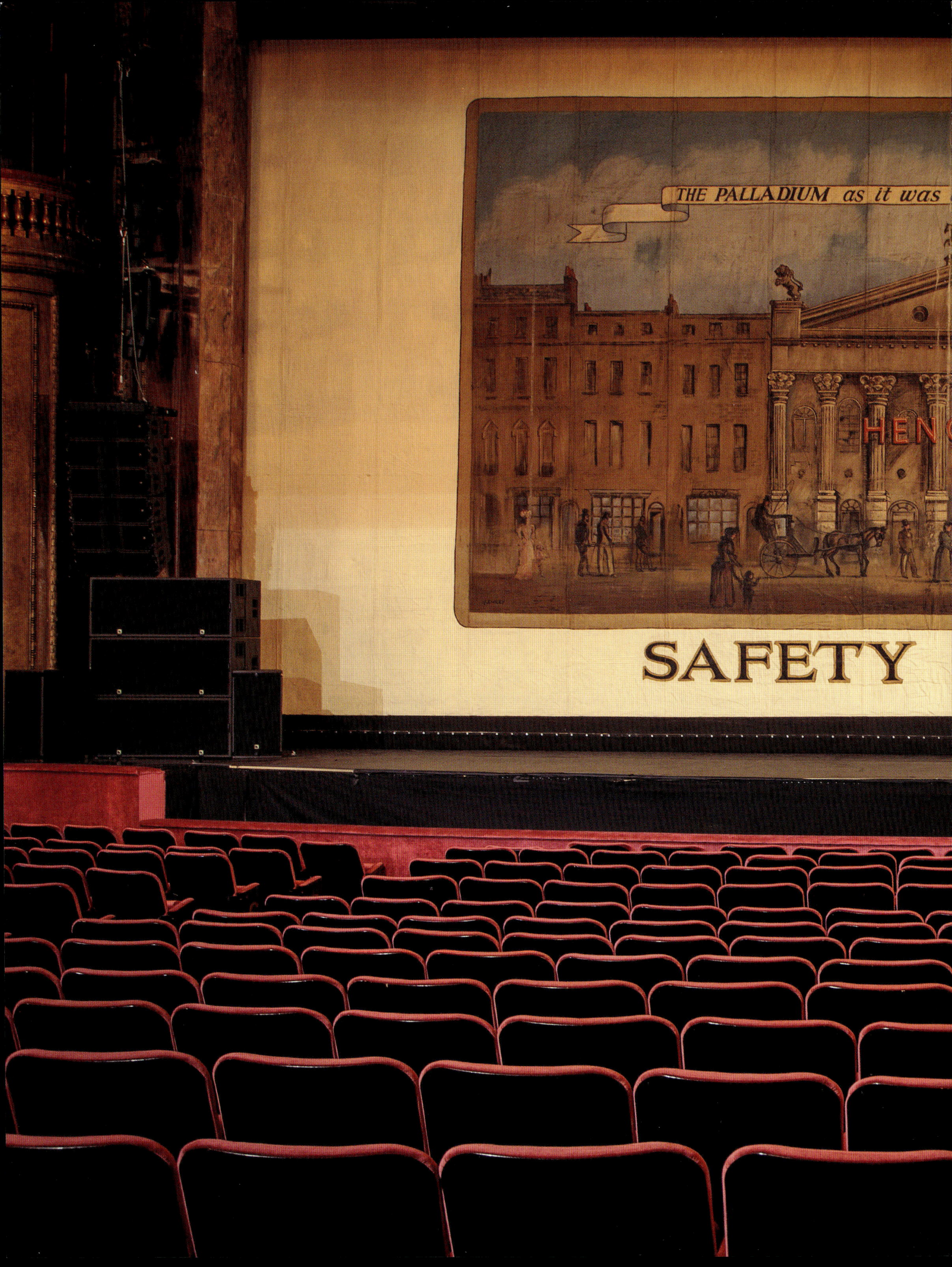
THE PALLADIUM as it was
SAFETY

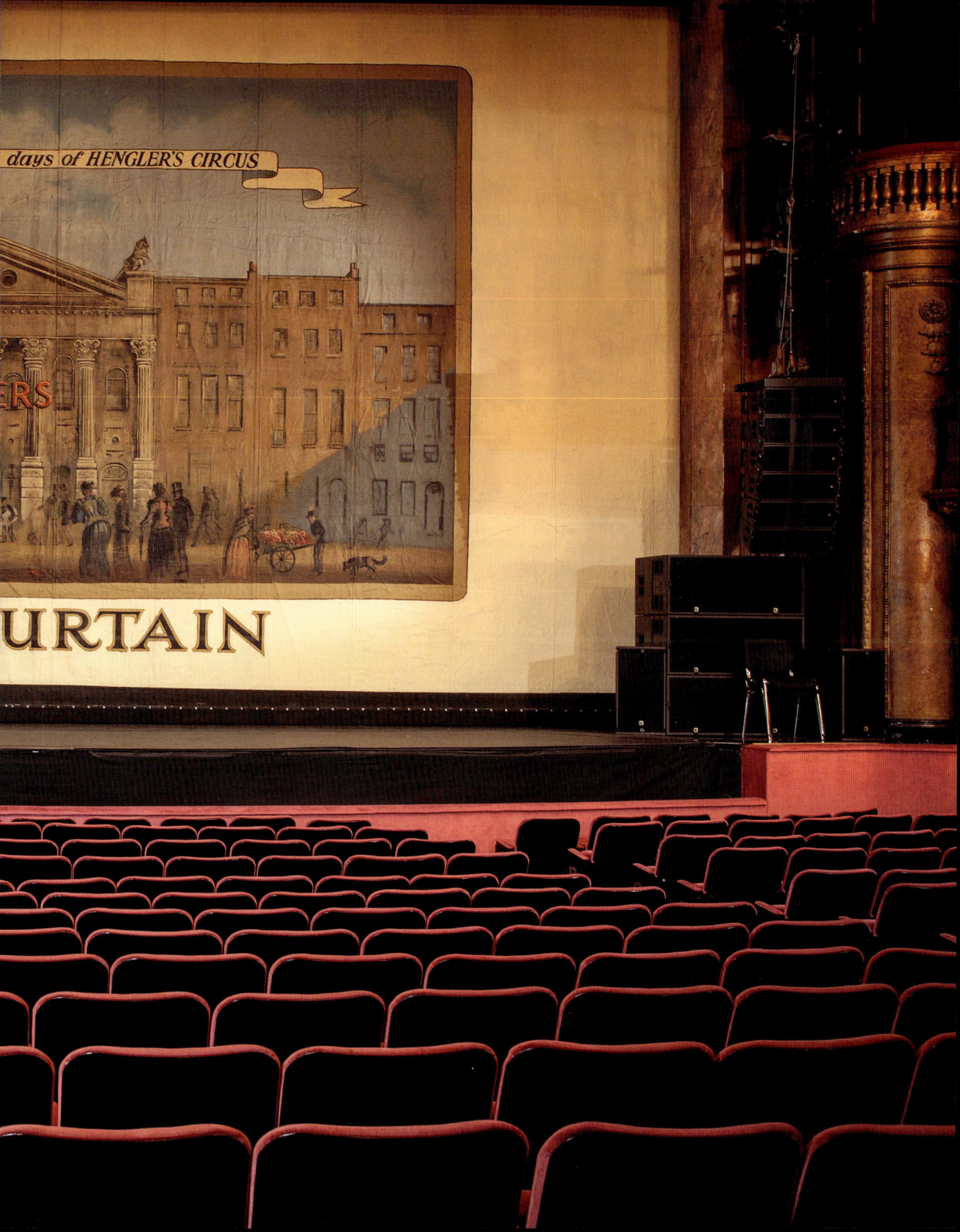
days of HENGLER'S CIRCUS
ERS
URTAIN

Then, in 1928, the impulsive Gibbons, now knighted, bought the theatre back and turned it into a cinema, presumably on the crest of the wave of enthusiasm that followed the development of sound. The experiment failed totally, and months later his resignation was sought, and received. Gibbons's luck, or judgement, had finally deserted him; he invested disastrously in venture after venture, finally bankrupting himself and dying, destitute, five years after being booted out of the theatre he had built. Variety was not to be trumped by some upstart new medium, and the Palladium reverted to what it was built for: spectacular live attractions. *Crazy Week*, a notion of the new intendant George Black, rapidly evolved into the Crazy Gang shows, which later moved to the Victoria Palace; triumphantly zany entertainments, their larky titles might be summed up by one: *Life Begins at Oxford Circus*. Even the bombs failed to stop performances during the Second World War, despite the theatre being hit by an ominously ticking parachute mine. A Royal Navy bomb disposal team was sent for and heroically dismantled it; the officer responsible won the George Medal, and the show went on, with proper bulldog spirit.

After the war, under a new managing director, Val Parnell, classic British style was given somewhat short shrift. Parnell favoured the big American stars; and so, in fairness, did the public. Carmen Miranda, Judy Garland, Sophie Tucker, Bing Crosby, Danny Kaye, the Andrews Sisters, Bob Hope, Liza Minnelli, Ella Fitzgerald, Frank Sinatra, Sammy Davis Jr, Frankie Laine, Johnnie Ray: all came, saw and conquered. The Americans were overpaid, oversexed and over here. It seemed symbolic: we won the war but lost the Palladium, or very nearly – Parnell's highly developed business instincts, which had made the theatre's name a household word with the massively popular television show *Sunday Night at the London Palladium*, told him in the mid-1960s that the game was up for live theatre, and he started planning to sell what remained of the Moss Empires theatre chain. A rival theatre owner, Prince Littler, moved quickly to save not only the Palladium but the Victoria Palace and the Theatre Royal Drury Lane, both of which also had their heads on the block.

Ironically, it was an American star who pointed to the new direction the Palladium would take and which effectively saved it. In 1968 the hugely loved Sammy Davis Jr appeared at the Palladium in *Golden Boy*, the theatre's first book musical; it was a smash hit. Increasingly, long-running shows held the stage there, a trend confirmed when Andrew Lloyd Webber acquired the theatre in 2000. But the Palladium has always been catholic, inclusive, diverse. Beatlemania started there in 1963; there Slade played a gig that resulted in the balcony nearly collapsing; there Rufus Wainwright played Judy Garland; and there Robbie Williams, joined by Kermit the Frog, Miss Piggy, Fozzie Bear, Gonzo, Statler and Waldorf, promoted his new album *Swings Both Ways*, the UK's thousandth No. 1 album. There was held Leon Robinson's astonishing and groundbreaking photographic exhibition celebrating one hundred years of black variety artists in Britain; there Vera Lynn's hundredth birthday party took place; and there Barry Humphries finally emerged as himself from under the skirts of Dame Edna (an image neither of them would especially relish).

That's show business. And that's what the London Palladium, more than any other theatre in the land, embodies.

PREVIOUS The auditorium with the lowered safety curtain shown in its full glory.

OPPOSITE A corner of the upstairs foyer. Its elaborate design almost disguises the fact that we are in a theatre.

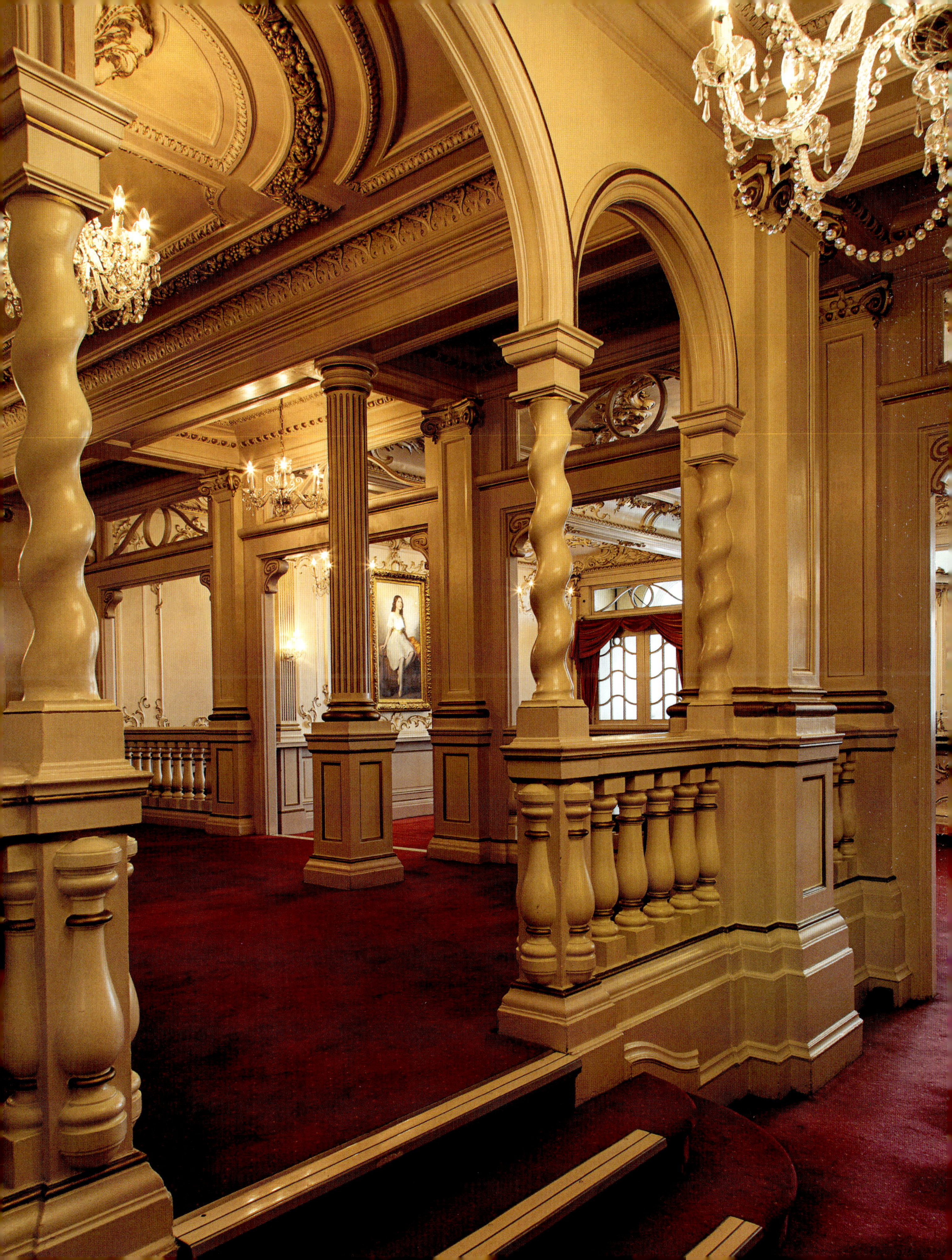

CRITERION

Among the less storied buccaneers who made the British Empire what it was are Felix Spiers and Christopher Pond, pioneers of mass catering. Spiers was a Scot, Pond from Essex. They met in Australia, where they had gone in the early 1850s to join in the gold rush; instead they took over the Café de Paris at the Theatre Royal in Melbourne, serving up to one thousand customers a day. They tried – and failed – to get Dickens to tour Australia; instead, in 1861, they brought over the All-England Eleven to play a series of matches. Returning to England in 1863, the pair successfully took over the Holborn Viaduct Hotel and embarked on a vigorous programme of opening restaurants in railway stations; by 1867 they had nine hundred employees. The following year they went back to their roots, opening a sumptuous new restaurant in the refurbished Gaiety Theatre in Aldwych, and in 1874 were sufficiently sure of themselves – by now they had restaurants in more than a hundred railway stations – to launch a bold scheme in the heart of the West End. They bought up the White Bear, a historic seventeenth-century posting inn located on the sloping ground that stretched between Jermyn Street and what was then known as Regents Circus (now Piccadilly Circus). On this substantial site they proposed to build a large restaurant with a huge ballroom above it and a concert hall right at its centre; to find an architect, they held a competition.

Thomas Verity, who had had a hand in designing the Victoria and Albert Museum and the Royal Albert Hall, was the winner; on the strength of his work for what became the Criterion he formed his own architectural practice, which in time was responsible for the Novelty Theatre, the interior reconstruction of the St James's, the Royalty and the Folly (all now defunct), and the Comedy Theatre (now the Harold Pinter); the firm also designed the French Hospital on Monmouth Street – the Covent Garden Hotel, these days – and the Pavilion at Lord's Cricket Ground. Verity's design for the new complex was on a grand scale, an early example of the monumentalisation of what only a century earlier had been a semi-rustic area. The broad facade of the building is in the fashionable French manner: Georges-Eugène Haussmann's expansive reconstruction of Paris was much imitated as central London systematically wiped out its sprawling honeycombs of dwellings and small businesses, transforming itself into a capital worthy of the Empire. The interiors were similarly sumptuous: Verity's Marble Hall and the Long Bar, with its gold mosaic ceiling and mirrored walls (it has since become the Criterion Restaurant), could easily have been found in an Austro-Hungarian capital, Prague or Zagreb. The first and second floors were originally given over to dining rooms, with the ballroom on the floor above. There was no mention of a theatre at this point; that came very late in the process, by which time Simpson & Sons had already decorated the walls of the foyers and bars with tiles bearing the names of great composers for the proposed concert hall; these were somewhat incongruously left in place as Verity rapidly improvised a theatre, never having done one before. The result is one of the most uncommon and

OPPOSITE Detail of a stairwell showing the majolica tiles bearing theatrical, musical and military motifs.

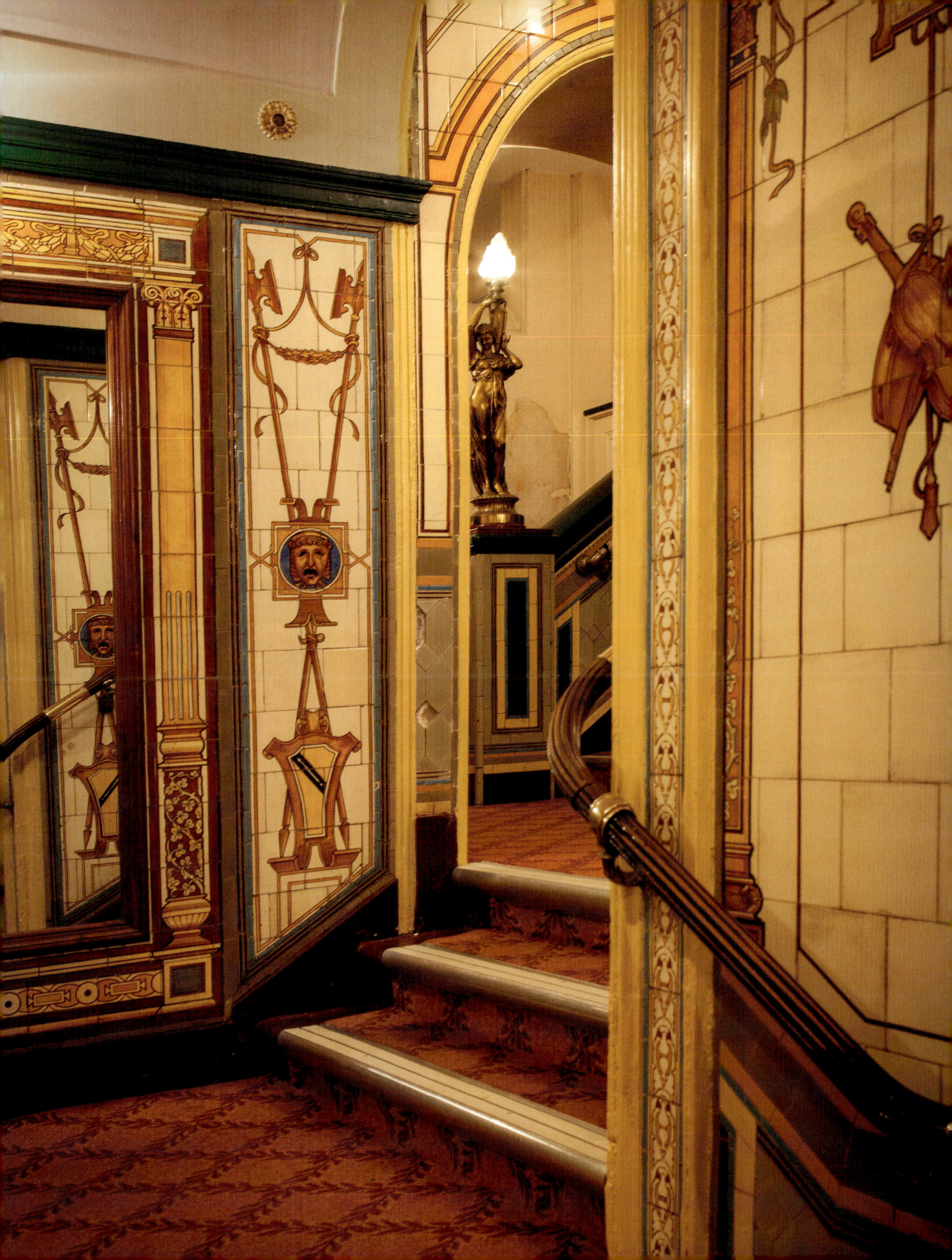

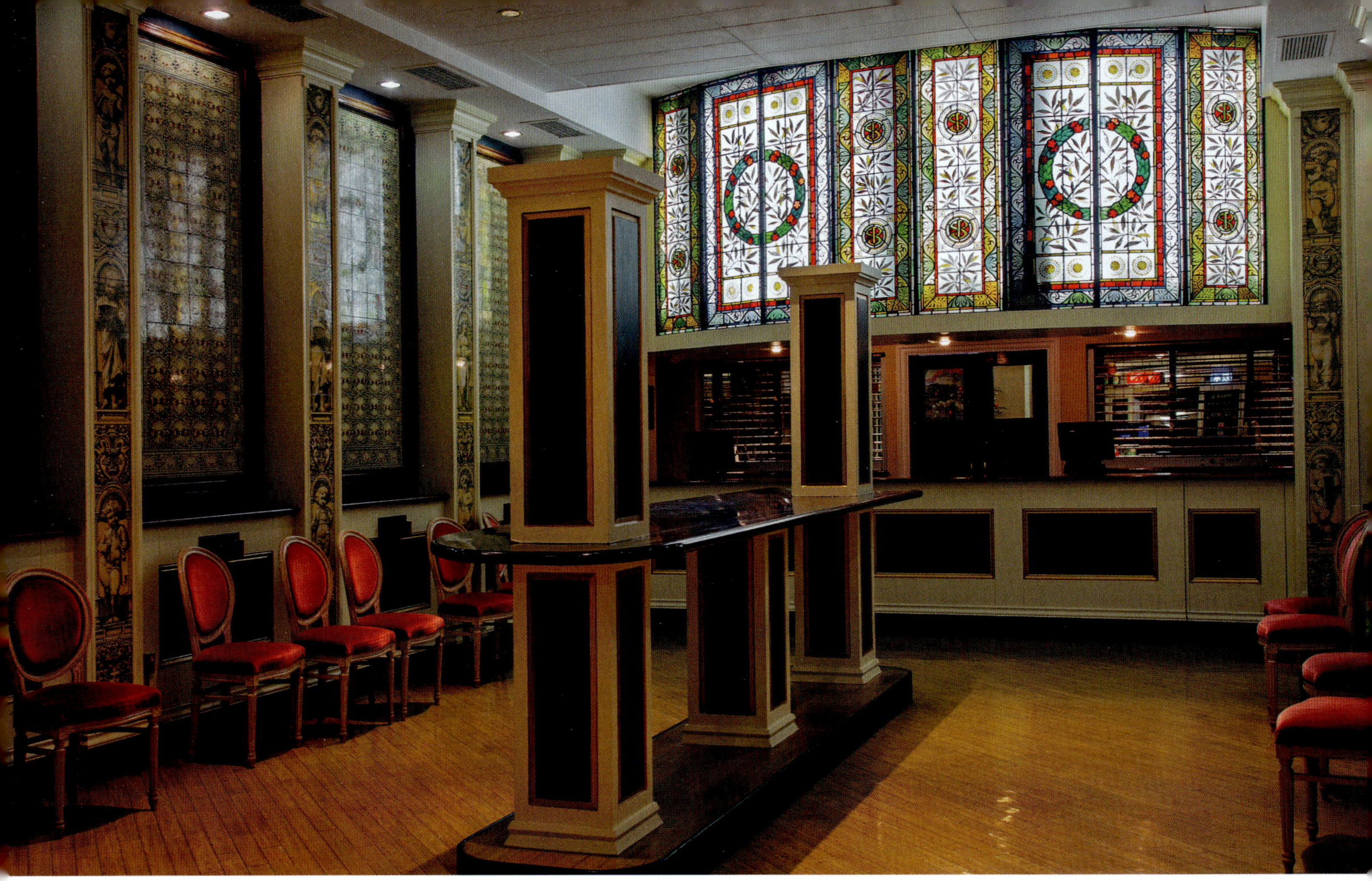

delightful playhouses in town: unique in that it is entirely below ground level, a perfect bijou theatre in its own right, holding no more than six hundred people and with its sturdy, serviceable, three-level horseshoe auditorium in close and direct contact with the stage. The original colour scheme was white, light blue and gold; the curtains were gold, too, in satin with folds of white lace. The seats in the stalls were oval-backed in blue satin, with white frameworks edged with a Louis XVI gold border. All this was in the exquisite French style of a hundred years earlier. Flying scenery here was (and is) problematic, and space in the wings is desperately limited, but that has only, over the years, sparked invention in directors and designers.

That the Criterion opened at all is something of a miracle. The Metropolitan Board of Works was anxious about the danger of toxic fumes, the theatre being entirely subterranean and lit by gas. Eventually, a year and two separate votes by the board later, it received its licence: its debut in March 1874 was packed to the rafters, and there was a large and volatile crowd in the streets. 'Here was an entirely new theatre, raised, or rather sunk, at a point which is familiar, to all fashionable and quasi-fashionable London,' wrote a reviewer in the *New York Times*, rather suggestively, drily adding: 'but which has hitherto been unexplored by theatrical enterprise.' An air of music hall hung about the place. Despite the magnificence of their latest venture, Spiers and Pond were populists at heart, well known for hiring attractive barmaids. Dickens had earlier described the women in their employ as 'bright-eyed, cheerfully obliging nymphs'; the same formula was repeated at the Criterion.

ABOVE The bar. Note the stained-glass windows and the majolica tiles, all creating a harmonious effect.
OVERLEAF The auditorium. Note the design of the front of the balconies, which are original.

The first lessees of the new theatre were the manager E. P. Hingston and the hugely popular actor-dramatist Henry James Byron, whose *An American Lady* opened the theatre in a double bill with *Topsyturveydom*, a fantasy by W. S. Gilbert that has disappeared and of which the author himself, as he confessed in a letter to T. Edgar Pemberton, author of a 1903 book on the Criterion, had little recollection a quarter of a century later: 'I don't even know what the piece was about!' If a contemporary's recollection is to be believed, this is to be regretted, for the show depicted, said Gilbert's friend E. A. Sothern, 'a world wherein everything was the reverse of what it is in this; how men were exalted by their follies, and degraded for their virtues; how they walked on ceilings, and looked up to floors; showed dislike when they wished to please, and used courteous expressions when they sought to be insolent'. Gilbert's work was often to be seen at the Criterion: *On Bail* in 1877; four years later the phantasmagorical *Foggerty's Fairy* (another of the author's pieces to feature extra-terrestrials); and finally, in 1892, *Haste to the Wedding*, a musical version of his earlier *The Wedding March*, itself an adaptation of the 1851 French farce *The Italian Straw Hat*. This last piece was an abject flop; its failure drove Gilbert back to Arthur Sullivan, with whom he had – not for the first time – fallen out. Gilbert's career in the theatre lasted fifty years and took a variety of forms, some of them highly experimental; he lived on into the reign of George V and was still writing for the theatre the year he died, 1911. Moreover, he was something of a pioneer as a stage director; his collaboration with Sullivan is unquestionably the thing that has secured his immortality, but he was a central figure in the later Victorian theatre.

Apart from *Topsyturveydom*, the Criterion had a rather shaky start; the Byron–Hingston management failed, and it was taken over in 1875 by Charles Wyndham, who – with an extraordinary career as a brigade surgeon during the American Civil War behind him – had been developing a strong reputation as an actor-manager with a flair for both light comedy and melodrama. He stayed at the Criterion for nearly a quarter of a century before he built his eponymous theatre in the Charing Cross Road, and even then he kept a lease on the Criterion and supervised its output. He rapidly established it as the home of stylish comedy, his own performance as Charles Surface in Sheridan's *The School for Scandal* setting the bar high. It was, however, his sensational appearance as David Garrick in Tom Robertson's adaptation of a French play about the eighteenth-century English actor-manager that proved to be his, and the theatre's, greatest success – to the point Where Wyndham came almost to hate it. He escaped from it into an extraordinary range of parts in plays ancient and modern. One of those latter that eluded him was Algernon in *The Importance of Being Earnest*: Wilde and Wyndham had been friends for some years when in 1895 Oscar offered him his newly written 'trivial comedy for serious people', suspecting that the rather high-minded George Alexander, the actor-manager at the St James's for whom he had initially written it, would dismiss it as lightweight. Wyndham delightedly agreed to do the play, but then Alexander, in urgent need of a new play in the wake of the abject failure of Henry James's *Guy Domville*, turned in desperation to Wilde – and had the biggest hit of his career. Nevertheless Wyndham continued to do very well at the Criterion, particularly with new plays by the endlessly prolific Henry Arthur Jones: including the melodrama *The Case of Rebellious Susan* (1894) and the comedy *The Liars* (1897), both smash hits.

In 1883 the theatre had finally fallen foul of the Board of Works that had threatened its opening a decade earlier: the ventilation of the auditorium was deemed inadequate and, at that depth, dangerous, so – at considerable expense and loss of earnings – a new shaft giving access to fresh air was installed, which meant losing a substantial section of the Criterion restaurant. Under the direction of Verity, the original architect, the opportunity was seized to modernise and refurbish both auditorium and backstage areas; electricity, safer and healthier, was installed. The result of all this expensive labour, during which the theatre

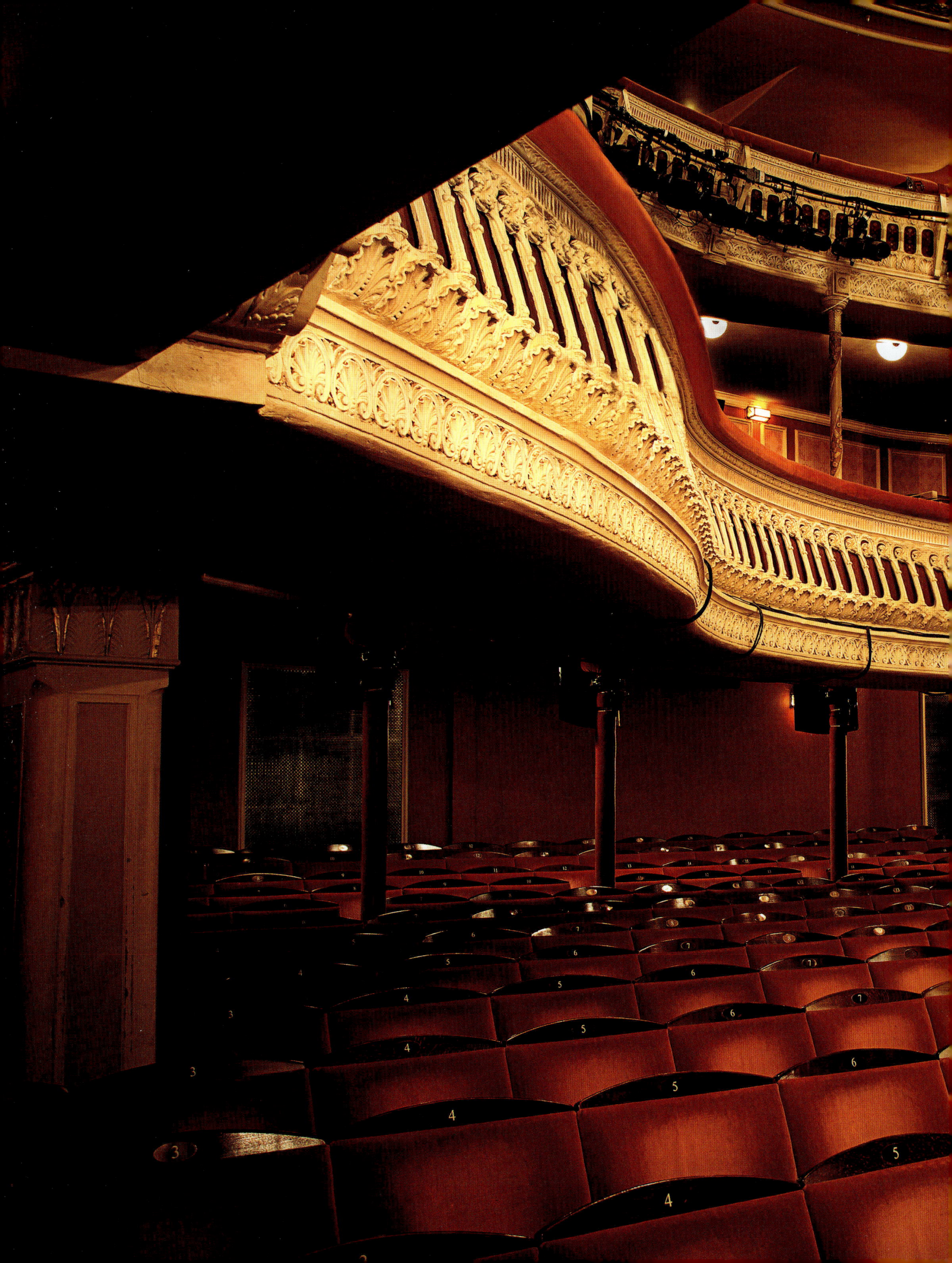

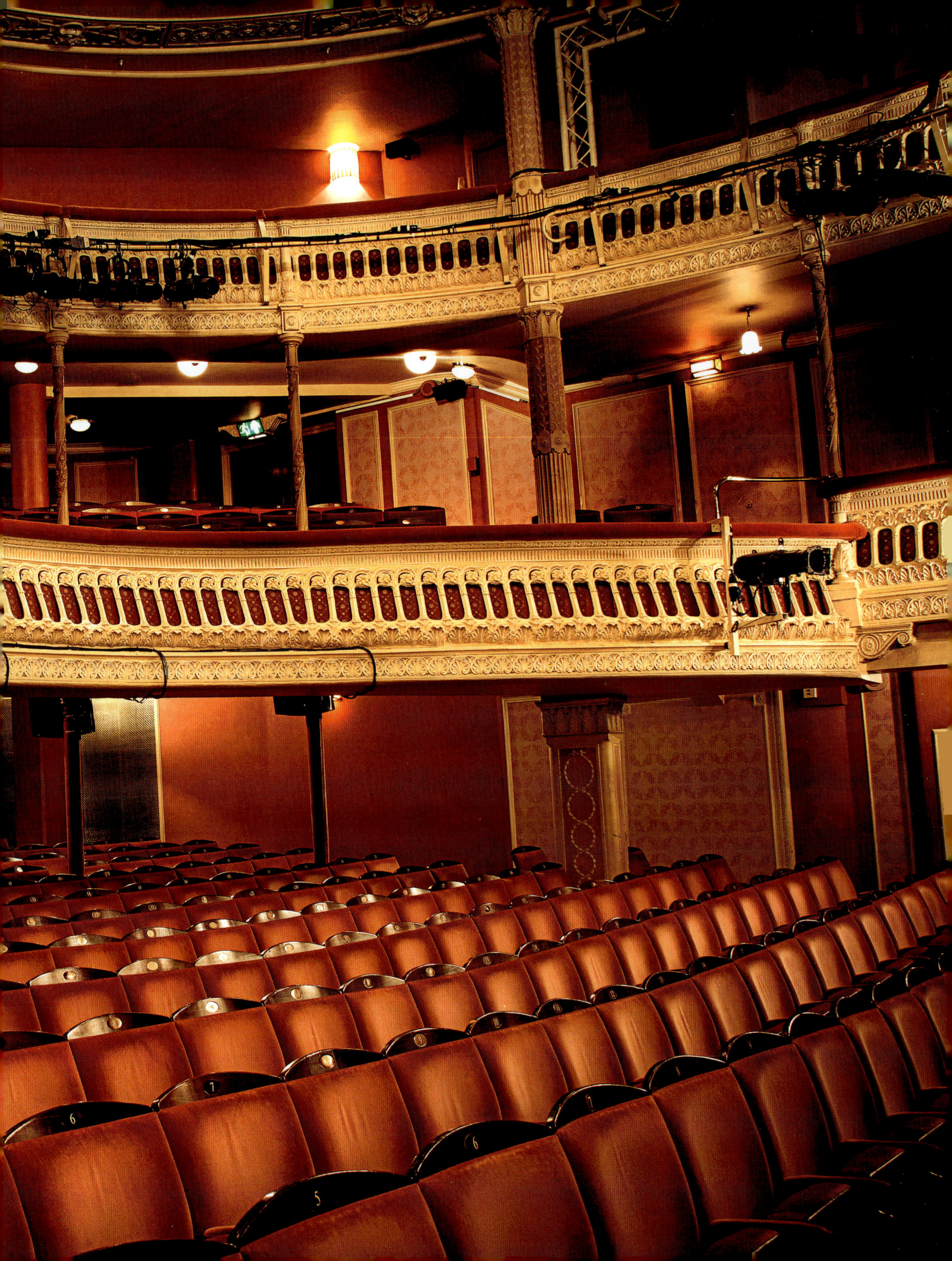

was closed for over a year, was judged a triumph: it was now, reported *Dramatic Notes* in 1884, 'a convenient, handsome, and well ventilated house . . . transformed from a stuffy band-box'; the auditorium was warmer, ruddier, more cheerful. Like most theatres during the theatre-building boom, the Criterion was in a constant state of evolution and innovation, always desperate to keep up with the competition; there was yet more extensive reconstruction in 1902–3, when it found its final form, a perfect and exceptionally well-preserved example of the late Victorian and early Edwardian theatre style.

Charles Wyndham died in 1919; his stepson, Bronson Albery, took over the management of the Criterion as well as the New Theatre (now the Noël Coward) and Wyndham's, where he produced a number of highly successful thrillers. In the 1930s he signed a contract with John Gielgud, fresh from his early triumphs at the Old Vic, to do three plays at the Criterion. Gielgud was determined to seek out new work; when a brooding young Scotsman, Ronald Mackenzie – who had worked down the mines and as a logger in Poland and Canada – sent him *The Discontents*, he quickly gathered together a fine group of young actors, including Jessica Tandy, Finlay Currie, Roger Livesey and Margaret Webster, under the great émigré Russian director Theodore Komisarjevsky. They had an immense hit with it, under the more audience-friendly title *Musical Chairs*. Gielgud himself was hugely acclaimed as the central character, the sensitive, mordantly witty young composer Joseph Schindler. 'Perfection in every detail', wrote James Agate of his performance, though Gielgud himself was as always severely self-critical: 'I act very badly in it sometimes,' he wrote to a friend, 'and such a small theatre as the Criterion is difficult for me, who am used to the wastes of the Old Vic and His Majesty's. If I play down, they write and say I'm inaudible and if I act too much, the effect is dire.' The play ran for nine months, towards the end of which the moody playwright was killed in a car crash in France.

Within a year or so the theatre had an even bigger success with the 25-year-old Terence Rattigan's first play, *French Without Tears* (1936), fielding a dazzling cast including Rex Harrison, Kay Hammond and Jessica Tandy; it ran at the Criterion for over a thousand performances. During the Second World War the theatre – being subterranean, and so not threatened by the Blitz – was commandeered by the BBC, its fare of light entertainment sitting very happily in the cheerful little auditorium. After the war it became home to some striking modern plays, including two notable transfers from the Arts Theatre under the direction of Peter Hall: Jean Anouilh's *Waltz of the Toreadors* in 1956, with Hugh Griffith as General Saint-Pé and Beatrix Lehmann as his hypochondriac wife, and, in 1955, *Waiting for Godot*, an altogether less likely candidate for a West End transfer. It had sold out at the Arts Theatre and was nominated in the Best New Play category for the new Evening Standard Drama Awards. Some of the panel were bitterly opposed to this; Sir Malcolm Sargent threatened to resign if *Godot* won. The impasse was broken with the creation of a new category, Most Controversial Play of the Year, which it won effortlessly; no such category has ever been heard of since. The Criterion continued to be at the forefront of sparky new plays: in 1968, after his triumph the previous year with *Rosencrantz and Guildenstern are Dead* at the National Theatre, Tom Stoppard produced *The Real Inspector Hound* from his bottom drawer. This endlessly witty and inventive satire of Agatha Christie, the critical fraternity and bad rep acting, written seven years earlier, gave him a second triumph in as many years (and incidentally introduced the notion of previews to the West End); it ran and ran. A little later, Simon Gray's darkly funny *Butley*, the first of his savage accounts of academic life, opened in 1971 and fielded a succession of brilliant leading actors, a new one every six months.

In the outside world, the Greater London Council Planning Committee, that sworn enemy of West End theatre, proposed to redevelop the site. This was met with a militant response from the profession, with John Gielgud, Warren Mitchell, Diana Rigg and Robert Morley taking to Piccadilly Circus, placards

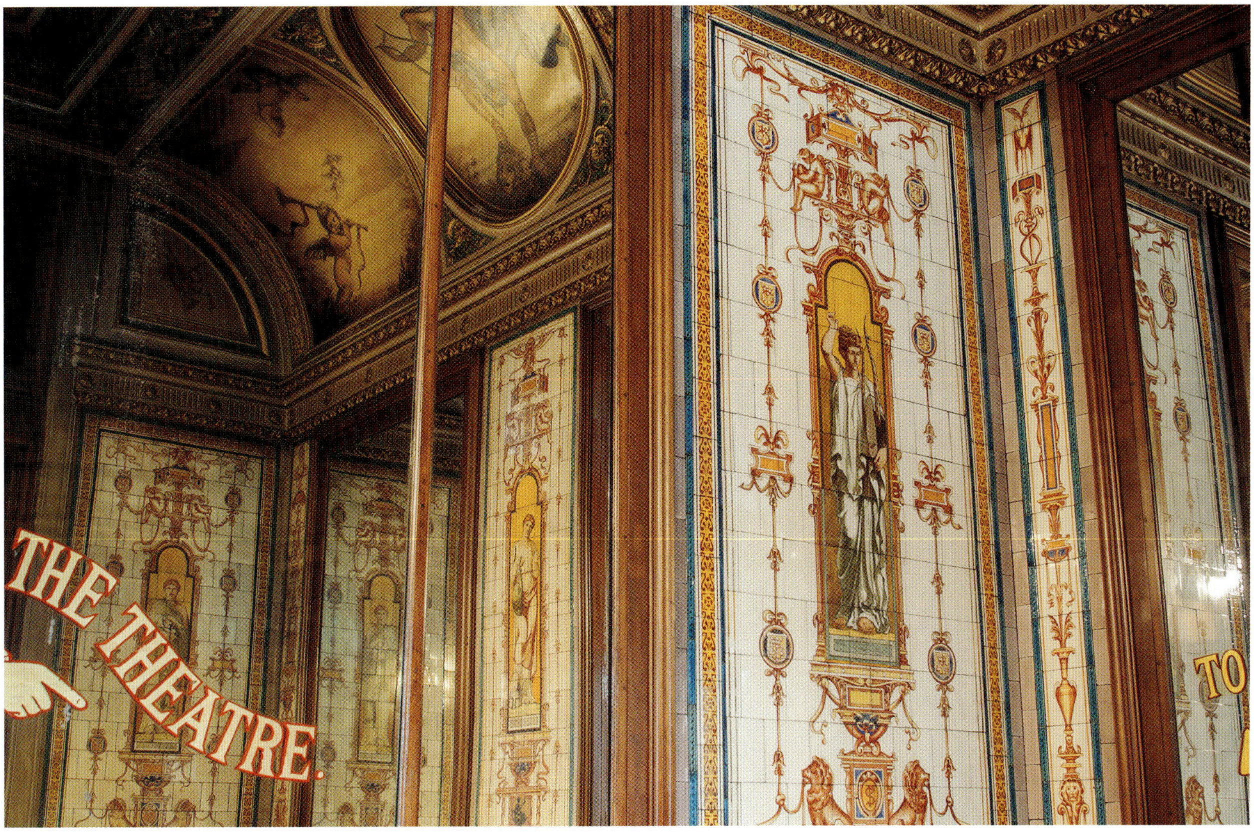

in hand – which terrifying spectacle persuaded the committee to the allow the theatre to continue in 'full, continuous and uninterrupted use' during redevelopment. But no one believed it. Equity's Save London's Theatres Campaign kept the pressure up; and then, in 1986, Margaret Thatcher abolished the Greater London Council, the only time she ever – albeit unwittingly – did the arts a favour. The property developer Robert Bourne then bought the theatre with his wife, Sally Greene, under the aegis of the Criterion Theatre Trust, a registered charity created to protect its future; from 1989 to 1992 it was renovated both back and front of house, and the block behind it, towards Jermyn Street, was built up to provide more office space. Under Greene's management, and despite a handful of short-lived ventures – including Jack: *A Night on the Town* (1994), a one-man show about John Barrymore, which proved to be Nicol Williamson's farewell to the British stage – it has had substantial successes with entertainments, starting in 1996 with the Reduced Shakespeare Company's *Complete Works*; followed ten years later by Maria Aitken's riotous *The 39 Steps*, which remained weirdly true to John Buchan while sending him up rotten; and most recently *The Comedy About a Bank Robbery* (2016), possessor of the funniest first act in post-war theatrical history. *Waiting for Godot*, *The Waltz of the Toreadors* and *Butley* sat very happily in the Criterion, but somehow shows like these three most recent long-running entertainments are perfectly suited to an auditorium that has more than a whiff of the music hall about it. H. J. Byron, who kicked it all off with *Topsyturveydom*, would certainly have approved.

ABOVE The majolica tiles reflected in mirrors. The design is in Renaissance style.

SAVOY

From time to time, a theatre so embodies the spirit of its creator that merely thinking about it conjures up his spirit – even when, as in this case, the theatre he built is no longer standing. Richard D'Oyly Carte was the altogether exceptional man who built the Savoy Theatre (and indeed the Savoy Hotel), a quintessentially Victorian entrepreneur who transformed everything he touched. But he was no buccaneer, as a glance at any photograph of him reveals: dapper, elegant, clear-eyed, with well-trimmed beard and neat coiffure. Nor was he a mere businessman. He was that too, none shrewder, but his clarity of thinking and certainty of purpose were at the service of what Americans like to call A Dream, but what he described as 'the scheme of my life', namely the creation of a native British tradition of opera, both comic and Grand. Almost from the beginning, Carte's path was clear. He was born in 1844 in Soho, into the music business: his flautist father ran a musical instrument firm and published music. Richard was brought up in Highgate in a bilingual bohemian atmosphere; he enrolled in London University but left after a year to join the family business, which he sedulously built up, all the while composing songs and comic operas. He produced, directed and conducted these, among them *Doctor Ambrosias – His Secret* and *Happy Hampstead*; Arthur Sullivan's *Cox and Box* was a notable success under his baton. Always simultaneously exercising both his managerial and his artistic instincts, Carte shortly afterwards established an operatic, concert and lecture management agency; the list was glittering, including the composers Clara Schumann, Charles Gounod and Jacques Offenbach, the singers Adelina Patti and Giovanni Matteo de Candia, the painter James McNeill Whistler, the poet and critic Matthew Arnold, and the young and madly flamboyant self-styled Professor of Aesthetics, Oscar Wilde.

Carte took a lease on the Opera Comique, a small theatre off the Strand where at first he staged popular French works. But his avowed intention from the start was to generate an English light opera tradition, and to that end he brought the playwright W. S. Gilbert and the composer Arthur Sullivan together again. Their first joint venture, *Thespis* (1871), had not been a success, but *Trial by Jury*, Carte's first commission from them, was a tearaway hit, and by 1876 he had been sufficiently successful as a manager to found the Comedy Opera Company; *The Sorcerer* and *HMS Pinafore* followed shortly after, the latter nursed by Carte, after a slow start, into a huge success. He, Sullivan and Gilbert then set themselves up independently as partners. The Comedy Opera Company tried to seize the physical production of *Pinafore* from them, but Carte's stagehands foiled them; the COC then attempted to mount a rival production, but it flopped, the original continuing its triumphant run of 571 performances. *The Pirates of Penzance* and *Patience*, equally successful, followed on both sides of the Atlantic (*Pirates* had its premiere in the US, to ensure

OPPOSITE The auditorium, looking towards a pair of leather-panelled doors – note the Art Deco motifs and silver finish of the walls. This could be the entrance to a law court or other public building.
OVERLEAF The auditorium viewed from the stage – a perfect example of an Art Deco auditorium.

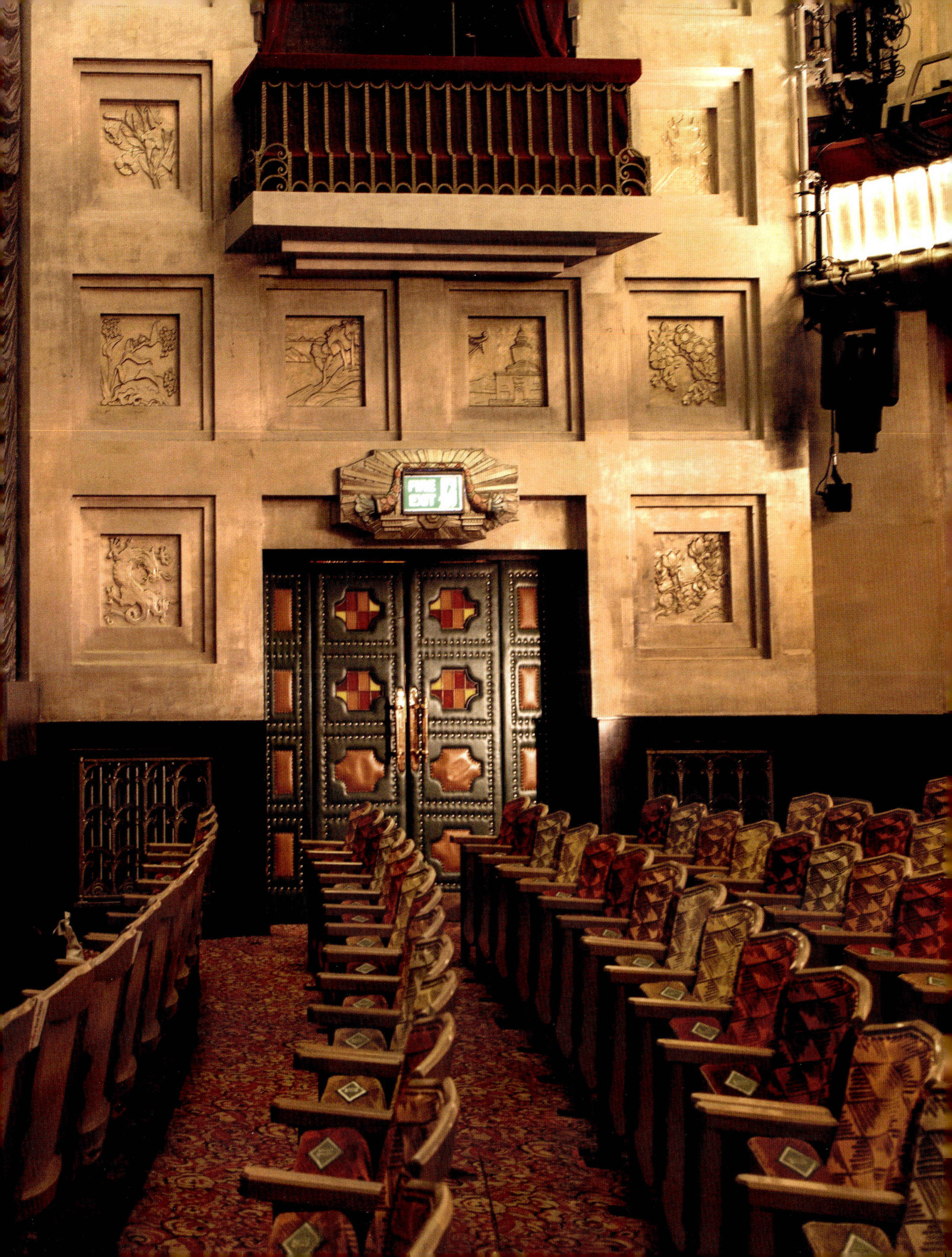
FIRE
EXIT

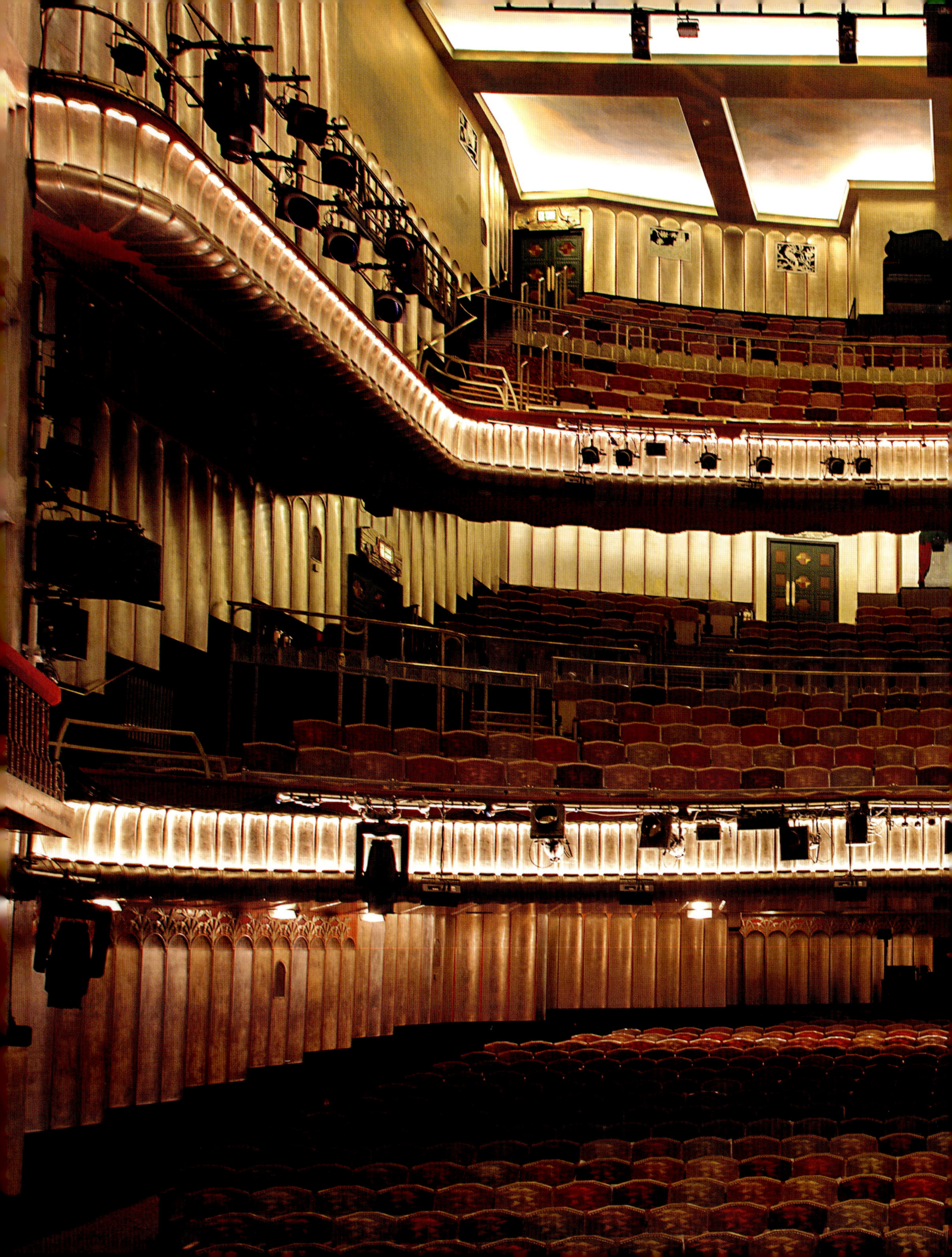

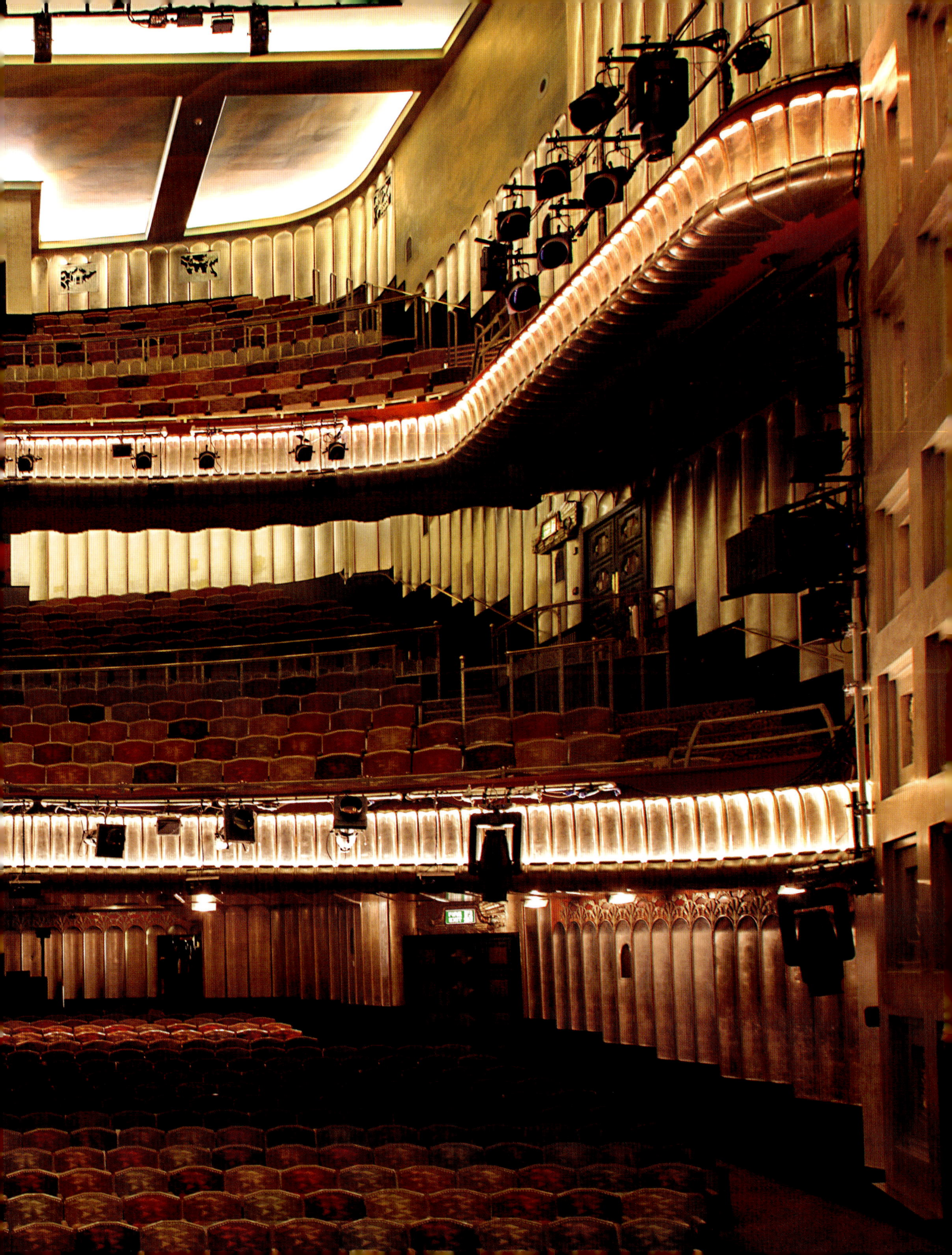

American copyright) as well as in Australia. The huge success of all these productions – to say nothing of amateur rights, which Carte was the first to organise on a proper formal basis and which proved massively lucrative, but also transformed standards – encouraged him to build a London theatre.

In 1880 he bought land on the derelict and fire-razed site of the old hospital buildings just off the Strand; it had once been the site of John of Gaunt's massive Savoy Palace, and Carte's property was bordered by the fifteenth-century Savoy Chapel. The City of Westminster required him to pay half the cost of building a street to run down the side of the new theatre, which he did; he even succeeded – and there can be no greater proof of his tenacity – in getting the authorities to cough up their half. At this point he sacked the young architect Walter Emden, who was rapidly rising as a theatre specialist, for increasing his estimated costs by 50 per cent. Despite these tiresome obstacles, Carte never faltered, engaging the astonishingly prolific Charles J. Phipps to build it instead. The Savoy was Phipps's 34th theatre, and indeed his second that year; he was only 46, and it eclipsed all his other theatres – among them the Theatres Royal in Brighton, Bath and Glasgow, the Vaudeville and the Olympic in London, and the Gaiety in Dublin – not least in its modernity, being the first public building anywhere in the world to be illuminated entirely by electric light, with 1,200 incandescent bulbs required to light the front of house alone (the stage itself continued to be lit by gas for a couple of months). At the first electricity-lit performance, Carte himself came onstage before the performance and, to show how safe the new technology was, broke a glowing light bulb in his hands.

Leading from the front as always, he made a speech at the new theatre's opening night in October 1881 in which he made clear the principles that had guided the design of its interior (by the firm of Collinson & Lock): 'Paintings of cherubim, muses, angels, and mythological deities have been discarded,' he said, severely, 'and the ornament consists entirely of delicate plaster modelling, designed in the manner of the Italian Renaissance.' Oscar Wilde, with his aesthetician's hat on, would have approved. Carte was harsh about what he called 'the Gingerbread school of decorative art', eschewing the use of gold on relief-work or mouldings. The stalls, he said, were covered with 'blue plush of an inky hue, and the balcony seats are of stamped velvet of the same tint'; the curtains of the boxes were of yellowish silk, brocaded with a pattern of decorative flowers in broken colour. Elsewhere, Venetian red prevailed. The *Times* felt, somewhat neutrally, that 'all reasonable demands of comfort and taste are complied with.' The auditorium was in classic horseshoe configuration and held 1,292 people, who benefited from Carte's front-of-house reforms: 'I believe a fertile source of annoyance to the public to be the demanding or expecting of fees and gratuities by attendants,' he announced at the opening. 'This system will, therefore, be discountenanced. Programmes will be furnished and wraps and umbrellas taken charge of gratuitously. The attendants will be paid fair wages, and any attendant detected in accepting money from visitors will be instantly dismissed.'

Patience, which had already enjoyed a hugely successful run at the Opera Comique, was the opening show at the new theatre. The following year saw the premiere of that wicked send-up of the House of Lords, *Iolanthe* – the first of Gilbert and Sullivan's shows to have its debut there, making it, strictly speaking, the first of the Savoy operas, though the whole G&S canon is now so designated. There followed an astonishing run of hits: *Princess Ida* (1884), *The Mikado* (1885), *Ruddigore* (1887) and *The Yeomen of the Guard* (1888). The latter was the last huge hit for the team; but as a worldwide franchise the shows were more than lucrative enough for Carte to expand his Savoy operation to include a hotel, which opened in 1889. It too was ablaze with electric light; even the lifts were run on electricity.

OPPOSITE A corner of the foyer. Both design and gilded finish create a wonderful effect of light and elegance.

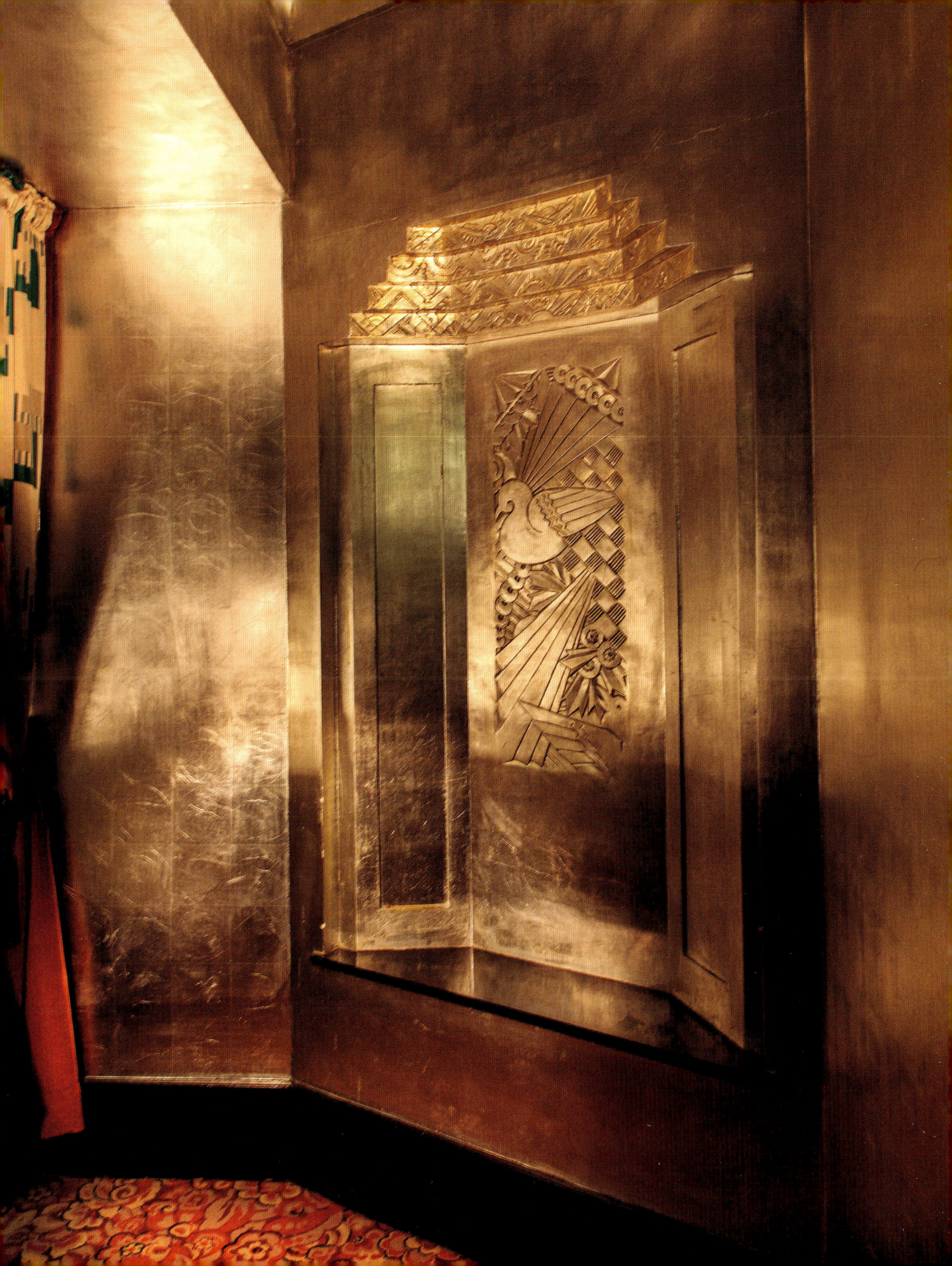

Carte guaranteed the hotel's success by importing the increasingly prominent César Ritz as manager, and Ritz brought with him Auguste Escoffier, 'the king of chefs and the chef of kings', as the publicity said. This formidable team introduced an entirely new level of culinary experience to London and the place was crammed to the gunnels with the *bon-ton*; but after nine years Ritz was summarily dismissed for fraud by the ever-decisive Carte. Ritz went off and founded the chain of hotels that bears his name, taking Escoffier with him. Carte meanwhile became a formidable hotelier himself, acquiring the Grand Hotel in Rome and Claridge's in London, as well as the restaurant Simpson's-in-the-Strand, which in its time had a higher financial turnover than the shows.

Meanwhile, there were considerable tensions in the theatre. Sullivan, Leipzig-trained and highly regarded for his Cello Concerto and his Symphony in E ('The Irish'), to say nothing of his large-scale choral pieces, was reluctant to write any more comic operas, though he had become dependent on the income from them; while Gilbert deeply resented being obliged by contract to produce work on demand, making him in effect Carte's employee. He publicly denounced Carte for charging the company in which he and Sullivan were partners for running repairs to the theatre; eventually he took him to court, and won. But somehow the triumvirate held together. Carte's managerial instincts were infallible: when, after the relatively short run of *Princess Ida*, there was no new work with which to replace it, he magicked a new double bill out of G&S's early works *Trial by Jury* and *The Sorcerer*, and programmed matinee performances of *The Pirates of Penzance* with a cast of children. Thus given time to work on a new piece, the team produced, in 1885, *The Mikado*, an outright smash hit – the most successful, indeed, of all the operettas. Carte supervised every aspect of the Savoy Theatre and its work; he was, said a colleague, 'a great stage manager. He could take in the details of a scene with one sweep of his eagle eye and say unerringly just what was wrong.' Even George Bernard Shaw, the scourge of managements everywhere, acknowledged the transformation in standards of musical entertainment synonymous with the name of the Savoy. Carte lived it and breathed it. His London flat, in the Adelphi building just down the road from the theatre, had been decorated by Whistler and boasted the first lift ever to be installed in private accommodation, but he was more often to be found in the theatre than in his private quarters.

Eventually things soured between the partners. Gilbert, especially, was implacable, though at Carte's urging he and Sullivan produced a highly successful light opera, *The Gondoliers*, which was a new departure for them and had a good run at the Savoy; *Utopia Limited* followed, an extravaganza whose cost made it impossible to recoup the investment. Finally there was a limp last effort, *The Grand Duke*, an undisguisable flop. Throughout the 1890s Carte continued to present various musical shows, many of them adapted from the French, as well as encouraging native composers like Edward German while attempting, elsewhere, to stimulate and encourage the composition of English opera – all the while pursuing his work as an international hotelier. But his health was, unsurprisingly, shot; he had not been well throughout the decade. Despite the animosity between them, in 1900 Carte and Gilbert took a bow onstage to celebrate their great partnership; both men were seen to be dependent on canes when they appeared. Sullivan was at home, on what turned out to be his deathbed; Carte died the following year, just short of his 57th birthday. Gilbert, astonishingly, lived to see George V crowned in 1911.

Carte's operation was taken over by his widow, Helen Lenoir, one of whose first initiatives was to move the theatre's entrance to the hotel's forecourt, Savoy Court. She almost immediately leased the theatre to William Greet, who continued the tradition of musical comedy at the theatre; then G&S returned, the core repertory under the direction of Gilbert himself. But from then on the repertory, galvanised and modernised by Richard D'Oyly Carte's son Rupert, played elsewhere, and the theatre was

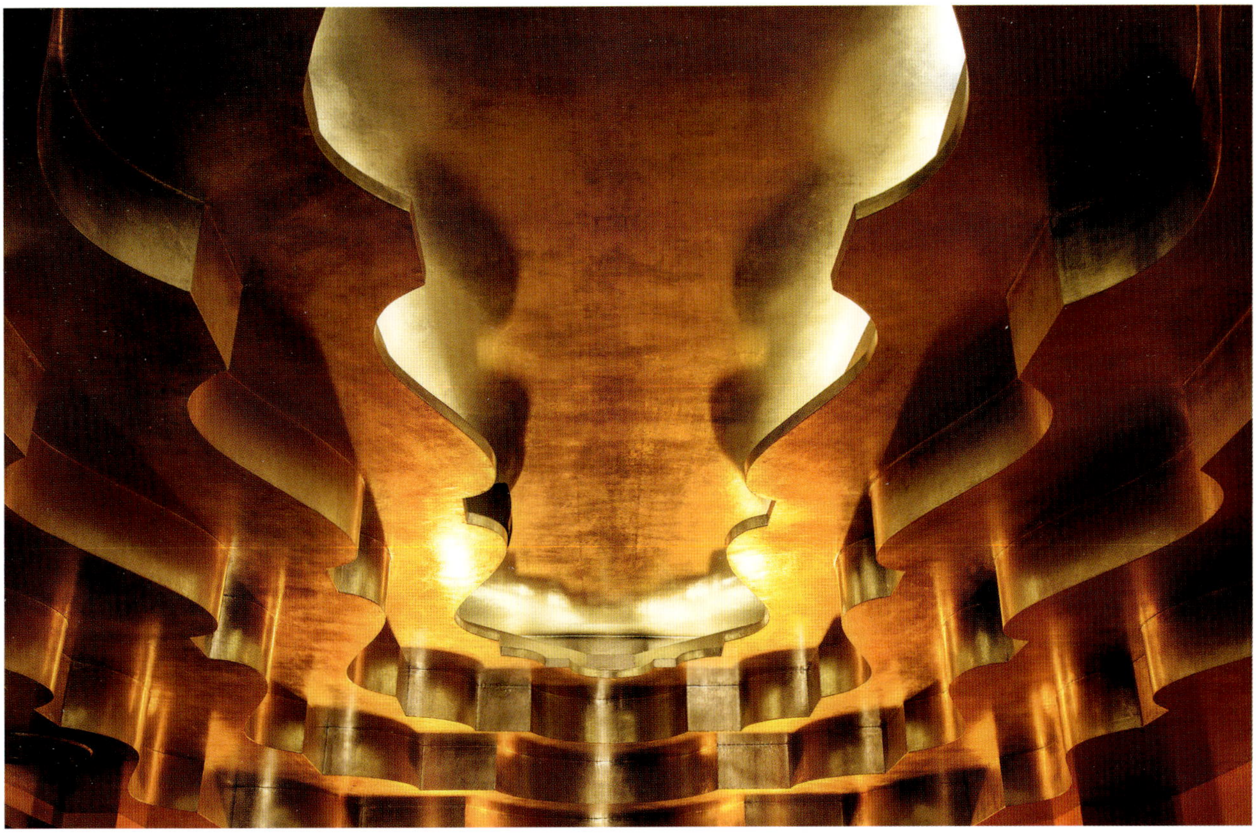

leased out to various managers. First there was a groundbreaking season of Shaw's plays, then Shakespeare directed with radical simplicity by Harley Granville-Barker, and for a while Henry Irving's son, H. B., took a lease on the theatre, playing an admired Hamlet. R. C. Sherriff's great First World War play *Journey's End*, after a wildly successful two-night run at the Apollo Theatre directed by a very young James Whale, transferred to the Savoy in 1929, without its original leading man, Laurence Olivier, but with an acclaimed successor in Colin Clive. This run too was very short, a mere stopgap; *Journey's End* went on o play for another two years, but elsewhere, because Rupert D'Oyly Carte had decided that the theatre needed to be completely redesigned.

Rupert's transformation of the Savoy was as bold as anything conceived by his father. He commissioned the veteran architect Frank Tugwell – formerly responsible for two Scarborough theatres, the Futurist and the Opera House, and Harrogate's Grand Opera House – to reshape the interior, a task he undertook with some ingenuity. The former cloakrooms and the bar at the back of the theatre were now on the side, and seventeen out of eighteen boxes were removed. The new auditorium had two tiers, leaving three levels – stalls, dress and upper circle; the capacity was thereby increased to 1,200. So far, so radical, but the most startling decision was the appointment of the ultra-modernist Basil Ionides as decorator. A wealthy aesthete and the influential author of *Colour and Interior Decoration*, Ionides had redesigned Pinafore, one of the Savoy Hotel's private dining rooms, and also, a little later, caused a sensation with the famous pink-and-cream ticket hall at Hounslow West underground station; he was the sort of chap ruthlessly satirised by Gilbert in

ABOVE The Art Deco foyer ceiling.

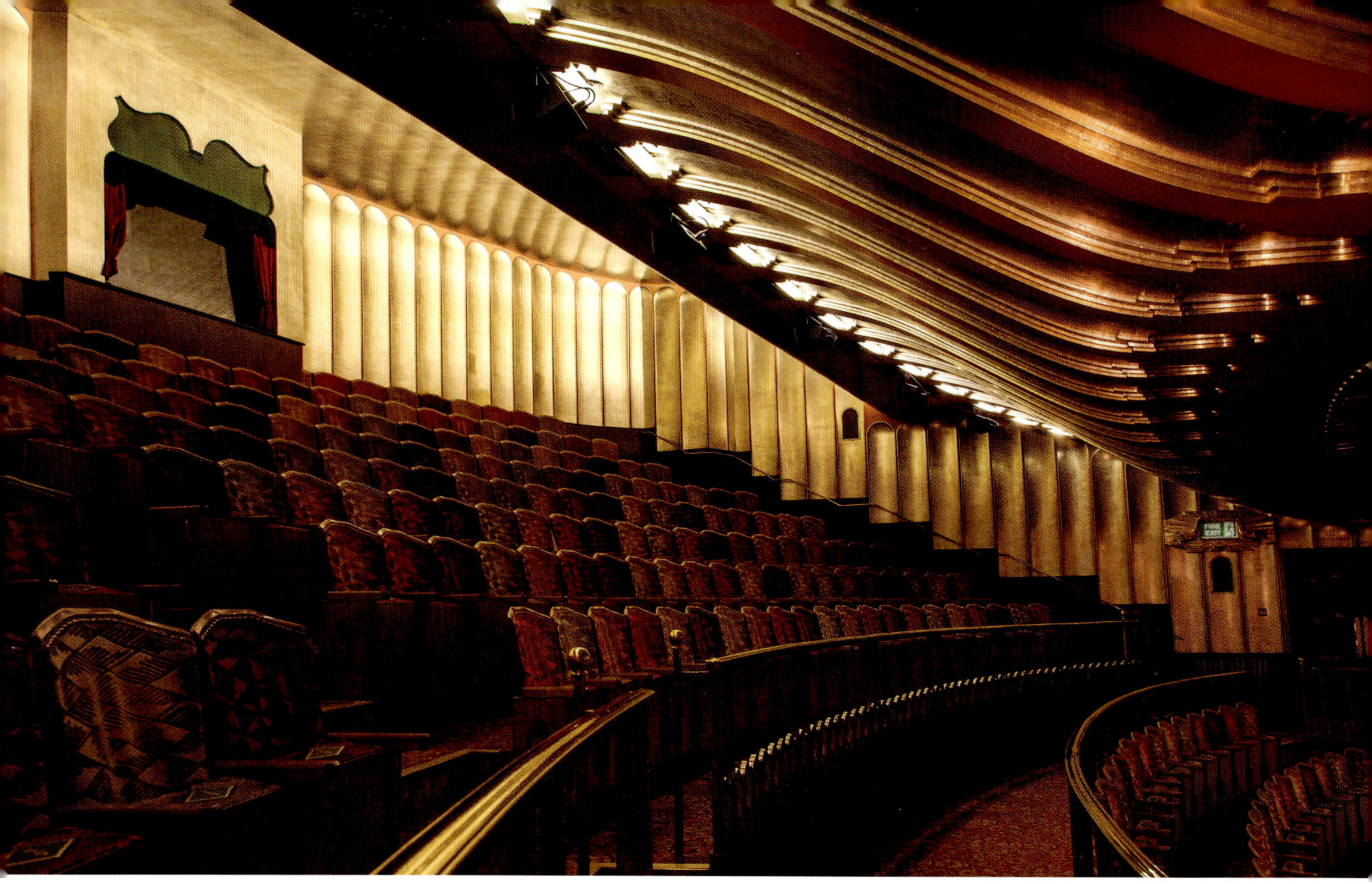

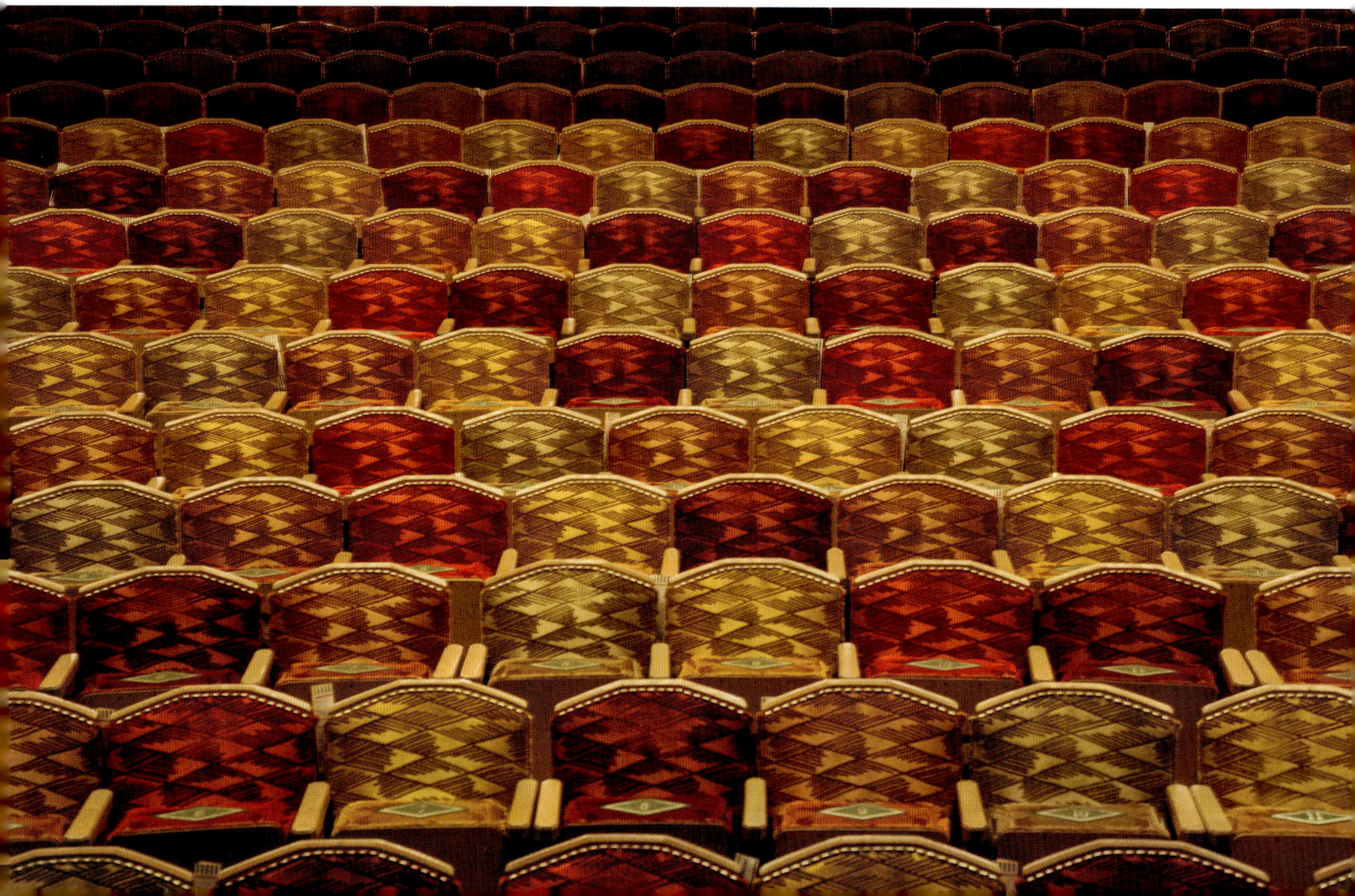

Patience, 'Distinctly a pallid and thin young man / A haggard and lank young man, /A greenery-yallery, Grosvenor Gallery, / Foot-in-the-grave young man'. All credit, then, to Rupert D'Oyly Carte for giving Ionides his head. The result is a classic of Art Deco design, both in concept and in execution. The materials are of the finest, each of the 82 side wall panels different and each inscribed with Chinese motifs that Ionides had spotted in the Victoria and Albert Museum as ornaments on a Ming–Qing lacquer screen. The high walls are rendered in aluminium leaf lacquered with transparent tints so they seem to glow in the dark, lending the auditorium a glamorous sheen possessed by no other London theatre. The ceiling is a painted sky with light clouds, the seats originally upholstered in elegant mushroom tones. Ionides confided in a journalist that he had taken the overall colour scheme from a bed of zinnias in Hyde Park, a remark that would have had Gilbert snorting with derisive laughter.

Predictably enough, it was with Gilbert and Sullivan that on 21 October 1929 the new theatre opened – but in operatic rather than operetta mode with *The Gondoliers*. Wittily conducted by Malcolm Sargent in a specially corrected edition that eliminated the sloppy habits of the past, the production was, astonishingly, designed by Oscar Wilde's friend Charles Ricketts, only 63 years old but seeming to belong to another world, a rare and improbable survivor of the naughty nineties. At the opening performance, in the only box, sat Gilbert's widow. The production marked a huge improvement in standards for the D'Oyly Carte Company, which continued to play at the Savoy, on and off, for another 75 years, until, exhausted, it finally disbanded. In its early seasons the transformed theatre hosted a number of distinguished and/or notable productions, including, in 1931, the very first performance on the English stage of Wilde's lurid *Salomé*. Soon after, the Savoy settled into a middlebrow repertory fronted by stars. *The Man Who Came to Dinner* with Robert Morley ran for two years, as did the Agatha Christie thriller *The Spider's Web*, written for its leading actress Margaret Lockwood, more famous for her film performances. In between the two was Noël Coward's *Relative Values* starring Gladys Cooper, a modest success in 1951. Later, a number of plays by William Douglas-Home, starring among others Peggy Ashcroft, Ralph Richardson and Kenneth More, provided mild entertainment; but the theatre really came into its own with *Noises Off*, Michael Frayn's delirious backstage farce, which ran for five years.

In 1990 the Savoy, in the throes of refurbishment, fell prey to that dread of Victorian managers, fire; it was effectually gutted. The usual proposal of building a new theatre was fiercely overruled by English Heritage; and, restored exactly as Tugwell and Ionides conceived it, with the sly addition of an extra floor above the auditorium to house the hotel's swimming pool, the theatre reopened with great fanfare in 1993. It has since largely concentrated on musicals – *Porgy and Bess*, *Fiddler on the Roof*, *Carousel*, *Legally Blonde*, *Let It Be*, *Dirty Rotten Scoundrels*, *Funny Girl*, *Dreamgirls* – which is very fitting, since Gilbert and Sullivan, whose works were the occasion for the construction of the theatre in the first place, laid the foundation stone for musical comedy as we know it. A recent revival of *Gypsy*, a musical perhaps less indebted than most to G&S, featured a performance by Imelda Staunton that counts among the very greatest performances the West End has seen for many years. And the wonderfully restored Savoy holds its place as the most beautiful twentieth-century theatre in London, with a very nice little hotel attached.

OPPOSITE TOP The upper circle – exuberant Art Deco.
OPPOSITE BOTTOM Stalls seats, remade to the original design.

THE PLAYHOUSE

The first theatre on the site of what is now The Playhouse was commissioned by a peculiarly energetic actor-manager and serial theatre-builder by the name of Sefton Henry Parry. Born in London in 1832, Parry was tirelessly peripatetic at a time when travel was a long and arduous business; by the time he was 23 he had toured extensively not only in England but in America, Australia and South Africa, all of which involved lengthy sea journeys. Once at his destination he rapidly assembled companies, some of them amateur, performing a repertory that extended from *Mother Goose* to *Hamlet* – in both of which, needless to say, he played the leading part. In Australia and South Africa he was something of a pioneer, proving a dab hand at knocking up theatre spaces when, as so often, available premises were inadequate. So it was entirely natural that when he returned to London in 1864, Parry – by then variously described as Australian, American or South African – should begin building theatres. In fact, with the New Greenwich Theatre he built the first new theatre in the metropolis since the Theatre Act of 1843 had abolished the notion of patent theatres. Thereafter he built the Holborn Theatre, a Globe Theatre on the Strand, and the New Theatre Royal in Hull. Then, in 1880, his ceaseless activity was halted for a moment by a severe attack of paralysis; but no sooner had he recovered from it than he was at it again, building what he called the Royal Avenue Theatre on Northumberland Avenue, just up from the Embankment. It was rumoured that he had chosen the site in the hope that Charing Cross station would need to expand and that he would then sell the site at a large profit, but it was not to be.

Whatever his ultimate intentions, Parry by no means stinted on the design or the finish of the new theatre. It opened in 1882 to great admiration, the work of Fowler & Hill, very much in the French style typical of so many late Victorian and Edwardian theatres, with a curving circle of curvaceous statues – *ooh-la-la* – on the exterior of the theatre; F. H. Fowler had earlier been responsible for the Opera Comique theatre in Westminster. And indeed the new theatre opened, with Jacques Offenbach's delicious opéra comique *Madame Favart*; even the manager, M. Marius, was French. The auditorium was voluptuous in the extreme, including a painted ceiling featuring portraits of dramatists through the ages, among them a very unexpected Joost van den Vondel, the great Netherlands playwright, known only in the non-Dutch-speaking world as a footnote in scholarly studies of the drama. The ornamentation of the auditorium was in the popular interior technique of *carton-pierre*, a kind of papier mâché imitation of wood, stone or metal. There was a great deal of elegant space in the front of house: 'there will be no obstructive entanglement in a labyrinth of tortuous corridors', tartly opined *The Era*, 'devised seemingly only for the purpose of bewildering and impeding the visitor.' There were some 1,200 seats. The new theatre was particularly admired for its unrivalled situation, looking up towards Trafalgar

OPPOSITE View of the proscenium arch with deliciously ornate safety curtain.
OVERLEAF The auditorium viewed from the stage – one can both see how the auditorium has been squashed into a small space and marvel at its grace. Note the unusual fronts of the balconies.

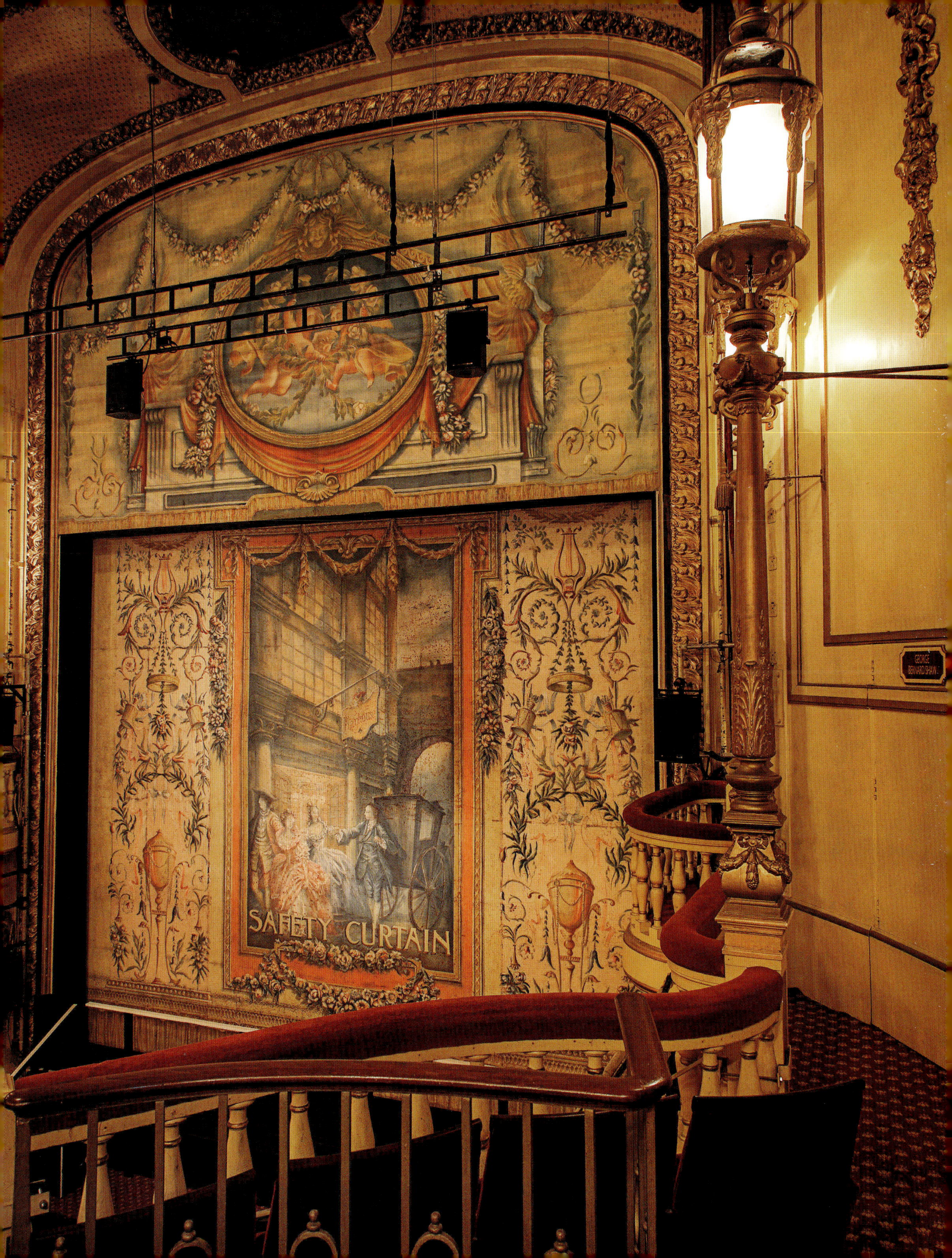
SAFETY CURTAIN
GEORGE
BERNARD SHAW

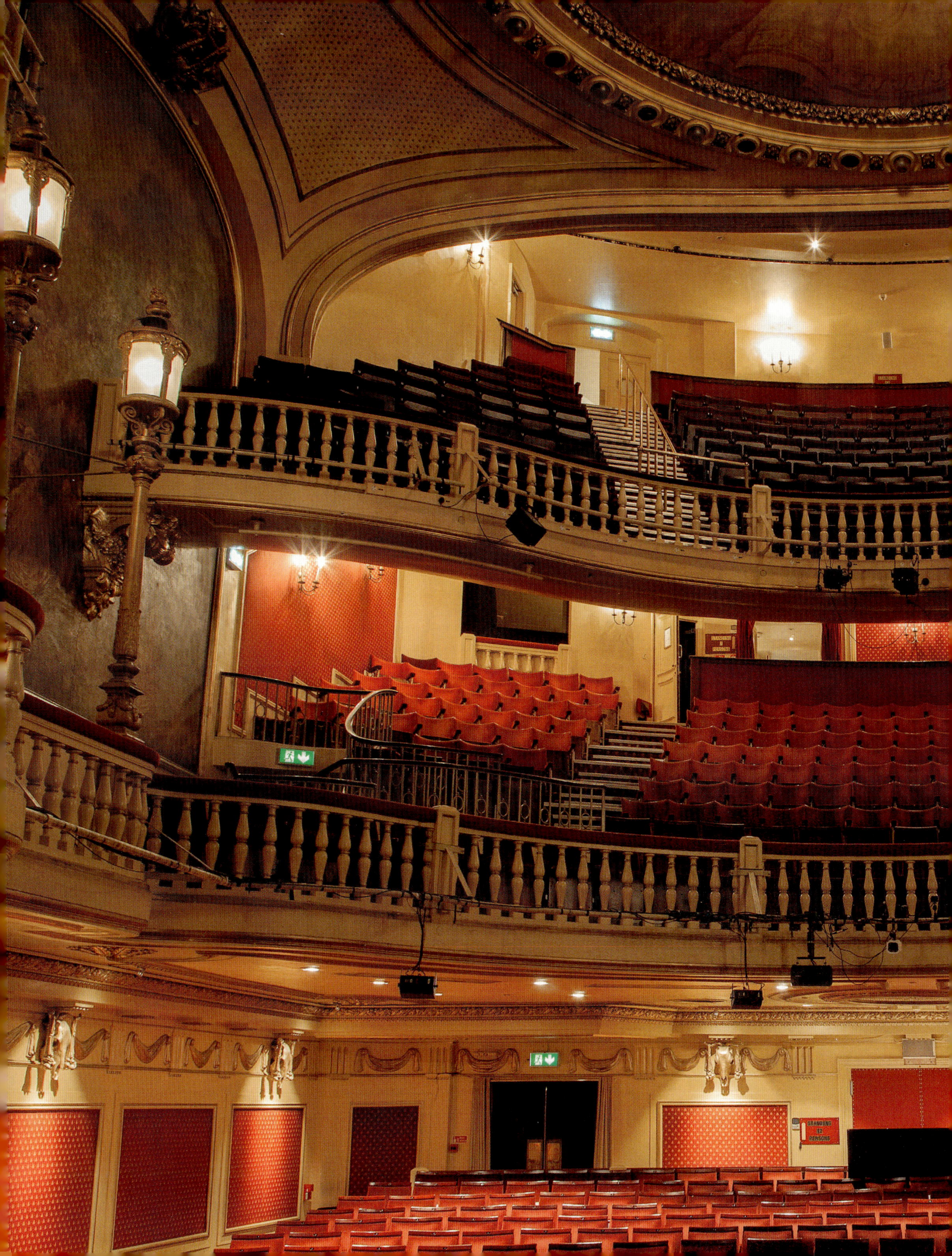

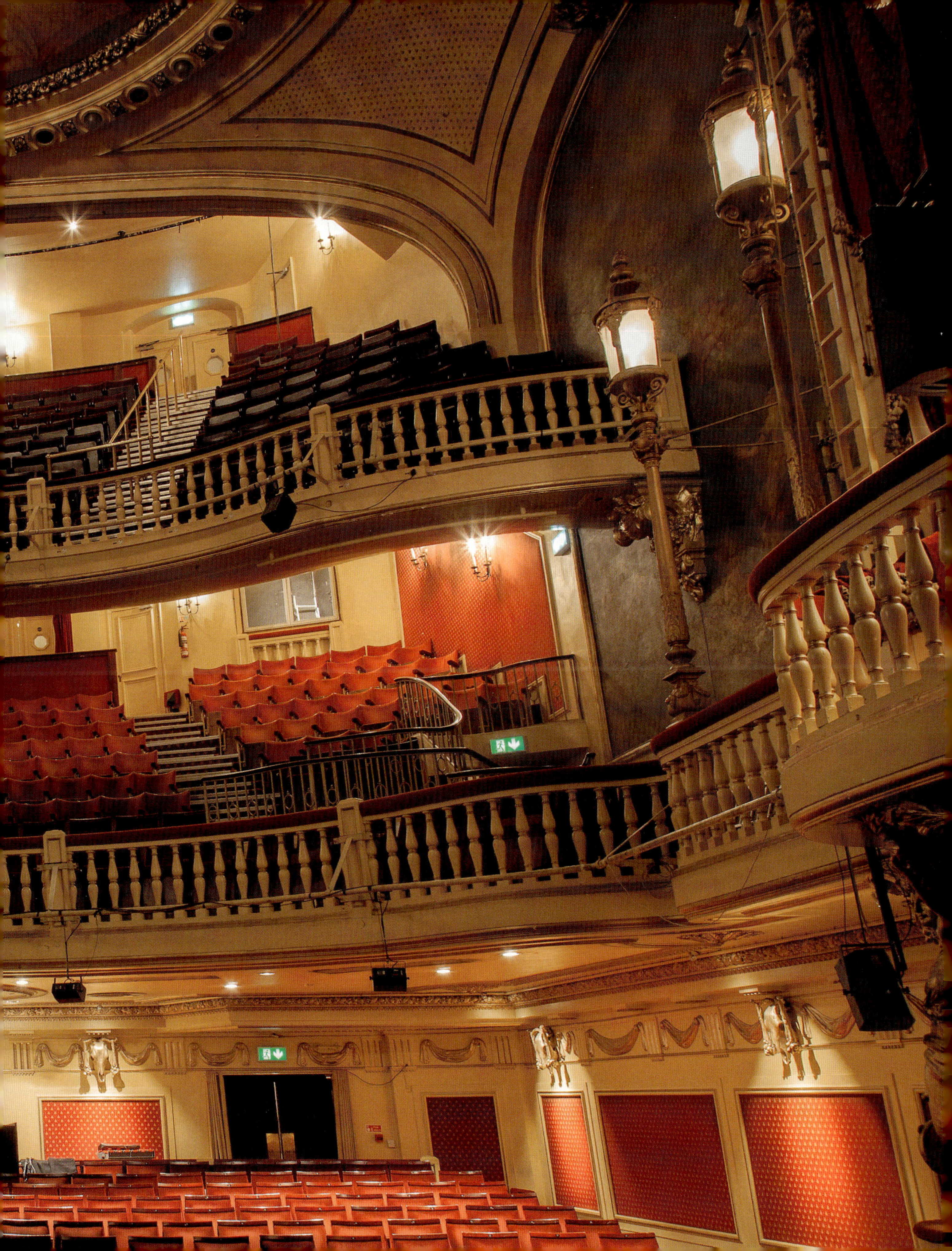

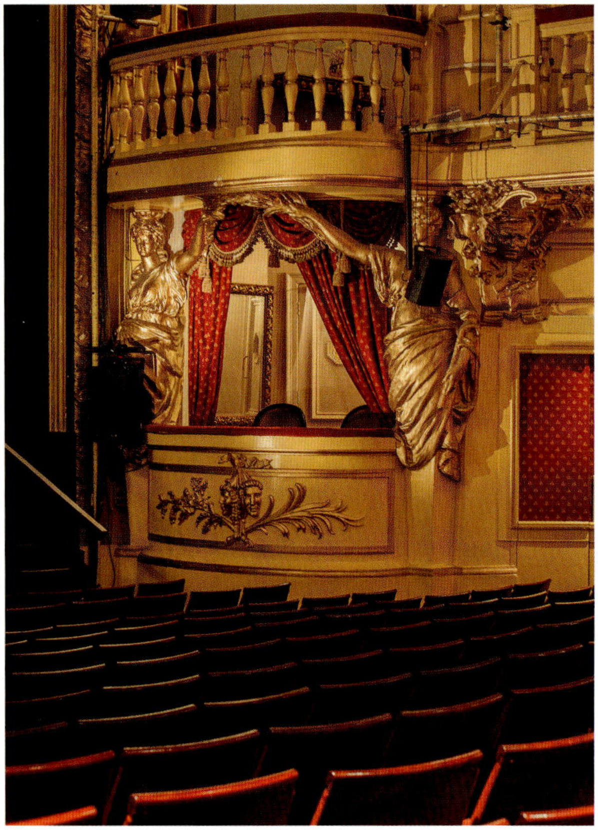

Square and down towards the river; being free-standing, it was also deemed to be without risk of fire. Little did anyone imagine that something much more alarming than fire was in the offing.

It carried on with its menu of Gallic delights until 1890; by then, the ever-active Parry had again been stopped in his tracks by another, this time lethal, attack of paralysis. The theatre was then taken by George Alexander, soon to enter theatre history (elsewhere) with his productions of Oscar Wilde's last two comedies, but in 1894 the Avenue Theatre – having, for reasons unknown, sloughed off its royal pretensions – now witnessed its first significant premiere, Shaw's anti-war comedy *Arms and the Man*, rarely seen nowadays but for over seventy years a guaranteed box office hit. The play, specially written for Florence Farr, the first of several female managers of the theatre, was Shaw's earliest commercial success; on the first night the applause was vociferously favourable, with only one lone booer. 'My dear fellow,' said Shaw from the stage, 'I quite agree with you, but what are we two against so many?' A similarly great but rather less long-lived success was *A Message from Mars*, in which a selfish young man is shown the error of his ways by an exiled Martian. It was presented by and starred the raffish, Eton-educated comic actor Charles Hawtrey; he later filmed it, making it the first British science fiction film. The theatre was less successful in subsequent years, prompting Cyril Maude, who had had a brilliant decade as actor-manager of the Theatre Royal Haymarket, to buy the theatre and rebuild it, reducing the number of seats and refashioning the auditorium, though the exterior remained as it was.

ABOVE A box flanked by two statues of goddess-like figures.

The new interior was designed by the fashionable partnership of Detmar Blow and Fernand Billerey, with interior decoration suggested by the celebrated Whistler pupil, world traveller, etcher and drypoint artist Mortimer Menpes: the keynote was rich brown and gold. Work was nearing completion when, without warning, 60 feet of the railway roof collapsed, smashing right through the side of the building and hurling bricks onto the stage, where the designers and the management were in the middle of a meeting. No one was harmed inside the building but, *The Times* reported, 'some 20 or 30 men who, suspended from the roof in swinging cradles, were . . . scraping and painting the ironwork of the bays, fell into the station below and were buried beneath a mass of debris that was variously estimated at between 50 and 100 tons in weight.' In the event, six people died and 26 were injured. After a respectful pause, work resumed, slowly. Maude temporarily transferred his operation to the Strand Theatre; the South Eastern & Chatham Railway company coughed up £20,000; and eventually in January 1907 the transformed theatre, now named The Playhouse, opened with a double bill of old Maude standbys, *The Drums of Oudh* and *Toddles*.

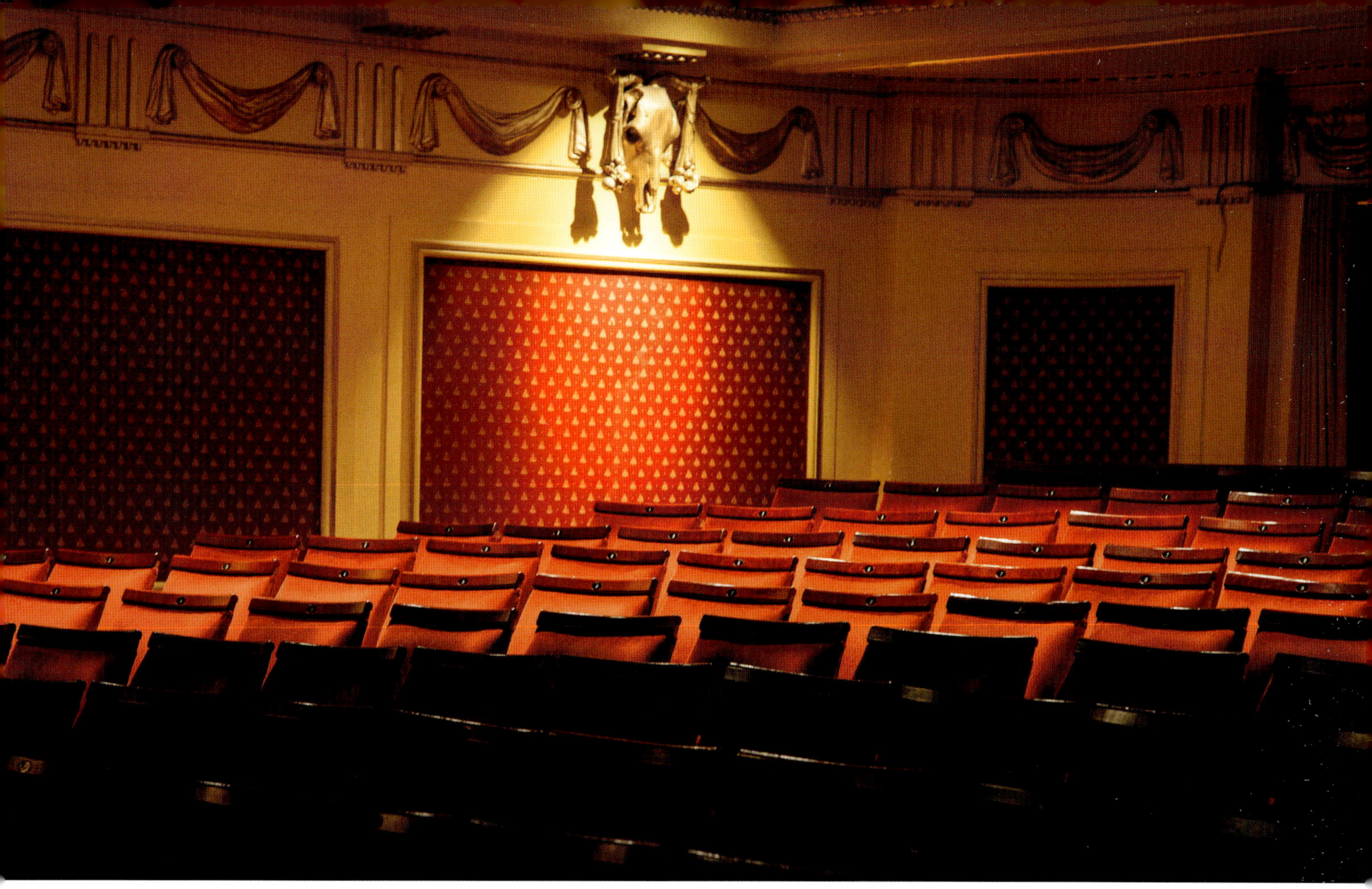

The event was made memorable by the performance of a curtain-raiser specially written by Shaw, a deliciously witty piece of meta-theatrical knockabout in which Maude appeared as Goldsmith, a nervous actor-manager, making a rambling historical speech about his new theatre, constantly spurred on by his wife (played, of course by Maude's own wife) to start the evening's play, *Pickles*. Goldsmith becomes defensive: 'you ask me why I don't play Hamlet instead of Pickles. Well, the reason is that anybody can play Hamlet, but it takes me to play Pickles. I leave Hamlet to those who can provide no livelier form of entertainment.' He departs in a huff, leaving Mrs Goldsmith to deliver the properly Shavian final words, reminding the audience that drama is not mere entertainment but has a higher purpose, so, though they aim to please, 'we will not please you except on terms honourable to ourselves and to you. But on those terms we hope that you may spend many pleasant hours here, and we as many hard-working ones, as at our old home in the Haymarket. And now may I run away and tell Edwin that his speech has been a great success after all, and that you are quite ready for *Pickles*?' *Pickles* was a wild success, as was the new theatre: its dress circle Empire lamp-posts, its French paintings on the walls and ceiling, its new cane-seated armchairs, its arch surmounted by figures of Fame crowning Thalia, goddess of comedy, were all admired, though *The Guardian* felt, as many people have since, that 'the general impression which the interior conveys is that there are many ideas in it, but that they have not quite shaped into a unity.' The paper also noted that 'the old line of statues round the roof has been chastened into a line of vases.' The auditorium has

ABOVE A detail of the stalls showing one of the 'horse skulls' flanked by plaster swathes of drapery.

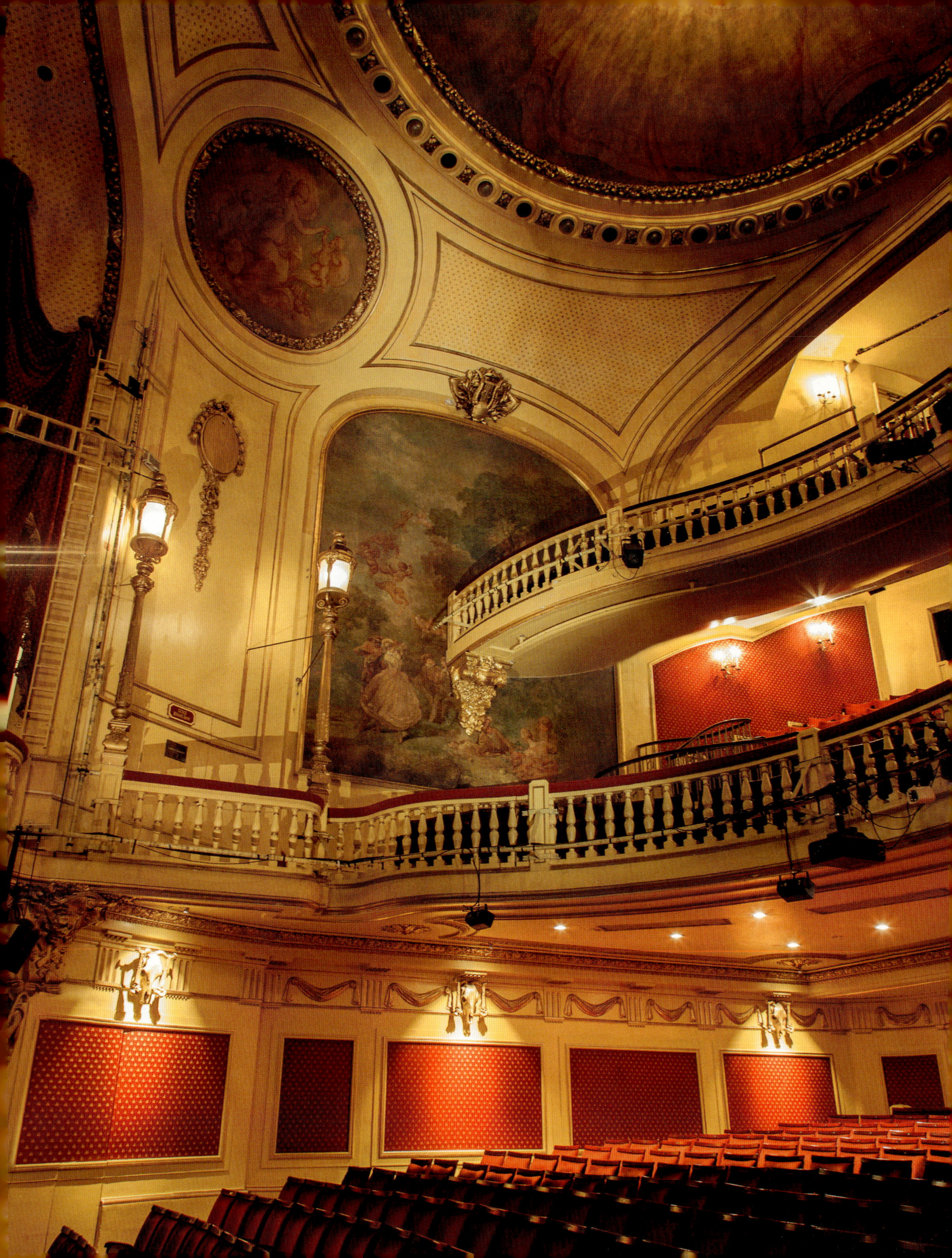

an unexpectedly open feeling to it which some commentators have felt gives it an airy delicateness. Certainly it has a unique character, almost like a set itself; and under the stage, in working condition but never used, is some remarkable stage machinery.

During his tenure of the theatre, Cyril Maude rose to considerable heights in his profession: he succeeded Henry Irving as the president of the Actors' Orphanage Fund and established the first orphanage for actors' children, inaugurated innovative fundraising schemes and events, attracted royal patronage and secured committee members from among leading actors of the day. He served until 1914 and carried on acting with great distinction until not long before his death in 1951, an astonishing survivor from the Victorian theatre. The Playhouse was subsequently run by a succession of enterprising actor-managers – Frank Curzon among them – but it is most closely identified with the great beauty Gladys Cooper, who was first Curzon's professional partner and then ran the theatre on her own, before pairing up with the highly regarded Gerald du Maurier in a series of Maugham revivals. But there were other costly failures, and eventually, after losing a great deal of money on *The Rats of Norway*, in which a very young Laurence Olivier appeared, Cooper admitted defeat. Thereafter, the theatre never entirely regained its momentum. Yet another actress-manager, but of a rather different kind, Nancy Price, brought her People's National Theatre there in 1938 and 1939; and the Old Vic, still nomadic while the bomb damage to its home was made good, visited. But by the time the 1950s began, The Playhouse had lost its profile. Luckily it escaped demolition when the BBC took it over, converting it into a radio studio, which it remained for a quarter of a century, producing some memorable, not to say classic, programmes – *The Goon Show*, *Hancock's Half Hour*, the radio version of *Steptoe and Son*.

Eventually the BBC moved on, and the theatre sat, empty and forlorn, for ten years before a romantically inclined property developer named Robin Gonshaw, intrigued, asked to be shown around and immediately fell in love with the place. He restored it to its original condition on the back of a commercial building he was able to erect above it. Ever since, a variety of owners, including Jeffrey Archer and Ray Cooney, have taken it on, often for quite brief tenures. In 1996 the quixotic American property magnate Patrick Sulaiman Cole purchased the theatre and lavished large sums of money on bringing it to a beauty of finish that would have impressed even Cyril Maude and old Sefton Parry; all this elegance still failed to draw audiences. Finally, the theatre was bought by the Ambassador Theatre Group. Many remarkable productions, notably by Peter Hall and Richard Eyre, and seasons by the Royal Shakespeare Company, have since lit up its stage. Despite its loveliness The Playhouse remains a slight oddity, and its situation, so much admired by the Victorian commentators, has not necessarily produced a steady flow of potential customers in the vicinity, even with the many thousands of people who pour out of Embankment station – one minute away – every day. But in spite of the windowless subterranean dressing rooms and Terry Farrell's Embankment Place of 1987–90 looming over it like a science-fiction barracks, there is no lovelier theatre in which to work; despite the transfers of remarkable immersive productions of *The Jungle*, about the Calais refugee camps, and *Fiddler on the Roof*, somehow, fancifully perhaps, the spirit of gallant and beautiful Gladys Cooper seems to permeate the auditorium in the most delicate and delicious way.

OPPOSITE The auditorium, looking up to the roof.

GARRICK

The southern end of Charing Cross Road has a quality all of its own, brought to a charming finish by the Garrick Theatre, built in 1889, its curving and colonnaded facade with balcony giving on to the street, leading straight down to Trafalgar Square. It faces the National Portrait Gallery, which, perhaps drawn by the charm of the theatre, opened in 1896 after various peregrinations across London, adding its own Renaissance character to the area. And then, in 1910, nearly ten years after Henry Irving's death, an imposing statue of the actor universally known to his colleagues as the Guv'nor was unveiled in the presence of some of his most distinguished former colleagues. The great actor-manager is, perhaps surprisingly, represented wearing the academic gown of an Honorary Doctor of Letters of the University of Cambridge, but it was an essential part of the image of profundity and respectability that he, the first theatrical knight, born John Henry Brodribb in a worker's cottage in Somerset, had so successfully cultivated; the street to the statue's left was renamed Irving Street in his honour. All of which lends a certain distinction to this this little enclave at the end of Charing Cross Road, a sort of bijou theatrical Mount Rushmore. David Garrick, who hobnobbed with kings and earls and who was the first actor to be buried in Westminster Abbey, would surely have approved. His magnificent full-length – rather larger than life, in fact – portrait stares straight across the foyer of the theatre named after him; the painting is a copy of a Gainsborough original, but startlingly lifelike for all that, as befits the famously mercurial actor.

It was another theatrical immortal, W. S. Gilbert, then nearing the end of his celebrated partnership with Arthur Sullivan, who built the theatre; it is not known why particularly he called it the Garrick – perhaps it was to be a sort of practical counterpart to the club of that name just round the corner. In fact the theatre very nearly didn't get built at all, as excavations in the subsoil revealed an unsuspected river dating from Roman times; Gilbert commented that he wasn't sure whether to build a theatre or lease out the fishing rights. In due course the foundation was secured, and the Garrick was ready to open its doors. It was jointly designed by two men: Walter Emden (who had built the greatly admired Globe, now Gielgud, and Royal Court theatres) and C. J. Phipps (of the Theatres Royal in Glasgow, Belfast, Northampton, Portsmouth and Exeter – the latter destroyed by fire two years after it opened, leaving Phipps under something of a cloud, which may explain why he was prepared to collaborate with a less productive and less acclaimed younger colleague). Gilbert invited his friend the noted character actor John Hare – who specialised in men-of-the-world parts, a kind of role sadly no longer on offer in the twenty-first century – to initiate the new theatre as manager and lessee. 'It was', said a contemporary report, 'altogether a pleasant and refreshing experience that awaited the public in Mr Hare's new theatre . . . they were introduced to what with propriety may be described as the most elegant and best appointed place of amusement in London – perhaps in the world.' A proud boast indeed. Once past the small but elegantly appointed foyer with its fine mosaics, one was in the dress circle; the stairs

OPPOSITE The auditorium, side view.

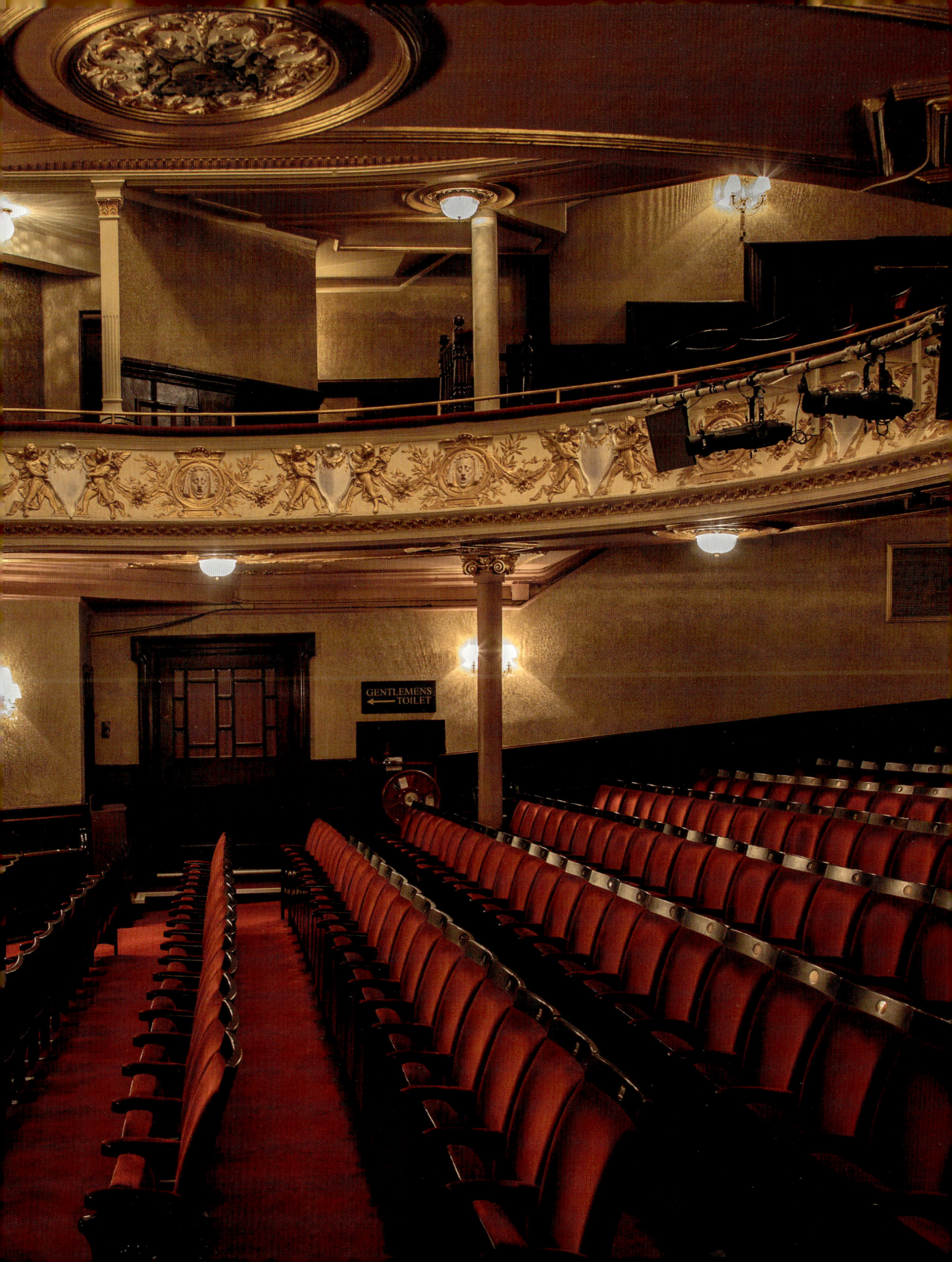
GENTLEMENS
TOILET

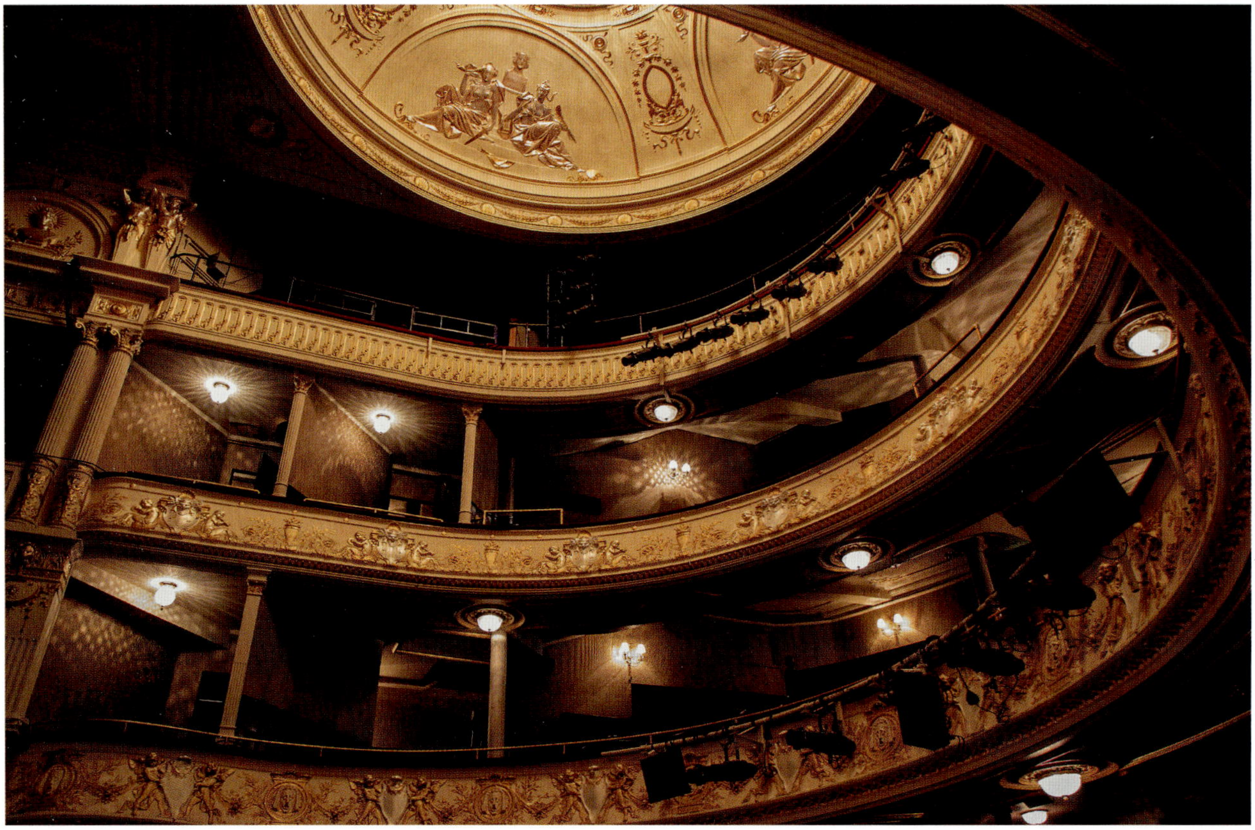

took one down to the stalls. The auditorium, recently restored to its original colour scheme, was white with gold ground. Cherry-red was the dominant note: the walls round the dress circle and stalls were hung with cherry-coloured silk, and the pit walls covered with Japanese paper of cherry-red and gold; the upper circle and the rest of the house followed suit. Even the box rests were in cherry-coloured satin. The seats were a great novelty: the 350 pit seats lifted up and had arm rests, arranged, *The Era* reported, 'so as to take the hat, coat, umbrella, and programme'. The 170 stalls seats were lounge chairs with circular padded backs, covered like the dress circle seats in, yes, cherry-red, with silk pockets for programmes and boxes large enough to contain a tall hat and an overcoat. No such luxury in the spartan gallery, which though bringing the capacity up to 1,200 was at a very sharp rake to the stage; it was soon permanently closed, being altogether too precipitous for comfort or indeed safety. With further reseating the capacity now stands at 656, making it a bijou theatre like the Duke of York's in St Martin's Lane, which stands back to back with the Garrick, the two closer even than the Wyndham's and the Noël Coward, with not even an alley between them.

For the opening of the new theatre, and his first venture into management, John Hare chose boldly. He had gained his reputation in the cup-and-saucer realist plays of Thomas Robertson (whose first success, by odd chance, had been *David Garrick* in 1864); Robertson was now long dead, and Hare chose instead to open his first season with a new play by his friend Arthur Wing Pinero, the English dramatist who had made his name in the 1880s with brilliantly contrived comedies – among them *The*

ABOVE In the auditorium, looking up.

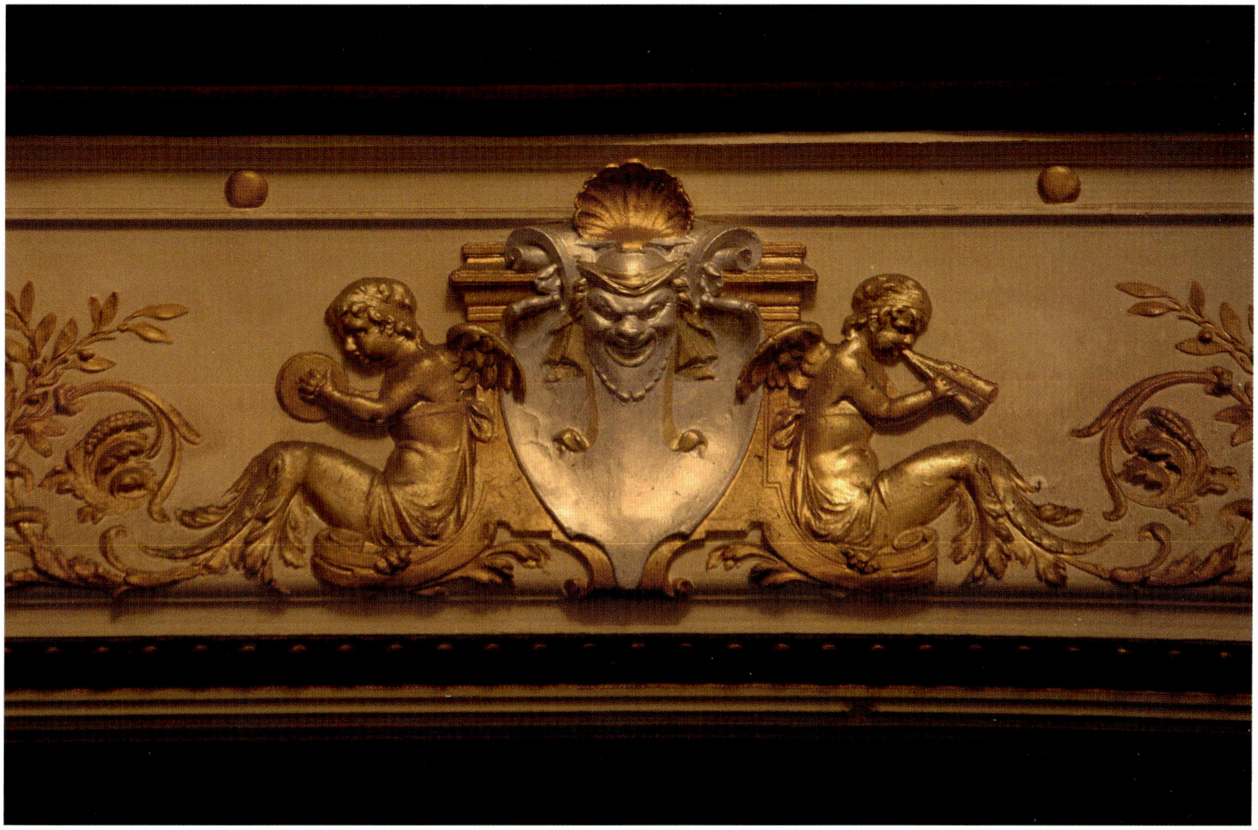

Magistrate, *The Schoolmistress* and *Dandy Dick* – which still hold the stage. Now he wanted to write in a more naturalistic vein, addressing serious matters. 'He evidently felt', Malcolm Salaman wrote in the preface to an edition of Pinero's plays, 'that the air was clearing, that the period was approaching when the British dramatist might begin to assert his artistic independence, and at least attempt to write plays which should, by means of simple and reasonable dramatic deduction, record actual experience flowing in the natural irregular rhythm of life, which should at the same time embody lofty ideals of conduct and of character.' Pinero accordingly wrote *The Profligate*, about a feckless man who, having wrecked all the lives around him, kills himself. He showed it to Hare, who was not yet ready to go into management on

ABOVE Detail of one of the balconies with a pair of winged cherubs.

his own, but begged Pinero to wait two years until he was. Pinero did not regret the delay: the play caused an absolute sensation, even though he was persuaded by Hare at the very last moment to change the ending and save his anti-hero. Despite this imposed last-minute redemption, audience and critics were astounded by the play's audacity:

> LESLIE . . . the burden of the sin you have committed I will bear upon my shoulders, and the little good that is in me shall enter into your heart. We will start life anew – always seeking for the best that we can do, always trying to repair the worst that we have done. Dunstan! Don't fear me! I will be your wife, not your judge. Let us from this moment begin the new life you spoke of.
> DUNSTAN Wife! Ah, God bless you! God bless you, and forgive me!
> LESLIE Oh, my husband!

'No original English play produced on our stage for many a day has stirred its audience so deeply at the time of its representation,' said *The Spectator*, 'or has sent them home with so much to think over, to discuss and to remember.' Hare, Lewis Waller, Jonston Forbes-Robertson and Kate Rorke all made powerful impressions in their roles. Pinero soon trumped the effect of *The Profligate* with, first, *The Second Mrs Tanqueray* and then *The Notorious Mrs Ebbsmith*. The latter play appeared at the Garrick in 1895, still under Hare's management, with Mrs Patrick Campbell sensational in the title role; the play's success was only enhanced when a woman by the name of Ebbsmith was discovered floating, dead, in the Thames, with two used halves of tickets for the play in her pocket. The mystery was never solved. In 1899 Hare had a final success at the Garrick with Sydney Grundy's Labiche adaptation *A Pair of Spectacles* before moving on to the Globe theatre; and in 1904, rather charmingly, W. S. Gilbert, who had built the theatre fifteen years earlier, finally presented a play there – his last, though he had another comic opera still in him. *Harlequin and the Fairy's Dilemma*, a 'domestic pantomime', is a piece of affectionate whimsy in which the playwright satirises the theatre of his youth: 'Fairy Rosebud', says the first stage direction, 'enters the Abode of Demon Alcohol, who complains bitterly about the law that requires demons to speak in verse; and indeed he is very bad at it.' Nobody got the joke.

The Garrick was now set on the rocky path of any commercial theatre, with its endemic vicissitudes. After a series of unsuccessful productions in the 1920s an attempt was made to turn the theatre into a music hall. Despite the appearance of number of stars from the good old days of variety, it failed, as did the revival of a number of musical comedies, and the piranha-like cinema owners began circling the theatre; despite well-advanced plans for its sale and conversion, it escaped – just in time to receive *Love on the Dole*, the Walter Greenwood classic of working-class life during the 1930s slump, which starred Wendy Hiller (his wife) and ran for nearly a year. During the Second World War the Garrick was converted into a 'Forces Theatre', but it was already back in regular business in 1941 with a rapid but lively turnover. Revues came and went. The great wafer-thin Scots hoofer-cum-fashion-plate Jack Buchanan, who made Fred Astaire seem somehow sloppy, took the theatre on for a decade, with some success; during his regime the bilingual satirical revue *La Plume de Ma Tante*, devised by and starring the great French comedian Robert Dhéry, ran for two and half years. In 1960, *Fings Ain't Wot They Used T'be*, also a revue in all but name, transferred from Joan Littlewood's Theatre Workshop in Stratford East and stayed for two years, ensuring the company's survival and bringing Miriam Karlin, Barbara Windsor, Toni Palmer, Bryan Pringle and a large number of other Stratford stalwarts into the mainstream.

Having fended off predatory cinema owners, the Garrick now faced a more formidable enemy: local government. The Greater London Council's nefarious 1968 scheme to wipe out a large part of the Strand and Covent Garden to make life easier for motorists stretched its tentacles as far as Charing Cross Road; fortunately it was defeated by a formidable alliance of rebels, from the actors' union, Equity, to the Covent Garden Community Association, to the Shadow Minister for the Environment. Had it gone ahead – and quite apart from the brutal obliteration of the piazza, Long Acre and Maiden Lane – the Garrick, the Vaudeville, the Adelphi, the Lyceum and the Duchess theatres would have been swept into oblivion. Instead, the Garrick, like the other threatened theatres, resumed its work of adding to the gaiety of nations, a phrase, as it happens, coined by Samuel Johnson on hearing of the death of Garrick: 'I am disappointed by that stroke of death which has eclipsed the gaiety of nations and impoverished the public stock of harmless pleasure.' The theatre named after him has a particularly genial aspect, and there is no more agreeable corner of London of an evening or at a matinee than this end of Charing Cross Road as

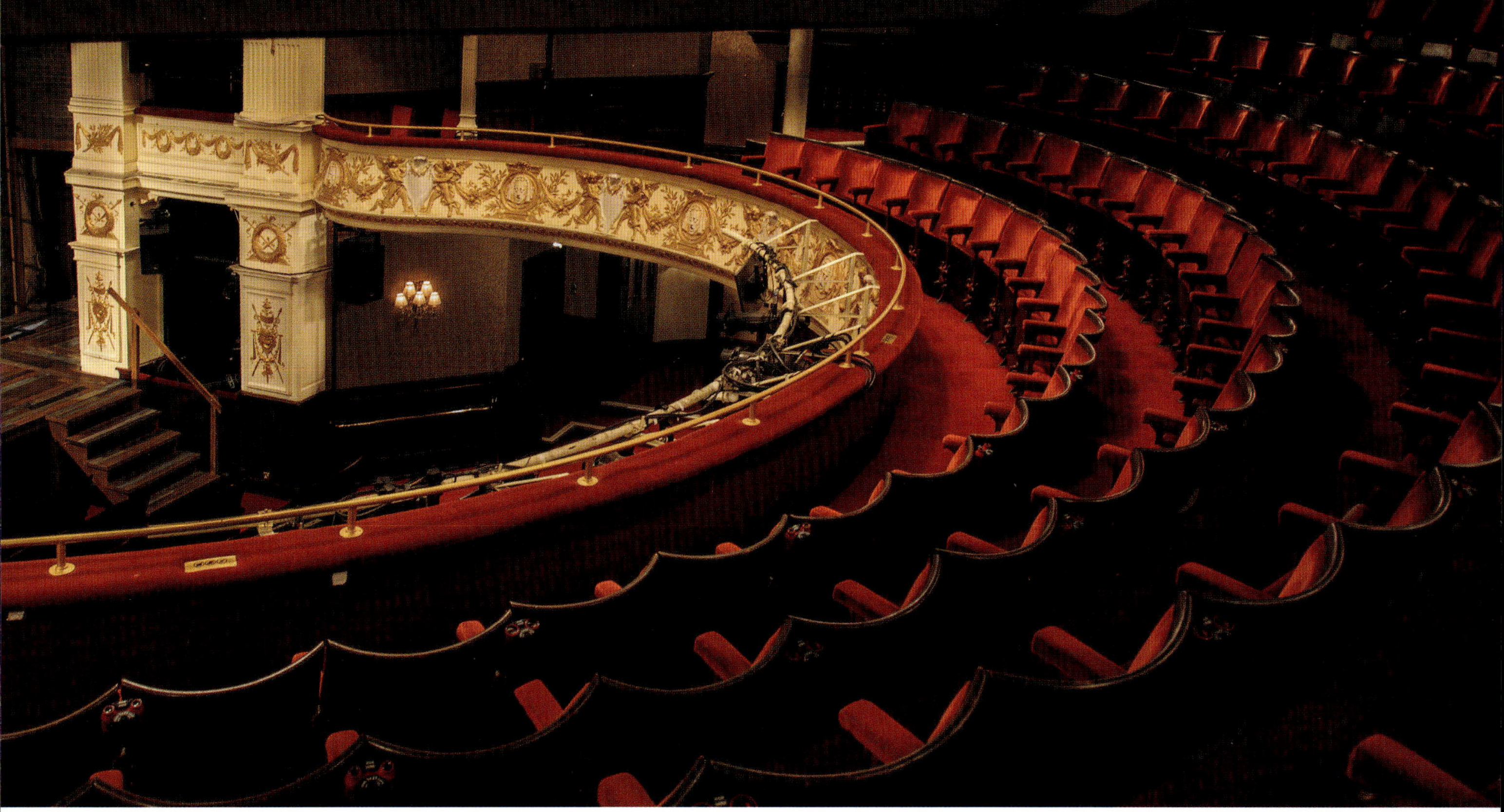

people flock into the theatre and, weather permitting, crowd onto the little balcony outside the dress circle bar, drinks in hand. It exemplifies the degree to which the West End is a village: the business of putting on shows and going to them an entirely normal, integral part of life; it's what we do.

The Garrick has been host to every conceivable kind of show, but for some reason it has been particularly hospitable to comedians; maybe the spirit of Gilbert has ensured that the comic muse is more often in residence there than her surly sister. Bea Lillie, Frankie Howerd, Paul Merton and Ricky Gervais were all, to put it mildly, memorable during their seasons there, but the most indelible of them all was surely Max Wall, the rubber-legged, lank-haired, tails-wearing genius of surreal fantasies and gallows humour who in 1975 made a glorious return to stardom after decades in the wilderness, igniting the audience into throat-aching laughter: a lord of misrule triumphantly enthroned, giving two fingers up to the developers. Henry Irving would probably not have cracked a smile, but Garrick himself would surely have seen that Max Wall represented the ancient antic spirit of theatre as well as anyone who ever trod its boards.

ABOVE The auditorium from the first circle, showing the horseshoe shape.

PALACE

Foremost among Richard D'Oyly Carte's many ambitions was the desire to found a school of English opera. He encouraged his team of resident geniuses W. S. Gilbert and Arthur Sullivan to move towards a loftier style, but this did not materialise; they carried on, somewhat dispiritedly, in their accustomed light vein. Carte had meanwhile quietly engaged the Leipzig-trained Sullivan (without his long-standing collaborator) to write a Grand Opera that would inaugurate the English Opera House he was building expressly to accommodate all the brand-new native operas he planned to commission. Sullivan, not in good health, toiled ceaselessly to finish *Ivanhoe*, his Very Grand Opera drawn from Walter Scott's medievalist novel, in time for the opening; he managed it, just. The theatre, too, only made it in the nick of time. It was no less ambitious than the music: a free-standing building of great splendour, located on Cambridge Circus (round the corner from Carte's birthplace in Greek Street) at the western intersection of Shaftesbury Avenue and Charing Cross Road, the view of its magnificent Northern Renaissance facade unimpeded by any other building. There was and is no other West End theatre in this style, not only in the extensive and distinctive use of red brick and terracotta mouldings, but also in the breadth and openness of its construction. It owes nothing either to the clean lines of the neoclassical model favoured by the former patent theatres, or to the florid embellishments in the French manner beloved of the latest boulevard theatres. The Royal English Opera House, Carte proudly called it. It was to be a sort of West End Bayreuth, custom-built for a whole new art form, one that in fact did not yet exist (and indeed never would).

Nominally the architect was the highly distinguished Thomas Collcutt, recent recipient of the Grand Prize for Architecture at the Paris Exposition Universelle. He had designed the Savoy Hotel for Carte and would go on to design what is now Wigmore Hall (originally Bechstein Hall), and there is a similar use of materials, notably an abundance of pale terracotta, in all three buildings. The interior of the Palace, with its magnificent staircases with alabaster balusters, its epic auditorium with three-tiered balconies and profusion of encrusted green marbles with gilded capitals and base, was of great splendour, as befitted its status as a grand opera house. As might have been expected of Carte, that passionate pioneer of electric light, ensured that the house was flooded in it: there were upward of two thousand bulbs, the power provided by the theatre's own generator. Backstage, the mechanical appointments were nonpareil: the stage machinery, replete with traps and chariot slots, was installed and supervised by the bewilderingly versatile Walter Dando, wizard of stage flying, promoter of India-rubber gymnastic springs and chest-expanders, official photographer to London Zoo and, before the century was out, director of the first film ever to be made from a Shakespeare play. Carte had spared no expense, and it was widely understood that, despite his crack team, the building owed everything in design and concept to him; it took three years to build. The opening was a triumph: the Prince and Princess of Wales (later to be King

OPPOSITE Sunlight catches the marble wall of the main staircase.
OVERLEAF The main staircase, as grand and original as any theatre's.

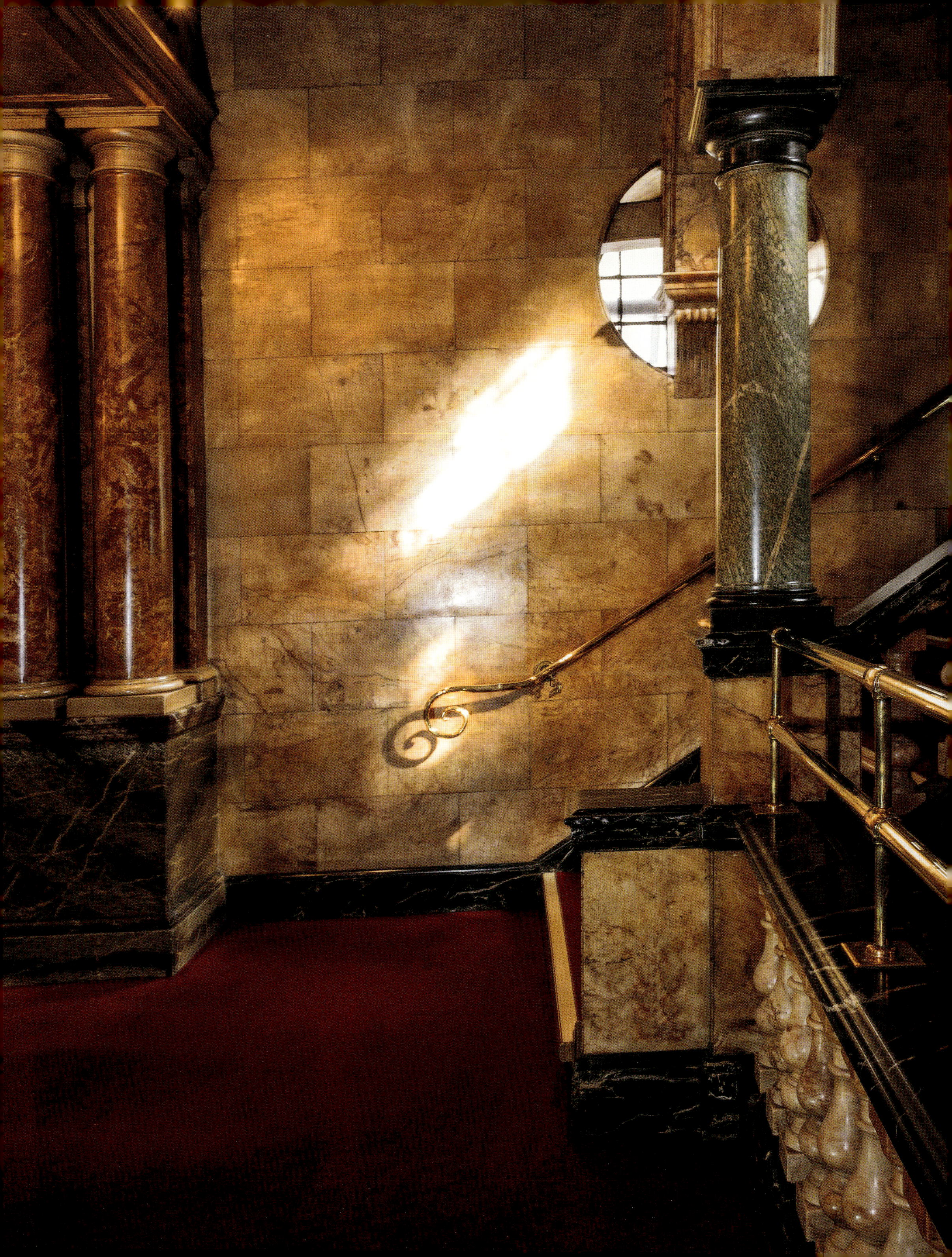

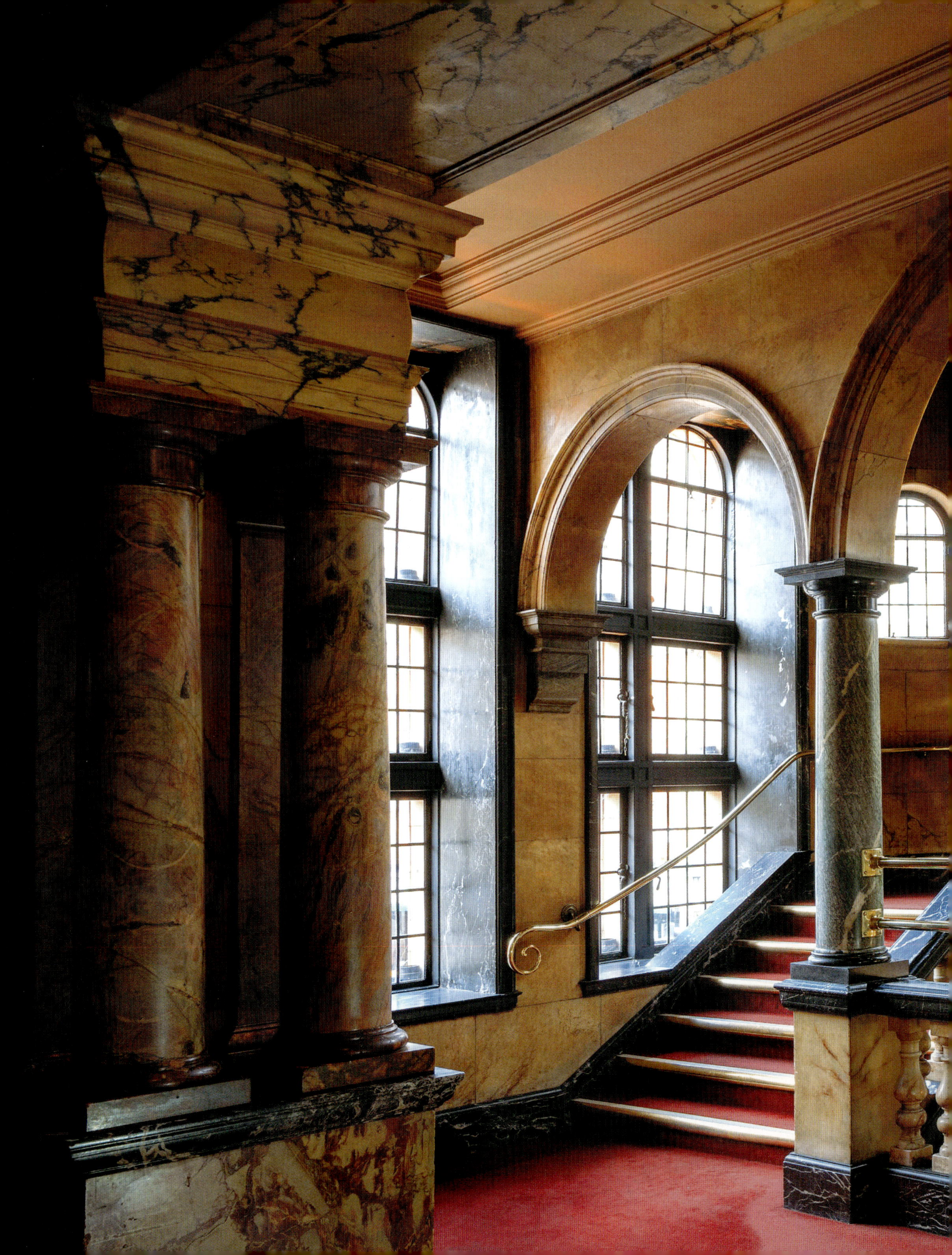

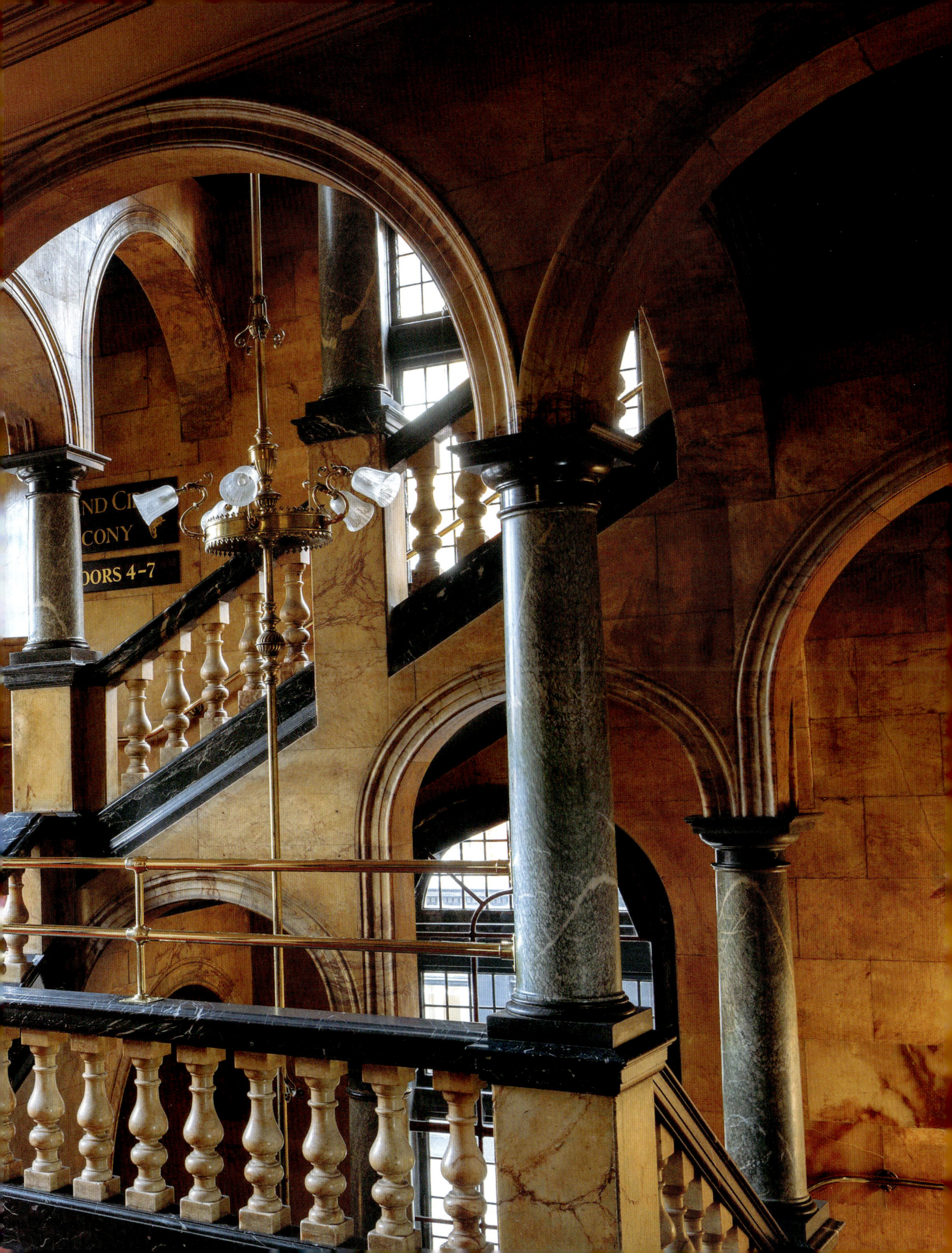

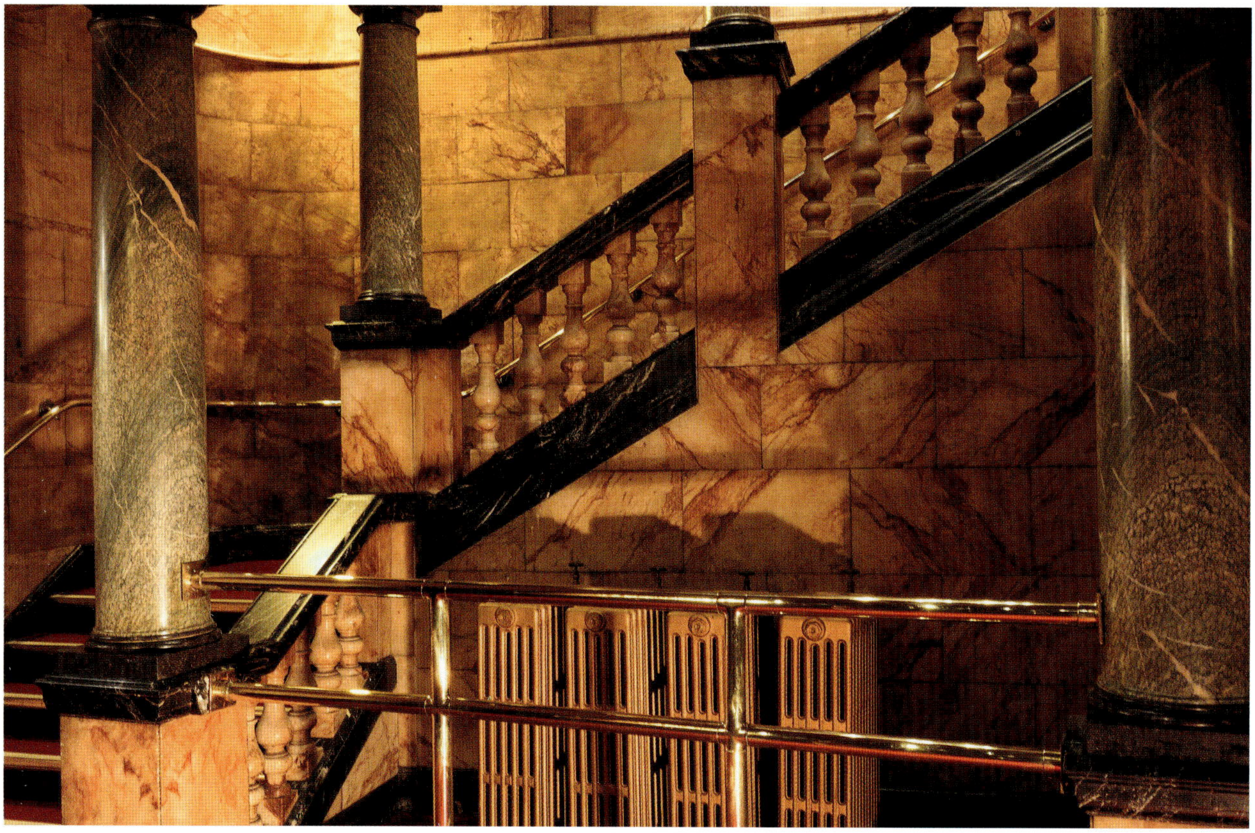

Edward VII and Queen Alexandra) and the Duke and Duchess of Edinburgh were in attendance, along with the cream of London society; every seat was taken, the streets outside filled with the many hundreds of people who been unable to get tickets to see what was widely expected to be Sullivan's masterpiece.

The first night audience, on 31 January 1891, were not disappointed. 'The work is one', wrote the critic Herman Klein, 'which rivets the attention of the spectator from the moment the curtain is raised; which is rich in melody and replete with musical interest and contrast; and which, finally, is presented with a perfection of executive detail such as English opera never enjoyed before.' There were two alternating casts with over two hundred performers onstage and 64 in the pit; 'every imaginable effect of scenic splendour' was supplied, said Klein, and each performance was sold out. *Ivanhoe* ran for six months, during which time it was given over 150 times – 'far and away', said Klein, 'the longest unbroken run ever accomplished by a serious opera'. The glorious future of English Grand Opera seemed guaranteed, but, alas, after the monumental effort of getting the new building open and the opera written, Carte seems to have been unable to persuade any other British composer to write for him. After a summer break the theatre reopened with a French operetta, which alternated for a while with a revival of *Ivanhoe*, sparsely attended, which then staggered on alone until Carte was forced to close it. Vigorous, melodious, colourful and fatally lacking in depth, it is the musical equivalent of a Victorian historical painting. Astonishingly, this most astute of managers had neglected to commission anything with which to follow it and threw in the towel, leasing the theatre to Sarah Bernhardt, then on a two-year world tour; among other favourites,

ABOVE One of the staircases, showing the architectural details.

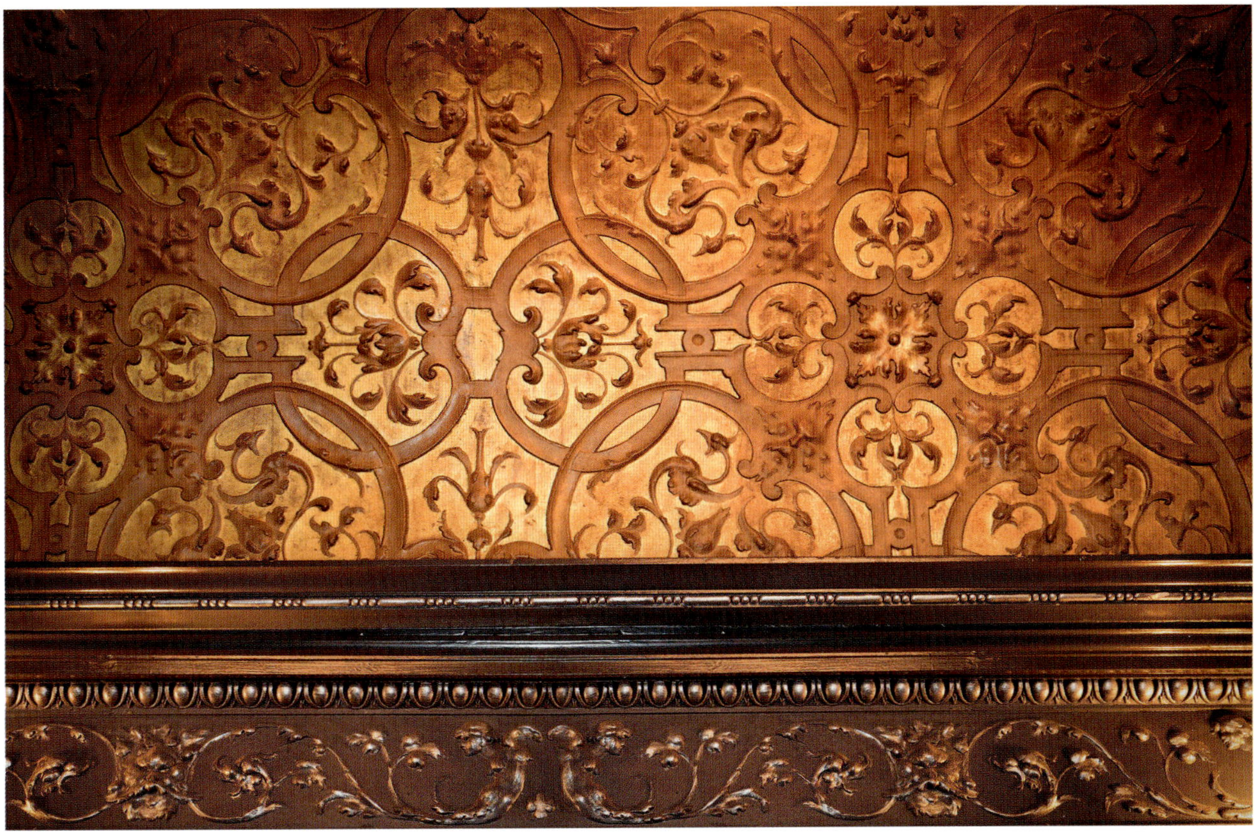

she gave Victorien Sardou's recent *Cléopâtre*. *Ivanhoe* led a twilight existence thereafter, rarely revived and then always unsatisfactorily. Carte withdrew, hurt, back to the Savoy. Shortly after, he sold the opera house of his dreams to Harry Newson- Smith's Music Hall Syndicate, which approached Charles Morton, the so-called 'Father of the Halls' – founder, with his brother-in-law, of the very first purpose-built music hall, the Canterbury, nearly half a century before, in 1852 – to take it over. Morton was 73 at the time and, after successfully making a go of the troubled Alhambra in Leicester Square, had finally retired; but the prospect of taking on a theatre as beautiful as the Palace was irresistible. It reopened, with modifications to the interior, under the new name of the Palace Theatre of Varieties, and it was suddenly a blazing success, as if that had been its destiny all along.

ABOVE Detail of a wall of the auditorium.

The champagne bar was crammed to the gunnels; if you bought a five-shilling Rover ticket, you could wander wherever you wanted, but not occupy a seat. The veteran theatre journalist W. J. MacQueen-Pope memorably evoked the atmosphere: 'Variety held the stage, but there was no trace of the roaring choruses, the noisy bonhomie of the ordinary music hall. Here white shirts and silk dresses filled the boxes, the stalls, and the dress circle. Here the carriages set down, and 'took up' at eleven. But although women, with their escorts of course, occupied many of the seats, it preserved a masculine atmosphere, as befitted a theatre of varieties. The air was blue with the smoke of good cigars. Champagne and whisky were the drinks in the bars – it even had a cigar bar at the back of the stalls, where good cigars were sold – for the Palace patrons knew a cigar and did not want inferior brands.' Morton retired, going happy to his grave soon after. He was succeeded by 26-year-old Alfred

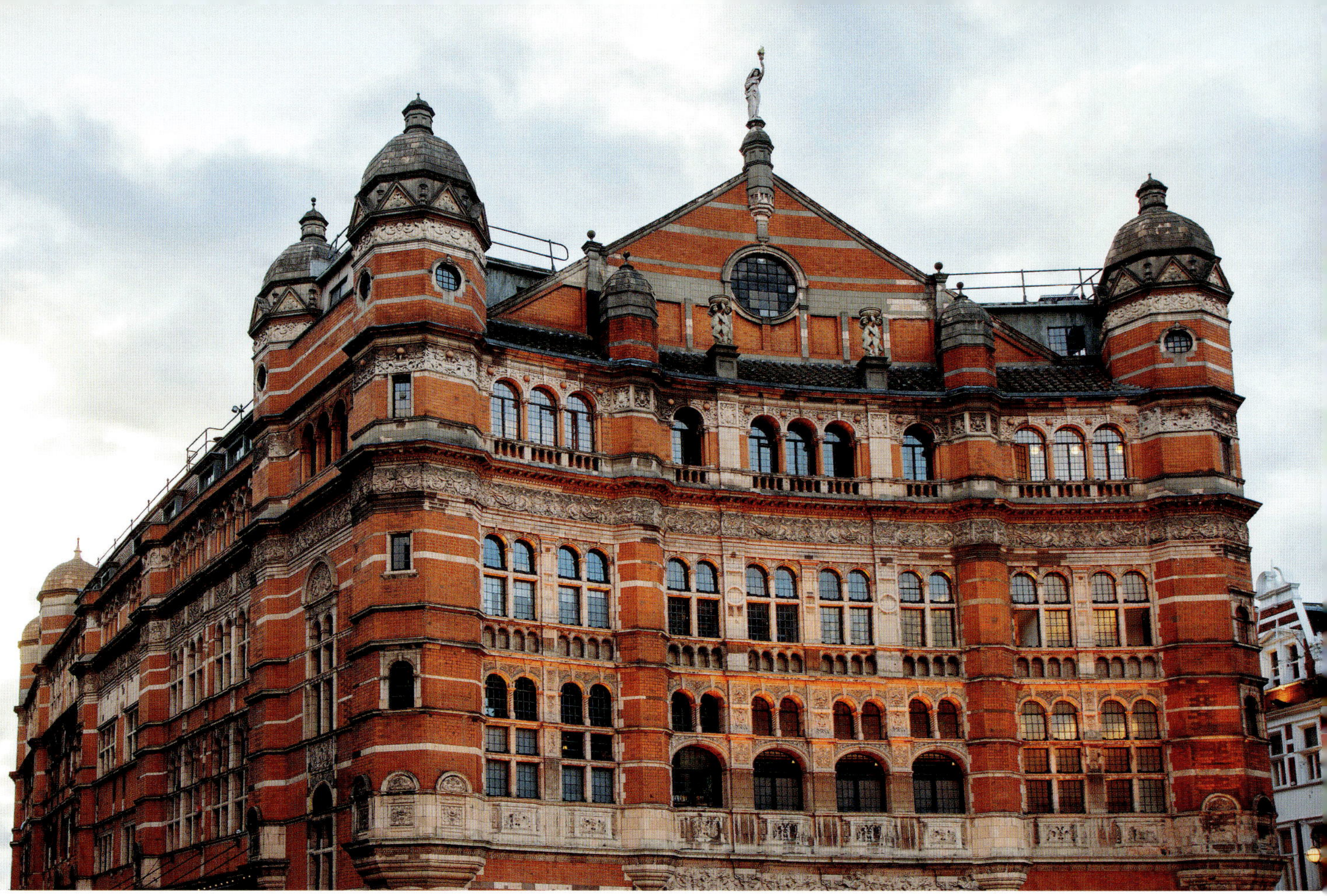

Butt, who ran the Palace Theatre of Varieties for fourteen dazzling years.

Variety certainly describes the theatre's fare in the early years of the twentieth century, from comedy to Maud Allan's *Vision of Salomé*, so risqué that she was taken to court; there was a specially written play by George Bernard Shaw, a solo recital by Hubert Beerbohm Tree, and the first appearance in London of the great Russian ballerina Anna Pavlova. The quality of the performers is justly, though rather forbiddingly, commemorated in a stone over the stage door: 'The greatest artists in the world have passed and will pass through these doors.' It seemed entirely fitting that the Palace Theatre (as it was now named) should be chosen, in 1912, as the venue for the first Royal Command Performance. 'The Cinderella of the Arts', said Sir Oswald Stoll, 'at last went to the ball.' Or rather, the King and Queen came to the Palace, bringing with them Grand Duchess George of Russia and Princess Victoria; the theatre was transformed into a bower of lovely blooms, all two thousand of Carte's electric light bulbs blazed at full strength and *le tout Londres* filled the place to the rafters. It was, in retrospect, Cinderella's final bow; the commencement of the First World War marked a climacteric for popular theatre: revue, a much more sophisticated form than the old variety bills offered, became the prevailing form, starting with *The Passing Show* in 1914 and continuing throughout the war with a succession of topical and modish entertainments.

For two years, reflecting the general crisis brought on by the arrival of the movies, the Palace showed films. In fact, film had been an integral part of shows there as early as 1904, but its life as a cinema was brief; by 1925, with *No, No, Nanette*, it firmly established

ABOVE The exterior. A completely free-standing theatre of red brick, with terracotta mouldings.

itself as a house for musicals, which, until recently, is what it remained. Here many of the greatest successes of the interwar years appeared, mostly Broadway hits – Cole Porter's *Gay Divorce* and *Anything Goes* and Rodgers and Hart's *On Your Toes*. After the war a mad concoction called *The Song of Norway*, based on Edvard Grieg's music, held sway for an improbably long run, followed by Ivor Novello's last and greatest success, *King's Rhapsody*; halfway through the run, Novello, playing the leading role, died, but the show completed a triumphant 839 performances. In between musical successes the stage door's proud boast continued to be fulfilled: distinguished foreign companies visited, among them Bertolt Brecht's Berliner Ensemble, whose season had a profound effect on the British theatre. Fittingly, John Osborne's 1957 play *The Entertainer*, widely felt to be influenced by Brecht, transferred there, with Laurence Olivier giving what many people felt was the performance of his life as the broken-down comic Archie Rice, bringing the Palace Theatre of Varieties full circle – though neither Morton nor Butt would ever have allowed a comic as seedy as Archie to disgrace its boards.

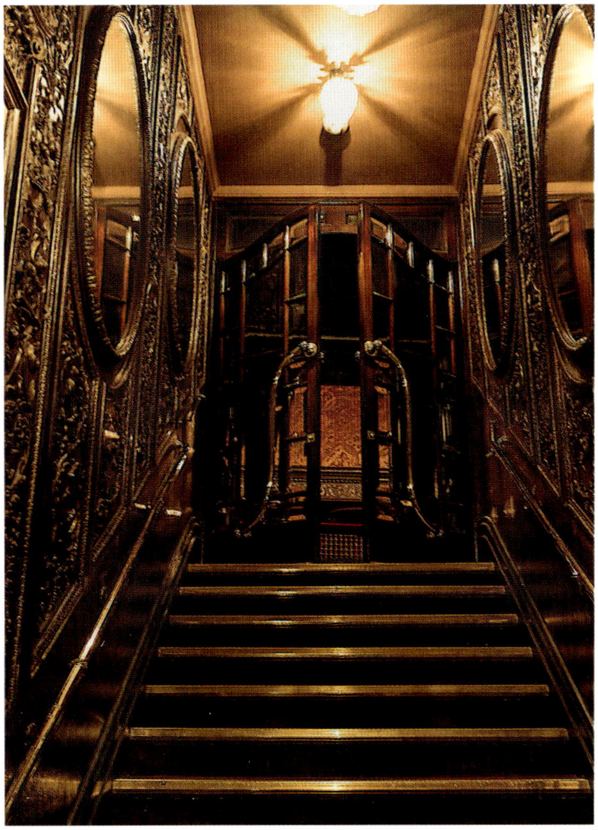

Sally Bowles would scarcely have made it to the top of bill at the old Palace, either, but when Judi Dench played her in Kander and Ebb's *Cabaret* she was unforgettably vulnerable, sassy and fearless. As was Danny La Rue – well, perhaps not notably vulnerable, but all the rest in spades. His act was of course quintessential music hall; drag had always been a part of its great tradition. There was a period during the late 1960s when the Palace seemed only to house flops, but that period came to an end with *Jesus Christ Superstar* (3,358 performances from 1972 to 1980), followed by *Song and Dance*, which played from 1982 to 1984. The composer of those shows then bought the theatre, which was a lucky thing, because Andrew Lloyd Webber is a Victorianist with a special passion for the fabric of theatres. To start with, he restored Carte's great facade, which had been obliterated by a huge neon sign. *Les Misérables*, panned by most critics when it opened at the RSC, then took up residence and was acclaimed nightly, and twice on matinee days, for nearly twenty years. In time for the opening of his own Victorian musical, *The Woman in White*, Lloyd Webber refurbished the auditorium, scraping off decades of accreted paint and wood – restoring it to its full late nineteenth-century splendour, very much in tune with the high melodrama of his show – and cladding the walls with original paintings from his fabled Pre-Raphaelite collection. Having returned this uniquely splendid theatre to a state in which Carte would have recognised it, he sold it on; presently it houses *Harry Potter and the Cursed Child*, a play that has brought a whole new generation into the theatre. It is hard to imagine a playhouse more likely to introduce them to the special delights of the Aladdin's cave that a theatre can be.

ABOVE Staircase leading to the auditorium.

DUKE OF YORK'S THEATRE

Narrow and drawing the eye intriguingly towards the epic vista of Trafalgar Square, St Martin's Lane is one of the most agreeable streets in the West End, a little off the beaten track, with alleys, now pedestrianised, running between it and Charing Cross Road; one of them is Cecil Court, London's last remaining street of bookshops. Giacomo Puccini, in London for the English premiere of *Tosca* in 1900, strolled down the Lane one evening and found himself standing in front of the Duke of York's Theatre, gazing at a poster for the current attraction, *Miss Hobbs* by Jerome K. Jerome (of *Three Men in a Boat* fame). There was a curtain-raiser: *Madame Butterfly: A Tragedy of Japan* by David Belasco. On an impulse, Puccini went in. Thus is musical history made.

The theatre was fairly new when Puccini visited it. Built in 1892 as the Trafalgar Square Theatre, it soon became the Trafalgar and then, in honour of the future George V, the Duke of York's. It was built by an actor-managerial husband-and-wife team, Frank Wyatt and Violet Melnotte. He was the more famous – having created the role of the Duke of Plaza-Toro in Gilbert and Sullivan's *The Gondoliers* – but she seems to have been the business brains; she kept control of the theatre until her death in 1935, by which time Wyatt had long gone to the great green room in the sky. The architect they commissioned was the slightly controversial Walter Emden, who despite having been born into the theatre – his father was the lessee of the Olympic Theatre – and having, at the age of 23, designed the first West End Globe theatre in Newcastle Street, was never accorded the respect given to his apprentice, W.G.R. Sprague (who, as it happens, built the second Globe, now the Gielgud). Emden was prolific, having by the time he designed the former Trafalgar Square Theatre already built the Tivoli Theatre of Varieties on the Strand (now reckoned to be his masterpiece) and the Garrick on Charing Cross Road, which sits back to back with the Duke of York's. The latter was free-standing and had a number of unusual features, some of them intended to make it infallibly fireproof, with fire exits wherever they could be put. Anxiety about fire was not unreasonable: there were 137 recorded instances of major fires in theatres in nineteenth-century London, many leading to death and destruction. The dressing rooms were in a separate block; access to the theatre itself was via fireproofed passages under a short, covered iron bridge. This uncommon arrangement, essentially practical, has with the passage of time and the addition of a lamp become picturesque.

The facade is plain and dignified, as is the auditorium, which has undergone an uncommon number of metamorphoses. When it first opened, *The Era* praised its decorations as 'chaste and refined'. In 1950, Cecil Beaton made it over, abandoning both chastity and refinement; by the 1960s, however, flamboyance had fallen out of favour and it was returned to something more restrained. In 1980 the purists turned the clock right back, restoring it with historical precision to the original scheme – with one exception: they removed the pillars in the

OPPOSITE Backstage. The ropes for controlling the backdrops could almost be on an old sailing ship.

OVERLEAF The auditorium, looking up to the shallow domed ceiling.

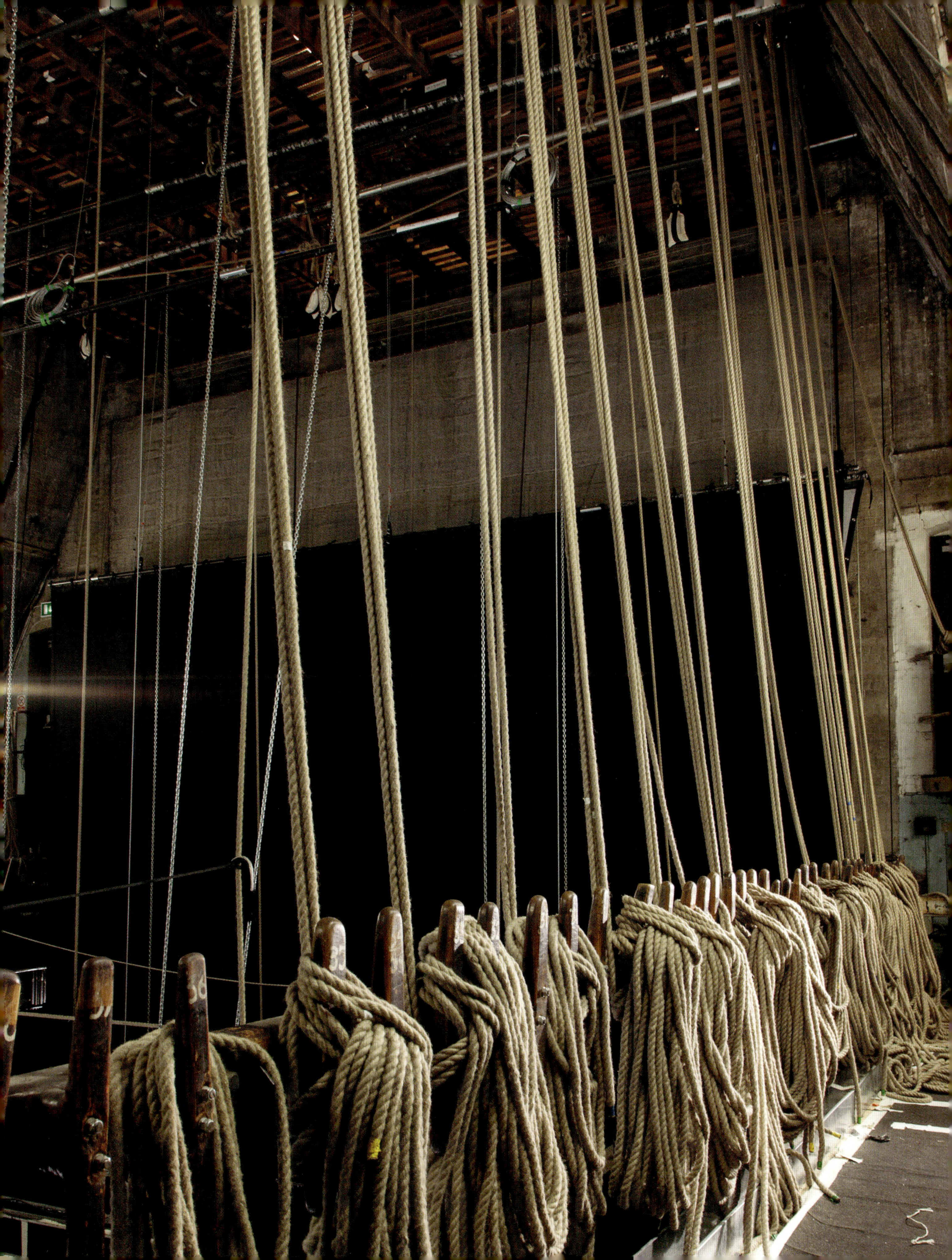

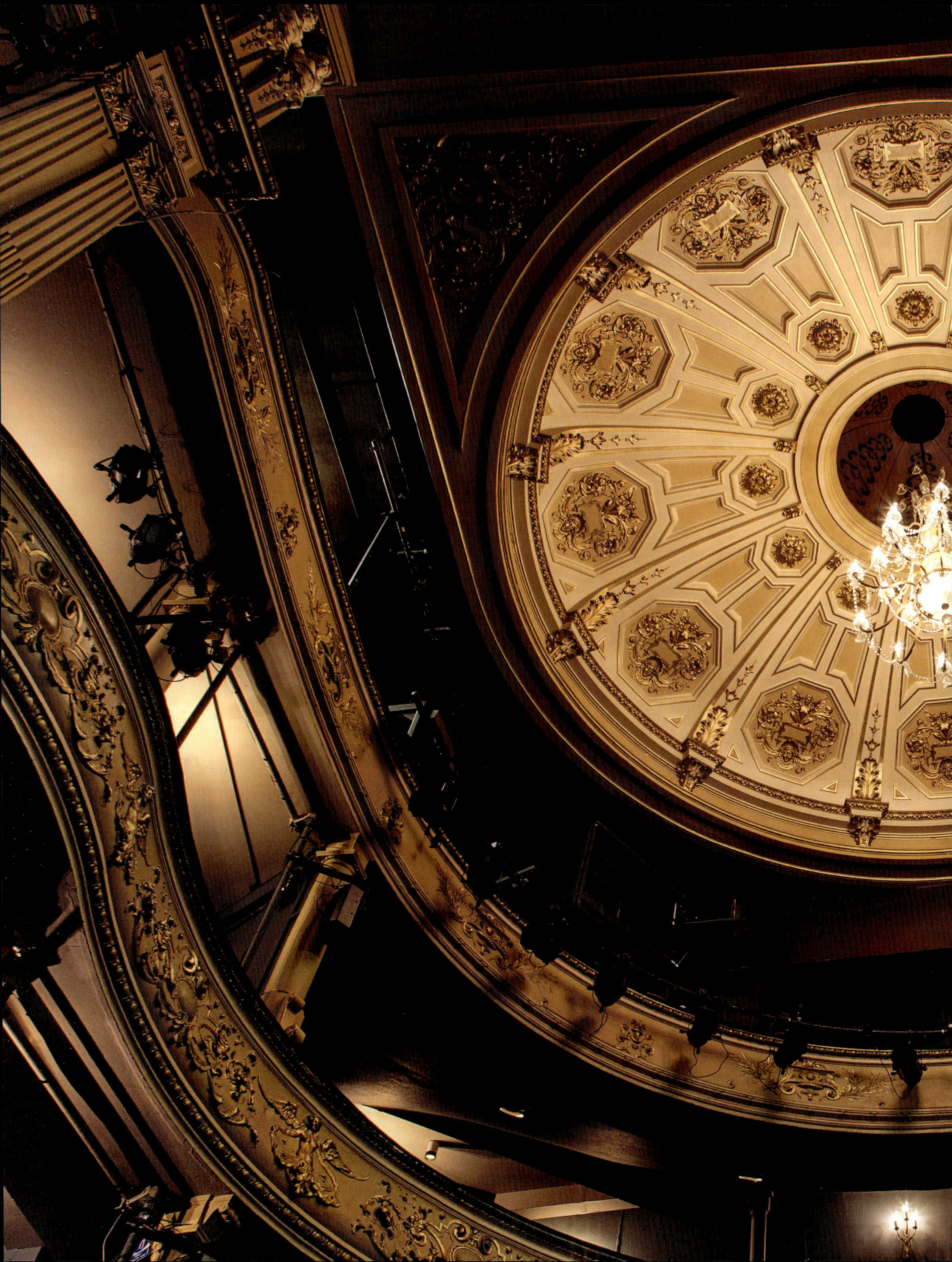

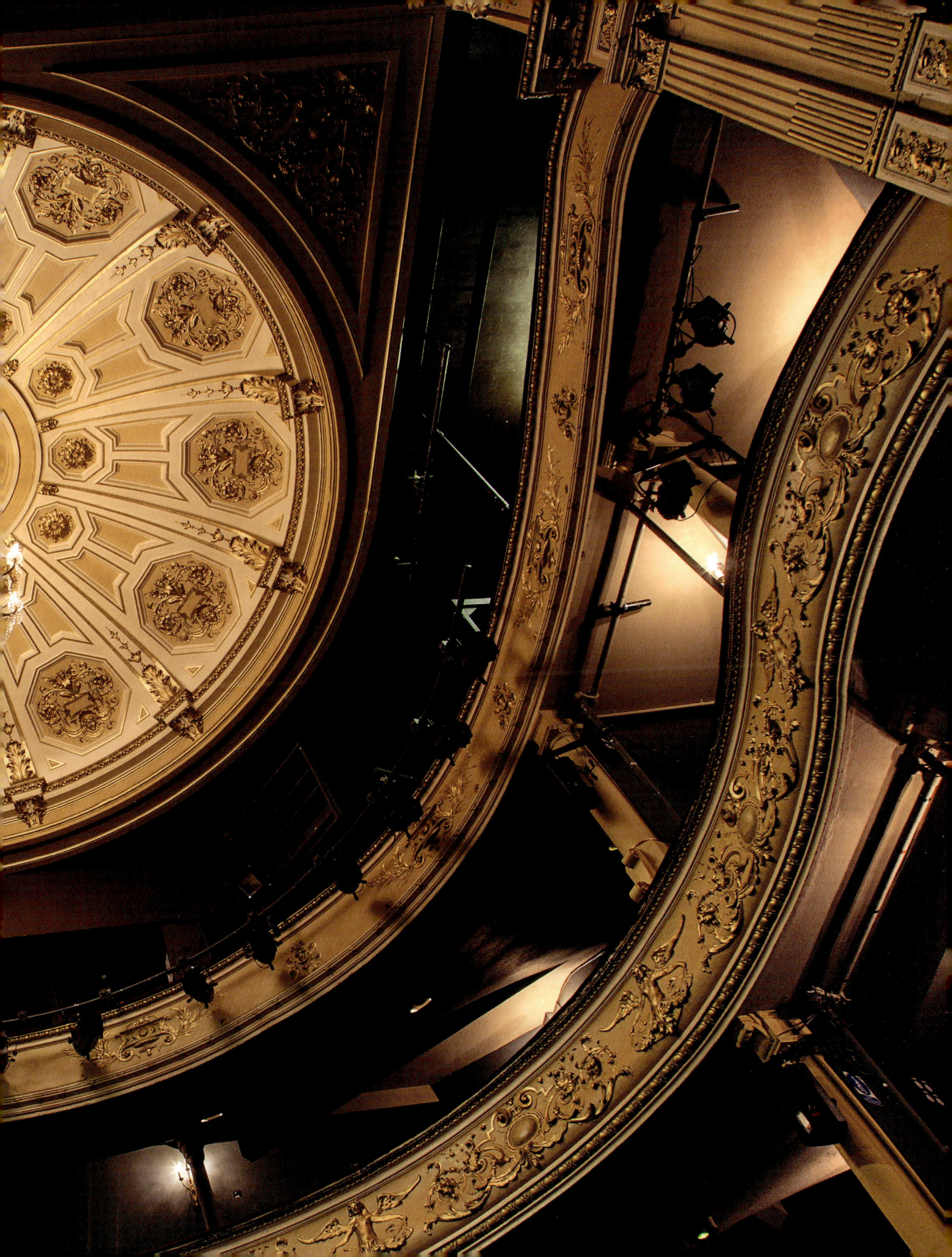

stalls, which had obstructed the view of a surprisingly large number of seats, instead securing the dress circle with a large beam; the new owners, Capital Radio, also blocked off the gallery and installed a sound studio in its place, thus turning what had been a fair-sized auditorium into an intimate one with a wonderfully direct relationship to its audience. The stage remains exactly as it was: small. How on earth, on 27 December 1904, the original director and designer of J. M. Barrie's *Peter Pan* managed to cram the Darlings' house, the Neverland, the pirate ship, and the crocodile-infested lagoon onto that little stage is a bafflement, to say nothing of the twenty or so named characters – Darlings, dogs, pirates, Lost Boys – plus sundry unnamed auxiliary 'redskins', pirates, mermaids, a pack of wolves and an ostrich. And then there was the flying. The director, Dion Boucicault Jr, who behaved in forgivably despotic fashion during the rehearsal period, somehow managed it all, and with such success that the show was repeated there every Christmas for ten years. Innumerable remarkable young actors figured among the Lost Boys in successive seasons, among them young Alfred Willmore (who in time became Micheál Mac Liammóir) and a thirteen-year-old Noël Coward. 'Coward was once Slightly in *Peter Pan*,' Kenneth Tynan famously remarked, 'and has been wholly in *Peter Pan* ever since.'

Nine months after the premiere of Barrie's play, an even more remarkably gifted youth sprang onto the little stage when sixteen-year-old Charles Chaplin, already noted as 'an impersonator, mimic and sand dancer', played the pageboy Billy the Buttons in the wildly successful play *Sherlock Holmes* opposite the celebrated American actor William Gillette, who had also adapted it. Chaplin had played Billy on tour with other Sherlocks, with some success, but appearing with Gillette was, he said, 'tidings from heaven'. He gave his Billy on one last tour, but this was the end of his career in the so-called legitimate theatre; soon Casey's Circus beckoned, which led to Fred Karno, America, and immortality. But Chaplin was not only a clown of genius, he was always an actor, too, and his few months on the Duke of York's stage opposite Gillette added a dimension to his work that was part of the extraordinary blend that made him unique.

Sherlock Holmes, *Peter Pan* and *Madame Butterfly* had all been produced under the management of the prodigious American showman Charles Frohman; his death on the *Lusitania* in 1915 was a serious blow for the British theatre. The Duke of York's remained an attractive venue, fielding a succession of ephemeral pleasures (ephemeral, but often long-running). Among these were two very different Noël Coward premieres. The first, in 1923, was the revue *London Calling!*, in which he was reunited with Gertrude Lawrence (they had earlier appeared together as child actors) and for which he wrote most of the songs, including the chilling 'Parisian Pierrot', the first of Coward's anatomisations of twentieth-century blues:

> Parisian Pierrot,
> Your spirit's at zero,
> Divinely forlorn,
> With exquisite scorn
> From sunset to dawn,
> The limbo is calling,
> Your star will be falling,
> As soon as the clock goes round.

Sobering stuff for the Bright Young Things sitting in the stalls. *Easy Virtue* followed in 1926; it was the 26-year-old Coward's sixteenth play, a moderately successful Wildean melodrama with jokes.

The Duke of York's was nothing if not varied in its fare: a season of Grand Guignol faux-horror plays in 1932 was succeeded by three years of Nancy Price's People's National Theatre. This noble enterprise was a sort of prototype of the National Theatre that was finally established in 1962 under Laurence Olivier; Price was a successful character actress who sold her yacht in order to bankroll the project. The last year of Price's tenure also saw the death of Violet Melnotte, who had maintained

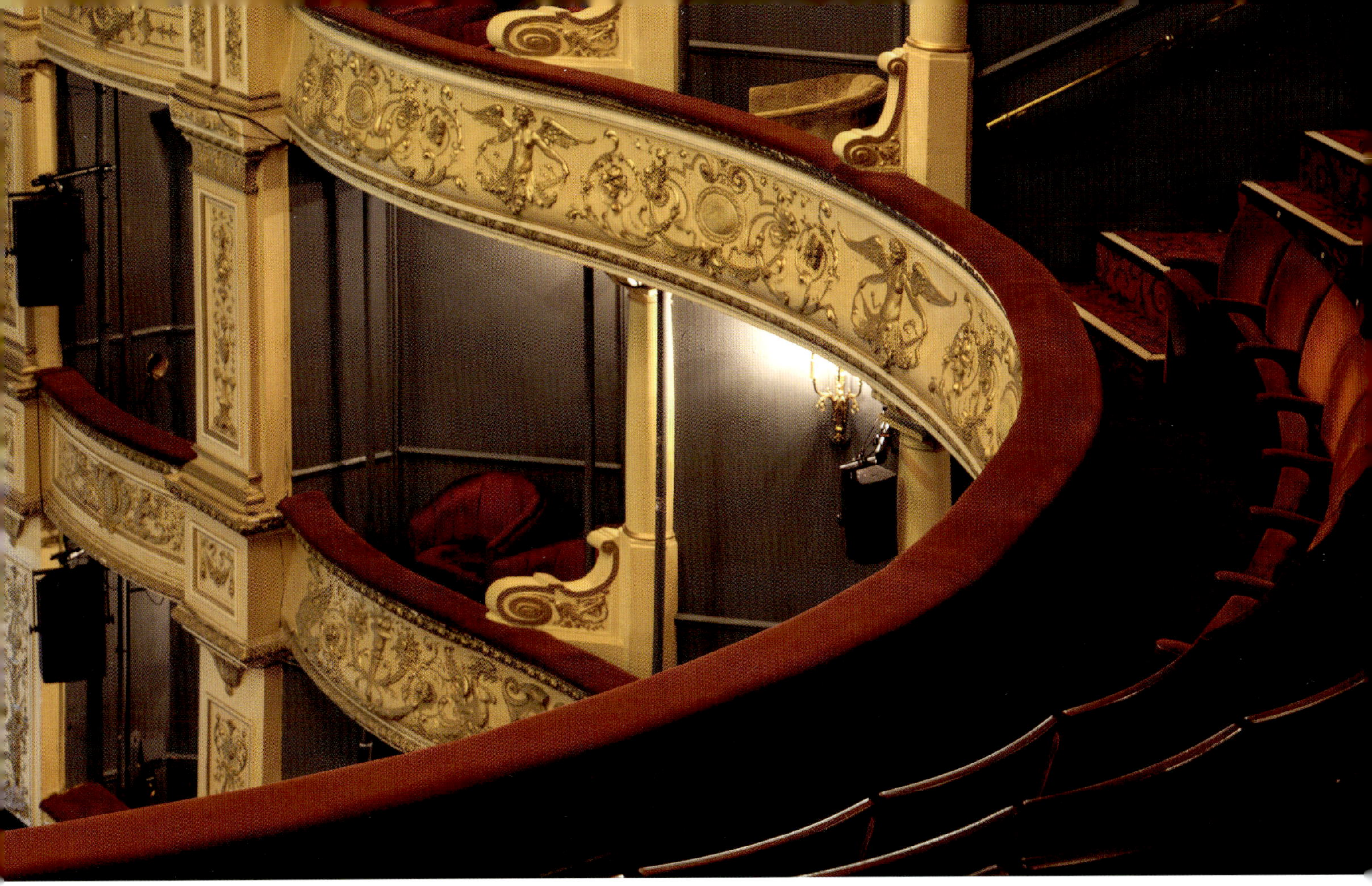

control of the theatre from its debut in 1892. It changed hands a number of times thereafter; bombs fell on it during the war, but it was soon enough back in business. It was especially suited to intimate revue, notably Binnie Hale's *One, Two, Three* (1947, with her brother Sonnie) and its sequel, *Four, Five, Six* (1948, with Bobby Howes). But one of the most startling manifestations ever to be seen in St Martin's Lane – positively epic in its impact, though in fact modest in means – was a production of *Moby-Dick* in 1955, brought to the stage by Orson Welles, deploying nothing more than a few ropes and a couple of rostrums to evoke Melville's heroic maritime universe. With a small company comprising, among others, Patrick McGoohan, Gordon Jackson, Peter Sallis and Kenneth Williams, plus Joan Plowright as Pip the cabin boy, Welles – playing a Victorian actor-manager playing Captain Ahab – summoned up whale, gale, vessel and ocean. Some good judges thought it was the best thing they had seen in any theatre, ever. It ran for three weeks to modest business, though this was very much better than the runs of the sadly unprophetic *All the Year Round* (three nights) and *Thirteen for Dinner* (one night, with the show abandoned halfway through).

Since then the theatre has hosted dazzling seasons from the Royal Court and many a glittering first night, but one stands out. Al Pacino's appearance in 1984, at the height of his film fame, in David Mamet's *American Buffalo* literally stopped the traffic in St Martin's Lane. Hundreds upon hundreds of fans poured out of the theatre for a glimpse of their hero face to face. This happened every night for the entire run – and every afternoon, too. How it would have gladdened Charles Frohman's Anglo-American heart.

ABOVE A corner of the auditorium from the first tier.

RICHMOND

There isn't an actor in England who doesn't love the Richmond Theatre. There is in the whole of the British Isles no more pleasant prospect on leaving a theatre than the vision of Richmond Green, swarming with cricketers, footballers, loafers, lovers, toddlers, mothers, fathers, all naturally congregating as if on the village common. The theatre is readily accessible from the metropolis and perfect in scale, in location, in relationship to the audience, in acoustics, in spacious bars and in comfortable seats. In some ways, it is everything that most West End theatres aren't. It should come as no surprise that it is the work of the master theatre builder himself, Frank Matcham, his most perfectly preserved auditorium. It is also perhaps no surprise that the Richmond Theatre is not the first playhouse to have been built on so ideal a site. Admittedly, the actor-manager who built the first theatre here in 1718, William Penkethman, late of the Theatre Royal Drury Lane (where he had a modest reputation as a low comedian specialising in donkey routines), was not inspired by the vision of ordinary people at rest and play: he had much bigger fish to fry. His 'handsome Theatre', he said, was 'for the Diversion of the Nobility and Quality who attend the Court of their Royal Highnesses the Prince and Princess'. It opened with a play called *The Busie-body.* 'There was a very great Appearance', the *St James's Gazette* reported, 'of Quality and Gentry.' Not enough of them to prevent the theatre from being rebuilt fifteen years later, evidently. But Mr Chapman, an actor, who undertook the rebuilding, had evidently misjudged it, because after six years it fell into decay and 'this temple of drama', recounted a melancholy chronicler of the Richmond theatrical scene, was put to use as a barn. Finally, it was demolished. It was another quarter of a century before Richmond Green had a theatre again, but when it did, it did so in some style.

This third Richmond Theatre was built by one Mr Sanderson of Drury Lane, and it opened in June 1765 under the management of an actor fetchingly known professionally as Mr Love (his real name was Mr Dance); it can hardly be a coincidence that the opening production was *Love in a Village*. He was a versatile fellow, James Love: as well as starring in the shows and directing and often writing them, he was the architect of the building itself; his brother was the distinguished architect George Dance, and he himself was Boswell's 'second best friend', according to the diarist. Love's purpose in Richmond was to show London theatres how it should be done: 'it has long been lamented', said his opening publicity, 'that the theatrical Entertainments there were as inelegant as the Company was respectable.' The new Richmond Theatre, built in red brick, was large and attractively furnished, the stage machinery was of the very latest and the scenery painted to the highest standards by craftsmen from the Theatre Royal Drury Lane. *Love in a Village* was not, it seems, burlesqued in any way. On the contrary, it was very seriously done, conducted, according to local reports, 'with so much Decency and Regularity, as seem to give a fair Earnest of the Endeavours of the present Company of Players to merit Encouragement'. The evening kicked off with a prologue written by

OPPOSITE The exterior. How self-confident it looks.
OVERLEAF The proscenium arch, ornate but harmonious.

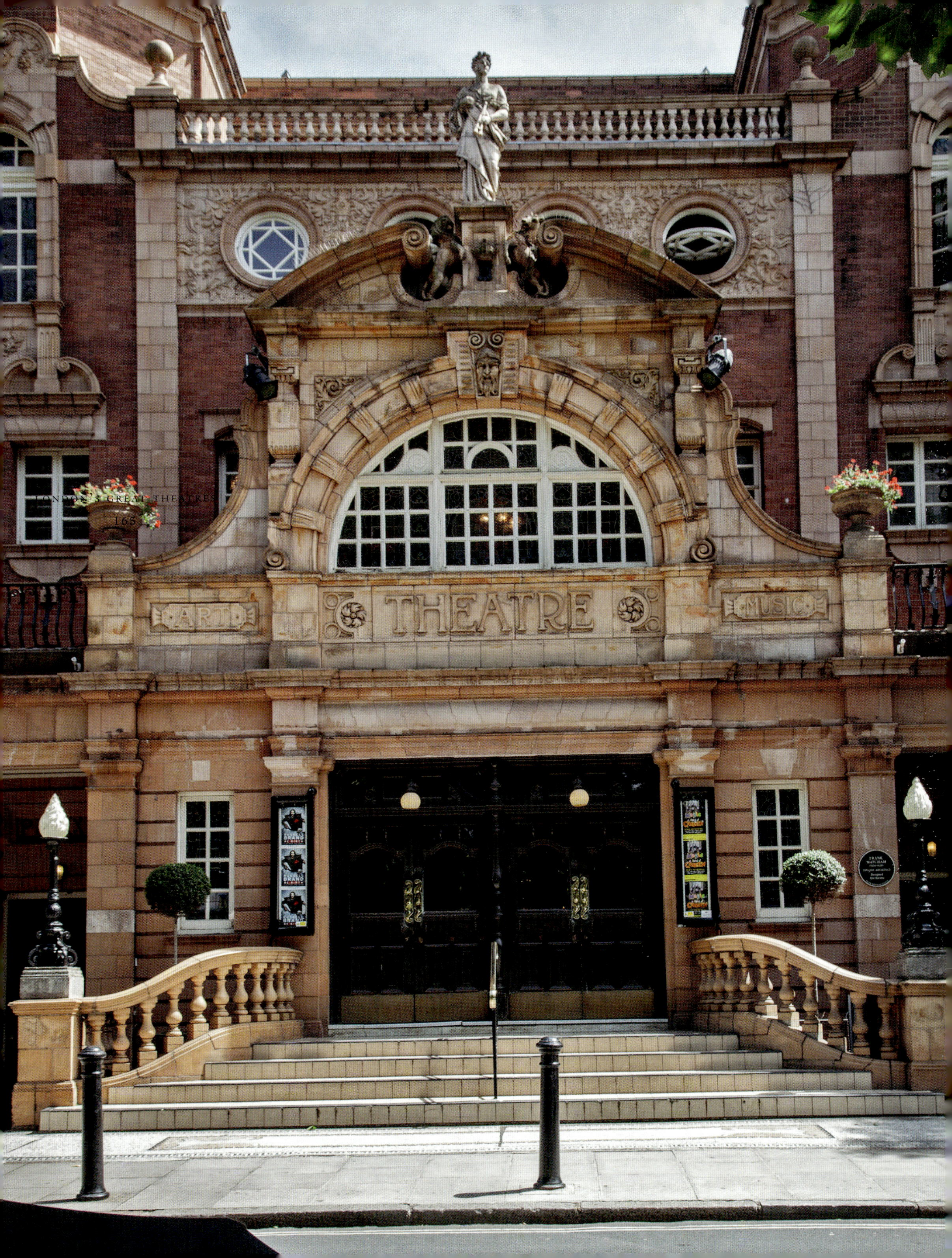
ART
THEATRE
MUSIC

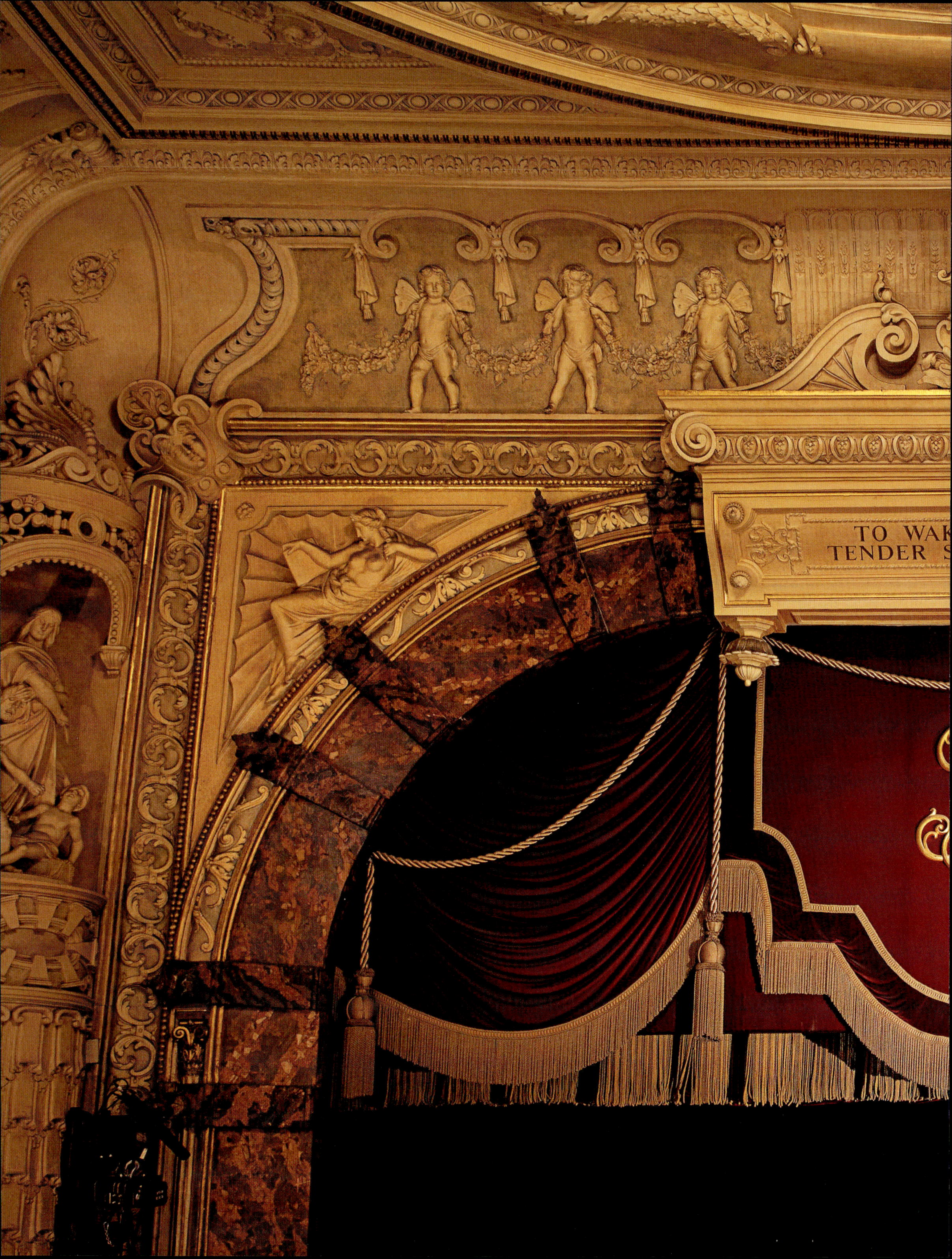
TO WAK
TENDER S

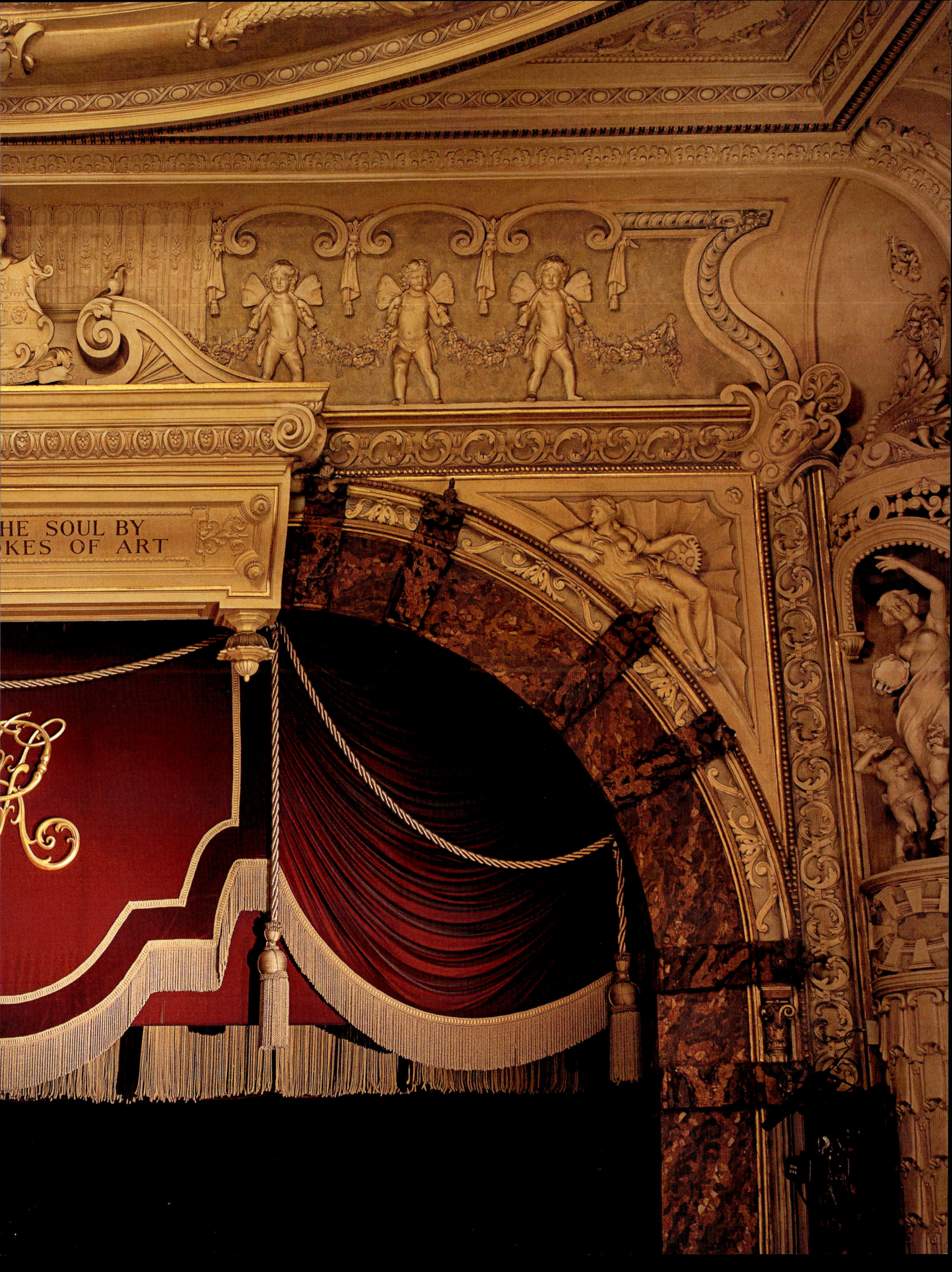
HE SOUL BY
OKES OF ART

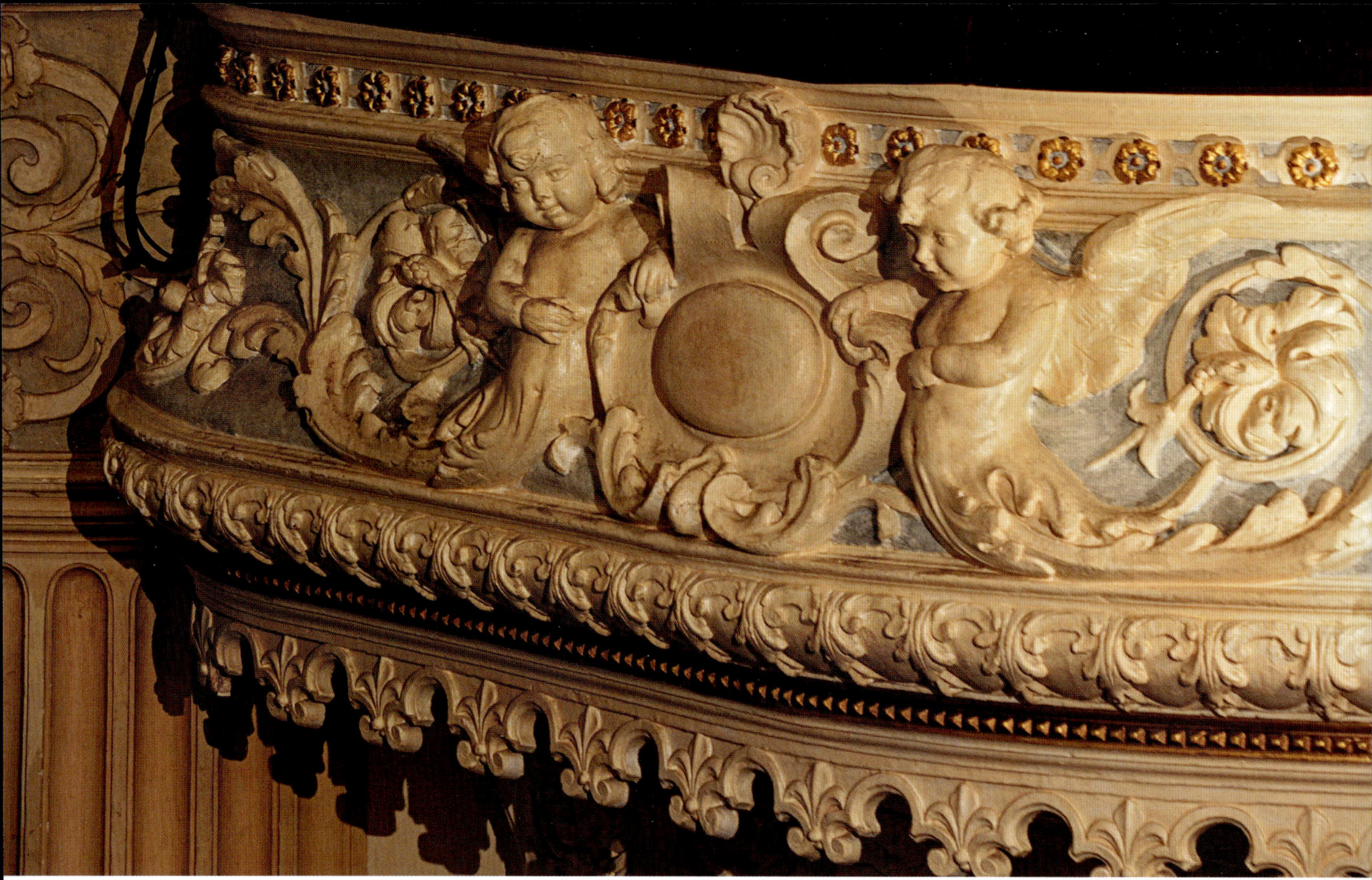

no less a superstar than David Garrick, so engagingly spoken by Love that it was repeated by popular demand the following evening before the second presentation, Sir John Vanbrugh's *The Provok'd Husband*. The season was a brilliant success and set the theatre on course for over a hundred years. The highest standards were maintained: it was kept immaculate, and the greatest actors of the age vied to appear there. At one point George III and his consort Queen Charlotte paid a state visit; thenceforth the playhouse was known as the Theatre Royal.

It passed from manager to manager until in 1831 Edmund Kean, the most dangerous actor of the age, took it on; he was only 44 years old but in visible and rapid decline. He lived in a little red-brick house next to the theatre; the actress Helen Faucit recalled an encounter with him outside it. He was, she said, 'a small pale man with a fur cap, and wrapped in a fur cloak. He looked to me as if come from the grave. A stray lock of very dark hair crossed his forehead, under which shone eyes which looked dark, and yet as bright as lamps. So large were they, so piercing, so absorbing, I could see no other feature.' The theatre was generally little more than a quarter full under his management; in 1833 he broke down during a performance of *Richard III*, his greatest role. Three days later he gave his Othello, and just ten days after that, playing the same part at the Covent Garden Theatre, with his son Charles playing Iago, he collapsed. In due course he was returned to the Richmond, where, six weeks later, he died in the manager's house. His funeral procession through the surrounding streets drew huge crowds; the cream of the theatrical profession came to pay tribute to the comet that had so suddenly been extinguished.

ABOVE Detail of a box in the balcony with cherubs. A typical example of the loving detail lavished on this theatre.

His son erected a statue outside the parish church (it is now inside) to the little genius, born of a brief encounter between a surgeon and a jobbing actress, who had so incongruously ended his turbulent existence in the genteel calm of Richmond.

The theatre had its troughs and peaks over the ensuing decades; eventually, by 1884, the building was beyond repair and it was torn down. It obviously held a place in local affections; Frederick Bingham somewhat histrionically lamented 'the evil day' in 1886 'when the angels of destruction descended on the doomed playhouse and removed it from off the earth, even using the very bricks and woodwork for enlarging some mineral water works in the town'. There was great interest across the country; the demolition seemed significant. Local photographers, Bingham reports, took snaps as the wrecking ball fell; some took wood from the stage and had it made into frames to put their photos in. There were other theatres in the vicinity, but none commanded the affection of the old Royal. The owner of one of them, F. C. Mouflet, who had converted a hotel into an Assembly Room where he presented plays, approached Frank Matcham to take the conversion further. Matcham dissuaded Mouflet, encouraging him instead to build a new theatre on the green, and lavished a great deal of affectionate imagination on the commission: it was his first important London theatre.

The theatre's facade in red brick and buff terracotta, with its twin towers, first-floor balconies and welcoming stone banisters stretching out to meet one on the pavement, might be described as possessing dignified exuberance – entirely fitting for a building whose proprietor named it Theatre Royal and Opera House. The opening show was *As You Like It*, performed by the Ben Greet Players, famous for their al fresco Shakespearean productions; perhaps they might have felt even more comfortable on the green itself, but the auditorium celebrates the Bard in fine style with a superb domed ceiling on which are depicted scenes from *Hamlet*, *A Midsummer Night's Dream*, *King Lear* and *Romeo and Juliet*. Above the proscenium arch is a motto from a local writer, Alexander Pope: 'To wake the soul by tender strokes of art', from his prologue to Joseph Addison's *Cato, a Tragedy* (1712):

> To raise the genius, and to mend the heart;
> To make mankind, in conscious virtue bold,
> Live o'er each scene, and be what they behold:
> For this the Tragic Muse first trod the stage,
> Commanding tears to stream thro' ev'ry age:
> Tyrants no more their savage nature kept,
> And foes to virtue wonder'd how they wept.

Oddly enough, despite these inspiringly lofty words, the Richmond Theatre is at its best in the more relaxed forms of dramatic art: comedy and, supremely, panto. The soul is left untroubled by these carnival sports, the strokes of art raucous rather than tender. An astonishing number of productions of every sort have traversed its stage, but Matcham, always interested in the happiness of his audiences, has created, in the lovely theatre he wrought on Richmond Green in the last year of the nineteenth century, a perfect venue – splendid but friendly, classy but popular – for the people to take their amusements.

APOLLO

The Apollo Theatre, which in many ways feels like the quintessential West End theatre, has a rather uncommon history in that it was built not by an impresario or an actor-manager but by a captain of industry, a rather sober one, at that. Henry Lowenfeld, Polish by birth, derived his fortune from his invention of a non-alcoholic beer called Kops. In fact, he was something of an inventor all round: the orchestra pit of his new theatre was personally designed by him, with a wooden sounding-board placed over the hollow oval floor space and on top of that a three-tier rostrum on glass legs. It was modelled, he said, on scant evidence, after Wagner's pit at the Bayreuth Festspielhaus. He also devised the innovative lighting rig, which hung limelights between the stalls and the dress circle box to avoid casting illusion-breaking shadows. As architect for his theatre he chose someone who had never designed one before, Lewen Sharp, who did a splendid job, with a generous facade in the French Renaissance manner, two pairs of shy Muses disporting themselves around the windows. There are twenty windows in all, lending a forthright quality to the expansive front piece, considerably wider and grander than its neighbour the Lyric, which preceded it by a couple of years. Shaftesbury Avenue had only been completed in 1884, wiping out great swathes of Dickensian slums; three theatres had already been built by 1901 when canny Lowenfeld snapped up the freehold on some land adjacent to the Lyric, making it a relative rarity among London theatres – the men who built the theatres rarely owned the land on which they stood.

The Apollo could justly claim to be the first London theatre to be built in the twentieth century, and – since Queen Victoria had just died – it was also the first Edwardian theatre, which it certainly feels like. Nothing Victorian about the Apollo; far too much fun. The auditorium, designed by the resplendently named Flemish artist Hubert van Hooydonk, is in Louis XIV style, originally white and gold with crimson panels (it has since become pinker and golder); sea gods paddle about in the shallow dome and fully realised human figures loaf about the walls. It is all very three dimensional; no doubt the fact that both the architect and the designer were new to theatre is responsible for them favouring reality over illusion. Between them – and presumably under the guidance of the ever-involved Lowenfeld – they also essayed a number of socially progressive innovations: the normally hard 'pit seats' at the back of the stalls, for example, were comfortably upholstered and could be tipped up to allow people to pass without difficulty. There were also dedicated foyers for each level, and promenade areas. Unexpectedly in a theatre named after the sun god, the auditorium's iconography makes no reference to him, or indeed to the Muses whose leader he was. This is because Lowenfeld had no idea what to call his theatre to begin with. Eventually he offered a prize of £100 plus a free box for the grand opening for the best suggestion, but none of the entries was sufficiently striking. For a brief while the working name was The Mascot, a curious one that can be explained by the presence in the dress circle of a motif that was derived, so the souvenir booklet proclaimed, from

OPPOSITE Two of the boxes – note the quality of the carvings and the gilding.

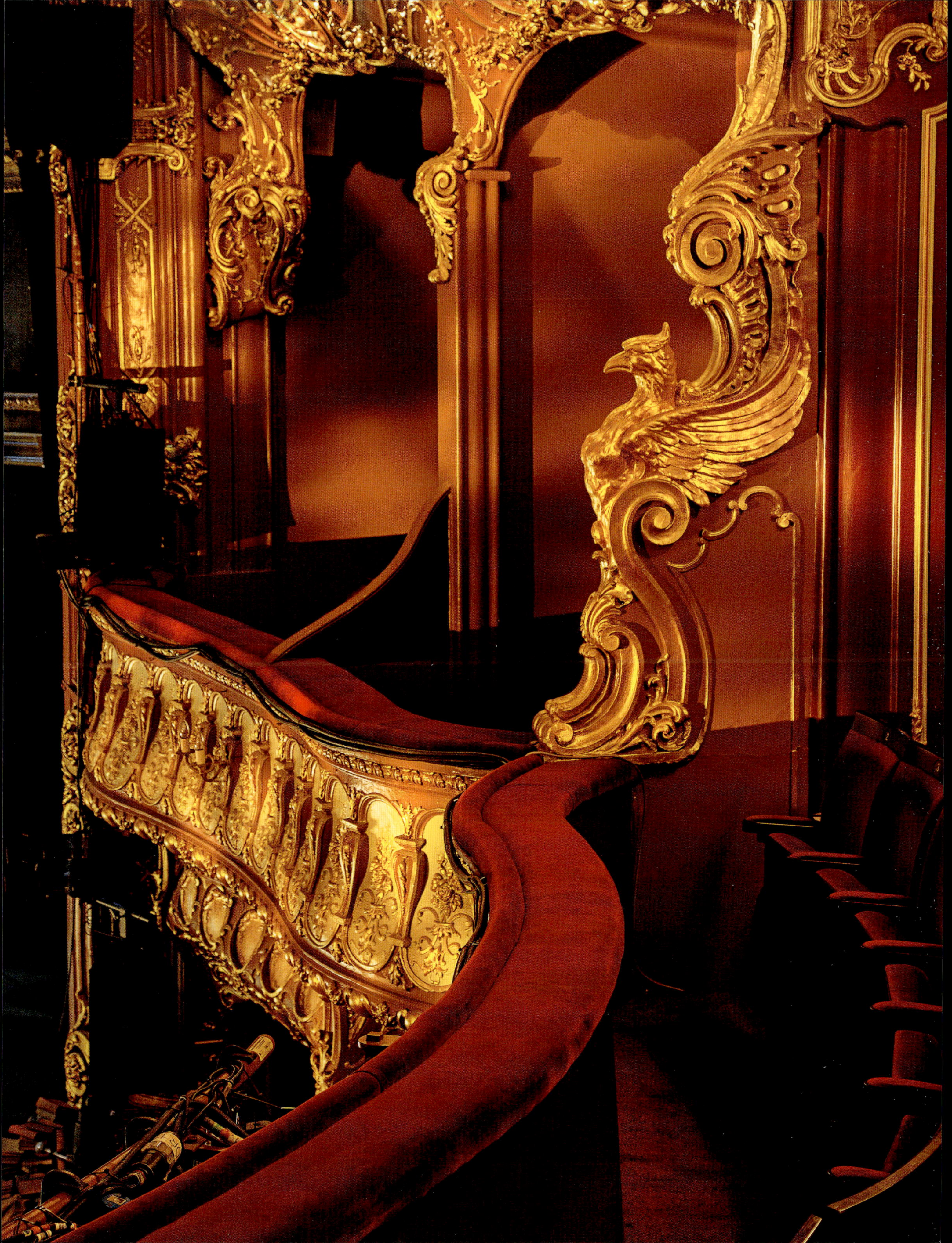

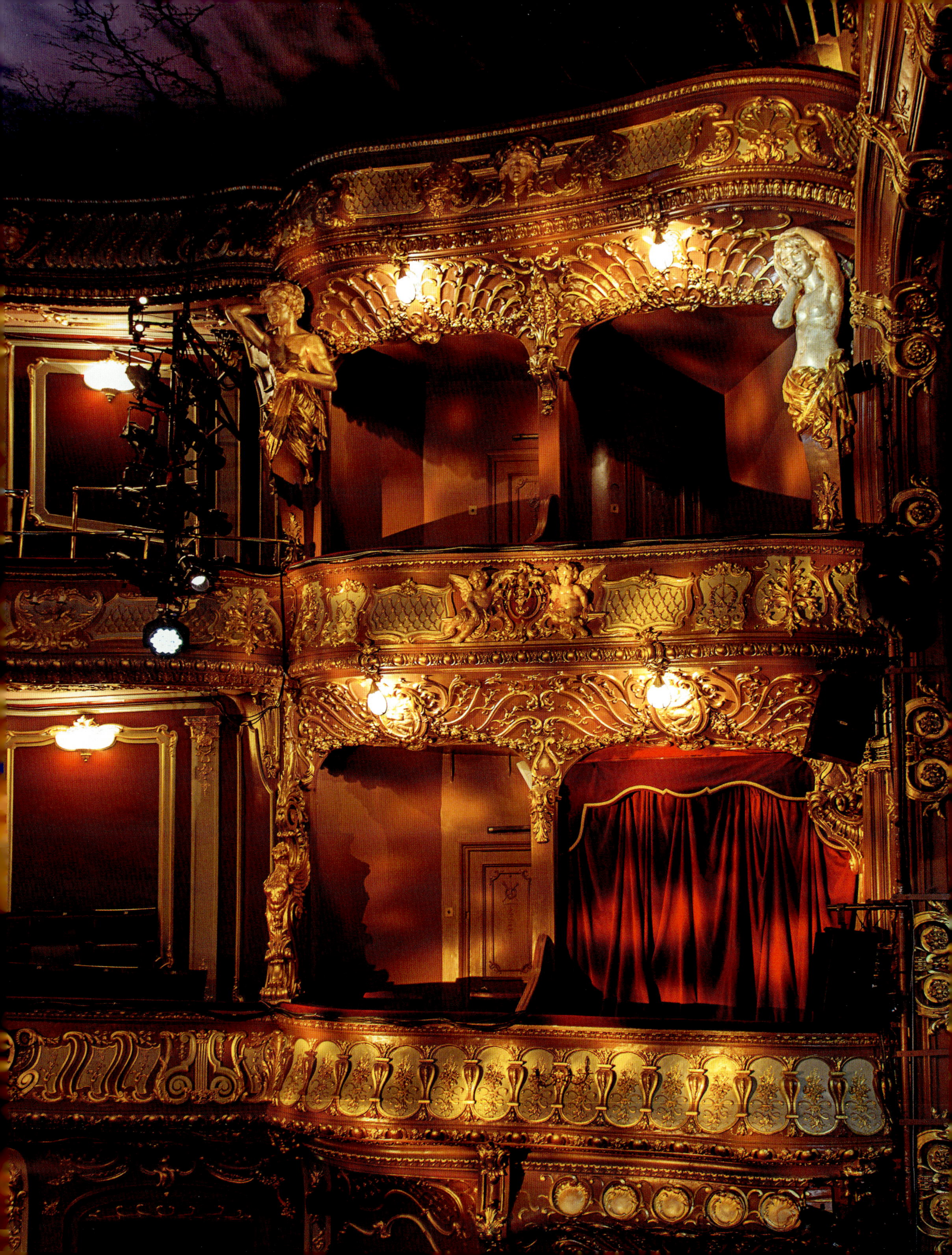

'the original badge of a German tribe of gypsies who are connected to the owner's family estate in Poland. It is a silver chain and buckle, on the buckle being a flying lizard supported dexter and sinister by lions rampant.' This design was carried into the new theatre's decorative scheme and appeared on the front of all its programmes: it was a good luck token, said Lowenfeld.

Alas, it didn't work. Lowenfeld alienated the press by having a grand opening for invited guests only, which the newspapers boycotted. Bad reviews for that first production, Harry B. Smith's musical comedy *Belle of Bohemia*, directed by the Broadway producer George Lederer, limited its run, and only a year after the opening the management of the theatre was taken over by the hard-headed impresario Tom B. Davis. He favoured more and better musical shows and operettas, which must have benefited from Lowenfeld's state-of-the-art orchestra pit. Later, H. G. Pelissier, 'that ever-to-be lamented genius of the grotesque', brought his wildly successful satirical Follies troupe to the Apollo; but he had overextended himself both physically and financially, having for many years written, directed and performed in the shows, and in 1913, amid madly extravagant scenic effects and a welter of debts, he suddenly succumbed to cirrhosis of the liver. He was 49.

Over the nearly 120 years of its existence the Apollo has seen the premieres of many plays that have since disappeared without trace, but also of great and enduring classics like Seán O'Casey's *The Silver Tassie* in 1929, starring Charles Laughton; Hugh Hastings's long-running wartime drama *Seagulls over Sorrento* (1950); and in 1962 the huge box-office triumph of Marc Camoletti's saucy comedy *Boeing-Boeing*. In 1959 it presented the last of the great revues, Peter Cook's *Pieces of Eight*, which starred Kenneth Williams and Fenella Fielding and also included a number of sketches written by Harold Pinter; and in 1960 there was Micheál Mac Liammóir's masterful one-man evocation of Oscar Wilde, *The Importance of Being Oscar*, which sat as perfectly in that exquisite auditorium as any play in its history. John Gielgud graced the Apollo three times, first with his miraculously judged performance in Alan Bennett's *Forty Years On*, in 1968, then a year later in *Home* by David Storey, which saw the beginning of his unforgettable double act with Ralph Richardson; it was also here, at the age of 83, that Gielgud ended his astonishing stage career by playing Sir Sidney Cockerell in Hugh Whitemore's *The Best of Friends*.

The Apollo's own career very nearly came to an end in 2013 when, during a performance of the hugely successful National Theatre transfer of *The Curious Incident of the Dog in the Night-Time*, the ceiling fell in: unusually heavy rain had built up pressure on Van Hooydonk's elaborate ceiling. Two people were trapped and 88 injured by the accompanying collapse of the lighting rig and part of the balcony; several were hospitalised, others treated for shock. It is little less than a miracle that the casualties were so relatively limited. The fourth level and the balcony were swiftly sealed off and a temporary floor installed while investigations continued; only four months later the theatre reopened, restored and reinforced, with an adaptation of the Swedish vampire novel *Let the Right One In*. The show had, as tradition demands, gone on. Or at least the theatre had. There was much debate about the viability of 'these old buildings'; a couple of years later, there was a scare about the Palace, itself just a little older than the Apollo. Ever greater vigilance is now the order of the day, although the rarity of such incidents is a tribute to the remarkable soundness and durability of these highly risk-prone buildings, certainly by comparison with their predecessors, which burned down on a regular basis. The Apollo continues to offer an experience of theatregoing that is deeply gratifying and unique: sumptuous, welcoming, highly theatrical – a remarkable achievement for a collaboration between a brewer of non-alcoholic beer, a man who had never designed a theatre before (and never did again) and a fashionable decorative artist.

OPPOSITE View of the auditorium showing four of the boxes – examples of skilled gilding and carving, and inventiveness of the design (slightly Art Nouveau). Opulence without vulgarity.

HACKNEY EMPIRE

Hackney, seemingly remote from the West End, is perhaps an odd place, on the face of things, to build a grand theatre. As it happens, the Hackney Empire was part of an almost continuous spread of large variety houses – pleasure domes, as they were habitually labelled – from the centre of town through to the outer suburbs. The Empire was not the only such theatre in the borough of Hackney: the magnificent Alexandra Opera House in Stoke Newington was already extant by the time the Empire was built in 1901, the work of the same man, Frank Matcham, the greatest of all British theatre architects. The Empire was planned on an even grander scale than the Alex. Its proprietor, Oswald Stoll, who, at first in partnership with Edward Moss, then independently, had been creating an enormous chain of variety theatres across the country, intended the Hackney Empire to be his flagship; its site, next to the Town Hall, was carefully chosen to reflect its status. Matcham, who had already collaborated with Stoll on the Nottingham Empire Palace, set to work with his habitual enthusiasm and flair, sparing no cost; the theatre was to be on the largest scale and, as befitted the headquarters of a large organisation, there were to be offices and a massive boardroom. In the event, the mercurial Stoll decided he needed an even grander and more centrally situated flagship, so the designs for Hackney Empire were at the last minute reduced in scale: backstage facilities (always the first to go) were trimmed back, the facade was condensed to half the size of the original design, and in a defiant flourish it was topped with a statue of Euterpe, Muse of music, bringer of delight; finally, shops and flats were added at the side of the building.

Despite all this trimming, there were no complaints at the opening of the theatre about any lack of splendour. The rose-tinted facade – which later caused Iain Sinclair, alluding to the famous John William Burgon poem about Petra, to dub Hackney the 'Rose-Red Empire' – has a faintly Indian quality about it, subtly and prettily suggested by sinuously curling motifs over and underneath the windows and under each of the towers. It is imperial, but unshowily so, an allusion to Empire rather than an assertion of it. The showiness began almost immediately you crossed the threshold. Entering by a grand vestibule, you proceeded up the sweeping staircase and on into the fabulously extravagant auditorium in Flemish Renaissance style, adorned with panels containing paintings representing Eloquence, Grace, Tragedy, Comedy and Music. Though the seating capacity was a relatively modest 1,500, the auditorium interior measured 76 feet from the curtain to the back of the stalls, the width at the back of the pit being 80 feet; there were three balconies with boxes at the back of the dress circle and on the sides of the house. All this, not for a grand opera house but for a variety establishment. It represented a further victory in Stoll's campaign to turn the bawdy, profane, unruly music hall into a place of edification and uplift for All The Family; no alcohol was served on the premises (to begin with, at any rate), a decision that drew a clear line

OPPOSITE Detail of the auditorium. Note the original and curious little dome – it serves no particular purpose, but adds to the exotic quality of this theatre.

OVERLEAF The auditorium, side view showing the Flemish Renaissance style of the interior.

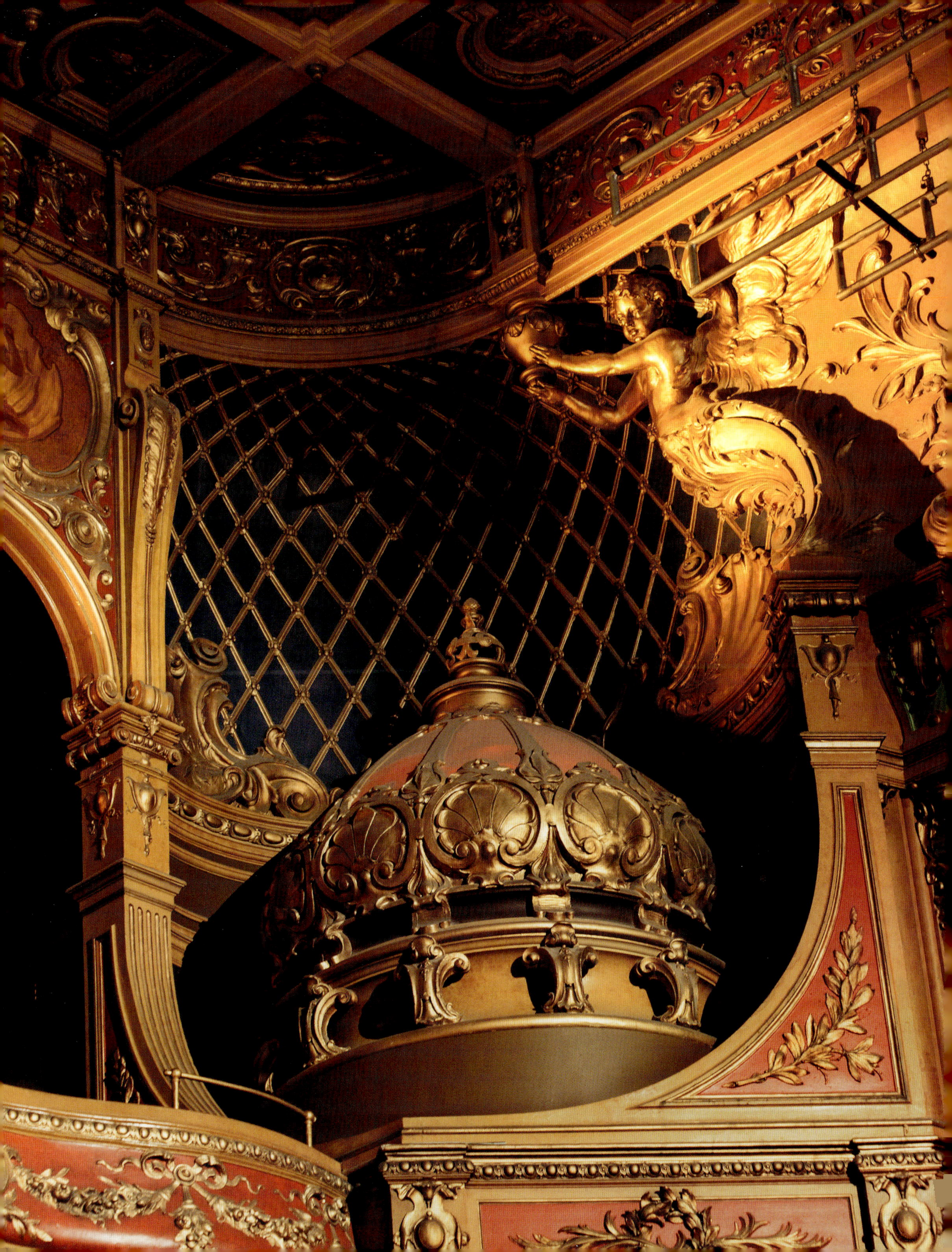

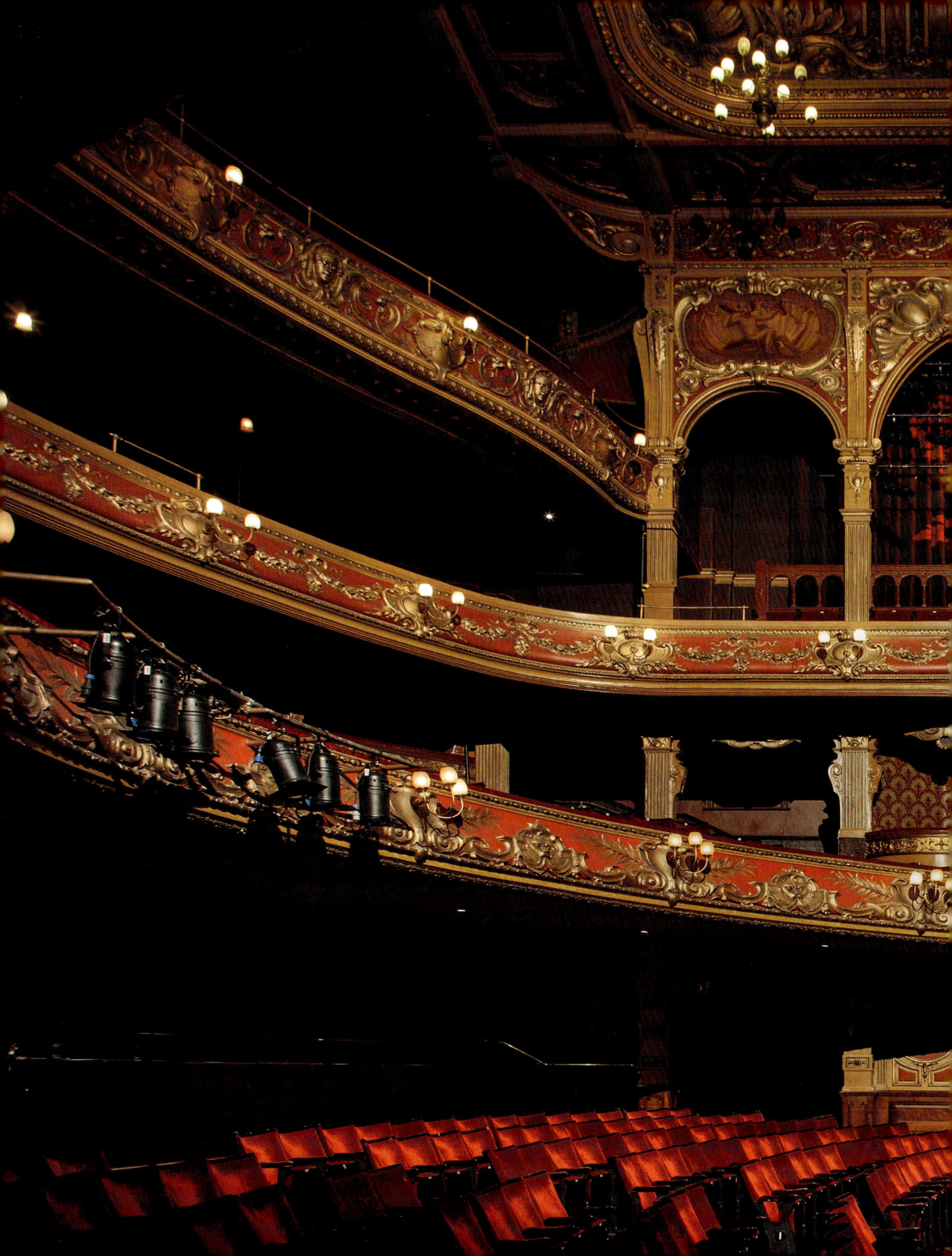

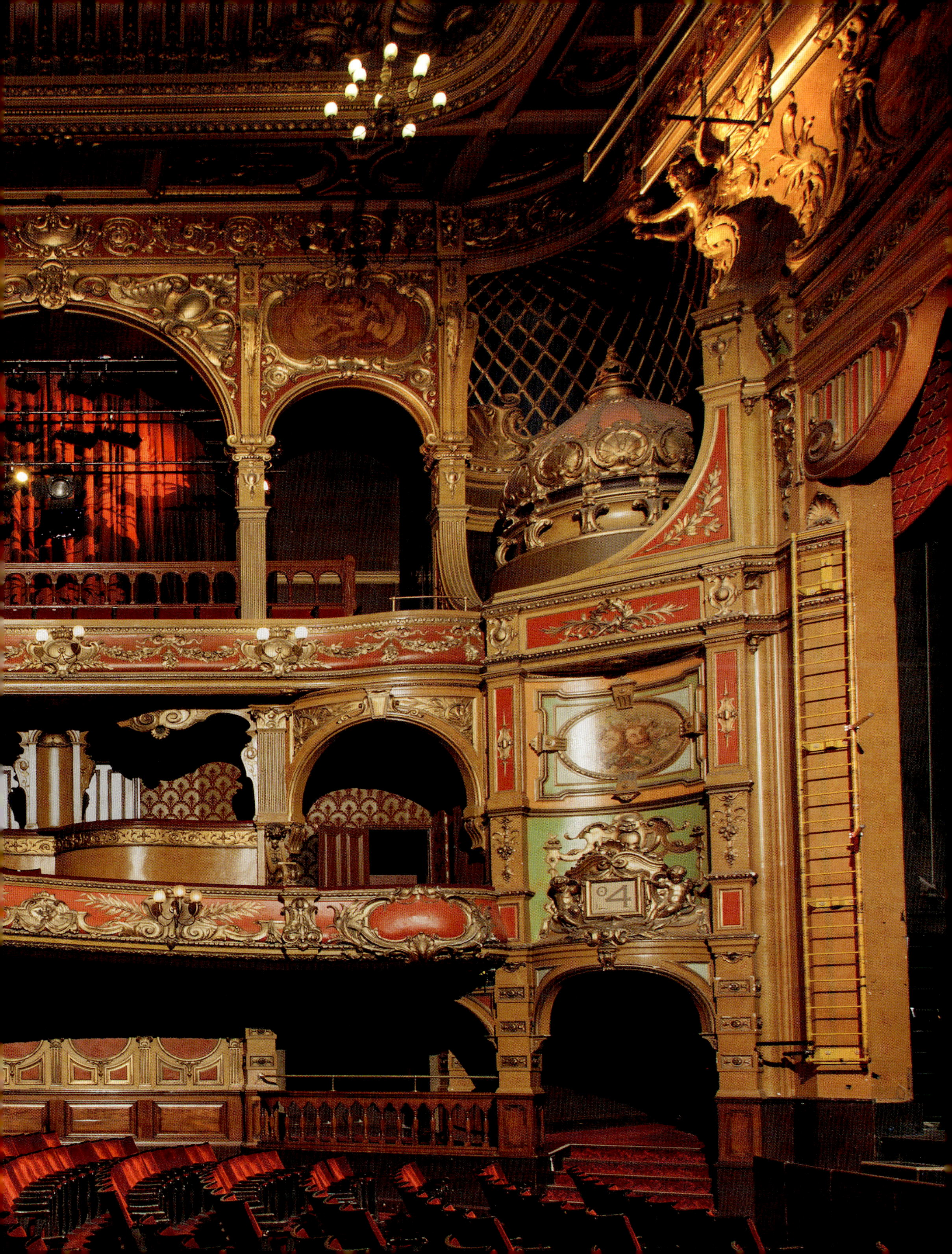

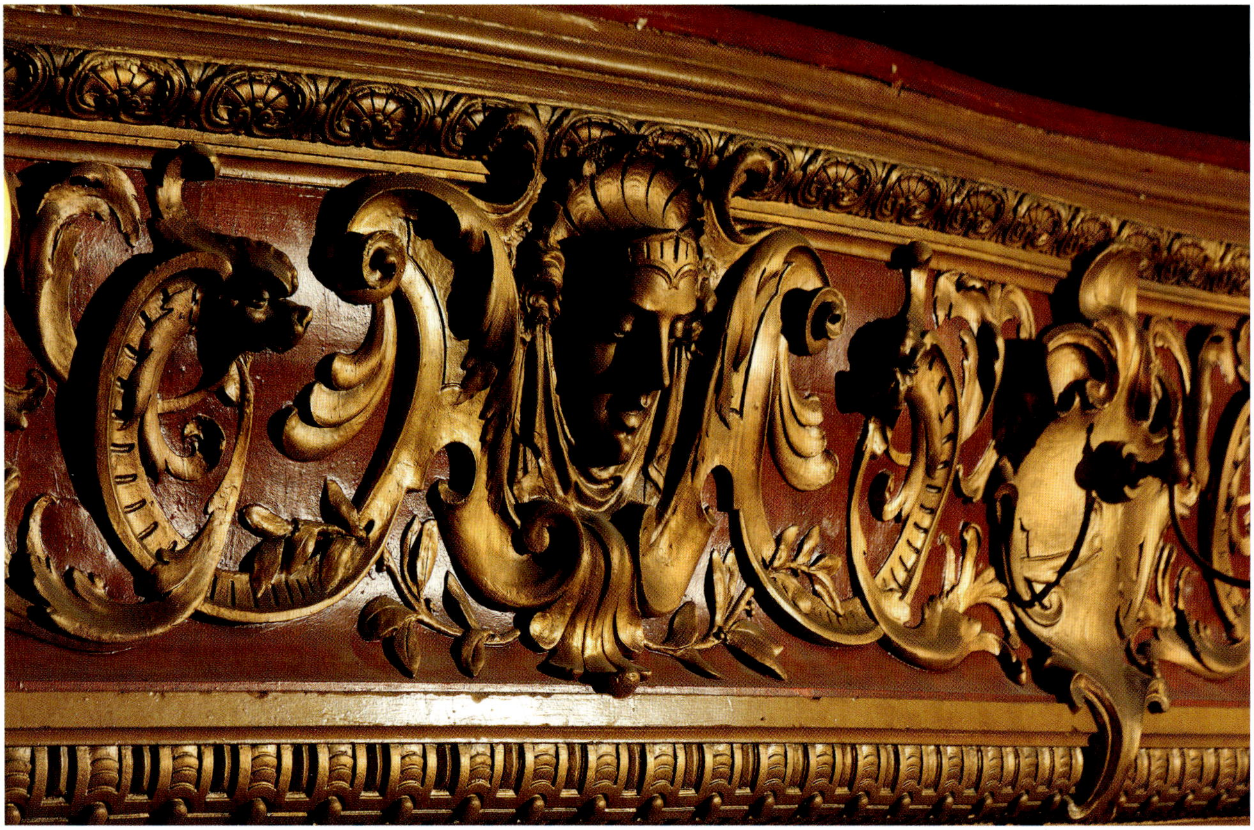

under the bad old traditions of the disreputable past. In their place was the intoxicating pleasure of the building itself. It was what might be described as an immersive experience: the theatre as an event in itself, not a mere prelude to something else. Before a note has been heard or a word spoken, the eye is drawn all over the auditorium, which with its allegorical figures and its allusions to earlier historical epochs and styles tells an intriguing story, one intended to be both pleasing and instructive. This improving approach would result in great wealth – and a knighthood – for Stoll, though by the time he died he had witnessed the simultaneous decline of his Empire theatres and the British Empire after which they were named, both empires coming to their full glory just as the game was up, crumbling and disappearing with astonishing rapidity.

Frank Matcham, the empire's architect, may have had a sense of this. His glorious career – in the course of which he designed some eighty completed theatres and a dozen others that weren't (to say nothing of his modifications of other architects' designs) – came to an end in 1911 for no evident external reason. He seems to have understood that the great expansion of theatre building, in which he was such a prime mover, had peaked. While he was working, however, he was the unquestioned king of theatre architecture. Stoll might have been 'the Napoleon of the music hall', as he was dubbed, but Matcham was its Leonardo. 'Matchless Matcham' and 'Magnificent Matcham', he was called. As early as 1891, at the opening of his Cheltenham Opera House (later the Everyman Theatre), the great celebrity Lily Langtry said in her prologue to the first performance,

ABOVE Detail of the balcony.

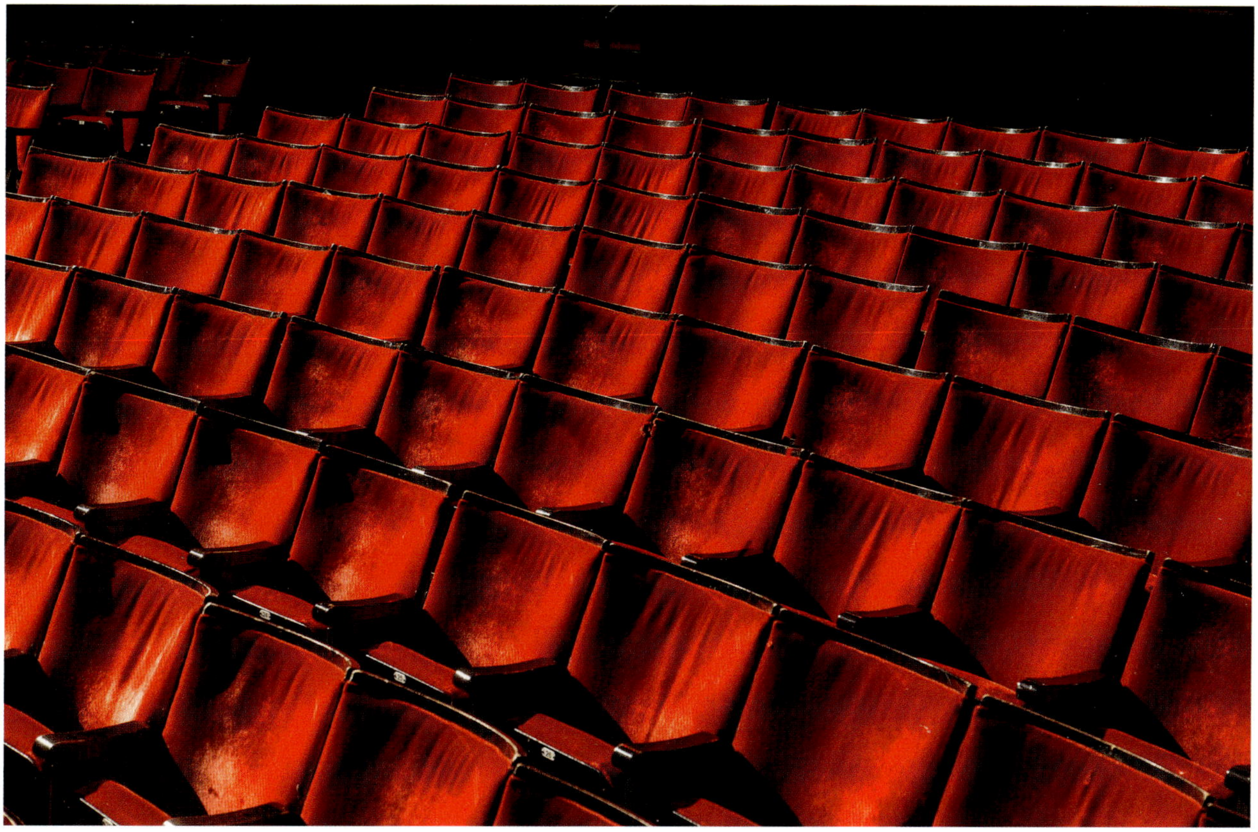

Nay, where (within this house you'll all agree)
Not only all can sit, but all can see –
The Architect's arrangements, if you'll *watch 'em*
(Like these two rhymes), 'tis hard to *Match 'em*

Allied to his extraordinary instinctive grasp of acoustics and sightlines, his application of the latest engineering principles (notably cantilevering) and his sense of fantasy – his theatres manage to be simultaneously grand and playful – was his consideration of the audience's comfort and safety, which transformed the experience of theatregoing: Matcham pioneered ventilation and was rigorous in his elimination of the risk of fire.

There may be a clue to his innate understanding of what made a theatre work in his own passionate devotion to amateur dramatics. He acted in plays, but also adapted, designed and directed them, notably a version of Dickens's *The Cricket on the Hearth*, bringing them to a high level of finish. It is also perhaps noteworthy that he was brought up in the seaside resort of Torquay, on the southwest coast of England; some of its holiday hedonism seems to have rubbed off on him. Certainly his theatres, without exception, celebrate pleasure rather than any more austere virtues. His personal appearance as portrayed in contemporary drawings and cartoons – shiny top hat, smart waistcoat, morning coat and elegant trousers, splendidly moustached and with neatly trimmed beard – suggests that he greatly enjoyed being himself. His practice was large, including at one time or another many of the next generation of theatre architects; in collaboration with his team he often worked on several theatres at a time, sometimes being spotted hurtling in high spirits, Mr Toad-like, in his spiffing Daimler-Benz

ABOVE The stalls seating – as red as could be!

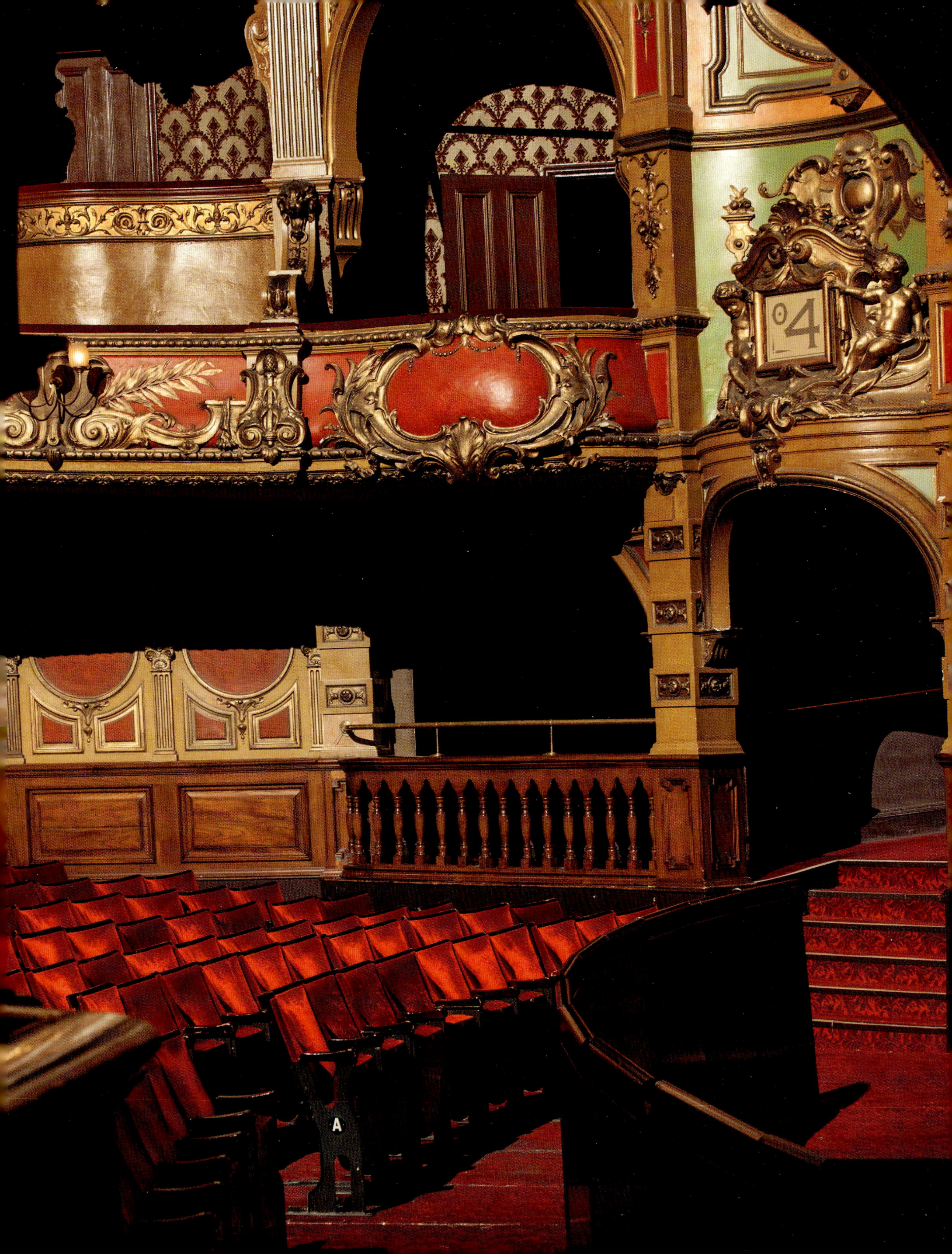
A

from London to Manchester or from Liverpool to Glasgow. But nothing was stinted, nothing rushed. He and his team were in complete command of the job; the speed with which Matcham adapted his plans for the Hackney Empire when Stoll changed his mind is astonishing.

The Empire was an immediate success, playing twice daily; over the years, W. C. Fields, Stanley Holloway, Stan Laurel, Marie Lloyd and Charlie Chaplin all performed there, as well as the so-called 'legitimate' companies; and in the mid-1950s Orson Welles filmed scenes there for one of his many unfinished films, *Moby-Dick*. But almost from the beginning, variety was threatened – first by the cinema, then by television. The Empire staggered on until 1956, purveying some pretty suspect stuff, including, rather later than you might have thought possible, that staple of the nineteenth-century circus, a freak show, which promised the biggest man in the world, and the smallest. The latter, who had no arms, offered a display of writing, smoking and scratching his head. Demand for such poor stuff scarcely existed, and eventually the fare turned into an imitation of itself: one of the last shows to take to the boards attempted to recreate the Victorian music hall, with The Empire Orchestra, Lotus & Josie, The Gelletto Bros and Moris & Cowley warming the house up for the sensational Act One closer, Tod Slaughter and his company in the blood-and-thunder melodrama *Maria Marten; or, The Murder in the Red Barn*. It was very nearly Slaughter's last performance; he died in harness soon after, having just performed the very same piece. In the second act, Cody & Oran (*Western Pastimes*), Charles Ancaster (*What's Cooking?*) and the blackface entertainer G. H. Elliott kept the audience, such as it was, breathlessly awaiting the arrival of the imposing Dawn White & Her Glamazons. Ms White was reputedly a class act, but it was all over for the variety theatres; television, which had contributed so substantially to their demise, now moved in to the grand, if by now somewhat run-down, old building, using it to transmit game shows and quiz shows of the ilk of *Take Your Pick!* and *Opportunity Knocks*, plus the occasional episode of *Emergency – Ward 10*. By 1963 the theatre itself was in A&E: television moved on and the Mecca organisation moved in, turning Matcham's masterpiece into a bingo hall, covering up the delicate rose-red facade with a gaudy billboard and brutally painting out the figures of Eloquence, Grace, Tragedy, Comedy and Music in Mecca's trademark primary colours. This was the Empire's nadir.

OPPOSITE Various details of the auditorium – note the red cartouche.

Even Mecca was defeated by the cost of maintaining the building. After twenty years in residence they were dealt a body blow: the theatre was awarded official Grade II listing, which meant they were obliged to restore the building to its original state, replacing the parts of it which they had quietly demolished – in the original materials. They finally threw in the towel in 1984, handing the theatre over to a radical theatre group whose name gave due warning of what they were about: CAST, the Cartoon Archetypical Slogan Theatre. Equally disgusted by Harold Wilson's Labour Party and the revisionist Communist Party, by bourgeois theatre and so-called socialist theatre, the group sought to create a genuinely popular, working-class theatre, one neither Brechtian nor Royal Court literary, nor even like Joan Littlewood's Theatre Workshop; much less would it be nostalgic 'traditional' fare. Their quest for pure popular theatre led them, somehow inevitably, straight to the Hackney Empire: 'We are talking, of course,' they said, 'of the Music Hall, Burlesque, Pantomime and farther back still, the Mediaeval Guild play. But analyse their success, study their techniques, consider their comment, and you will find pungent direct social commentary – plus artistry, so pure and honest, based on a good sense of the social archetype; thus giving a direct relationship and meaning to the audience. Therefore, it became reflective and relevant to its time and, at the same time, indisputably entertaining.' And so for

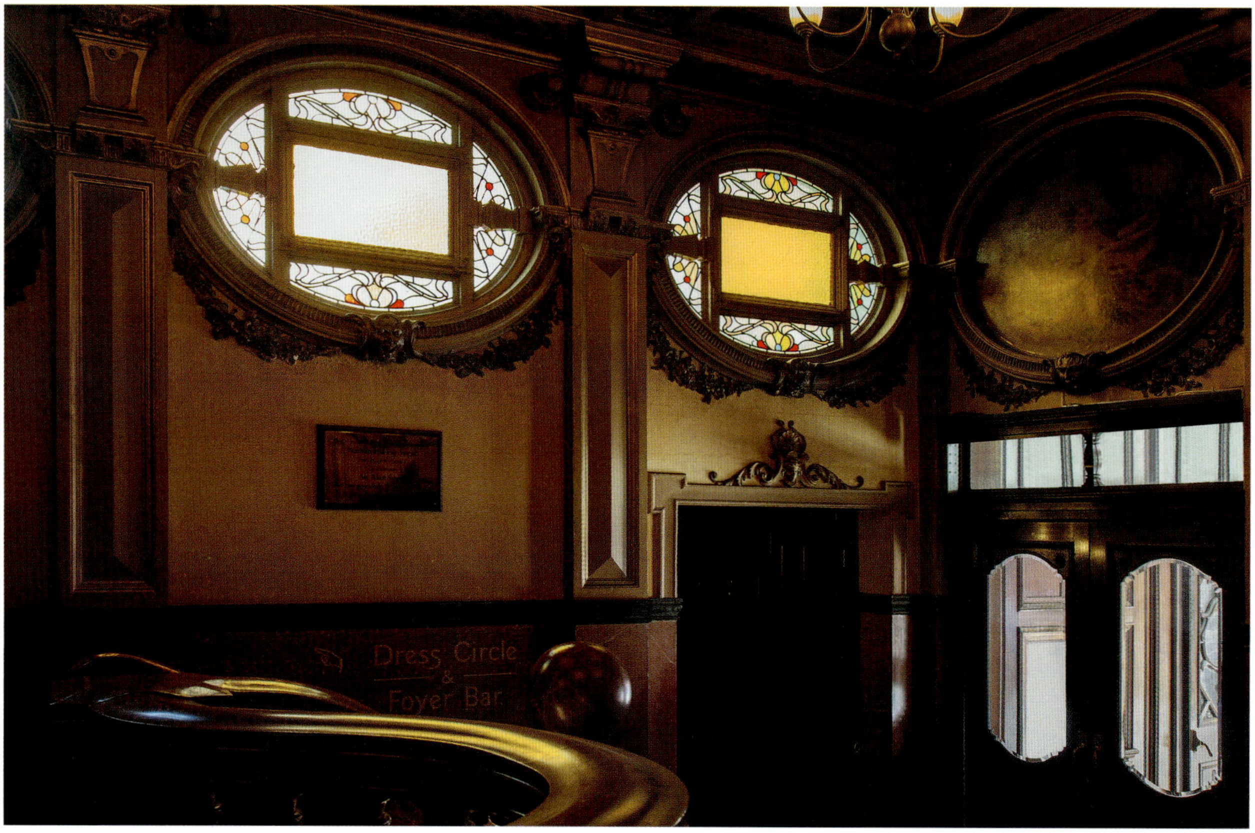

a twenty-year period the old theatre went back to its original character – or rather to its pre-Stoll, anarchic, subversive roots. It became a forum for every crazy voice in comedy, the temple of the alternative.

Paradoxically, perhaps (or perhaps not), it was during CAST's radical tenure that the physical fabric of the theatre was restored to its old glory. Finding that the building was in a perilous state of physical repair, the group mounted a successful campaign to buy back the freehold, and the restored building duly opened on 9 December 1986, precisely 85 years since its triumphant first opening at the beginning of the Edwardian era. CAST and the alternative comedians did not hog the stage; among others, Ralph Fiennes played his Hamlet there with huge success, and, perhaps most indelible memory of all, the great Russian clown Slava Polunin gave his *SnowShow* there: popular theatre at its sublime best, its ancient novelties working their familiar unfathomable magic. Thanks to a demonically possessed Griff Rhys Jones raising funds with a fury, there was further refurbishment, after which there was a new dispensation, less radical but more diverse, under which opera, plays, pop concerts and the annual legendary panto now regularly rub shoulders. Oswald Stoll would have beamed.

ABOVE Detail of the foyer.
OPPOSITE The exterior. Note the bizarre domes, which contribute to the eclectic effect. Inside and out, eccentric is a word that springs to mind when describing this theatre.

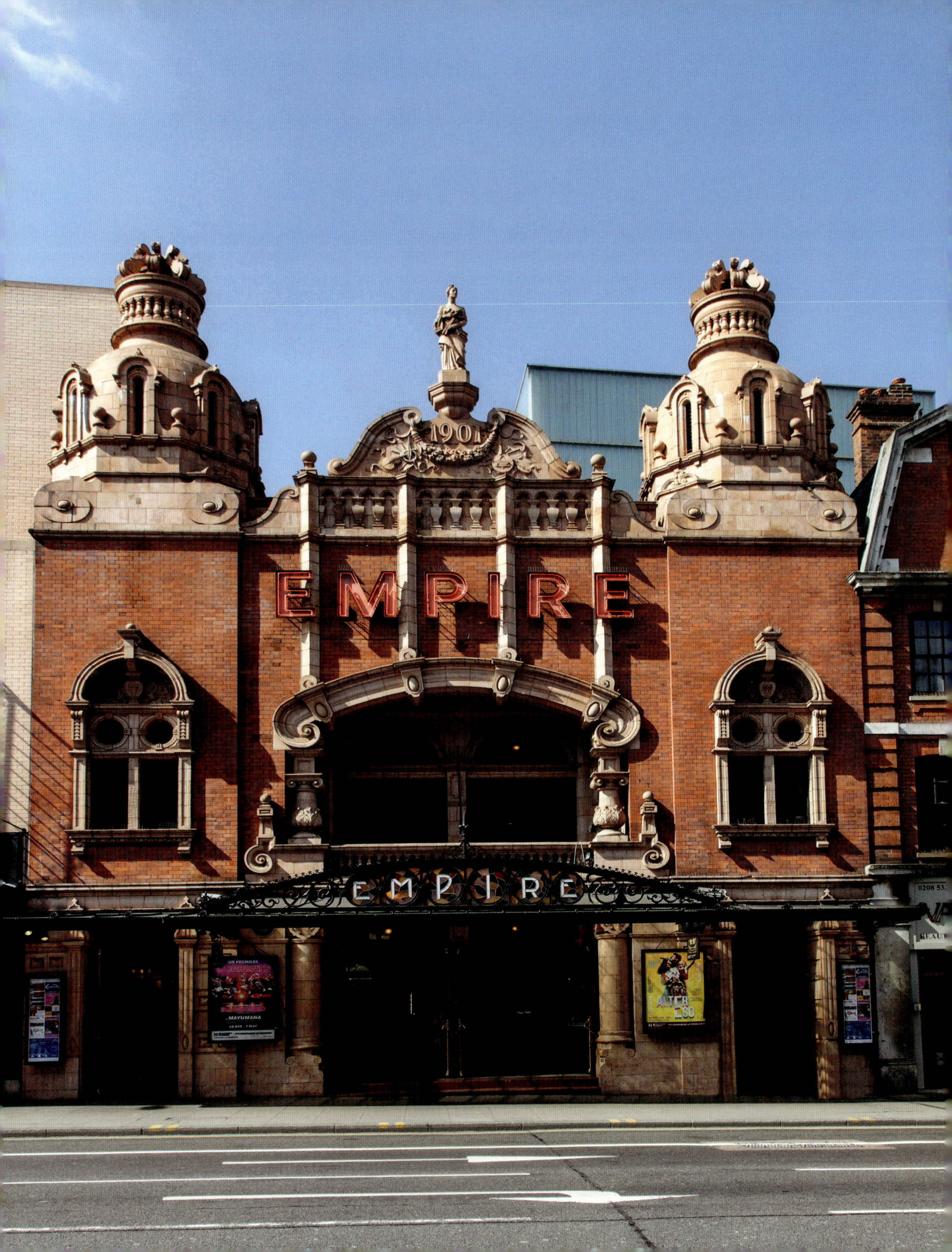
1901
EMPIRE
EMPIRE

NOËL COWARD

There's scarcely a theatre in the West End that hasn't changed its name at one time or another. Most of them have emblematic, often classical, names; a few bear the names of the people who built them. Often a new lessee wants to put his or her stamp on the theatre; and sometimes names are changed to avoid confusion. The Globe Theatre on Shaftesbury Avenue became the Gielgud when Sam Wanamaker's Globe opened on Bankside, with the additional bonus of honouring the greatest and best-loved classical actor of the twentieth century. Recently, Cameron Mackintosh renamed the Strand Theatre after Ivor Novello (who lived – and died – round the corner from it) and the Albery Theatre after Noël Coward, who made his West End debut there in 1920 as Bobbie Dermott in his own play *I'll Leave It to You*, the first of his plays to be produced. It was a long-overdue accolade, but there was a drawback: the renaming was in danger of blurring the historical record. The present Noël Coward was previously, from 1973, the Albery, in honour of the family that had managed it for 85 years; before that, it was the New. The name was only changed because of the creation of the New London Theatre, on the site of the old Winter Garden Theatre in Drury Lane – which has now, with nice irony, itself been renamed the Gillian Lynne. The widespread resistance to the New Theatre's change of name was the fear that the golden memory of the old New Theatre, and what it represented, might be lost. It was, for a while, a name to bring a mist to the eyes of older theatregoers, the site of an unprecedented sequence of epoch-making productions and – for a brief but heroic few years – the epicentre of Britain's theatrical culture, a rallying point for the celebration of national identity at a time when that was desperately needed.

The theatre was built by the actor-manager Charles Wyndham, who after a highly successful few years at the Criterion in Piccadilly Circus had been persuaded by Lord Salisbury – who happened to be prime minster at the time – to build a theatre on Charing Cross Road in the vicinity of Leicester Square. Salisbury owned the freehold to a large part of the area around St Martin's Lane and refused to allow anyone but Wyndham, of whose work he was a devoted fan, to build there. Wyndham was duly persuaded and commissioned W.G.R. Sprague, architect of the Lyceums in Newport and in Sheffield, one-time assistant of Frank Matcham and collaborator of Bertie Crewe, to design it for him. It was Sprague's first solo West End theatre; they named it Wyndham's Theatre, and from the moment of its opening in 1899 it was a great triumph for both men.

Wyndham, who would be knighted three years later, was one of the most remarkable men of the theatre of his time. A qualified surgeon, he only started acting in his mid-twenties; finding work scarce he went to America, then in the throes of the Civil War. Still unable to get a job as an actor, he enlisted as a battle surgeon in the Union Army, serving at Fredericksburg, Chancellorsville and Gettysburg. Finally, he managed to find work onstage, appearing at one point in New York City where he acted with John Wilkes Booth the same year the American actor assassinated Abraham Lincoln. He remained in America for ten years;

OPPOSITE The auditorium seen from a box.

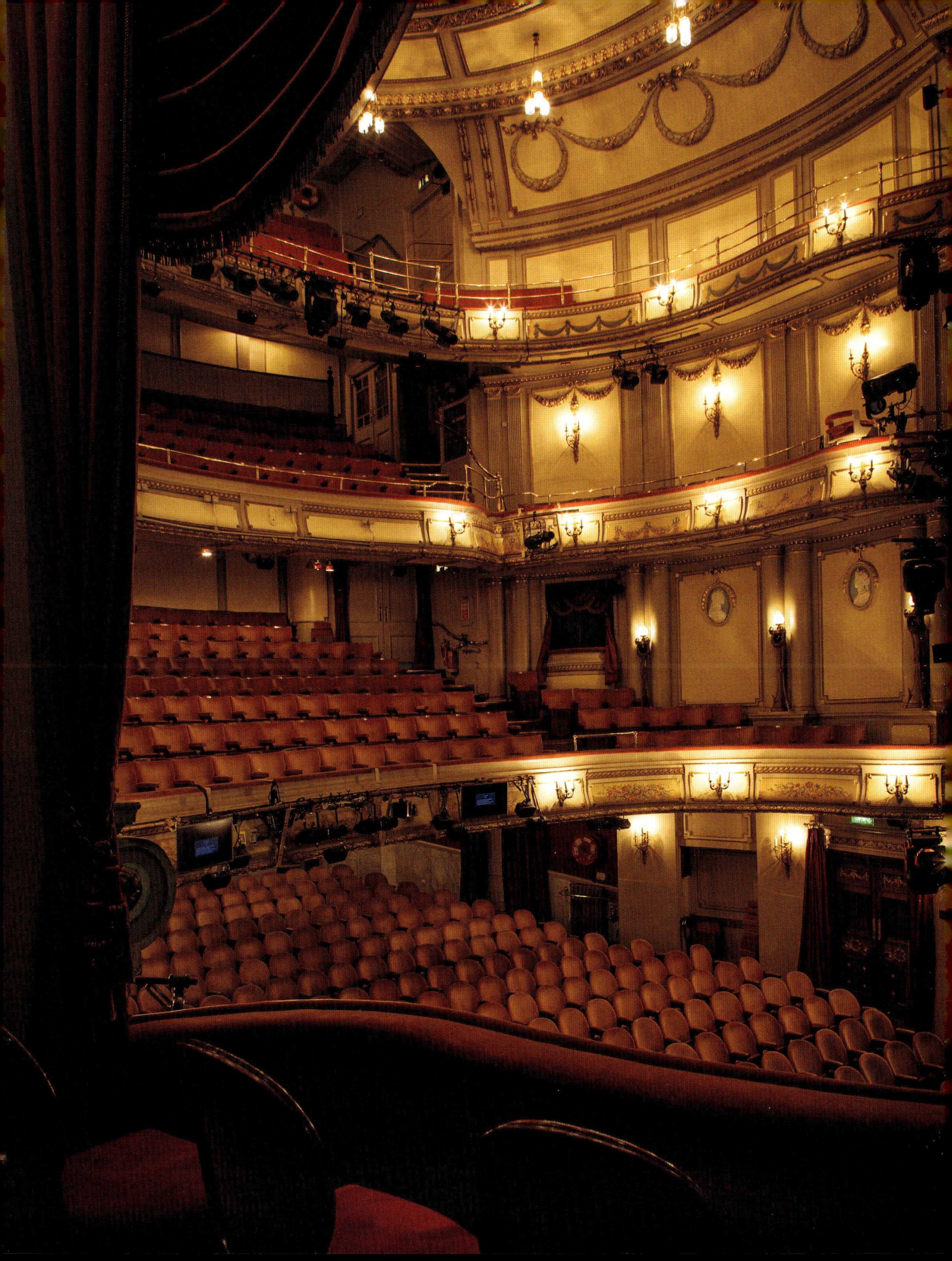

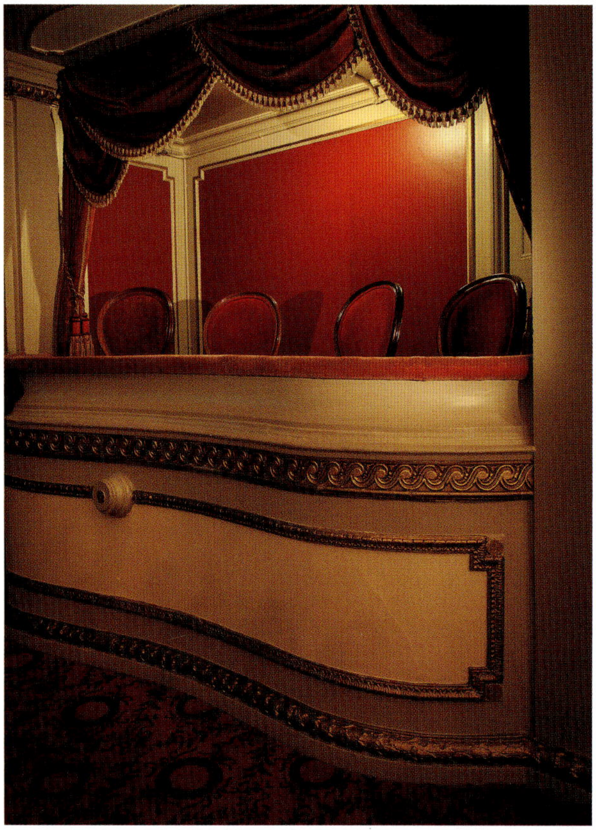

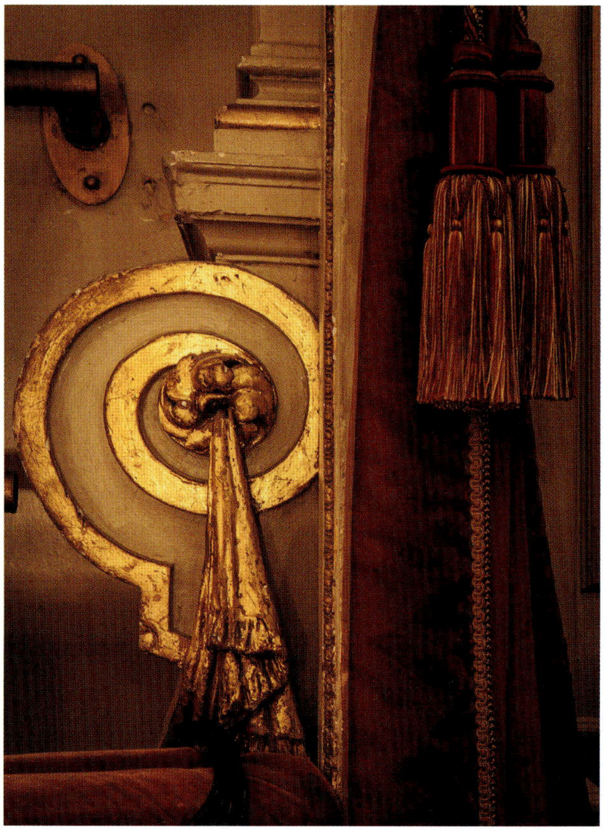

returning to England in 1872, he had an immediate hit with the American play *Saratoga* by Bronson Howard, triumphantly anglicized as *Brighton*. His tenure at the Criterion was notable for a series of plays by Henry Arthur Jones; he opened Wyndham's Theatre by reviving his performance as David Garrick in Jones's play of the same name. It and the theatre had an enormous success.

Behind Wyndham's was a plot of land of equal size giving on to St Martin's Lane which Wyndham had been obliged to buy along with the Charing Cross Road site. He had intended to sell it on, but when the deal fell through he decided to build a sister theatre, again to be designed by Sprague. 'What's going up on that site?' people would enquire. 'Sir Charles Wyndham's new theatre,' would be the reply, and so, by default, it named itself; it opened in March 1903. Unusually, the two theatres were linked by passages both underground and overhead, and it was rumoured that Wyndham's co-star and fellow manager, the delicious comedienne Mary Moore, liked to visit each other during shows; this seems improbable, since they were always acting together. They were certainly amorously entangled after the death of Moore's husband, the dramatist James Albery, in 1899, and finally tied the knot when Wyndham's long-ailing wife died in 1916. When he himself died three years later, he was buried next to his first wife, to be joined by Moore when she finally went to the great green room in the sky, in 1931.

The opening of the New was another triumph for both Sprague and Wyndham. It was, astonishingly, Sprague's thirtieth theatre (he was just forty). It is a modest auditorium, luminous in cream and gold, with wonderful sightlines (not a pillar to be seen),

ABOVE LEFT A box of restrained elegance.
ABOVE RIGHT Detail with carved swag of a curtain.

and its capacity of just under a thousand is an ideal size for the dramatic theatre. Wyndham and Moore starred in the first production, a revival of the romantic comedy *Rosemary*; thereafter the early years were dominated by another acting couple, Fred Terry and Julia Neilson, whose high romantic version of *The Scarlet Pimpernel* was brought back again and again by popular demand. During the First World War, the director-producer Dion Boucicault had a number of successes in a row, and revived his production of *Peter Pan* – originally staged at the Duke of York's Theatre just down the road – on several consecutive Christmases. The great Canadian-Scottish barnstormer Matheson Lang sent shivers down the spine with a series of melodramas, including his infallible standby *The Wandering Jew*, in the early 1920s; and in 1924 the play considered at the time to be George Bernard Shaw's masterpiece – *Saint Joan* – had its first British performance there, with Sybil Thorndike creating an indelible impression as the girl warrior from Lorraine.

From the early 1930s, the New was favoured by classical actors and directors: Harley Granville-Barker did a revolutionary monochromatic production of *Twelfth Night*, the set and costumes all in black and white; and then John Gielgud, just coming into his own as a leading actor and manager, appeared there in the sensationally successful *Richard of Bordeaux* by Gordon Daviot, otherwise known as the crime novelist Josephine Tey. Shortly after, he played his first Hamlet there; it had 155 consecutive performances, the second-longest run in the play's history, and seemed to contemporary audiences to be definitive – Gielgud's speed of thought and entirely natural way with verse, speaking it as if it were his normal form of expression, supremely equipped him to claim the part as his own. In 1935 he directed *Romeo and Juliet*; he took a gamble by alternating the roles of Romeo and Mercutio with the classically inexperienced Laurence Olivier, who prowled around the stage, sex and energy personified, in both parts, astonishing the town with his animal attack, his emotional dynamism and his extraordinary physical beauty. The critics were underwhelmed ('Mr Olivier does not speak the verse badly,' said the *Sunday Times*, 'He does not speak it at all') but audiences, especially young ones, found it electrifying, as did Gielgud himself. This was Shakespeare transformed, although many people were glad to hear Gielgud give full measure to the music and the fantasy of the verse. Peggy Ashcroft was Juliet, Edith Evans the nurse, and the production, with graceful and fluid designs by the Motley team, set new standards for Shakespeare.

Two years later, in 1937, the Old Vic transferred three very successful Shakespeare productions, variously featuring Michael Redgrave, Edith Evans and Olivier, back again, this time as Macbeth. Soon London was engulfed in war, and when both the Old Vic and Sadler's Wells were bombed out of their homes it seemed entirely natural that both companies would move their operations to the New, which they did in 1941. During the dark and terrifying days of the Blitz and after it, the appetite for theatre, and especially classical theatre, was immense, and the New Theatre became a pivotal part of the pressing task of maintaining wartime morale. Starting in 1944 the Old Vic company, under its new directors John Burrell, Laurence Olivier and Ralph Richardson (the last two newly released from service), presented a now legendary two-year programme at the New. In the first season, Ibsen's *Peer Gynt*, with Richardson in the title role; *Richard III*, starring Olivier; Shaw's *Arms and the Man* and Chekhov's *Uncle Vanya*, these last starring both Richardson and Olivier, joined by Sybil Thorndike. The second season featured *Henry IV, Parts 1* and *2* starring Richardson as Falstaff and Olivier as Hotspur and Justice Shallow, followed by a double bill of *Oedipus Rex* and Richard Brinsley Sheridan's satire *The Critic*; in an astonishing feat of versatility and virtuosity, Olivier played the title roles in both plays, seemingly made of steel in the Greek, light as a feather as Sheridan's Mr Puff. These productions, excellent in themselves, acquired an extraordinary resonance in the circumstances. In 1944 London was plagued with flying bombs; both actors and audiences needed nerves of steel to give themselves over to the theatre. But they did, affirming the power of the great communal act that theatre can be: the citizens coming together to be reminded of what civilisation means, and telling each other the stories with which we confront the truth about what it is to be human. Nobody who was there at the New Theatre in those dark days has ever forgotten the experience; there in St Martin's Lane, the Old Vic company lit a beacon whose light spread across the country and across the world. All this perhaps explains why changing the theatre's name was no mere rebranding exercise; it seemed to draw a line under a heroic past.

Of course, nothing can continue at that level. With the end of the war the Old Vic played five more seasons at the New, including Olivier's first (and only stage) *King Lear* and a sparkling *School for Scandal* with Vivien Leigh, Thornton Wilder's *The Skin of their Teeth* and Anouilh's *Antigone*. Then, in 1949, Olivier and Richardson were suddenly and summarily dismissed from the directorship of the company that was increasingly being seen as a national-theatre-in-waiting. The New, meanwhile, continued with distinction – T. S. Eliot's *The Cocktail Party* had its London premiere there; Katharine Hepburn gave her only British stage performance in Shaw's silly *The Millionairess*; and Charles Laughton returned to the British stage in 1958, after over twenty years' absence, in Jane Arden's quirky *The Party*, garnering few good reviews but introducing the young Albert Finney to the West End. In 1960, Lionel Bart's *Oliver!* burst forth in all its raucous, sentimental tunefulness and stayed for seven years, glorious years. And then in 1971 the National Theatre, under Laurence Olivier's directorship, came for a season of new productions which it was fondly hoped might scale new heights, but which turned into something of a nadir. One flop followed another with a sickening thud: Georg Büchner's 1835 French Revolution play *Danton's Death* with Christopher Plummer; *The Rules of the Game* by Luigi Pirandello, starring Paul Scofield; *Tyger, Tyger*, with words by Adrian Mitchell and music by Alan Price; and Jean Giraudoux's *Amphitryon 38* with Geraldine McEwan and Christopher Plummer. Everything hinged on the last production of the season, Eugene O'Neill's *Long Day's Journey into Night*, starring a still-convalescent Olivier. The first night, 21 December 1971, had an extraordinary nervous electricity about it; much was hanging on it and there was widespread anxiety, even among the general public, about Olivier's health. But from the second the curtain rose, the unmistakable gut-wrenching, breath-stopping electricity of greatness, such as Olivier had so often commanded in the theatre but never would again, was in the air. Somehow, 1944 and 1971 joined hands, and the elegant playhouse on St Martin's Lane was instinct with the meaning and purpose of theatre.

Symbolically, almost, the first show after the theatre's name change to Albery in 1973 took it into another world of expression: *Joseph and the Amazing Technicolor Dreamcoat* had its West End debut there, a supreme piece of pop theatre, as far away as humanly possible from the Tyrone family's long day's journey into night: joyous, vital and very, very popular, bringing a whole new generation of theatregoers into the West End. Charles Wyndham and Mary Moore never had any objections to successful runs of entertaining shows. The Noël Coward Theatre, like any other West End playhouse, is a commercial venture and has its ups and downs, its highs and lows. Its classical past is an exception to the West End rule, but it is a curious fact that classical plays feel exceptionally right in it. Coward himself, of course, is nowadays a classic, and perhaps of all its recent successful ventures the delicious and fierce revival of *Private Lives*, directed some fifteen years ago by the late Howard Davies with the late Alan Rickman and the ever-dazzling Lindsay Duncan, is the show that brought all its traditions together.

OPPOSITE The ceiling of the auditorium.

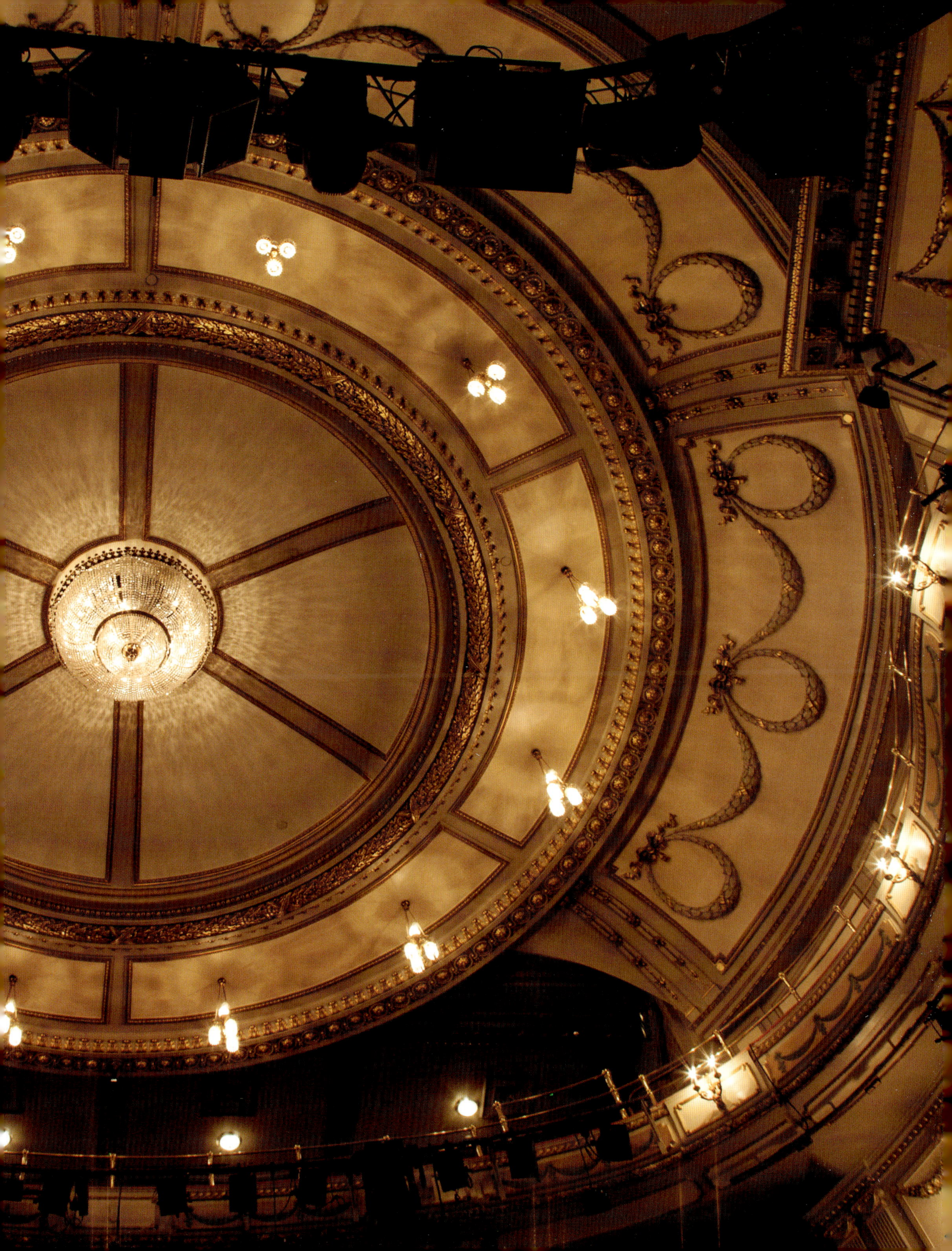

LONDON COLISEUM

This is the theatre that Sir Oswald Stoll finally built as his flagship, after the great impresario decided that the Hackney Empire, which he had commissioned three years earlier, wasn't quite grand enough. As its name suggests, the London Coliseum looks beyond the British Empire to the Roman one: Stoll was now not merely the Napoleon of the music hall but its Hadrian, or perhaps its Nero. Perhaps in the back of his mind was the sobriquet accorded to Sir Augustus Harris, the late manager of the Theatre Royal Drury Lane, the theatre the Coliseum was designed to eclipse: Augustus Druriolanus, they called him. Did Stoll aspire to being Oswald St Martinslanus? Certainly he went about buying up the southern end of that once modest street with a vengeance, steadily acquiring the freehold in an acre and a quarter of land there. Only two freeholders resisted his considerable financial blandishments: a jeweller and a publican, whose respective premises remained defiantly intact, as they do today. The continuing existence of those two premises required considerable ingenuity on the part of Frank Matcham, whom Stoll engaged to build the Coliseum: he had to design the great behemoth at an angle. Behind the mighty facade, which is of course flush to the street, the building is on a diagonal. Needless to say, this massive technical challenge presented no problem to the architect; it was all in a day's work. His brief was straightforward: to create the most splendid variety theatre that had ever existed. The Coliseum was to be the Valhalla of Variety.

And so it was, unquestionably the apogee of both Matcham's and Stoll's careers. It was more than a theatre: it was a manifesto. Stoll was a single-minded man, and all his thoughts, from boyhood, had tended towards this point. Even though as a young man he had written a few music hall numbers for Vesta Tilley – 'Is Marriage a Failure?' and 'The Tablet of Fame' among them – he was by all accounts a curiously charmless fellow, fiercely focused on his objectives; he passionately embraced the philosopher Herbert Spencer's 'social Darwinism'. Stoll had been born in Australia to an actor father, whom, it is said, Stoll was already managing at the age of ten; by the age of fourteen, when most boys would have been severely chastised for attending a music hall, he was running one. His father had died and he had been brought to England by his mother and her new husband; as soon as he could, the boy left school to help his mother manage the Parthenon Music Hall in Liverpool, and then a regional theatre company she had acquired. By the time he was twenty, in 1886, he and his mother had gone into partnership, buying a lease in Levino's Music Hall in Cardiff, which they proceeded to transform into the Cardiff Empire Palace of Varieties. Only six years later, in addition to the Philharmonic in Cardiff, they had acquired two more Empires, the ones in Newport and Swansea. Another six years and Stoll merged his business with that of the highly successful Edward Moss; the older man became chairman of Moss Empires, with Stoll as its managing director, controlling 37 variety theatres across the country, many of them built or adapted by him. From the beginning he was obsessed with the idea of raising standards, backstage and onstage; like the good

OPPOSITE The auditorium with some of the boxes. Note the two domes, which lend an air of importance to the boxes below.

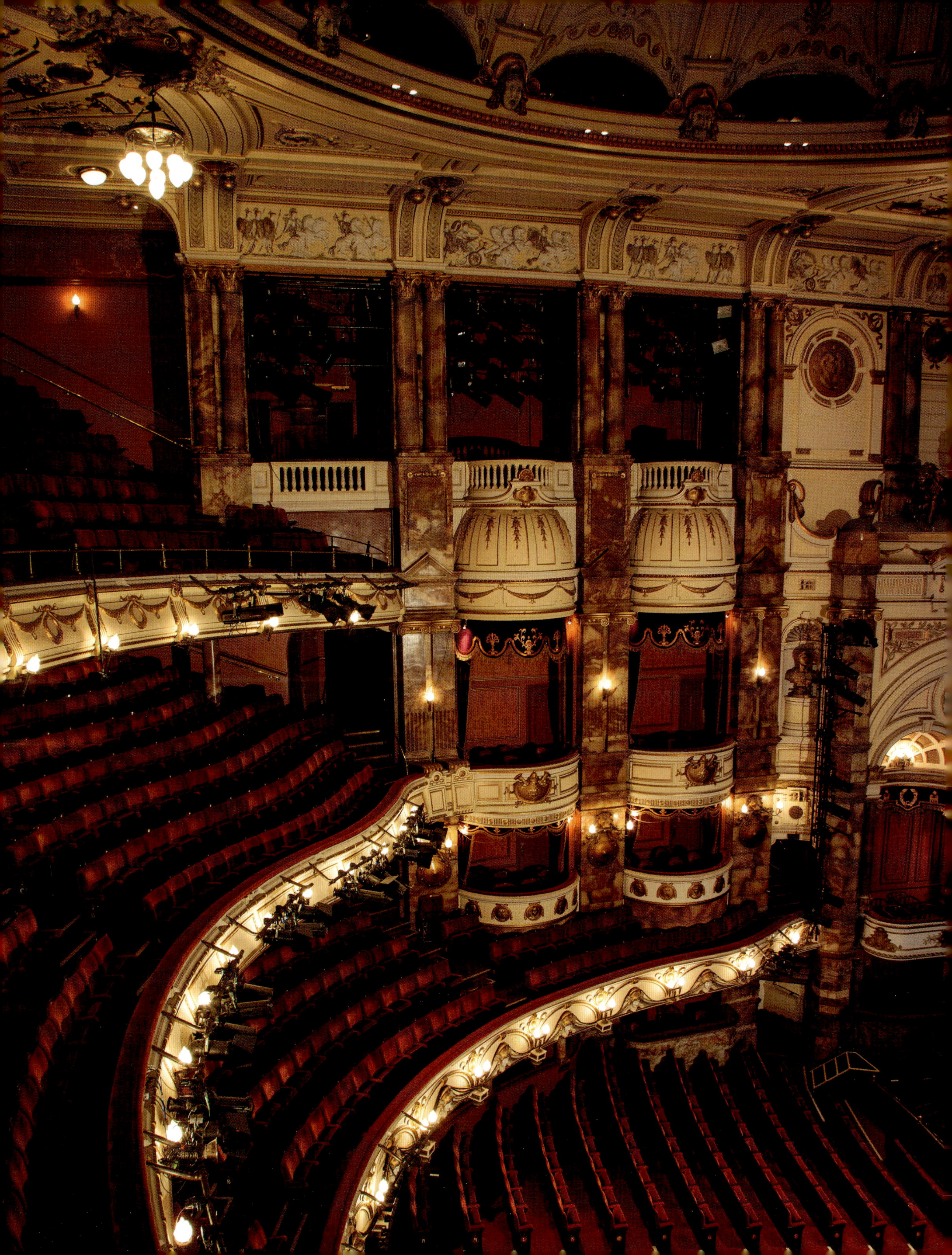

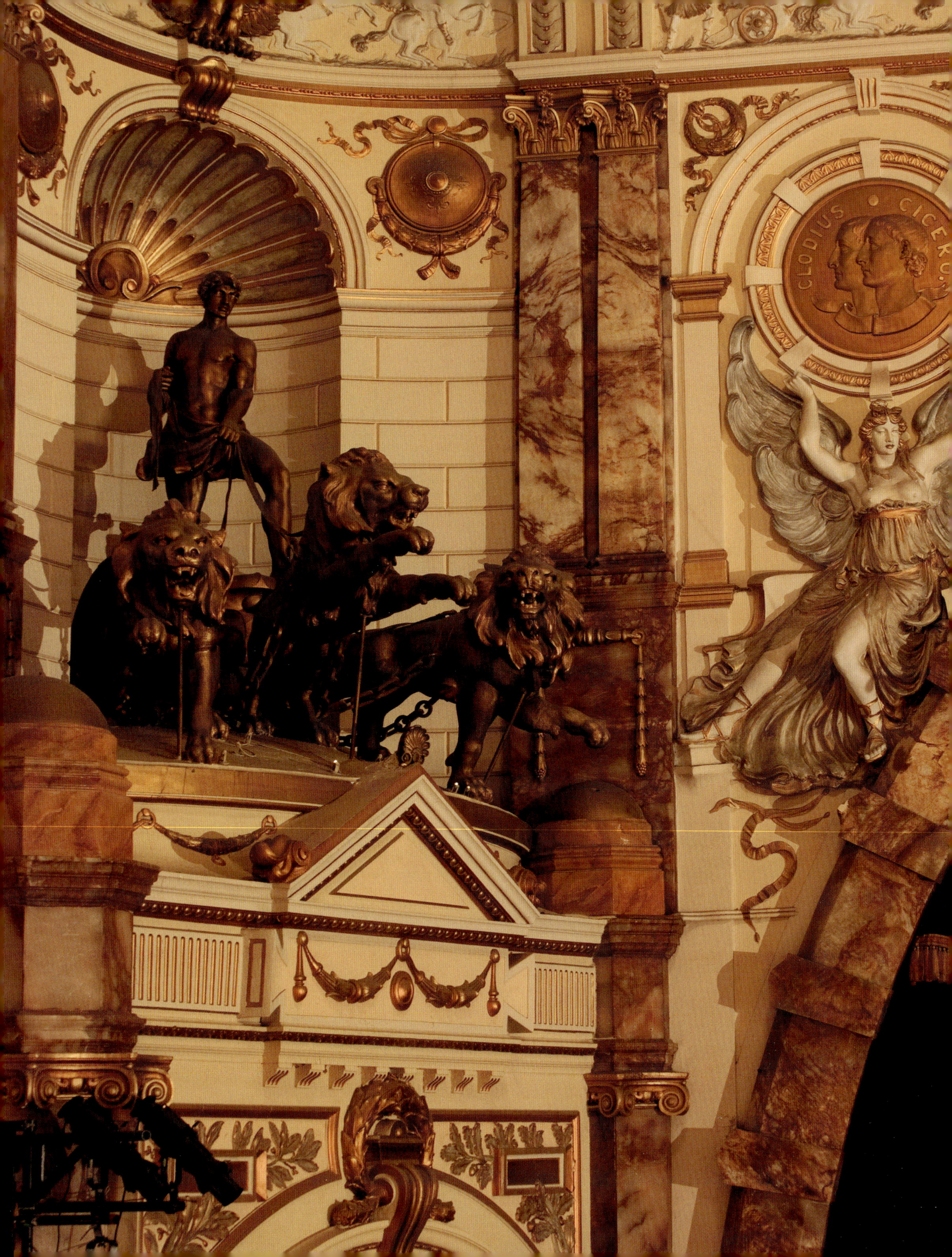
CLODIUS • CICERO

Victorian that he was, he saw the theatre as a vehicle for moral improvement. 'The Shakespeare of the stage, the Balladmongers of the music-hall, the Griffiths and the Chaplins of the screen,' he said at a reception celebrating the knighthood he received in 1919, 'are the educators of our emotions . . . they are the schools, not of the intellect, but of the practical, as distinct from the purely religious, emotions. They show in action the consequences of right and wrong emotions.' Hifalutin stuff for an impresario, a mere manager of mountebanks; but the Coliseum embodied Stoll's elevated ideas at every level. A plaque inside the theatre proclaimed its motto: 'Pro Bono Publico' – for the public good.

The facade was a dominating great series of arches that rose up, on the right side of the roof, to a great tower with bold carved figures at the corners representing Art, Music, Science and Architecture; they were guarded by sculptured lions, while eight cupids supported a huge iron revolving globe, electrically lit and visible for miles around, spelling out the word COLISEUM. Along the front was a novel device, also electric, announcing the current performance; there were two different shows a day running in tandem, the first at noon and at six, the second at three and at nine. On entering the foyer, if your seat was in the dress circle, you made your way to a lift, a state-of-the-art facility offered by no other theatre in Europe. If one were royal, one stepped into a richly furnished lounge which at a signal softly moved in its entirety along on a track formed in the floor, through the salon and into a large foyer, finally arriving at the entrance to the royal box. The lounge car then remained in position, serving as an ante-room should one need to stretch one's royal legs during the performance. Mere commoners who fancied a cig proceeded down the marble staircase to the Baronial Smoking Hall. Dainty snacks at moderate charges could be obtained all day in the theatre, while if it was tea you were after – and you could drop in off the street for a cuppa even if you weren't going to see the show – there were spacious tea rooms on every tier: the Terrace Tea Room, the Dutch Tea Room, the Balcony Tea Room, the American Bar, the Smoke Room, and the Chocolate and Cigar Bar. In each there was a kiosk where seats for future performances could be bought. In addition, to the left of the grand entrance there was an information bureau; doctors and others expecting urgent telephone calls or telegrams could leave their seat number with the clerk in case of emergency. Brief messages could be typed and dispatched from the bureau, telegrams could be sent, letters penned and stamps bought. When you'd written your letter you could pop it into a letterbox in the foyer; or, if you wanted to be absolutely sure, you could send a messenger.

OPPOSITE Details in the auditorium – note the references to ancient Rome, and the provocatively dressed angel supporting a medallion with the heads of Clodius and Cicero in relief.
OVERLEAF The auditorium. Again note the references to ancient Rome – and the craziness of the whole. What fun the designer must have had: it's more Cecil B. DeMille than Cecil B. DeMille. So extravagant as to be almost a satire.

All this, as Stoll intended, was about as far as humanly conceivable from the makeshift premises in which the British music hall had been born and in which it flourished. 'It combines', purred the publicity, 'the social advantages of the refined and elegant surroundings of a Club; the comfort and attractiveness of a Café; besides being the Theatre de Luxe of London and the pleasantest family resort imaginable.' The experience seems to have resembled nothing so much as travelling on an oceangoing liner.

Entering the auditorium brought its own rush of excitement, decorated as it was with all the appurtenances of the ancient coliseum: chariots, lions, ensigns, standards, shields, armed guards. It was enormous in every direction, width, depth and height, and held nearly three thousand people, making it by far the biggest theatre in England. The stage itself was 55 feet wide and 92 feet deep; embedded into it was a triple revolve, a miracle of modern engineering. The flies were 43 feet above the stage and were suspended from lattice girders 68 feet long and weighing about 7 tons each; a travelling

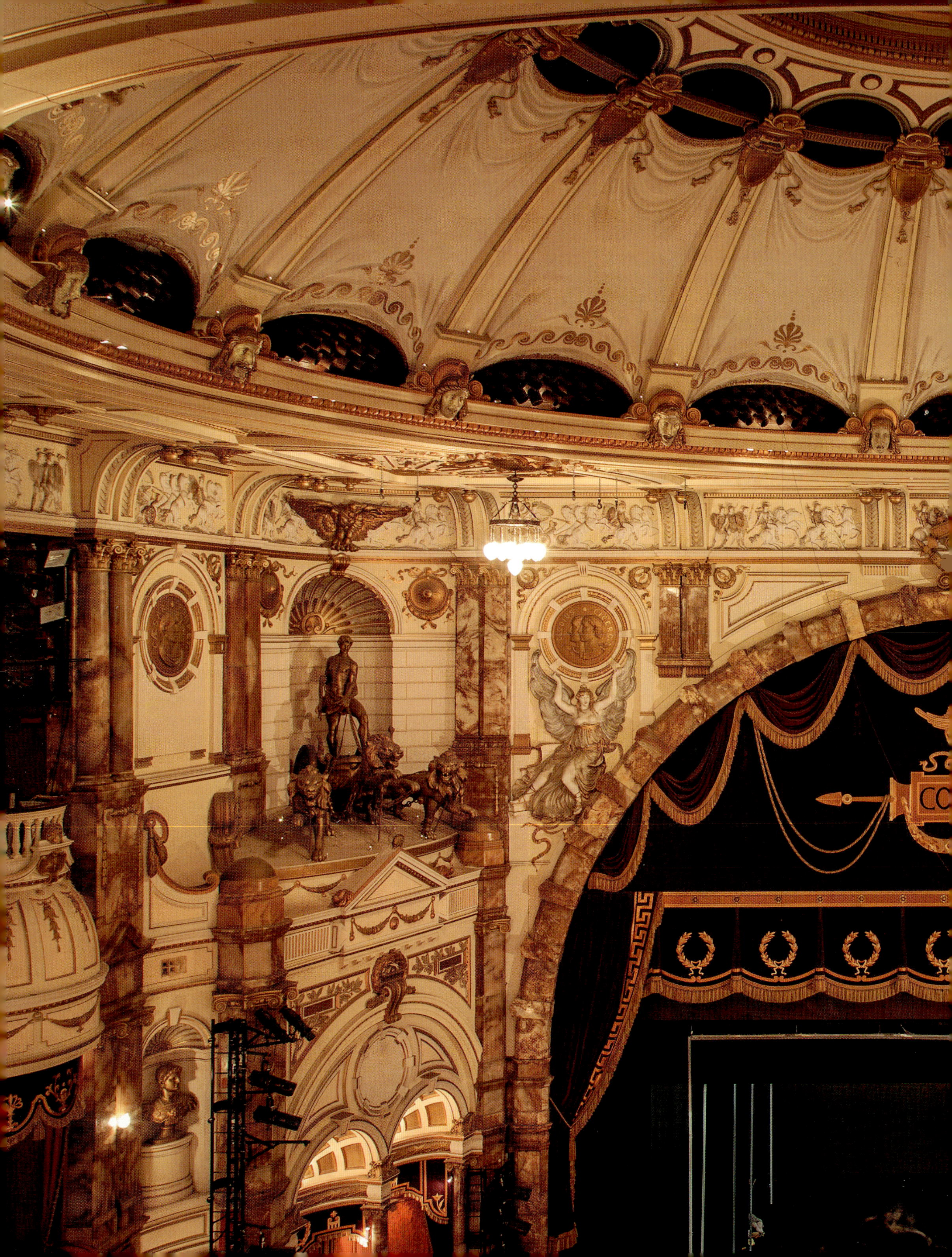

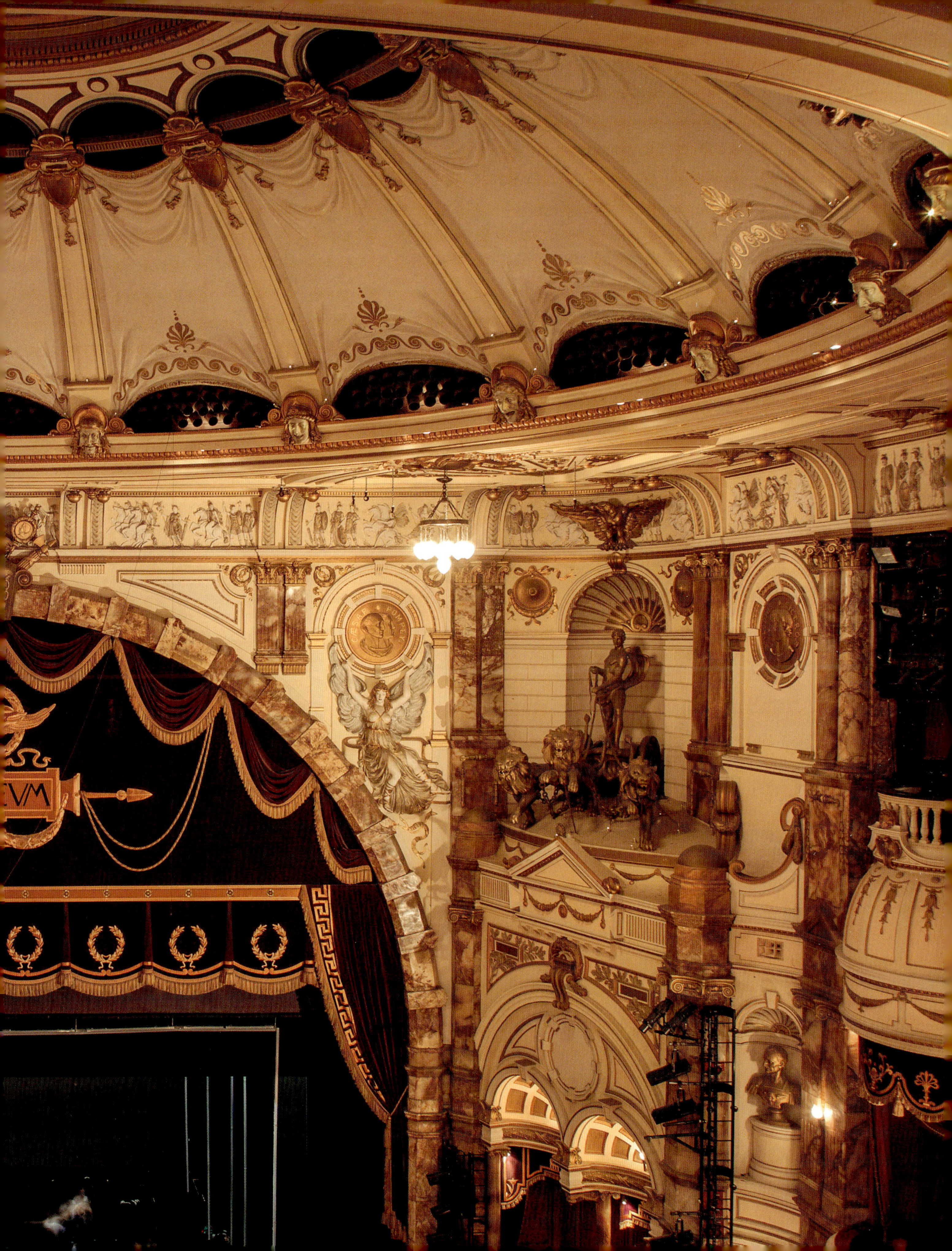

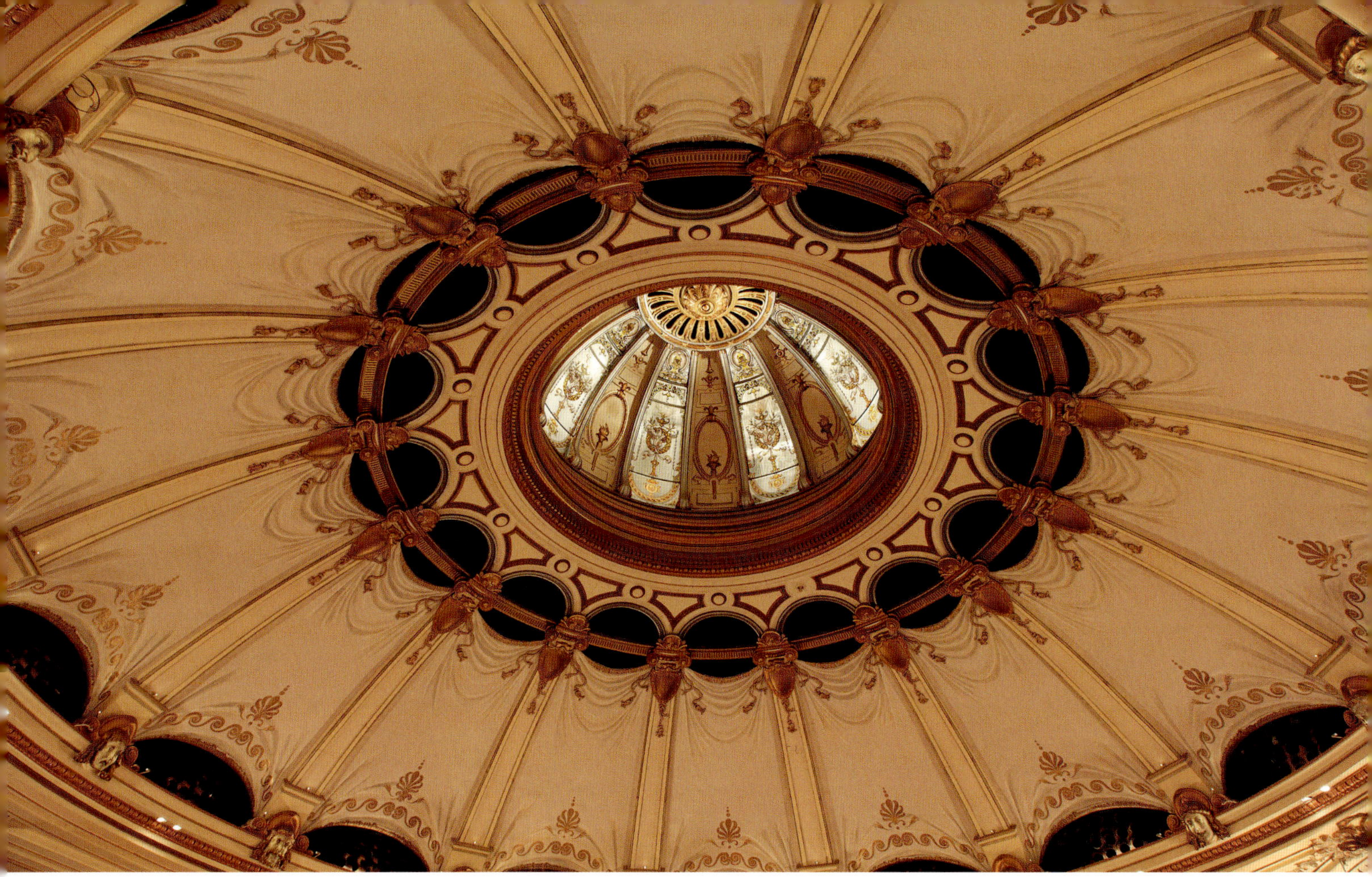

runway for suspending panorama scenes was carried by a 100-foot-long girder. The auditorium itself, constructed entirely of steel and concrete, was equally prodigious: the sweeping cantilevered balcony, unsupported by columns, weighed 9 tons. The huge proscenium arch was emblazoned with the acronymic motto 'SPQR', signifying not, as wags suggested, Small Profits, Quick Returns, but *Senatus Populusque Romanus*, the senate and people of Rome. The Coliseum opened in a blaze of glory on Christmas Eve 1904; onstage were the greatest performers of the age, not only variety artistes but classical singers, instrumentalists, dancers and actors.

It almost immediately faltered. The public simply didn't pitch up in sufficient numbers, and after eighteen months it closed. Things had not gone quite as Stoll intended: the revolving globe, somehow symbolically, never turned, banned by the London County Council; the royal moving lounge was only ever used once. The theatre closed for eighteen months, its emptiness all too visible – there was nowhere for the Coliseum to hide. But Stoll was not to be beaten; the theatre reopened with a new business plan, and it stayed open until 1931, by which time pretty well every variety artist of note had appeared there, as well as Diaghilev's Ballets Russes (three separate visits), Sarah Bernhardt and Ellen Terry. But having passed through the Roaring Twenties, survived the Great Crash and quivered on the brink of the Terrible Thirties, theatregoers craved escapism rather than skills, and saucy, subversive comedy; for the next quarter of a century the Coliseum became the home of the musical, starting with Erik Charrell's *White Horse Inn*, adapted from the German, with all the satire taken out and a lot of schmaltz added, plus spectacle: there

ABOVE Detail of the shallow domed ceiling of the auditorium.

were 160 performers, three bands and countless chorus. *Casanova*, *Blackbirds of 1934*, *The Golden Toy* and the real ice spectacle *St Moritz* followed. After the war, the American musical ascendancy led to a box-office bonanza with a succession of freshly minted masterpieces: *Annie Get your Gun*, *Guys and Dolls*, *Can-Can*, *The Pajama Game*, *Damn Yankees*, *The Most Happy Fella* and *Bells Are Ringing*. It was with this last that the apparently unbreakable run of hits came to an end, and after a couple more lame ducks the great building was turned over, with indecent haste, to cinema.

It was not the Coliseum's first encounter with celluloid. Indeed, Frank Matcham, ever prescient, had included a projection booth and projector in his original plans for the theatre, and from time to time short Bioscope films had been shown as novelty items. In 1933, after the long run of *White Horse Inn* ended, films took over for a year, including, sensationally, *King Kong*, which ran for some months; it was estimated that 10,000 people a day saw the film. In 1961, MGM leased the theatre, starting, rather stalely, by rereleasing *Gone with the Wind*. The following year, altogether more fittingly, *King of Kings* had its premiere, no doubt feeling very much at home among the Roman trappings of the building. Then came a residency by Cinerama in which the theatre matched the epic excitements of three-strip, three-screen presentation; but the supply of films in this format was not sufficient to fill the programme, and in 1968 Sadler's Wells Opera, in a wildly ambitious move, took up residence, exchanging its 1930s modernist, thousand-seat premises in north London for the grandest of all West End theatres, more than two and a half times the size. It seized the opportunity to restore the building to much of its former glory; the experiment, after a little uncertainty, worked, and after five years it proudly adopted a new name, English National Opera, offering an English-speaking, theatrically experimental, reasonably priced alternative to its grand rival in Covent Garden.

The vastness of the building has sometimes proved challenging, both in attracting audiences and in filling the stage with sufficiently dynamic action, but it persists in its mission, one that Oswald Stoll (who died in 1942, long outliving the world of theatre in which he had grown up) might have endorsed: the presentation of inspiring, thrilling work in stimulating surroundings for everyone. 'What he has done', they told him at the reception celebrating his knighthood, 'has been to improve the old music-hall out of all recognition. In the old days they produced and fostered plenty of fun and frolic, but it was for Sir Oswald Stoll and few other men to give them a beauty of many colours and an interest of many kinds which were undreamt of before.' And the revolving ball has finally been made to work, visible from miles around.

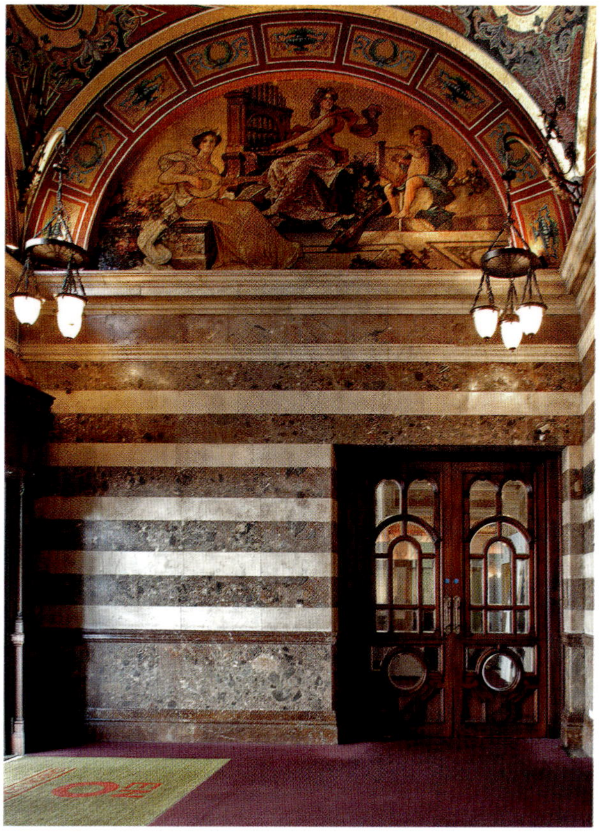

ABOVE The entrance foyer. Strips of marble on the walls and mosaic above give a sense that money was no object.

NOVELLO

What's in a name? In the case of the great actor-composer Ivor Novello's case, rather a lot, since his continued existence in the public imagination depends on the annual song award named after him and on this theatre – in which, as it happens, he never performed, though he lived, and died, in a flat above it. This theatre has had more changes of identity than perhaps any other London playhouse, being successively the Waldorf, the Strand, the Whitney, the Strand again and now – who knows how long for? – the Novello.* It was conceived from the beginning as a sibling of the Aldwych Theatre, flanking the grand hotel that occupies nearly the whole of the northwestern side of Aldwych, which it preceded by six months; the hotel itself – also the Waldorf – it preceded by three years. There the two theatres stood, looking in opposite directions, one on the corner of Drury Lane, the other at the corner of Catherine Street, with a gaping hole between them, part of the massive programme of urban regeneration that had remade the whole of the old Covent Garden theatre district.

Both theatres were the work of the same architect, the prodigious and prolific W.G.R. Sprague, who, fresh from Wyndham's and the New Theatre, was becoming something of a specialist in twinned playhouses; the Gielgud and the Queen's on Shaftesbury Avenue would soon follow. The facades of the two theatres on Aldwych are strongly related, as are their interiors, but the Novello seems bolder, facing down to the ever bustling Strand and the river, shamelessly flaunting its wares on its broad marquee, with the vast and magnificent Theatre Royal looming impressively behind it and the bijou Duchess and Fortune theatres sitting modestly in the background: a little community of playhouses. The Novello has, in the course of its more than a century of active life, been home to many rip-roaring popular successes, some on the brink of the risqué. This was by no means the way it started out, however, and indeed not the way it was designed. Sprague's interior was in consummate good taste, French in inspiration, though looking less to *fin de siècle* Paris than to the court of Louis XIV, with violet- and dove-coloured marble and the ubiquitous (for this period) *rose du Barry* furnishings; the circular ceiling is decorated with a panoramic painting in the manner of the Sun King's favourite painter, Charles Le Brun. Mirrors were everywhere in the foyers, an *hommage* to Versailles. The Sun God, Apollo, his chariot drawn by four horses and attended by a goodly retinue of goddesses and cupids, rides triumphantly over the proscenium, which is supported by delicate *fleur de pêcher* marble pilasters. It was all extremely elegant and refined: the American Shubert brothers, who commissioned it, were not to know that it would one day house *No Sex Please, We're British.*

The Waldorf's opening programme in May 1905 consisted of a rather ill-assorted operatic double bill of Leoncavallo's *Pagliacci* and Ferdinand Paer's *Il maestro di Ballo*; these two alternated in repertory with performances by the great Italian actress Eleanora Duse, among them a version of Arthur Wing Pinero's

OPPOSITE View of the auditorium from a box.
OVERLEAF Side of the auditorium with two boxes – note the extravagance of the marble veneer and the generous carving of the decoration.

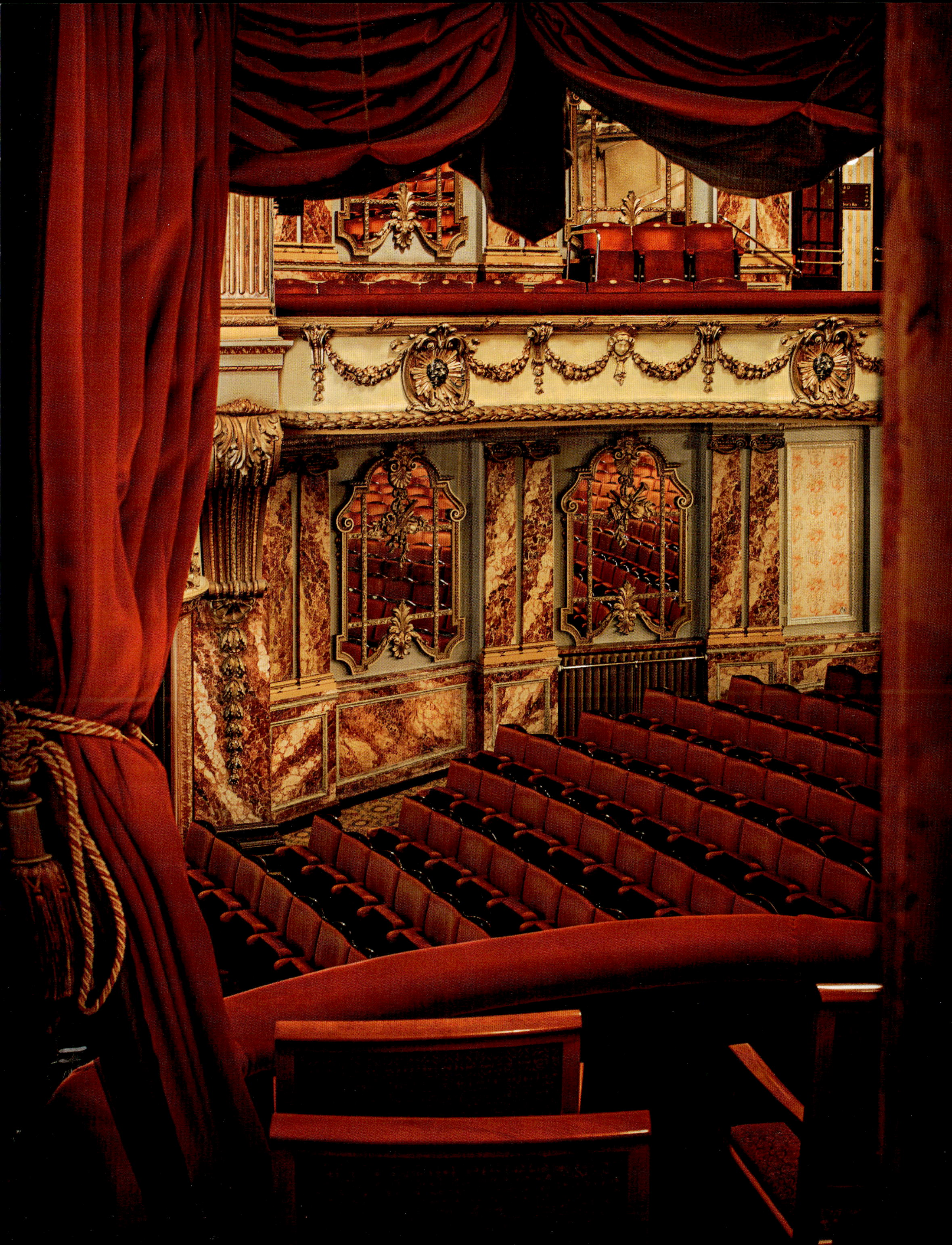

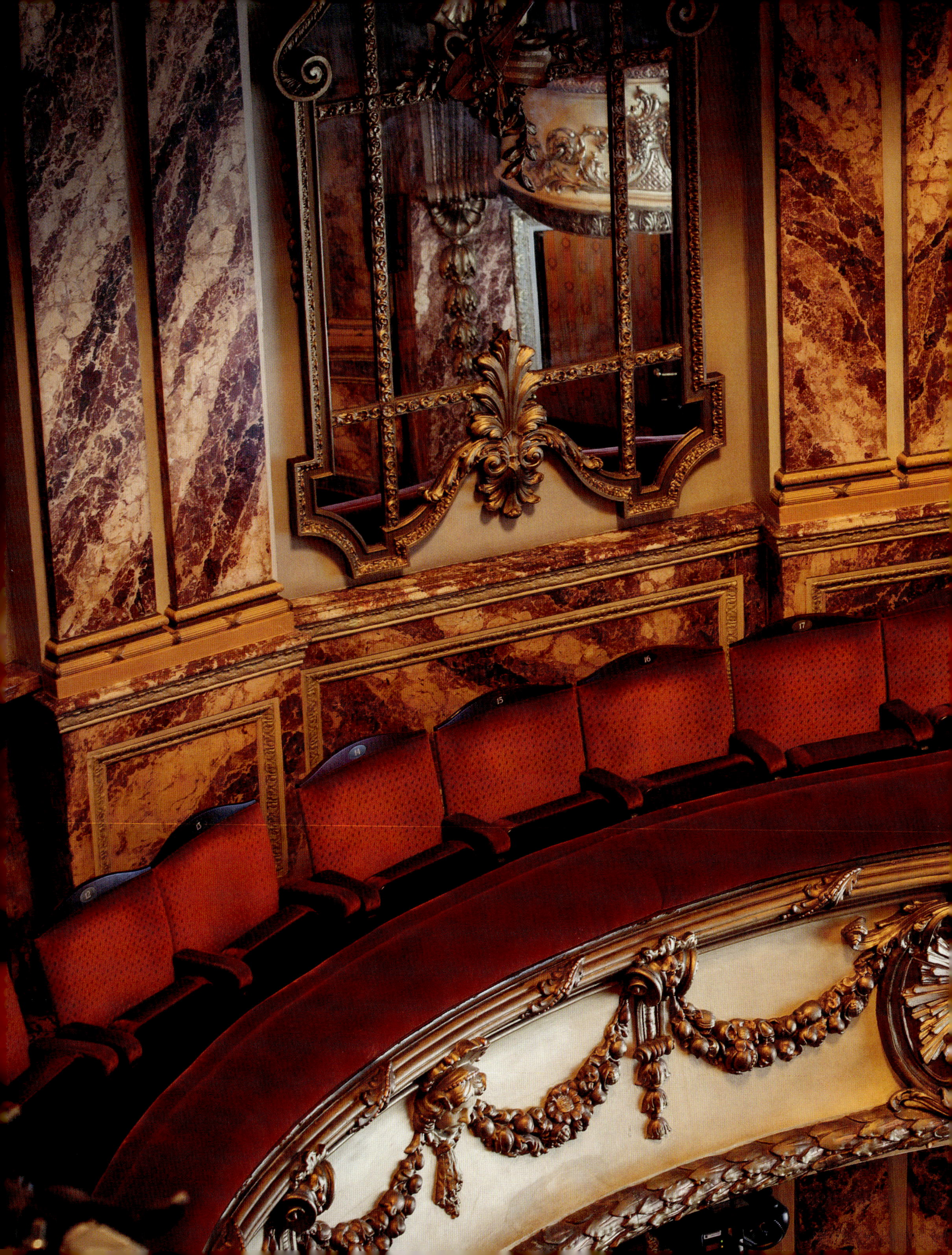

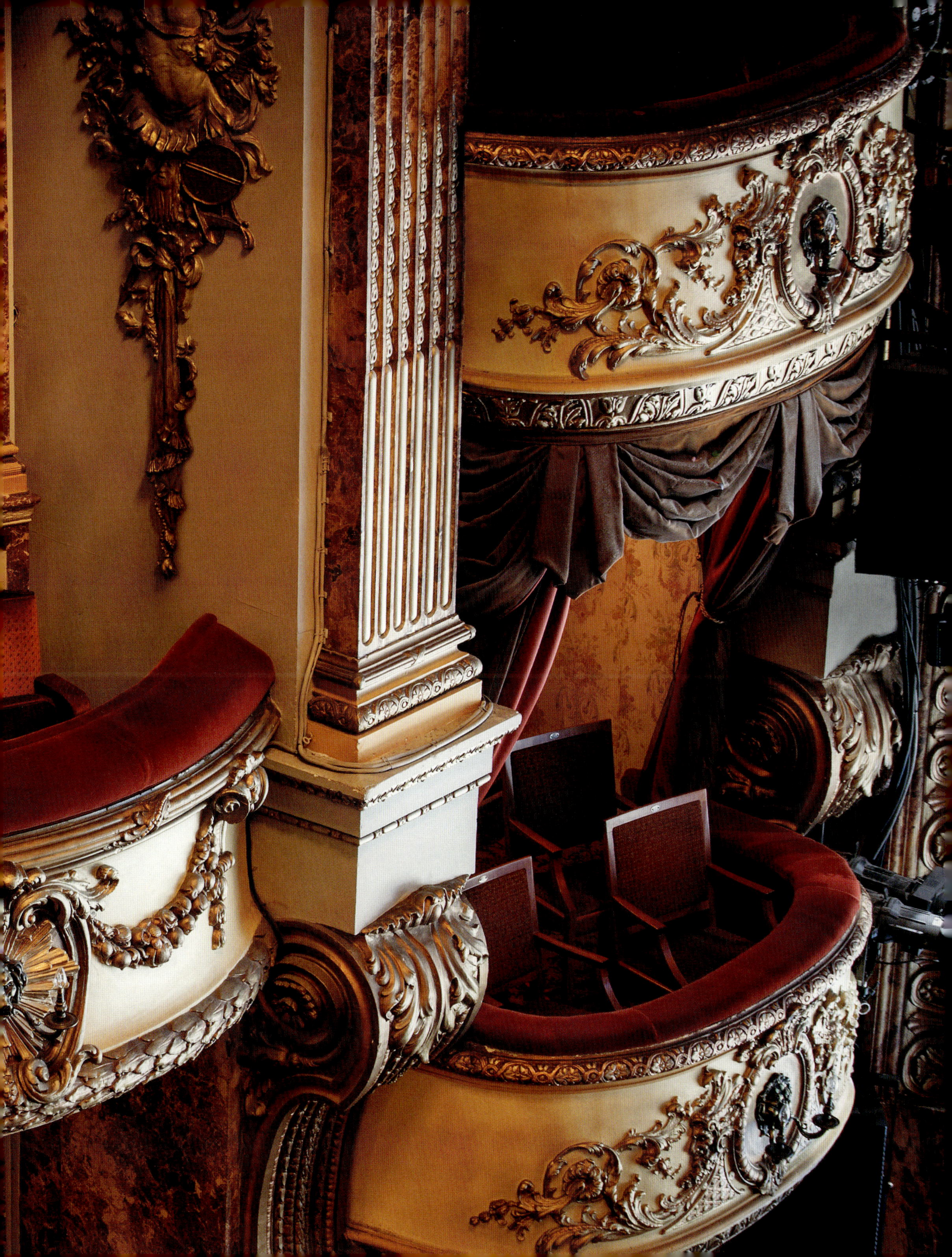

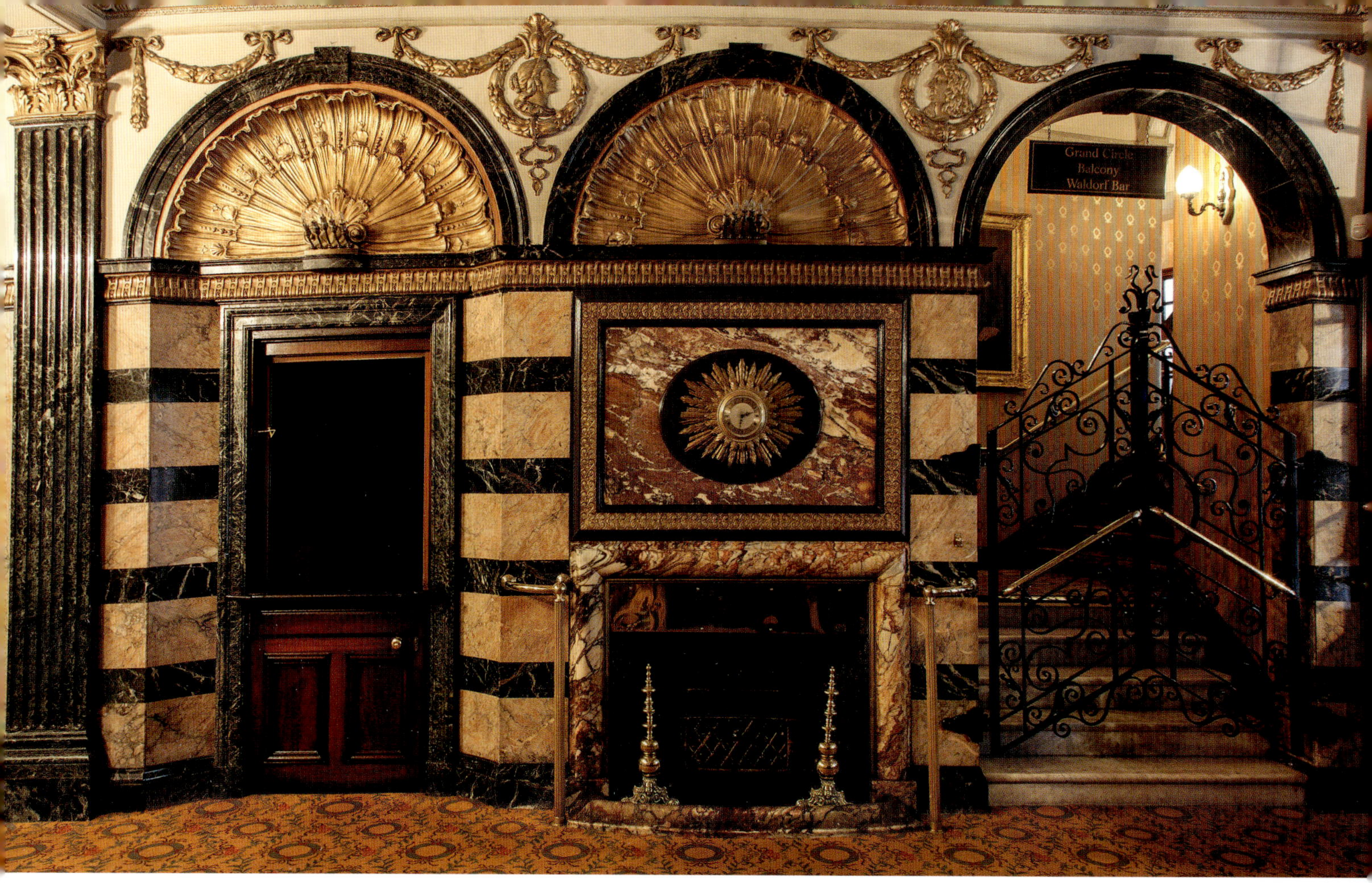
Grand Circle
Balcony
Waldorf Bar

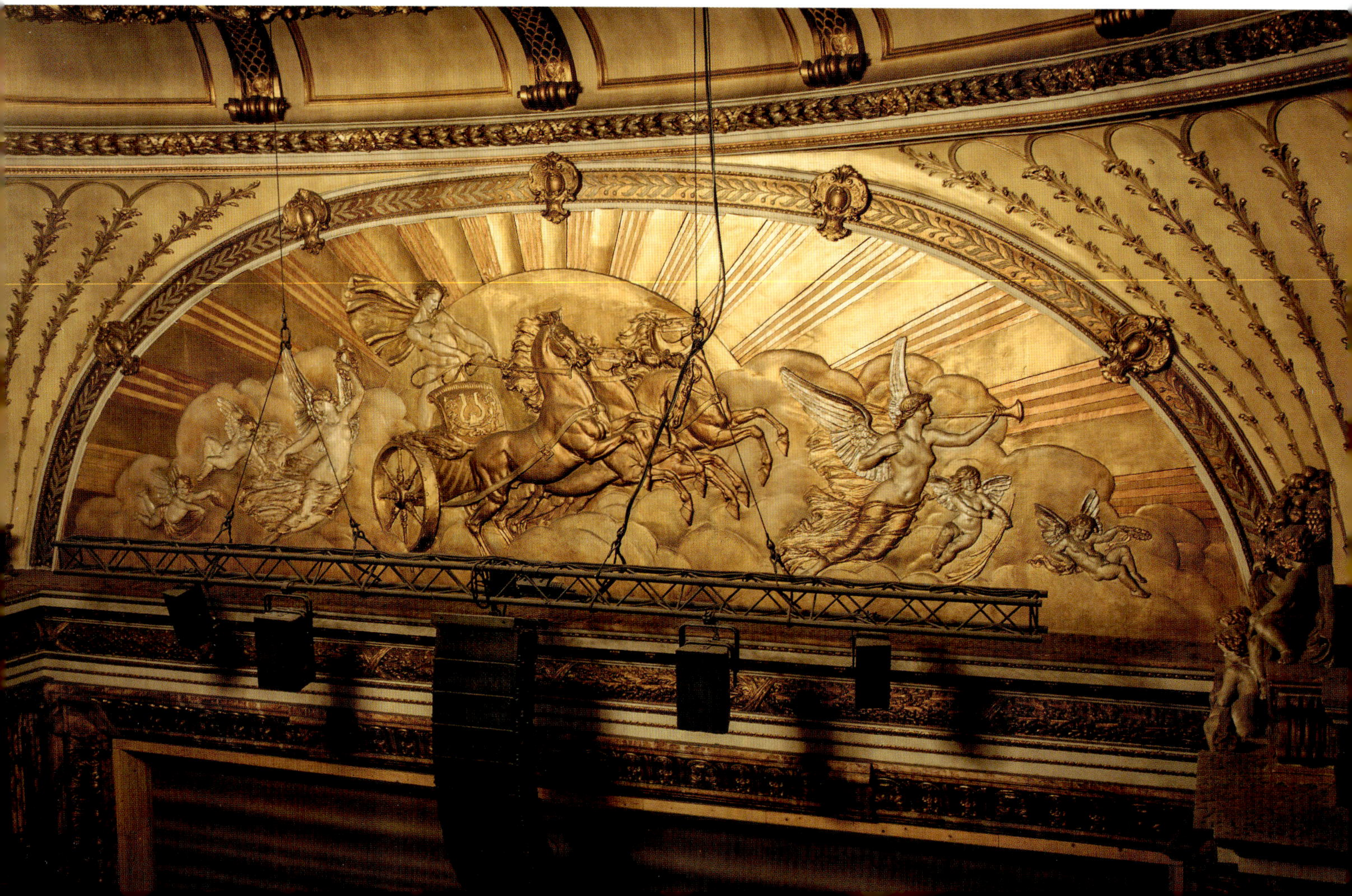

The Second Mrs Tanqueray. Enterprising, no doubt, but no way for a new theatre to create an identity for itself. Soon after, while the proscenium arch in their own theatre was being repaired, Herbert Beerbohm Tree and his company decamped from His Majesty's Theatre with their production of *Oliver Twist*; the following year, after the Avenue Theatre was destroyed by the collapse of a bridge on top of it, its lessee Cyril Maude moved into the Waldorf Theatre with some success, returning to his own theatre when it was rebuilt. There were yet more visitors in the form of the distinguished American Shakespeareans E. H. Sothern and Julia Marlowe; but somehow the theatre hadn't taken off. Gallingly, Seymour Hicks at the Aldwych was doing a roaring trade.

It was time for a change of name. J. A. Harrison redubbed it the Strand Theatre in 1909 and announced, with some fanfare, Leo Fall's operetta *The Merry Peasant*. It failed; two years later, the American manager F. C. Whitney took the lease, seizing the opportunity to rechristen the theatre in his own name. He failed, too, and the theatre fell into the hands of Louis Meyer, who changed the name back to the Strand, which ended the building's ontological crisis – for the next ninety years, at least. And with its new-old nomenclature, the theatre at last had its first copper-bottomed success, the premiere of *Mr Wu*, starring the intensely Caucasian barnstormer Matheson Lang as a most unlikely Chinese patriarch. The play remained at the core of his repertory for the rest of his acting life; his autobiography, indeed, is entitled *Mr Wu Looks Back*. Thereafter, Fred Terry and Julia Neilson delighted their public yet again with *The Scarlet Pimpernel*; after the First World War (in which the theatre sustained substantial damage during a Zeppelin raid) the magnificently farouche actor Arthur Bourchier, an old Etonian and Oxford graduate – founder, in fact, of the Oxford University Dramatic Society (OUDS) – took over the Strand and stayed there for over ten years, with great success. His career had its ups and downs – after his Hamlet, W. S. Gilbert observed that 'at last we can settle whether Bacon or Shakespeare wrote the plays. Have the coffins opened and whichever has turned in his grave is the author' – but he finally found his ideal role: Long John Silver in *Treasure Island*, which became the theatre's regular Christmas standby for many years. Still the lessee of the theatre, this splendid theatrical magnifico died in 1927. He had just been selected as a Labour candidate for Parliament, leaving behind him a pamphlet entitled 'Art and Culture in Relation to Socialism'.

OPPOSITE TOP The foyer of the Novello.
OPPOSITE BOTTOM Detail showing the bas relief over the proscenium arch, with Apollo in his chariot, the rays of the rising sun behind him.

Manager followed manager, and the fare became increasingly popular: George Grossmith, pioneer of revue and cabaret, took the theatre for a while, as did the dear old Terrys again; in the mid-1930s the great comedian Leslie Henson and his collaborator Firth Shephard had a big hit with *It's a Boy!*, swiftly followed by *It's a Girl!*; *Party* and *Night of the Garter* were not far behind. The Strand was by now mirth central: in 1935, *1066 and All That* took to its boards and ran for over a year, followed by a couple of plays by the greatest of English farceurs, Ben Travers, more normally to be found at the Aldwych; one of them, *Spotted Dick*, was playing as the Second World War broke out. There was a sudden appetite for spiritual nourishment, or at any rate for dramatic substance. The last of the actor-managers, Donald Wolfit, who had as usual been roaming the land with the giant masterpieces of the theatre repertoire – *Volpone*, *Macbeth*, *King Lear* – hastened to the Strand, where, at the height of the Blitz, like Myra Hess with her piano recitals at the National Gallery, he fed that appetite by offering hugely successful 'lunchtime Shakespeare' programmes. Then, in January 1942, he presented *Richard III* at the Strand, giving a performance so acclaimed that Laurence Olivier later admitted that his own conception of the part was largely governed by the desire – even the need – to do something different from Wolfit. But with his Richard Crookback, Wolfit

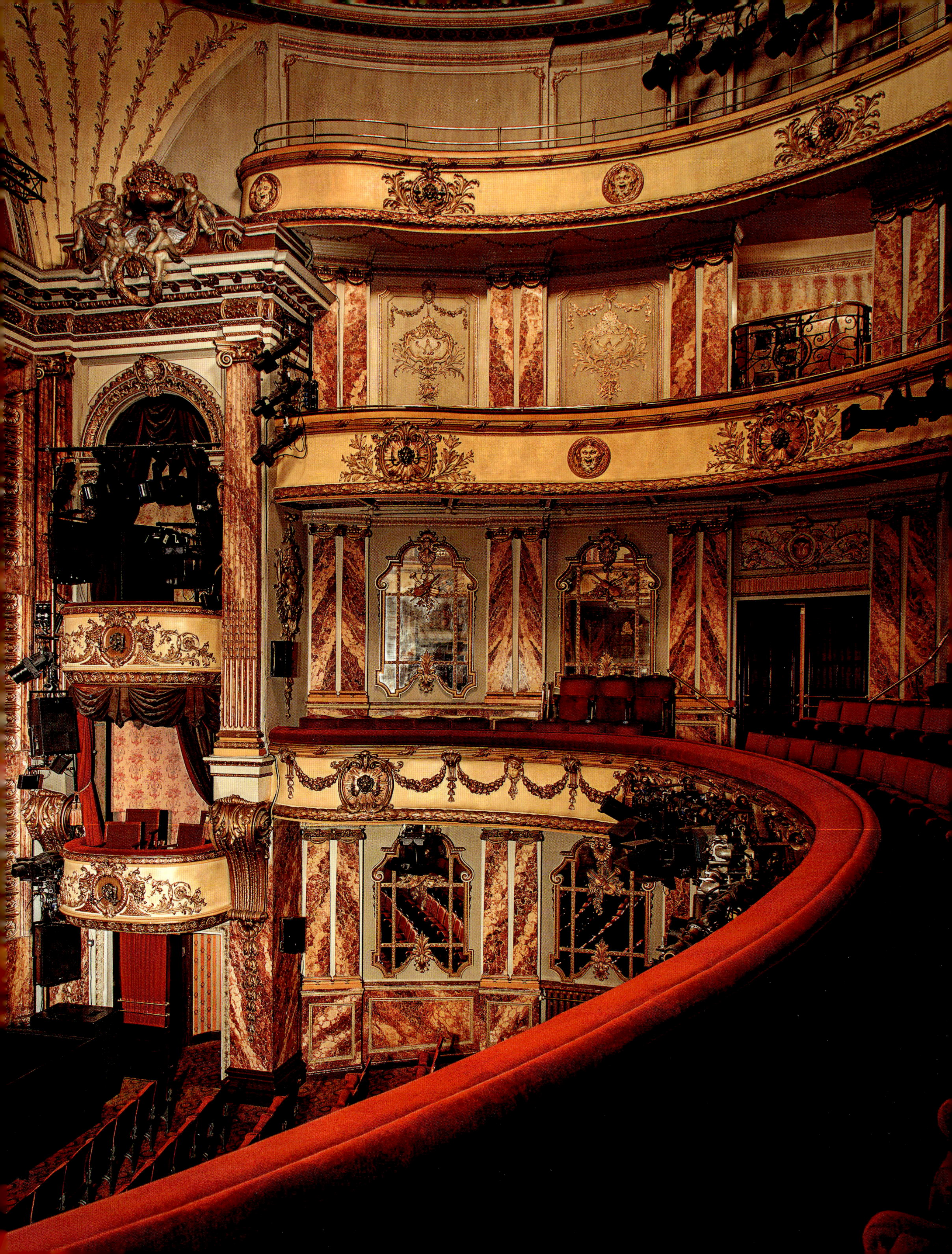

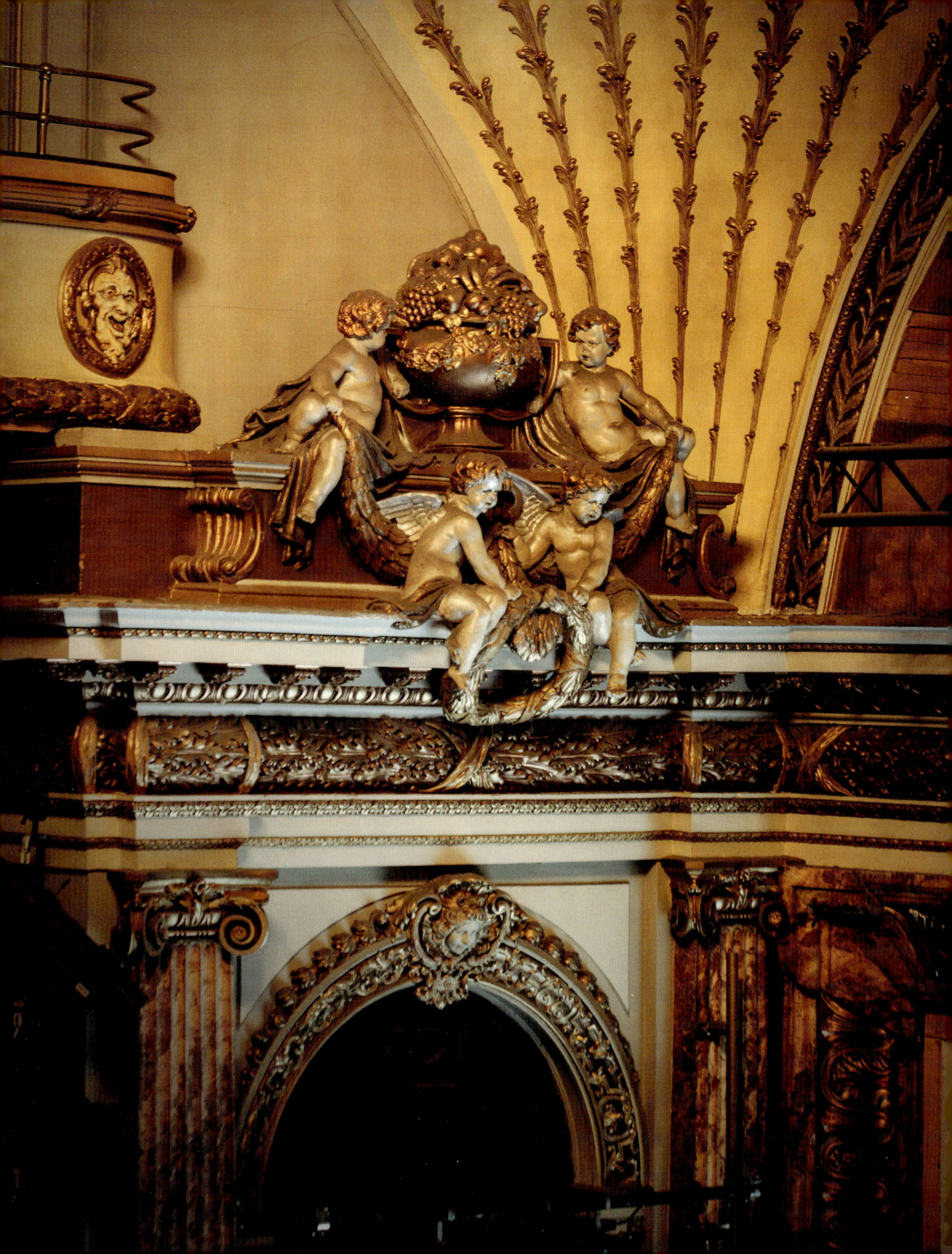

had exhausted the capacity of Strand audiences for seriousness, and shortly afterwards it reverted to type with a three-year run of *Arsenic and Old Lace*, satisfying the war-weary need for something blackly funny.

After the war there was more froth, culminating in another three-year run, this time the riotously bawdy *Sailor Beware!*, a Donald McGill postcard come to life. The ever-so-slightly shocking *For Adults Only* helped to pave the way for the sexually liberated 1960s. Before that, the Strand had suddenly and uncharacteristically gone avant-garde with Laurence Olivier and Maggie Smith in Orson Welles's production of Eugene Ionesco's expressionist allegory *Rhinoceros*, a transfer from the Royal Court; it did capacity business for its brief run. Perhaps inspired by its popular success, a new three-act American ballet, *The Princess*, whose heroine has 'lost the gift of laughter', tried its luck, only to be brutalised by the critics, who had clearly lost the gift not only of laughter but of ordinary human politeness. 'The ballet originated in Palm Beach', wrote Clive Barnes, 'and apparently shows American civilisation at its lowest ebb. Yet perhaps village-hall entertainment is the same the world over.' Nothing daunted, the management invited the public to attend without paying, an experiment that predictably failed: even fewer people went for free than had gone as paying customers.

In 1963 the theatre was full again with Stephen Sondheim's *A Funny Thing Happened on the Way to the Forum* starring Frankie Howerd, which ran for nearly two years. But its success was dwarfed by a noisy romp called *No Sex Please, We're British*, starring a young Michael Crawford (doing a faultless harlequin dive through the window, night after night) and the supremely elegant Evelyn Laye, then celebrating 55 years in the business; the show opened in June 1971 and was still running five years later when it transferred to the slightly smaller Garrick Theatre. Tom Stoppard's *The Real Thing*, in a rare excursion for the Strand into the dramatic theatre, ran for two years with Roger Rees and Felicity Kendal; perhaps encouraged by that, Kendal and Alan Bates not long after appeared in a repertory of *Much Ado About Nothing* and Chekhov's *Ivanov* in tandem. But it was the musical *Buddy* that seemed more at home there, happily running for seven years; the compilation show *The Rat Pack* was the last thing to play at the Strand Theatre, closing after a mere three years. Cameron Mackintosh had bought the theatre, and he inaugurated his regime not only by changing the theatre's name but by refurbishing it to a high level of finish and authenticity, so that the auditorium is now exactly as Sprague and his interior decorator, Hubert van Hooydonk, intended it.

The Novello opened in a blaze of classical splendour with a season of four plays given by the Royal Shakespeare Company. It is perhaps ironic that the company, peripatetic for so long since abandoning its residency as the Barbican, should have ended up in the sister theatre to the Aldwych, where it had had its base for so many glorious years. The company returned to the Novello the following year and the next, but has since retreated to its former (self-designed) fortress at the Barbican. A number of shows have come and gone since – some rather abruptly: the sophisticated musical *The Drowsy Chaperone* lasted just two months; its successor *Desperately Seeking Susan* only one, at a loss of £3.5 million. Finally, Abba became the name of the game: *Mamma Mia!* took hold in 2012 and shows no signs of ever letting go. The show is the almost exact late twentieth-, early twenty-first-century equivalent of Novello's Ruritanian fantasies: no crown princes or gypsy lasses, but every bit as escapist.

PREVIOUS LEFT The Novello Theatre auditorium.
PREVIOUS RIGHT Detail of the auditorium showing four plump and cheerful cherubs. Note the theatrical masks and the general feeling of enjoyment in the design.

*Ivor Novello himself had undergone a change of name, of course, since he was born David Ivor Davies in Cowbridge Road, East Cardiff.

OPPOSITE A mirror in the auditorium and cartouche with ancient Roman trophies.

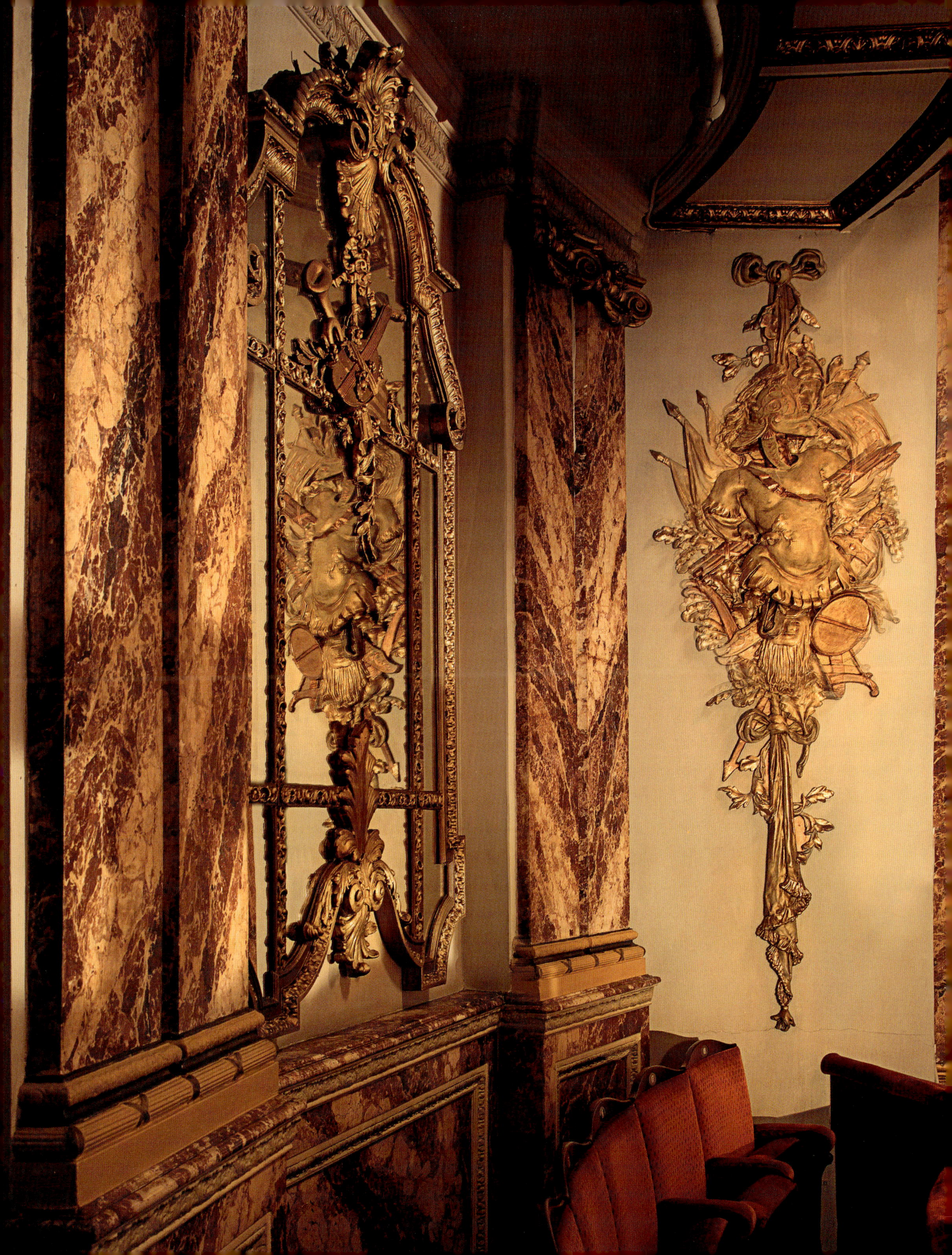

ALDWYCH

The Aldwych Theatre sits, raffish and handsome, at the corner of Aldwych and Drury Lane, a sort of bookend to the adjacent and expansive Waldorf hotel, whose other extremity is flanked by the Novello. These new buildings were all part of the stupendous Edwardian reshaping of the sizeable area from Holborn to the Strand, which wiped out what *The Standard* called 'foul and decaying congeries of streets' – the London Dickens knew. In place of its rickety-rackety warrens, the mighty boulevard of Kingsway now rolled down unchecked from Holborn to the newly created (and newly named) crescent of Aldwych, which was eventually completed, thirty years later, to the greater glory of Empire, by towering India House and Bush House. It was entirely fitting that the American Waldorf Astor hoteliers, building an empire of their own, should seek to establish a presence here with a kind of hotel new to Europe. But it was equally fitting that there should be theatres in this swaggeringly self-celebrating new development, since no fewer than four playhouses – the Olympic Theatre in Wych Street, the Opera Comique in the Strand, the Globe Theatre in Newcastle Street and the Gaiety Theatre in the Strand – had fallen under the developers' swingeing pickaxe.

The two new theatres were, as it happens, built before the hotel; both are the work of the same man, the astonishingly prolific architect W.G.R. Sprague, responsible for no fewer than eight London theatres, all still standing, all still in business. Sprague insisted on handsome facades for his theatres: he sought to create a stir of excitement in the theatregoer before she or he even entered the foyer. And indeed the exterior of the Aldwych Theatre has a lovely, curvaceous, come-hither quality. The architectural analysts of English Heritage describe it as 'lively Free Classicism of vaguely Beaux Arts derivation', which seems about right; it would not be at all out of place on the Champs-Élysées. It had *tous les conforts modernes*: according to a writer in *The Era*, 'one of the innovations that will be greatly appreciated by the male members of the audience is a commodious "smokers' gallery" above the entrance hall.' The *Daily Mirror* noted that 'a novel effect is produced by a circular balcony in the spacious grand saloon, giving a view of the fine crush room and the marble staircase leading from the principal entrance at the corner of Aldwych and Drury Lane,' which makes it one of the most attractive dress circle foyers in London.

Sprague was an avowed fan of Italian Renaissance style, but the Aldwych is not at all Italianate – it's all frou-frou and the promise of nocturnal naughtiness, which makes the choice of opening show in December 1905 all the more surprising. *Bluebell in Fairyland* was a Christmas fairy tale for children by Seymour Hicks, the vivacious actor-manager-writer who had commissioned the theatre. That out of the way, it embarked on a much more appropriate series of sparkling musical comedies under the management of the legendary American producer Charles Frohman. Frohman went down on the *Lusitania* in 1915, in heroic circumstances, but by then Hicks had long gone from the theatre he built, taking to the road and making movies; in his absence his theatre was occupied by some remarkable figures. In 1911 Chekhov's 1903 play *The Cherry Orchard*

OPPOSITE Side doors to the entrance lobby.

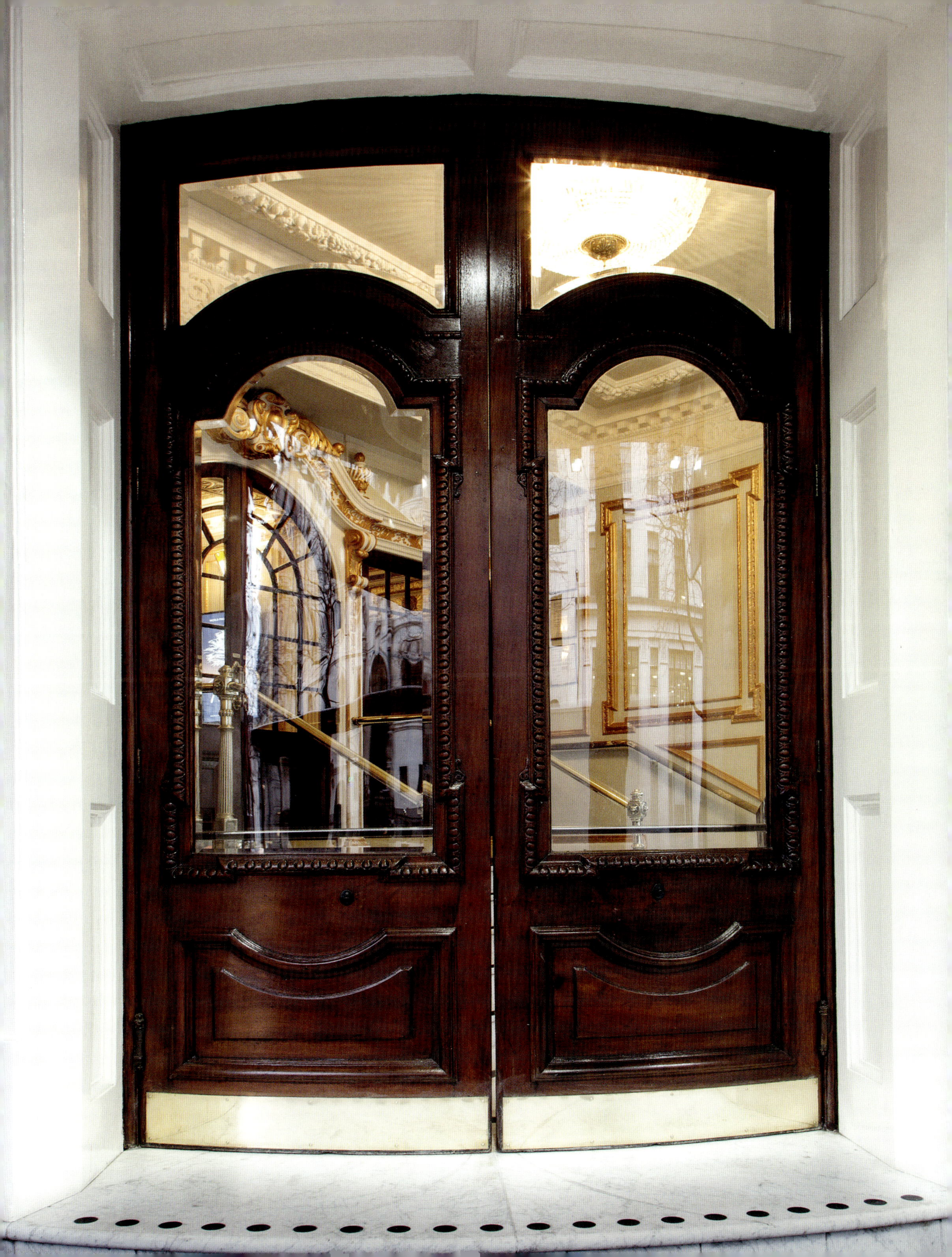

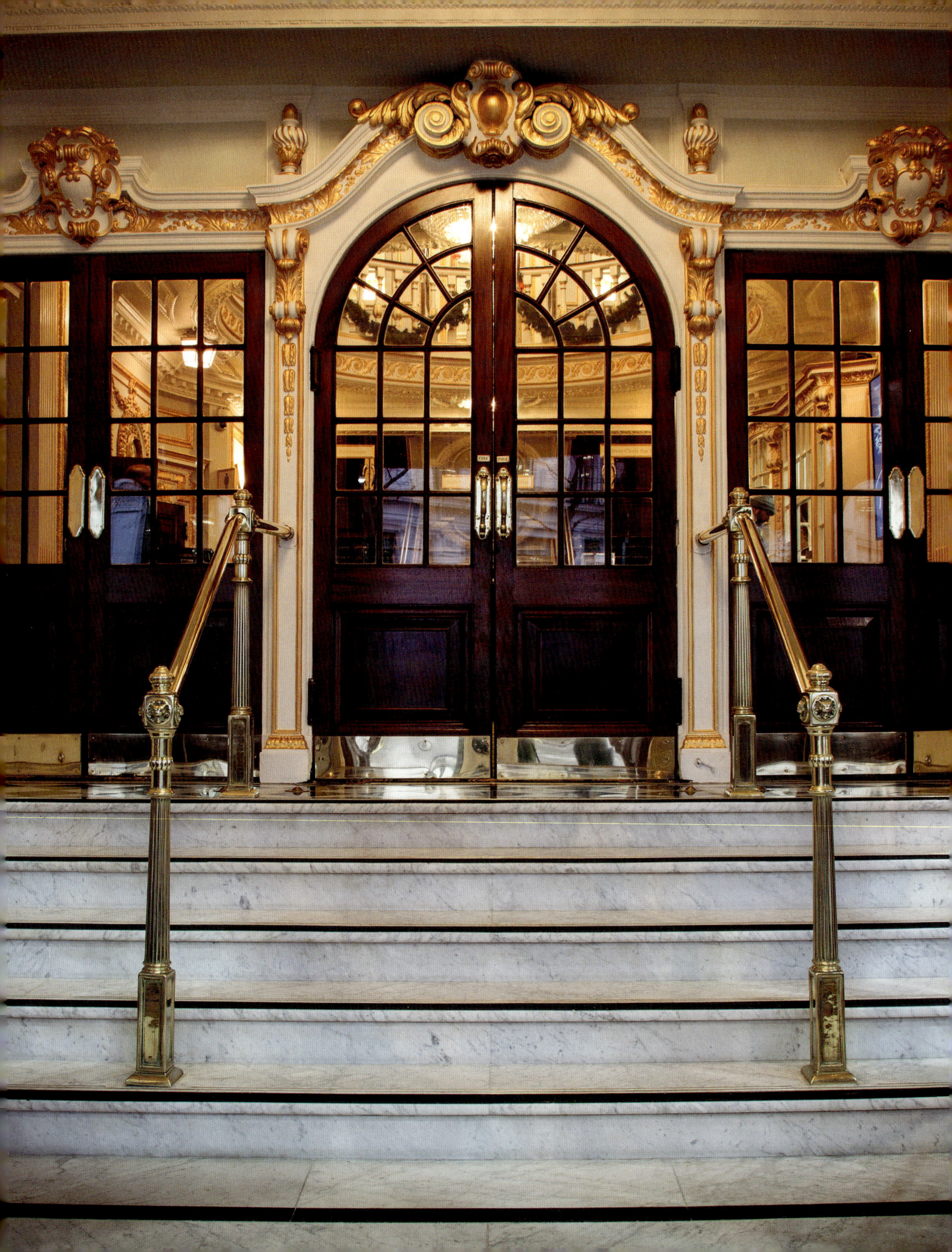

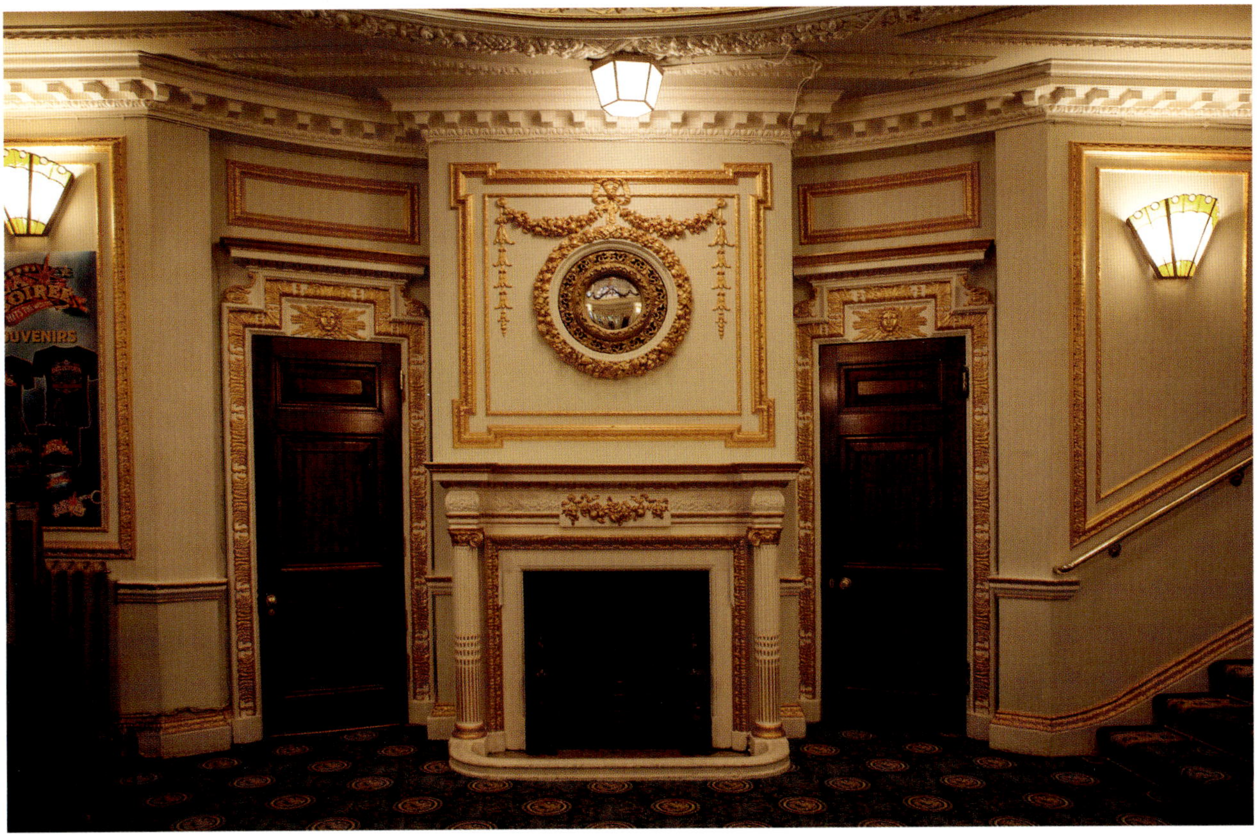

had its first production in English there, and two years later, continuing the Russian presence, it was hired by the great impresario Sergei Diaghilev for his brilliant young lover Vaslav Nijinsky to try to get to grips with *The Rite of Spring* before its premiere in Paris; the stage of the Aldwych Theatre was thus the first to hear the music of the future. Despite its frivolous exterior, the Aldwych has often found itself associated with high and sometimes positively radical art.

During the First World War the theatre was severely bombed; a drinking club for Australian servicemen was established in its ruins. But then it was rebuilt exactly as it had been, and from 1923 to 1933 was host to as crack a team of farceurs as England has ever assembled, performing the work of the most consistently and madly inventive of all English comedy writers, Ben Travers. Beginning in the mid-1920s the 'Aldwych farces', as they were called, included among their number those sublime masterpieces *Thark*, *Rookery Nook* and *Plunder*. One of the last of the Aldwych farces was called *Turkey Time*; by 1933, alas, it had been turkey time once too often. *A Bit of a Test* was their swansong; its plot – hinging on the attempts of the England cricket captain to keep his star batsman under control in Australia during an Ashes series – sounds highly promising, but it ran a mere 142 performances, which spelt curtains for the Aldwych farces. The great Austrian tenor Richard Tauber then swept into the theatre with his version – in German – of the operetta *Lilac Time*, an almost entirely fictive account of Schubert's love life; Schubert scholars might have thought it too was an Aldwych farce. Nonetheless, it clocked up more than six hundred performances.

OPPOSITE The main entrance doors.
ABOVE Fireplace and stairs in the lobby.

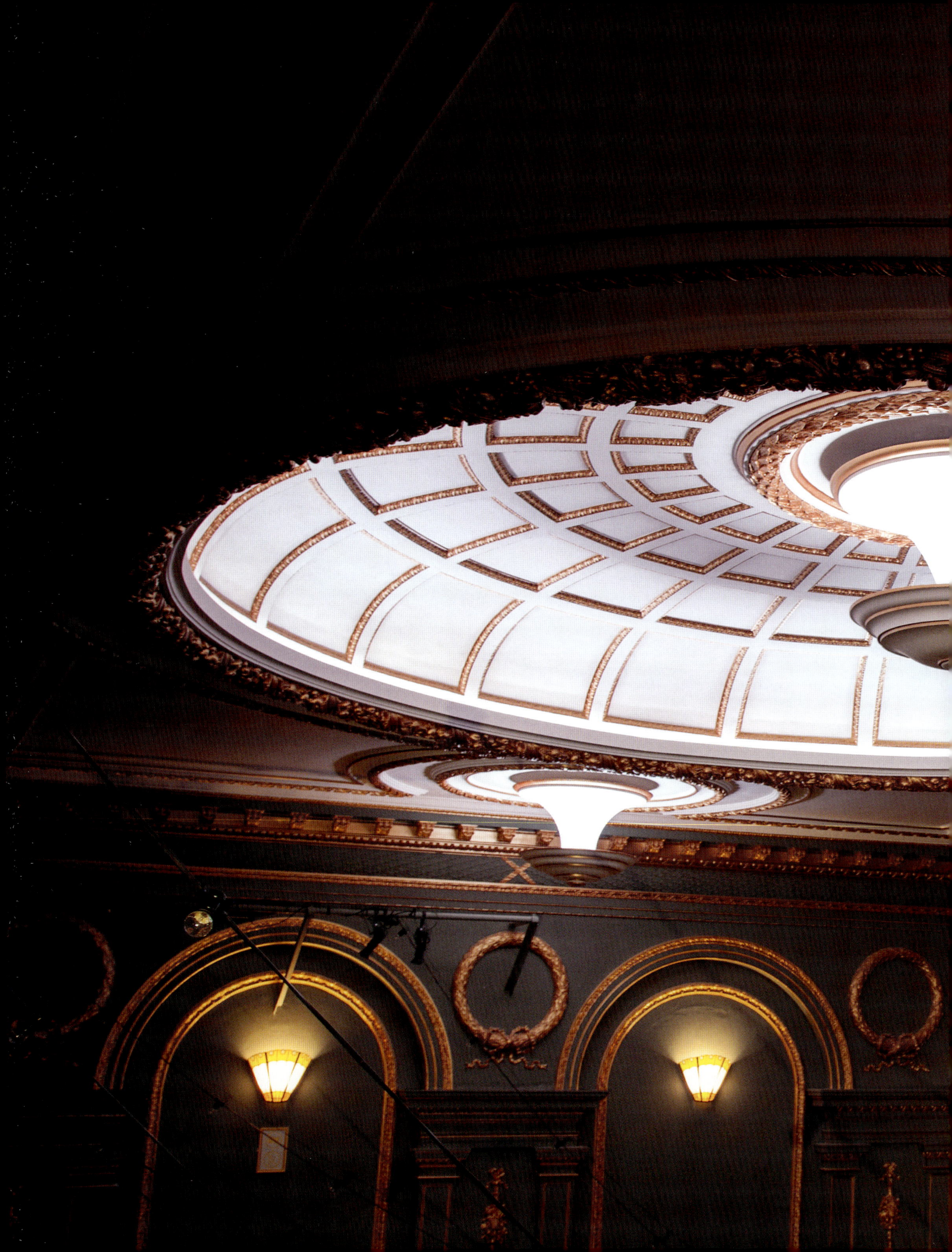

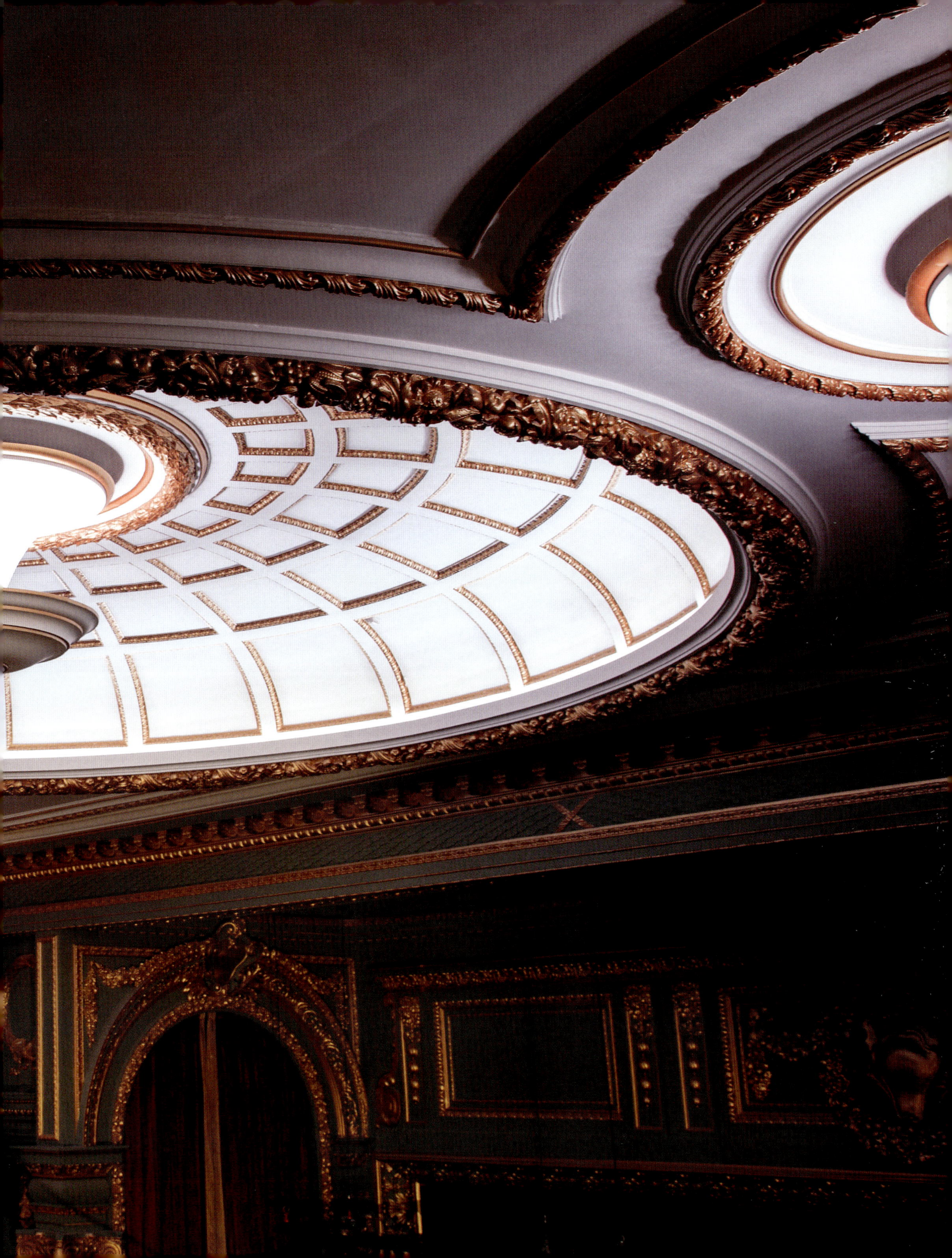

The Aldwych hit its stride again after the Second World War with what was then the *ne plus ultra* of drama, Tennessee Williams's neurotic masterpiece *A Streetcar Named Desire* in 1949, starring Vivien Leigh (before she had played Blanche in the film version) and directed by her then husband, Laurence Olivier. After *Streetcar* success was patchier, and like many another West End theatre in the 1950s the Aldwych was threatened with demolition. It was saved in 1960 in the nick of time by what was intended as a temporary London residency for the Shakespeare Memorial Theatre. The temporary stay lasted 22 years and constitutes what is probably the most glorious period in the history of Sprague's playhouse. Not that the new incumbents paid much respect to the master theatre-builder's original scheme: the elegant auditorium in *dix-huitième* Beaux-Arts style, with its two cantilevered balconies and ceiling with coffered dome, stucco work and finely executed pendants, trophies and beribboned wreaths, was painted a sombre black and gold; an apron stage was installed for greater connection between actors and audiences, losing two hundred seats in the process.

The work itself was extraordinary in its power and its urgency: not only were Stratford's finest productions, from Peter Hall's Wars of the Roses to Peter Brook's *A Midsummer Night's Dream*, automatically transferred to the Aldwych from the huge barn of the Memorial Theatre, happily relaxing into the Aldwych's much more intimate scale, but an unparalleled procession of new plays was first seen there, with John Whiting's *The Devils* (1961), Pinter's *The Homecoming* and *Old Times* (1965 and 1971), Tom Stoppard's *Travesties* (1974) and David Edgar's miraculous rendition of *Nicholas Nickleby* (1980) representing a tiny fraction of the company's world premieres. But there was more: when the RSC vacated the building during the summer, London theatregoers gorged on an astounding diet of great plays from across the world for three months every year, for ten years starting in 1964. The Moscow Art Theatre, the Comédie-Française, the Piccolo Teatro of Milan, Indian Kathakali theatre, Jean-Louis Barrault, Eduardo De Filippo, Anna Magnani, Núria Espert, Innokenty Smoktunovsky – the greatest performers on the face of the globe passed through the Aldwych's stage door, crammed their sets onto its narrow stage and squeezed themselves into those tiny dressing rooms for the glorious decade of World Theatre Seasons, convened by the maverick one-armed impresario Peter Daubeny. Its impact was immense. Laurence Olivier, artistic director, and Kenneth Tynan, literary manager of the new National Theatre then resident at the Old Vic, would nip across the river and sign up one director after another to come and work for them, resulting in the extraordinary range and audacity of much of the National Theatre's early work in the Waterloo Road. By the mid-1970s the newspapers that had sponsored the massively expensive event were themselves floundering, and it all came to a much-mourned end.

When the RSC, as it had now named itself, departed, the stage was restored to its former dimensions, the auditorium emerged from its black and gold coating, and the Aldwych resumed the up-and-down life of a commercial theatre. Sprague's facade remains as alluring as it ever was, his elegant auditorium with its marvellous acoustics still splendid to sit in. There has been a succession of plays, among them Anthony Minghella's darkly brilliant *Made in Bangkok*, Tom Stoppard's subtle *Indian Ink* and a two-year transfer in 1993 of Stephen Daldry's National Theatre rediscovery of *An Inspector Calls*, but for the most part the Aldwych has become a home to the musical theatre, including two not entirely successful Lloyd Webber shows (*Whistle Down the Wind* and *Stephen Ward*), a dazzling *Top Hat*, and much frequented shows celebrating, respectively, Carole King and Tina Turner, all very much in the spirit of Charles Frohman over a century earlier.

PREVIOUS The ceiling of the auditorium with extremely shallow dome.
OPPOSITE Stairs from the foyer. Quite Edwardian in feeling.

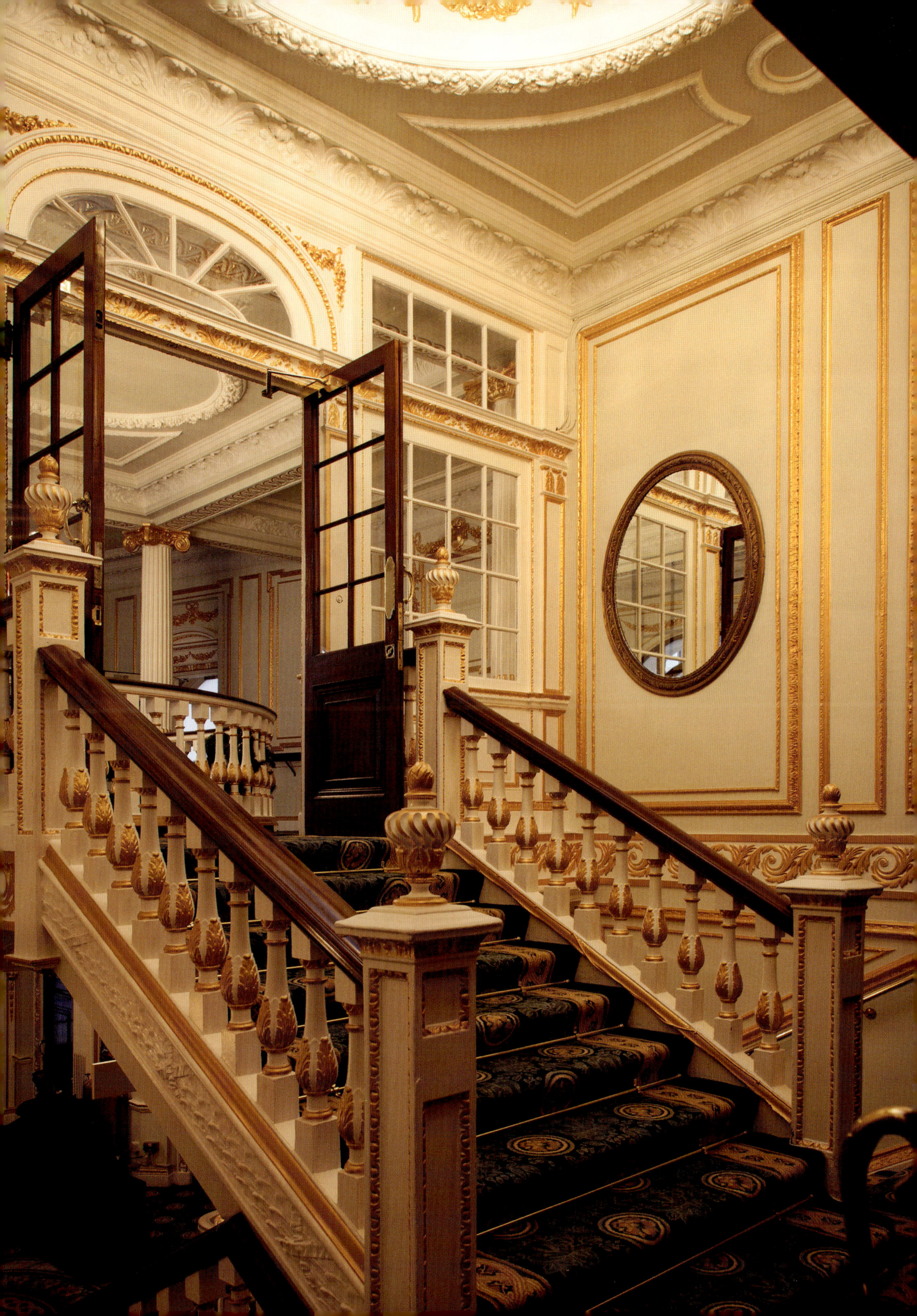

ST MARTIN'S THEATRE

West Street, just off Shaftesbury Avenue, is for a small road remarkably rich in theatres. The Ambassadors and the St Martin's were planned as twin – though not identical twin – theatres by Richard Verney, the Baron Willoughby de Broke, who owned the land. The Ambassadors opened in 1913, but the declaration of war a year later held up the second theatre – which was to have borne the name of the actor Sir Henry Irving – until 1916, when it opened as the St Martin's with a bit of froth called *Houp La!*, produced by the greatest of all impresarios of revue, C. B. Cochran. 'It must add one more to the many puzzles which English characteristics have afforded the Hun', said the *Financial Times*, 'that anyone should have the courage to build and open a new theatre in war time.' It was not achieved without difficulty; even the first night had to be postponed, twice.

The architect was the great Australian-born W.G.R. Sprague, responsible in London alone for designing the Queen's Theatre, the Gielgud, the Novello, the Aldwych, Wyndham's and, of course, the Ambassadors; it was his last theatre but one (the massive Streatham Hill Theatre, now empty and unused, was his swansong). Sprague was only 53 when the St Martin's opened and at the very zenith of his trade. All his theatres have distinctive characters, but this bijou playhouse (capacity 505) is unlike any other theatre in London. Wood-panelled, it has little of the red-and-gold, slightly operatic feel of many London auditoriums, having, rather, a sense of the sort of library in somebody's country seat in which murders are carefully explained by the all-knowing detective to the dumbfounded participants in hideous events. Indeed, the current incumbent of the theatre, Agatha Christie's *The Mousetrap*, takes place in just such an environment, so that the audience almost feels as if it is in the room with the characters – perhaps even as potential suspects.

The theatre's facade is rather more conventional than its interior, with recessed columns above the awning, at the centre of which was once a cartouche with the Willoughby de Broke coat of arms; this fell off in 1940 during the Blitz and was never replaced, even though the family (after a period during which the theatre fell into other hands) part owns it again. The theatre is notable – or was until 1974 – for its variety of fare; its scale and modest overheads make it possible to run fairly recherché material there. After the giddiness of *Houp La!* the St Martin's hosted *Damaged Goods*, Eugène Brieux's hard-hitting play about syphilis; Clemence Dane's *A Bill of Divorcement* (1920), about hereditary insanity; and, a little later, *The Likes of Her*, set in an East End slum, in which Hermione Baddeley scored a huge success. *Spring Cleaning* (1925), one of a string of smash-hit comedies, witty and sexy, by Frederick Lonsdale, caused outrage by including a prostitute among the dramatis personae, and in 1933 Mordaunt Shairp's *The Green Bay Tree* sensationally hinted at the sexual corruption of a young man by 'a rich hot-house sybarite'.

All this intensity was partly due to the management of the theatre, from 1920 to 1937,

OPPOSITE The stage seen from a box. Wood everywhere – pilasters, columns, balconies, panelling – which gives the effect of a toy theatre or the interior of a cigar shop.

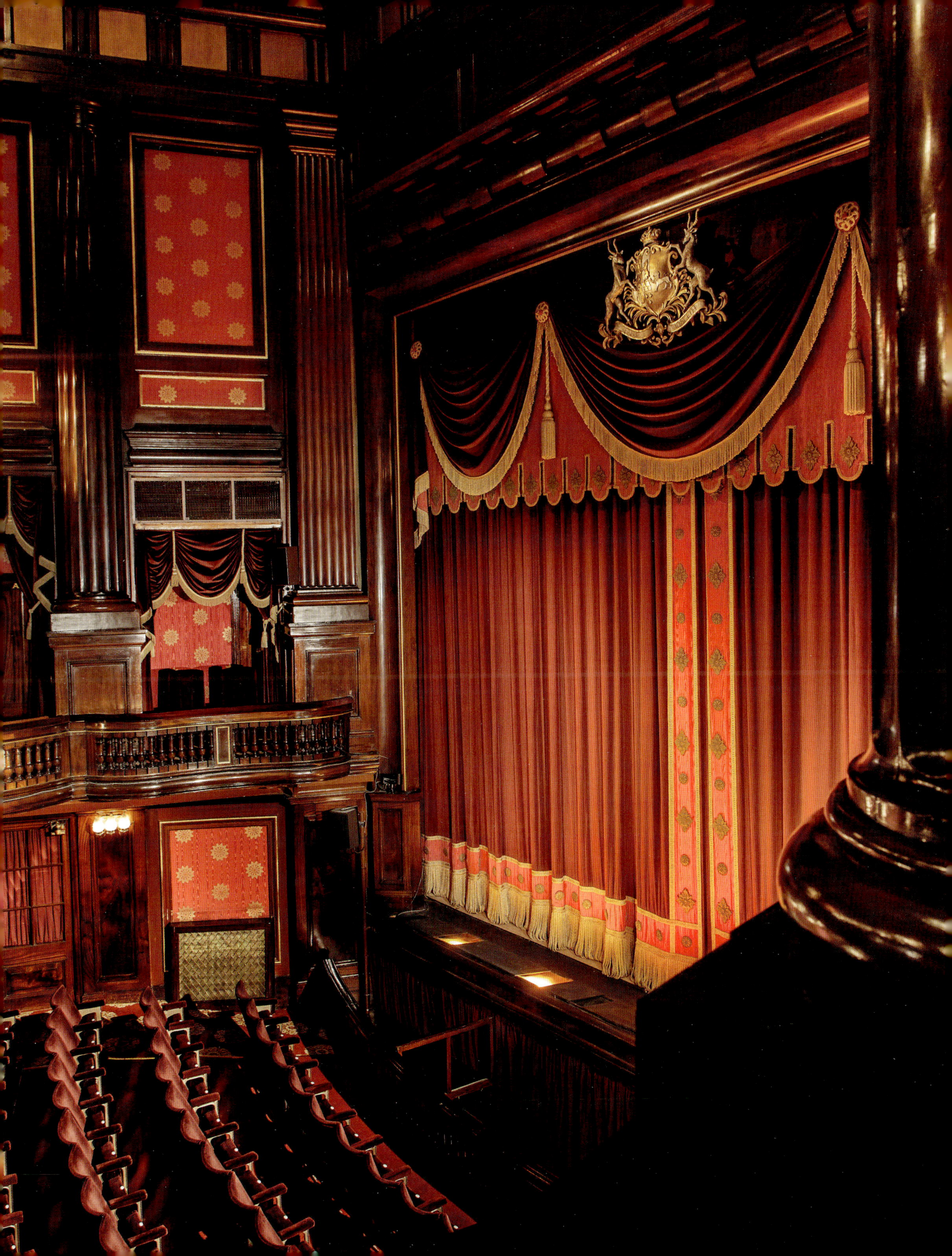

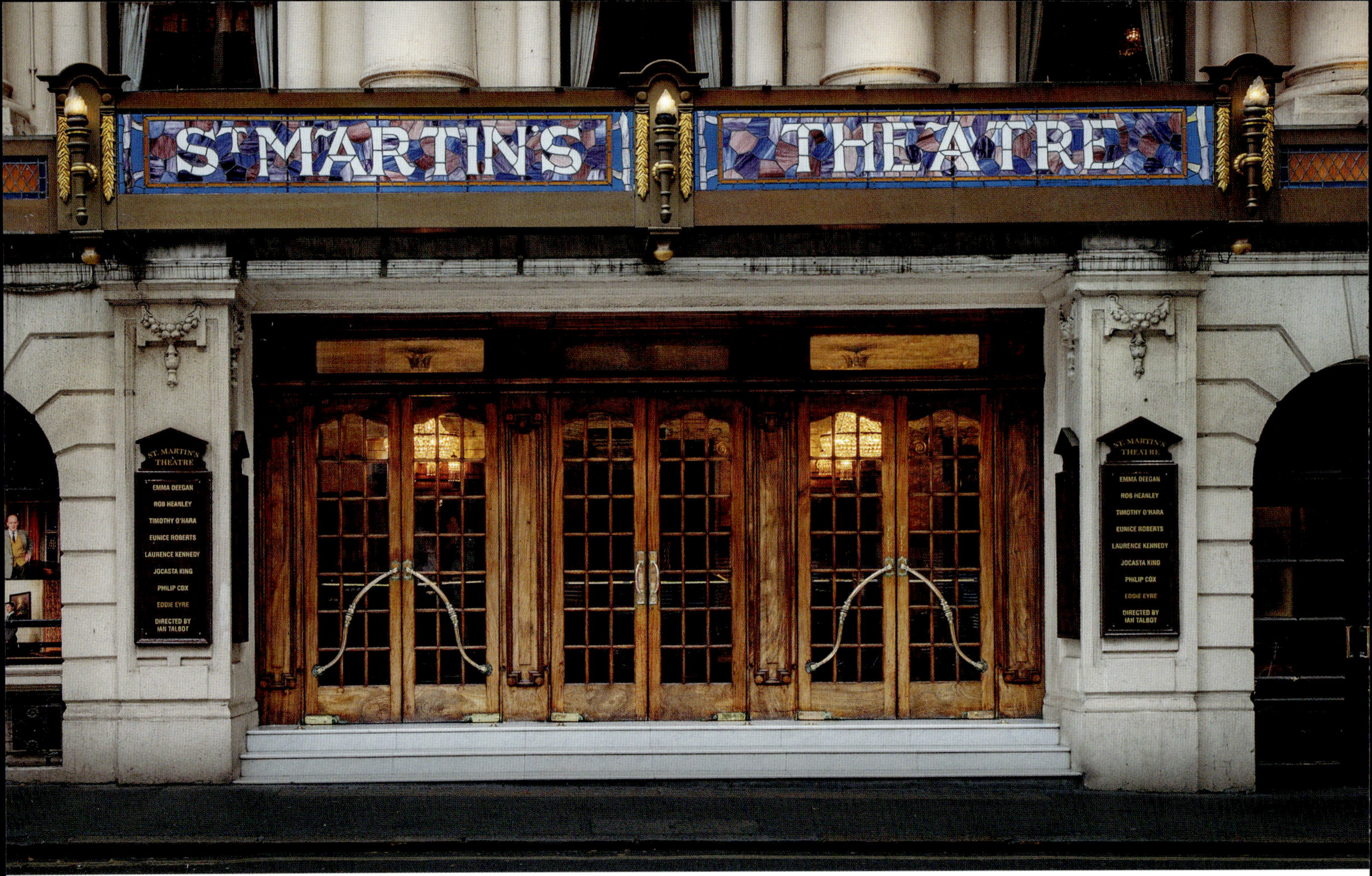
ST MARTIN'S
THEATRE
ST. MARTIN'S THEATRE
EMMA DEEGAN
ROB HEANLEY
TIMOTHY O'HARA
EUNICE ROBERTS
LAURENCE KENNEDY
JOCASTA KING
PHILIP COX
EDDIE EYRE
DIRECTED BY
IAN TALBOT

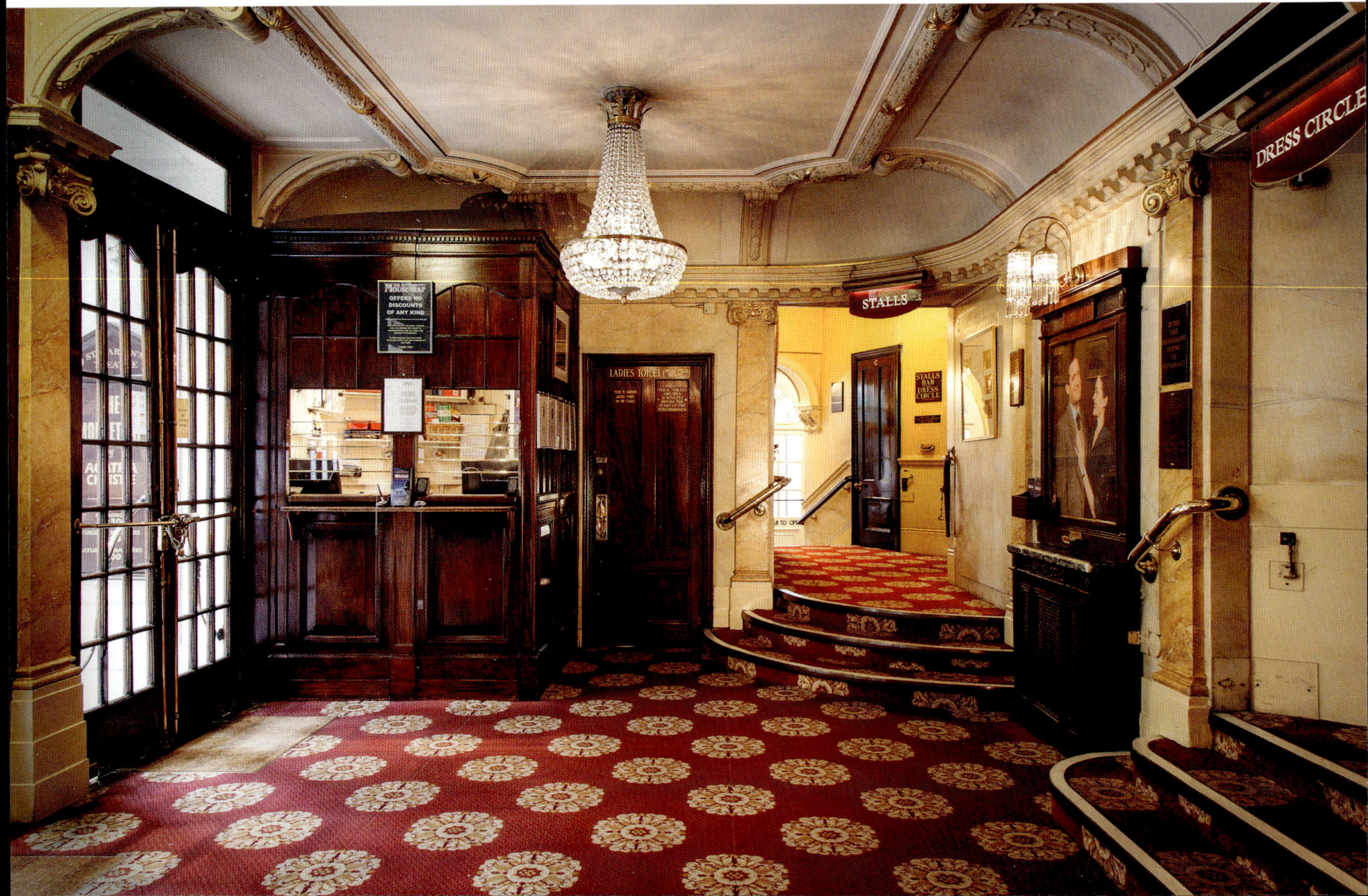
DRESS CIRCLE
STALLS
STALLS BAR DRESS CIRCLE
LADIES TOILET
OFFERS NO DISCOUNTS OF ANY KIND

by the famously high-minded and rigorous director Basil Dean and his associate Alec Rea. But they were by no means averse to commercial success, which they had with a number of John Galsworthy plays and, in 1925, the original production of *The Ghost Train*, a runaway hit written by the actor Arnold Ridley, apotheosised over forty years later on television when he created the role of Private Godfrey in *Dad's Army*.

Other commercial triumphs in the 1930s were the Broadway hits *Meet the Wife* and *The Wind and the Rain*, and the premiere of J. B. Priestley's magnificently subversive comedy *When We Are Married*, now a classic, regularly revived. It was the occasion for the author's debut as an actor. Six weeks into the run, the actor playing the wonderfully funny role of the photographer was knocked down by a car, and Priestley took over. 'I don't know how it will turn out,' the great man said during late-night rehearsals with the rest of the cast. 'Although I wrote the part, it isn't so easy to remember it. Just how many lines there are I don't know, and I shouldn't like to know; but there it is. As things are at present I shall appear tomorrow night; and now I must get on with my rehearsals.' He had a quiet triumph, but assured the audience at the curtain call that he would not be forsaking his primary calling. Shortly after he relinquished the role in November 1938, the show was transmitted live from the theatre by the infant television service at Alexandra Palace, a forerunner of today's hugely popular live transmissions which seem – paradoxically, then as now – to make theatregoing more popular.

The St Martin's Theatre's association with murder most foul was confirmed after the Second World War by the inexplicably long run of the mediocre thriller *The Shop at Sly Corner*, written by a sitting Tory MP, Edward Percy. The late 1940s and 1950s were fallow years for the theatre – despite the transfer from the Watergate Club of the radical revue *Cranks*, devised by the brilliant and radical South African choreographer John Cranko, with a witty score by John Addison for harpsichord, doubled by piano and harp. Anthony Newley and Annie Ross led the small company; it seemed to be the acme of sophistication, ideally suited to the intimacy of the wood-panelled auditorium.

By the end of the 1950s the Willoughby de Broke family, dissatisfied with the management of the theatre, took a controlling interest again. The independent television company Associated-Rediffusion took a long lease on the St Martin's in 1960, but in the company's expansion and reconfiguration little came of the relationship, and despite decent successes like John Mortimer's *The Wrong Side of the Park* it drifted on until – murder again, or at least planned murder – Anthony Shaffer's fiendishly ingenious *Sleuth* arrived triumphantly in February 1970, staying there until March 1973.

The rest is history: *The Mousetrap*, after occupying the Ambassadors Theatre for 34 years, transferred to the St Martin's in 1974, where it seems permanently installed. It's a little sad, perhaps, that whole generations of playgoers who have either seen *The Mousetrap* at the Ambassadors in their childhood or are simply untempted by the prospect of catching a seventy-year-old run of a play whose thrills have become rather mild, will never know the unique delights of Sprague's exquisite playhouse.

In 1968, when Dame Agatha's play was still at the Ambassadors and was boasting of its '15th staggering year!', Tom Stoppard, newly famous for *Rosencrantz and Guildenstern Are Dead*, was persuaded to revive an earlier play of his entitled *A Walk on the Water*, which was duly staged (as *Enter a Free Man*) at the adjacent St Martin's. The play was not liked by the critics, despite Michael Hordern's consummate performance in the leading role, and bookings were sluggish, the advance negligible. Stoppard begged his management to allow him to put up a sign outside the theatre saying 'Second staggering week', but, sadly, they refused his request.

OPPOSITE TOP Exterior of the main entrance.
OPPOSITE BOTTOM The foyer with box office.

APOLLO VICTORIA

For a while, from the late 1950s, it seemed as if the live theatre was doomed: once noble playhouses were condemned to the wrecker's ball, while the lucky ones – but oh, the humiliation – were converted into cinemas. The Saville Theatre, the Prince Edward Theatre, the London Coliseum: all at one point were given over to motion pictures; only the Saville stuck with celluloid, becoming the Odeon Covent Garden, the glorious bas-relief frieze on its facade, celebrating the performing arts, barely noticed above all the neon-lit posterage below. The reverse process was a great deal less common, the most remarkable example being the transformation of the New Victoria, the flagship of Gaumont-British Pictures, into the Apollo Victoria, home of mega-musicals. The transformation is all the more remarkable because the original building was considered at the time of its opening in 1930 to be the triumphant apex of cinema architecture, synthesising American and European – more particularly German – modernist influences into an extraordinary and enormous people's palace along the lines of Berlin's Grosses Schauspielhaus, which Hans Poelzig had designed as a live theatre a decade earlier. The architect of the New Victoria, Ernest Walmsley Lewis, acknowledged that astounding building as his chief influence, but a sojourn in America had also profitably introduced him to the work of Frank Lloyd Wright, with its emphasis on organic forms. These exalted influences, however, resulted in a building that, though austere from the outside – all parallel lines in the German Deco style, and with identical entrances on either side of the building – is a positive riot of sensual titillation inside. Once you pass through the magnificent foyer, the auditorium, designed by William Edward Trent, plunges you into a subaquatic wonderland in Art Deco style – a nod, it appears, to the managing director's passion for messing about in boats. Lit in pale blues and greens and adorned with naughty mermaids, it was as sumptuous and sexy as any of the great Los Angeles movie palaces. 'Imagine a mermaid's dream of Heaven', rhapsodised the *Gaumont British News*, with 'huge submarine flowers against the walls that branch up and out and throw mysterious light towards the realms above, and glassy illuminated stalactites hanging from the ceiling; and a proscenium like a slender host of silver trees, and silvered organ pipes that shoot up to the roof'. This wonderland opened with the rather sedate film *Old English*, starring George Arliss (who had just won an Academy Award) in the title role, but the evening included – as most cinema bills still did – a variety show, this one entitled *Hoop-La!*, as well as the first performance by the great Reginald Foort on the New Victoria's stupendous three-manual, fifteen-rank Compton organ.

These theatrical elements died away as cinema sound equipment – and it is worth remembering that the New Victoria opened only a year after the introduction of sound – got better and better. But the fact that they had once existed meant that when cinema attendances started to decline rapidly in the 1950s, the theatre was well enough provided with a stage and dressing rooms for it to be spared from the

OPPOSITE The staircase ahead of the entrance. Art Deco top to toe, including the carpet.

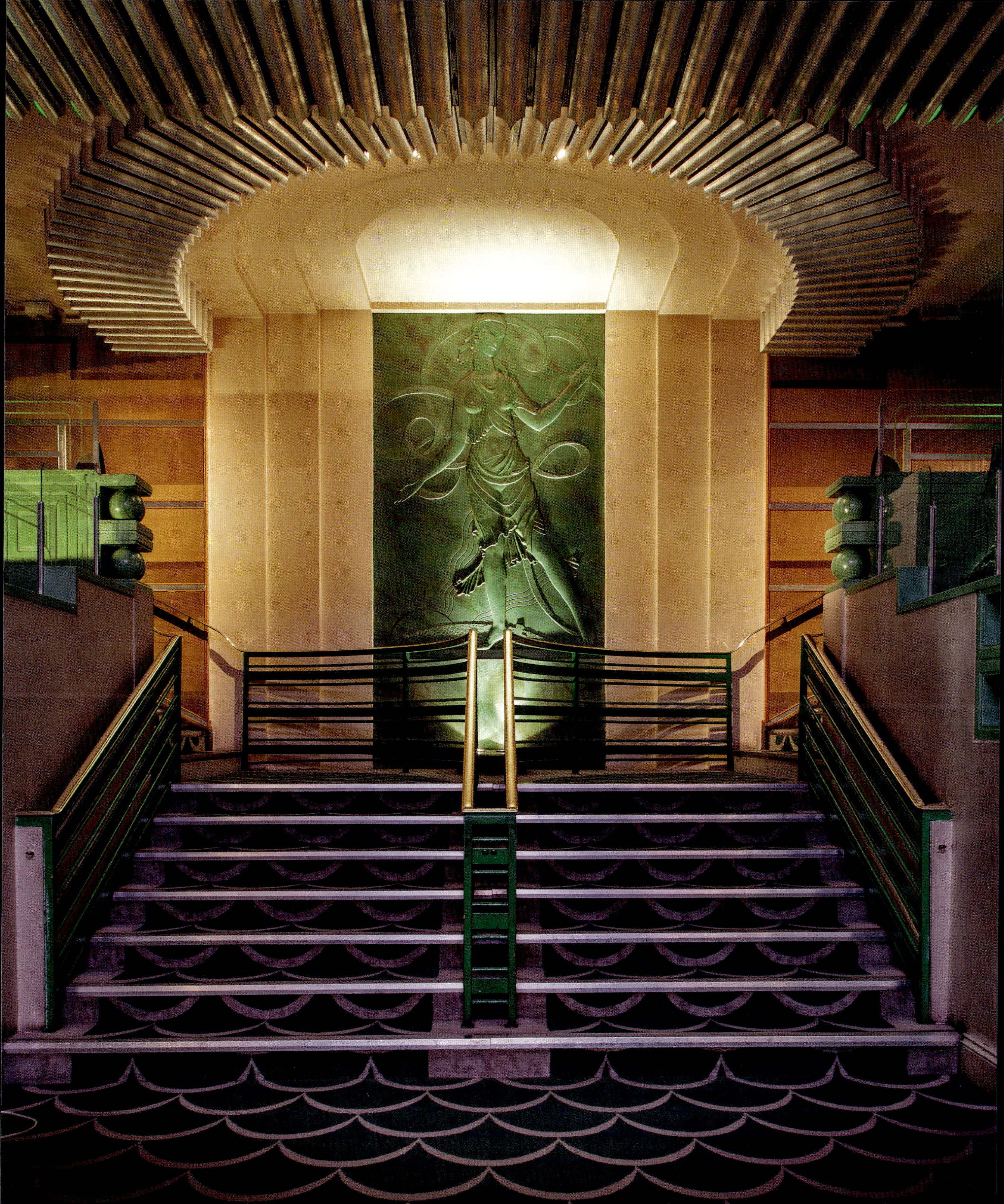

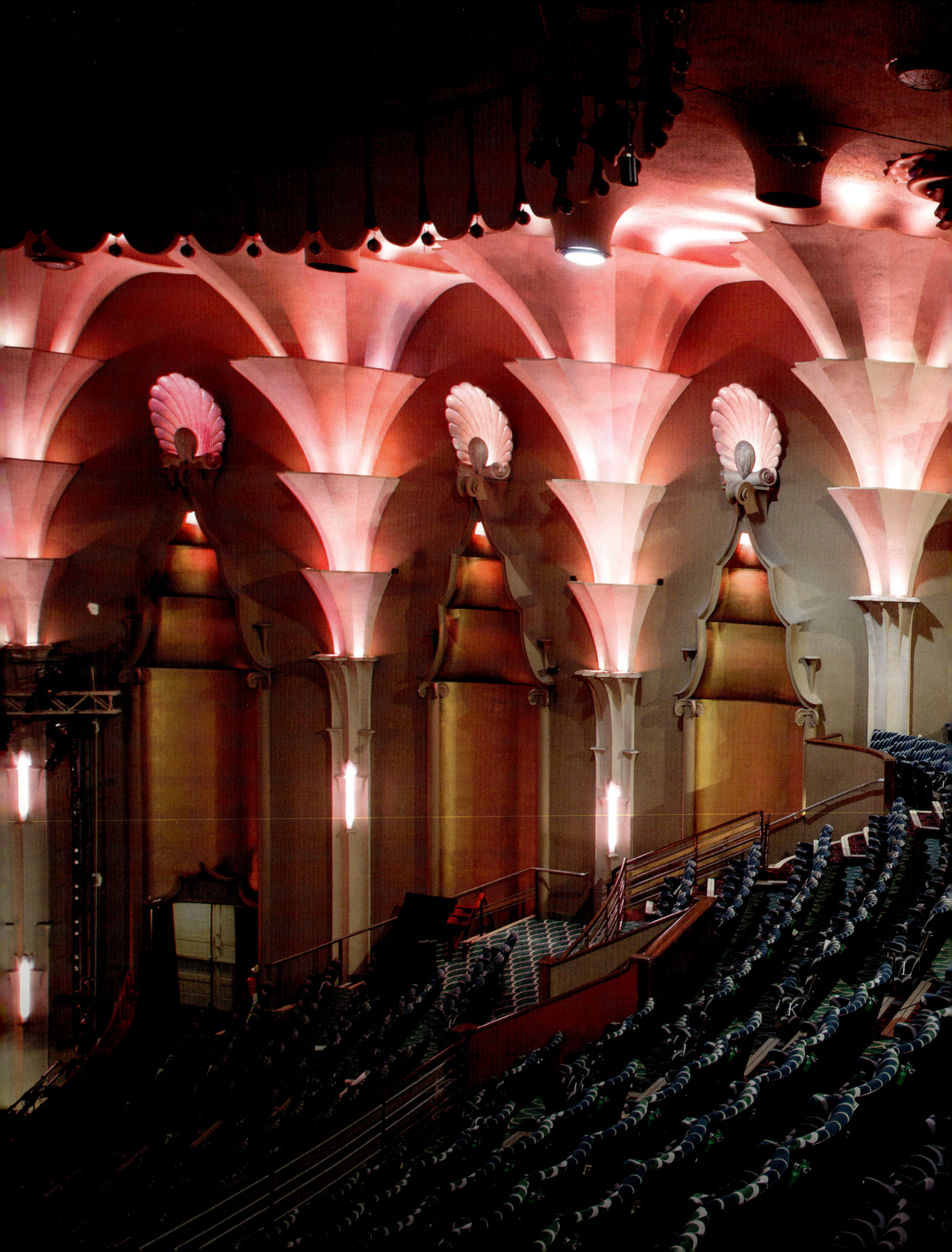

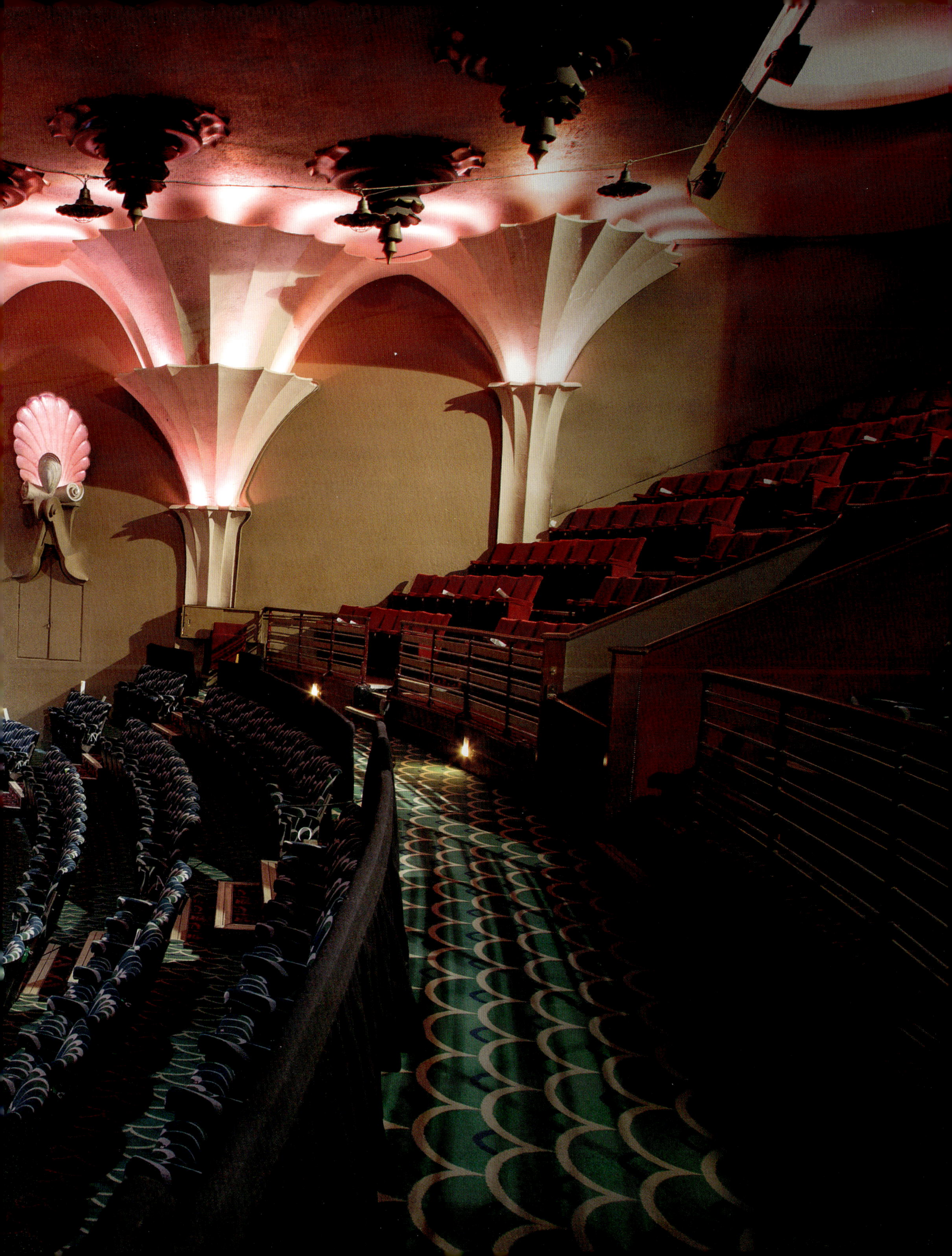

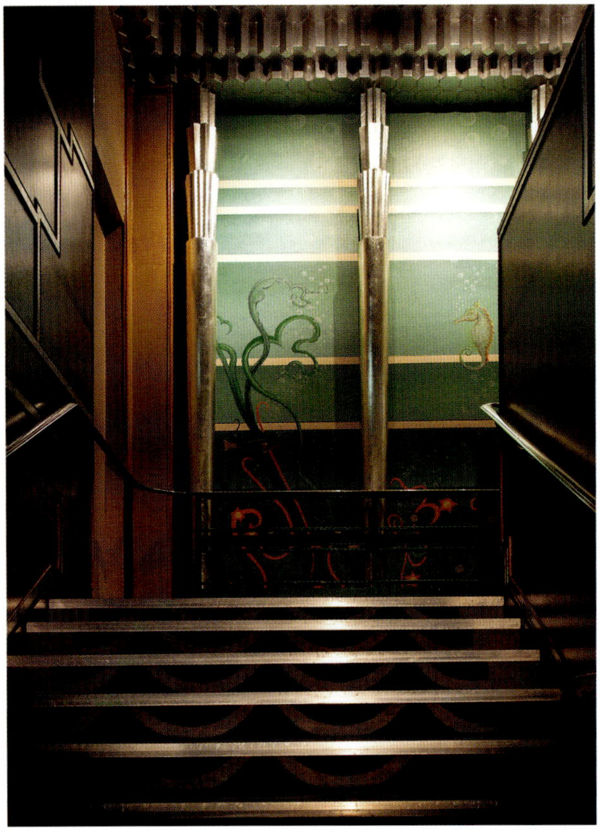

wreckers' ball, allowing for theatrical performances, principally ballets and live shows, to take place in tandem with movies. But it became increasingly difficult to fill its nearly three thousand seats with moviegoers, and in 1975 the cinema as such came to a bloody end with a Gothic double-bill comprising *Legend of the Werewolf* and *Vampire Circus*. It fell dark for nearly five years, until it was leased by Apollo Leisure, who renamed the theatre after themselves, thereafter hosting a number of big-name concerts – Shirley Bassey, Dean Martin, Liza Minnelli – and musical revivals (*The Sound of Music*, *Fiddler on the Roof*, *Camelot*). In 1984, Andrew Lloyd Webber installed his new show *Starlight Express*, which had nothing to do with Algernon Blackwood and Victoria Pearn's 1915 fairyland play for children, and everything to do with getting a cast of thirty whizzing around the auditorium on roller skates over tracks that looped into and around the auditorium and right up to the balcony, lifted and tilted by a six-tonne steel bridge connecting the different levels of the set. Needless to say, Lewis's delicately shaded underwater seascape pretty well disappeared from view under a tangle of metalwork. The show was a stupendous success: there were 7,500 performances over eighteen years. Even allowing for the loss of a thousand seats to make way for the machinery, this meant that by the end close to 15 million people had crossed the foyer of the theatre via one or other of the entrances on either side.

After the last skates had been hung up and the machinery was shunted into storage, the theatre closed and the auditorium was restored to something very close to its original 1930 decor, in which state it hosted *Bollywood Dreams*. Its current attraction, *Wicked*, opened in 2006 and – in reference to Oz's capital, the Emerald City – the auditorium was flooded with green light, but otherwise the Art Deco glory of the theatre is intact; some of the organ's silver pipes have even been incorporated into the show's design. Combining the fantastical glories of the golden age of cinema design with the epic splendour of the German modernist movement, the Apollo counts as one of the most extraordinary theatres in the land. 'A symbol of hope', the modernist critic P. Morton Shand called it in 1930. Though perhaps not quite that any more, it is nevertheless a gorgeous grotto from which to watch a spectacular show. And that is certainly one of the things that the theatre is all about.

PREVIOUS The auditorium – such fantasy, like a palace beneath the ocean.
ABOVE Part of the staircase.

OPPOSITE TOP The staircase from the dress circle.
OPPOSITE BOTTOM Looking at the entrance doors from inside the foyer.

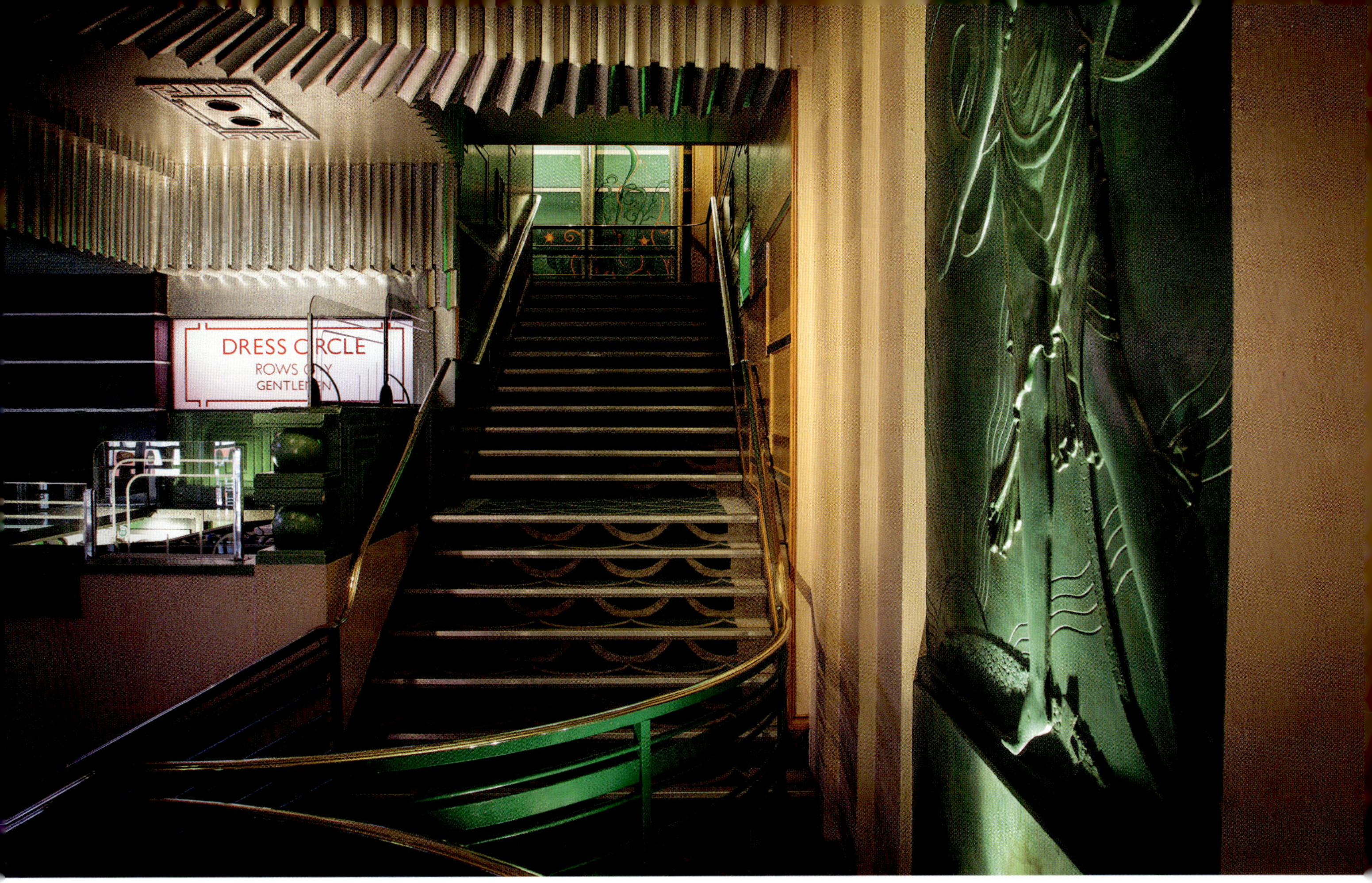

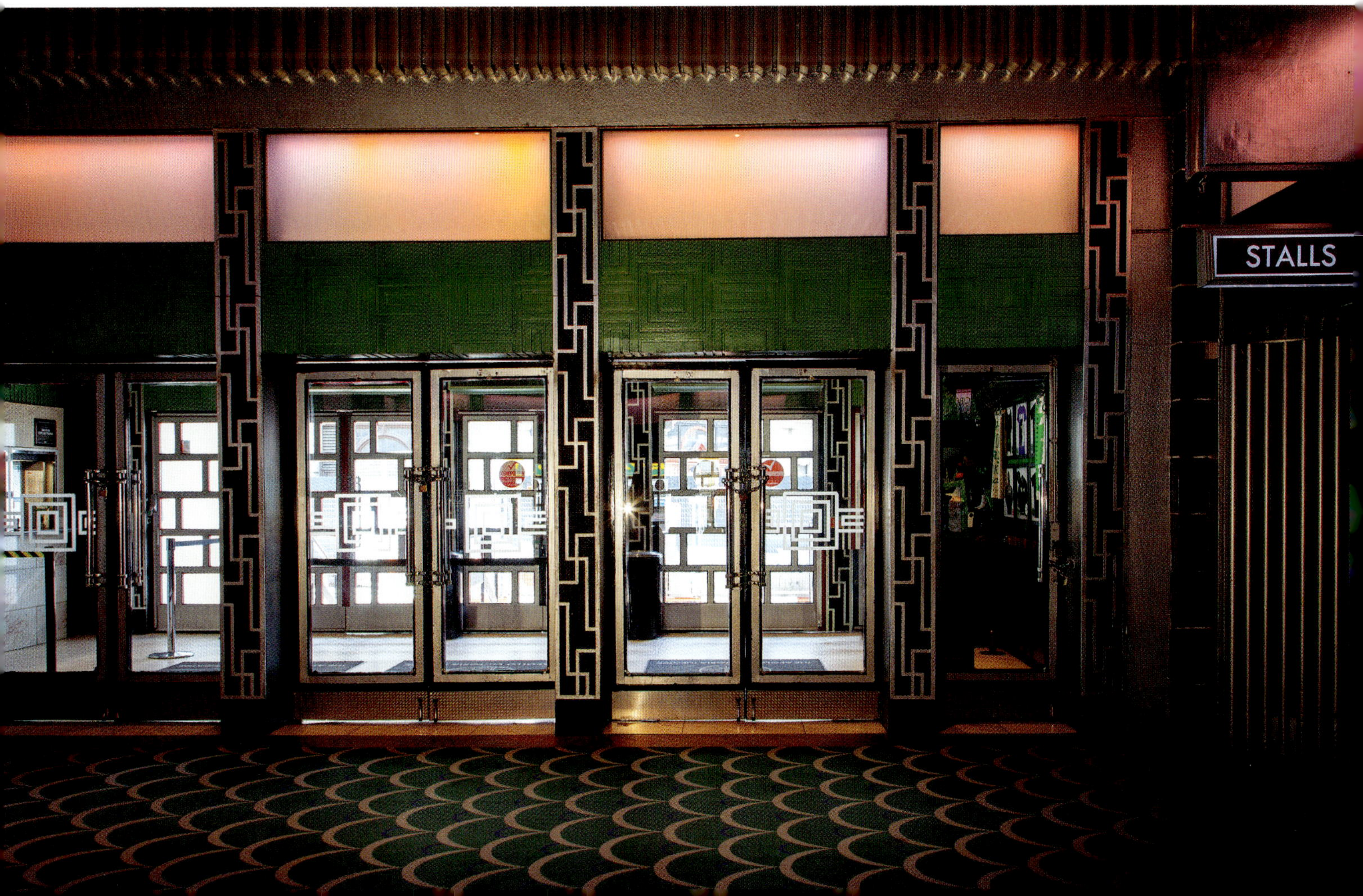
STALLS

ROYAL COURT

In the annals of theatre history, certain theatres have a significance that is belied by their physical form. The rather chunky Old Vic, for example, is much less beautiful than many other theatres, but the survival of the art of classical acting owes more to that theatre than any other. Similarly, the exterior of the Royal Court Theatre in Chelsea, pleasing as it is, gives little sense that over its 130 years of existence it has, at certain periods, been a powerhouse, not only of new writing – the West End is full of new writing that feels decidedly old – but of the kind of new writing that breaks every taboo and remakes the conversation with the audience. At those periods it has been both a breeding ground and a playground, a funhouse and a madhouse, a forum for rigorous class analysis and a gymnasium for the imagination. All that behind the very plain facade with which Walter Emden and Bertie Crewe endowed their theatre on the east side of fashionable, busy Sloane Square. There's nothing fancy about the interior, either. It originally held eight hundred people and was comfortably appointed, but with no hint of the Frenchified fantasy, gilded statuary and extravagant imagery of so many other theatres of the period. It opened, in 1888, with a comedy, and a French one at that – *Mamma*, or *The Surprises of Divorce*, a current Paris hit – but it distinctly lacks the front-of-house frivolity such a piece seems to call for. It was at first called the Court Theatre, but the palatial element that name leads one to expect is entirely absent; if it is a court, it must be a very severe Northern one.

As it happens, the first night of the new theatre was accompanied by something a lot more in keeping with its future: a riot. A class riot, at that. 'It seems that, by a curious blunder,' reported *The Era*, 'the pay-box had been placed at the bottom, instead of at the top, of the pit staircase, and the stream of pittites, gathering momentum in their descent, had found themselves hurled with embarrassing velocity against a wooden barrier at the bottom of the steps.' Had it not been for the timely breakage of the barrier, there might have been serious consequences, and the pittites were not to be easily mollified. 'For some time the pit was a veritable pandemonium,' continued *The Era*, 'not only a palpitating, but an exceedingly angry, mass.' This somewhat eighteenth-century outburst rumbled on all evening, because not only had the pit dwellers fallen down the stairs, they found when they arrived at their destination that they were packed in very tightly indeed. Throughout the evening there were cries of 'Manager!' 'Mr Chudleigh!' and even 'Architect!' But by the end the players – including Mrs John Wood, one of the co-lessees of the theatre – had won them over.

The theatre had in fact been commissioned by another actor, by the name of John Clayton; this Clayton, alas, died before the building was finished, and Mrs Wood and Arthur Chudleigh had taken it over. Clayton had been the actor-manager of an earlier Court Theatre on the other side of the square, or rather just off it, in George Street. This theatre had been a notable success. The work of the same Walter Emden, just 25 years old and startlingly confident, it was a colourful adaptation of an earlier, rather more sober adaptation of a Nonconformist church. Commenting on these serial adaptations,

OPPOSITE Detail of the first and upper circles.

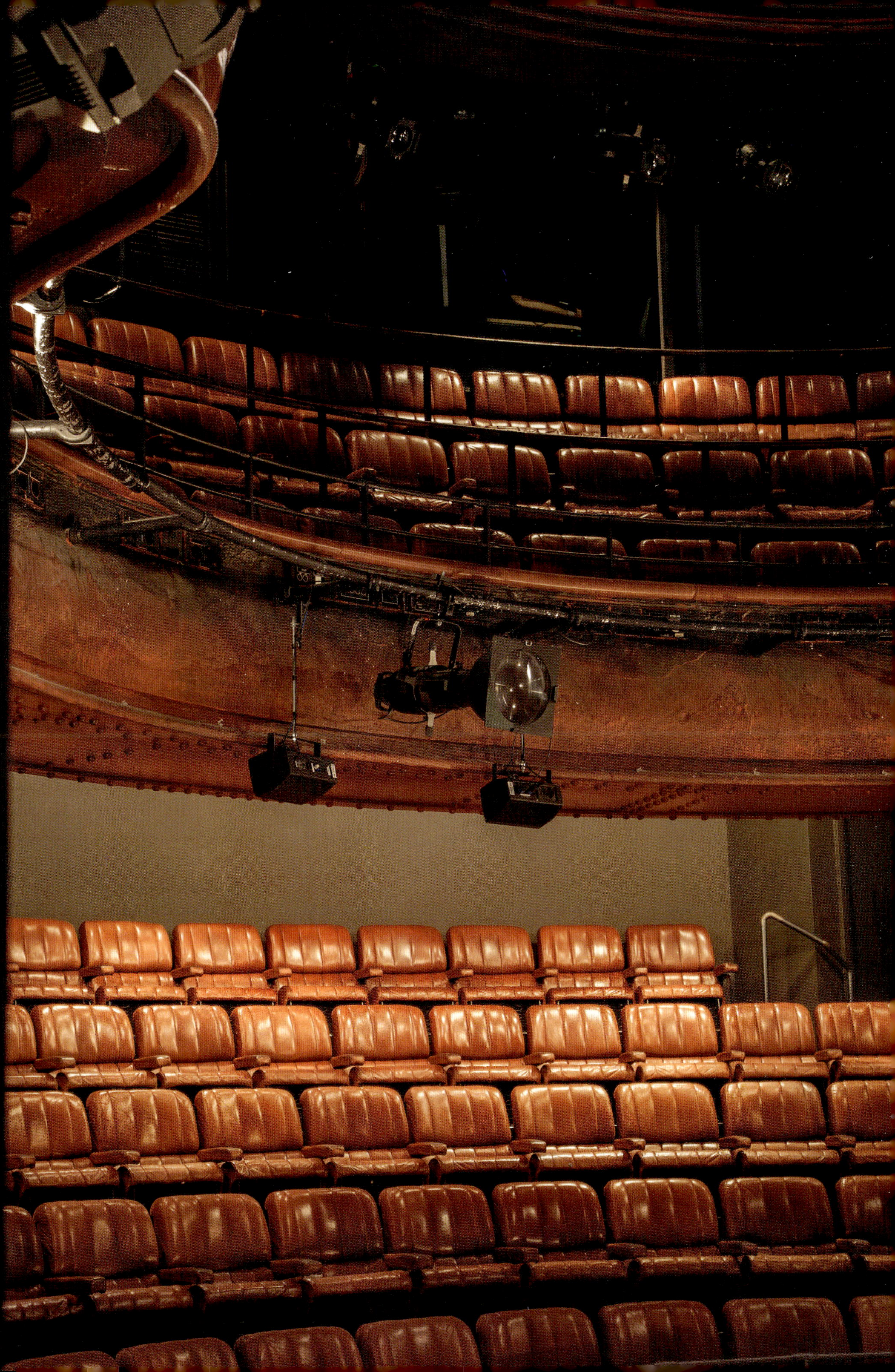

The Era enjoyed the idea that 'a dissenting chapel . . . which had, perhaps, been the means of converting thousands, might itself be advantageously converted into a Theatre'. This first Royal Court Theatre, which opened in 1870, had been more or less thrown up in six weeks and was adorned with frescoes representing incidents in the life of St George of England. It was committed to new writing, if not quite in the sense that the second Royal Court Theatre meant it. It particularly featured the work of the Tory satirist W. S. Gilbert, later, of course, to become indivisibly linked in the public mind with the composer Arthur Sullivan. One of the plays performed at the first Court was his *The Happy Land*, a pointed musical satire on popular government, specifically on William Gladstone's Liberal administration, in power at the time; characters unmistakeably based on the Prime Minister and two of his colleagues were heavily featured. The Prince of Wales (later to be Edward VII) was outraged by the piece and tipped off the Lord Chamberlain, who, as censor of plays, tried to have the show closed. He succeeded only in preventing the actors from making themselves up to look like their real-life counterparts. The resourceful manager of the theatre, a Miss Litton, had a large sign placed in the foyer saying that 'Miss Litton begs to inform the public that the Lord Chamberlain has forbidden Messrs. Fisher, Hill, and Righton to make up their faces in imitation of Messrs. Gladstone, Lowe, and Ayrton', thus guaranteeing that every member of the audience knew exactly who the actors were supposed to be. Game, set and match to Miss Litton: the Lord Chamberlain was made a laughing stock, his powers of censorship mocked. Alas, his privilege remained in force until the 1960s, its absurdity having been demonstrated over and over again by the second Royal Court in the early years of the twentieth century, when Harley Granville-Barker was presenting the plays of George Bernard Shaw, and then again in the 1950s and '60s when the firebrands of the English Stage Company defied the censor almost as a matter of course.

The first Royal Court presented many more of Gilbert's plays (including adaptations of *Great Expectations* and of the great Labiche/Marc-Michel farce *The Italian Straw Hat*) and not much later gave the premieres of a number of comedies by Arthur Wing Pinero, among them his masterpieces *The Magistrate* and *Dandy Dick*. Pinero was only the second playwright to be knighted (the first was Gilbert), so there was nothing wrong with the managerial instincts of Mrs Wood and Arthur Chudleigh. But by 1887 the building, so rapidly erected, had had its day, and Emden, still only forty, was again approached to design a second Royal Court, this time in tandem with his brilliant younger colleague Bertie Crewe, who would grow to be one of the masters of Edwardian theatre design. Apart from the riot, the early days of the new Royal Court were pretty tranquil. Then, in 1900, J. H. Leigh, a wealthy amateur, took the lease on the theatre with the intention of presenting Shakespeare, with his wife in the leading roles. To the surprise of no one but Leigh this proved unsuccessful, and he turned to the distinguished critic William Archer for advice. Archer recommended that he bring in the distinguished actor, dramatist and director Harley Granville-Barker, who agreed on one condition: that he would be allowed to revive Shaw's controversial *Candida*, in which Barker had created the part of Marchbanks, at matinees. This agreed, a manager was hired – J. E. Vedrenne, utterly committed to new writing – and a policy established: challenging new works would be presented on afternoons, featuring West End actors who were in other shows by night. Thus it was that a whole succession of highly provocative plays by Shaw had their first performances at the Court: *John Bull's Other Island*, *Man and Superman*, *Major Barbara* and *The Doctor's Dilemma*. The great and the good flocked to these matinees; on one occasion the prime minister, Arthur Balfour, attended a performance of *John Bull* with his entire cabinet, noted its criticism of his government's Irish policy, and duly changed it.

Having set new standards of acting and staging, and having pushed the theatre right into the heart

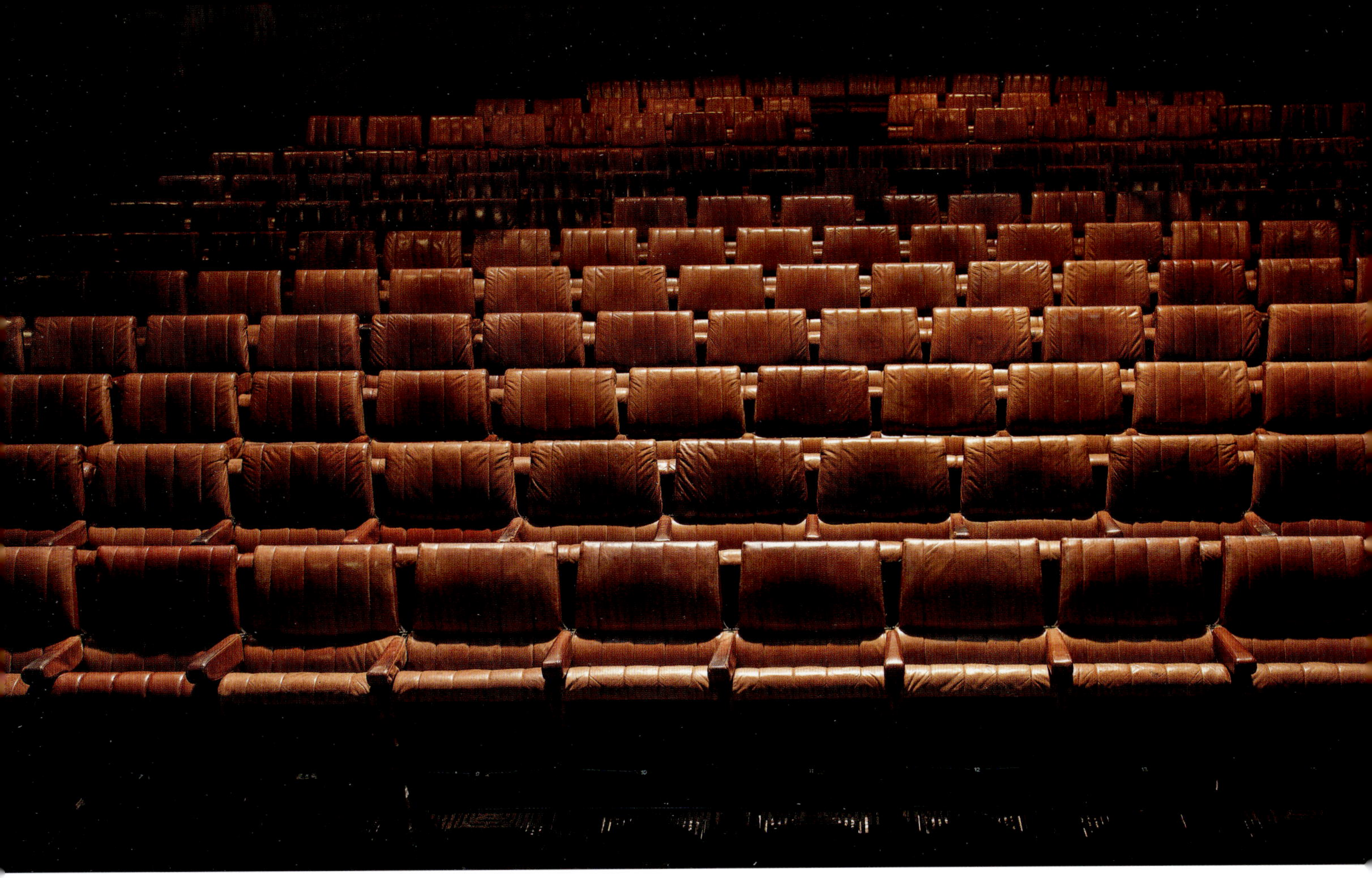

of the national debate, Barker, as he would do throughout his life, threw in the towel at the Court in 1907, after which it reverted to being a receiving house. W. Somerset Maugham's first successful play, *Lady Frederick*, was premiered there in 1907, and there were two London premieres, first of the play many people consider his masterpiece, *Heartbreak House*, in 1921, and then, in 1924, of his hugely ambitious, chronically diffuse pentalogy *Back to Methuselah*; there were also regular visits by the Macdona Players, dedicated to performing Shaw's canon. The Court was, in effect, Shaw's temple; he described the audience as 'this congregation'. But theatres cannot live by Shaw alone; by the early 1930s the place had declined, and in 1935 it underwent the humiliation of being converted into a cinema. It remained as such until a bomb hit it during the Blitz, its aim not the theatre but the adjacent station: the thing that was supposed to make the Court more attractive and accessible to theatregoers proved to be its undoing. The theatre stood stricken for a decade, until it was reopened in 1952 by the eminently worthy London Theatre Guild, the interior reconstructed by Robert Cromie and the number of seats reduced to under five hundred. The revivified theatre was host to *Miss Hargreaves*, a Margaret Rutherford vehicle; then a very successful revue; and then, in 1956 – a harbinger of what was about to come – the highly successful first British production of the Brecht–Weill *Threepenny Opera*, directed by the American actor and visionary man of theatre Sam Wanamaker, with designs by the great Caspar Neher and the music under the direction of Berthold Goldschmidt; it transferred to the West End, after which an organisation calling itself the English Stage Company took a lease on the Court with the intention of promoting new and foreign writing.

ABOVE The stalls seats – note the fine leather.

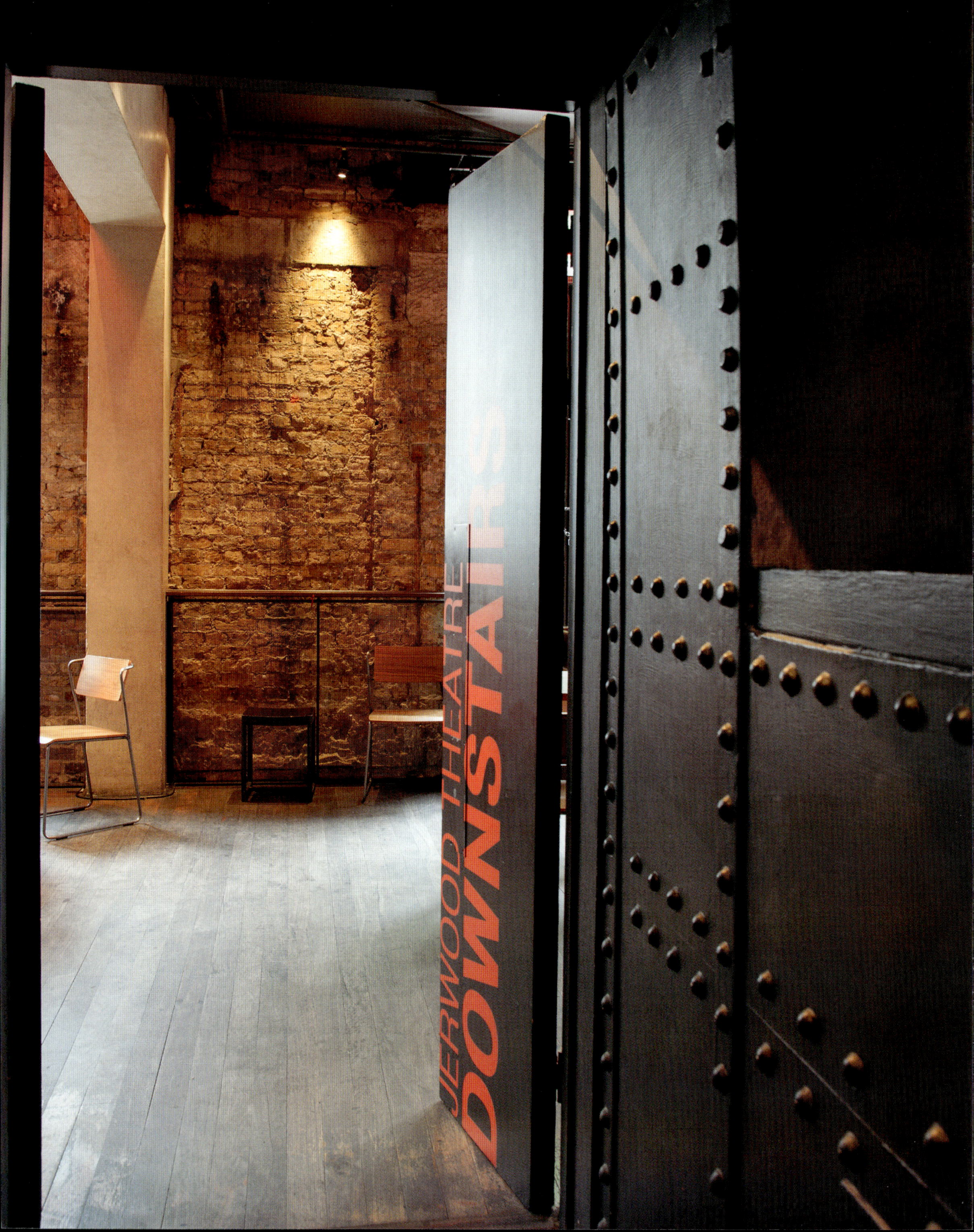
JERWOOD THEATRE
DOWNSTAIRS

At first, the ESC's plan was to encourage novelists to write for the stage, but with the overwhelming success in 1956 of its third production, a play by an unknown young actor called John Osborne, the theatre committed itself to a much less literary path. Though *Look Back in Anger* was in many ways a highly conventional play, it spoke with a voice that had not been heard before in the British theatre, the voice of a generation that rejected a great deal of what Britain currently seemed to stand for. The theatre had run its standard up the flagpole, and the young and the radical flocked round it. Under a highly disparate group of directors – ranging from the paternal George Devine to the theatrically flamboyant Tony Richardson, from the intellectually rigorous Bill Gaskill to the classically austere Lindsay Anderson – it was always alive, always challenging, both politically and theatrically. It combined, in some unfathomable way, Brechtian political clarity, Joan Littlewood's proletarian earthiness, a respect for texts, an awareness of conventions from other cultures – the use of masks, for example – and a desire to shock. And it quickly became a magnet for actors. As well as generating its own informal ensemble of young players of regional and/or working-class origins like Albert Finney, Alan Bates and Joan Plowright, it welcomed the grandees of the West End and the classical theatre – Peggy Ashcroft, John Gielgud, Ralph Richardson, Alec Guinness and, perhaps most startlingly, Laurence Olivier, whose Archie Rice in Osborne's *The Entertainer* was a devastatingly brilliant rapprochement between the skills and personal magnetism of the older generation and the actuality and relevance of the new writing. His celebrity forced mainstream theatregoers to take note of what was happening, radically changing the theatre and yanking it – just in time – into the twentieth century.

OPPOSITE Looking towards a foyer, these doors could be the doors of a prison. Also note the bare brick on the back wall.
ABOVE RIGHT The upstairs bar area.

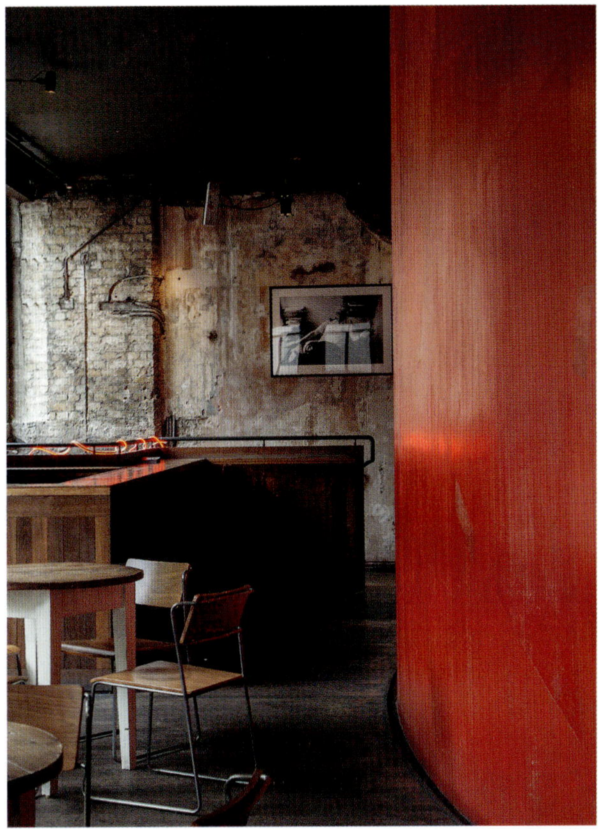

The building, in its simplicity and intimacy, was perfectly suited for work that directly engaged its audience but aimed for a certain epic distancing from the material. The auditorium was reconceived in 1964 by designer Jocelyn Herbert, and then in 1997, during Stephen Daldry's epoch, it closed for a year for a reconstruction that involved building right out under Sloane Square to expand the front of house and include a restaurant. The auditorium, rendered in battleship hues and textures, was denuded of any vestige of the decorative; the seats were made marginally less comfortable (quite an achievement). But these modifications gave the experience of seeing a play there even more edge than before. It feels as fresh and as combative and as impossible to ignore as it ever has, a centre of turbulence and truth-saying, wonderfully incongruously stuck in one of the most plutocratic parts of town, defiantly facing down the meccas of the haute-bourgeoisie.

NATIONAL THEATRE

The National Theatre, the youngest theatre to be featured in this book and therefore the one with the shortest history, is, like the Old Vic from which it sprang, an idea as much as a physical entity. The pragmatic British are famously resistant to ideas, which partly explains why this theatre took so long to come into existence: over a hundred years of frustrated idealism, of broken promises, of false starts from the first adumbration of the notion to its realisation in (literally) concrete form.

The first theatres in London, in the mid-sixteenth century, had been speculative ventures run by actor-managers; the successful ones (like Burbage's, with which Shakespeare was most closely associated) had formed relationships with great nobles, or, if they were very lucky, with the Crown, as of course did Burbage's company. But the Crown did not support these companies; it hired them. James I was particularly keen on spectacle, and his court staged lavish masques, but still there was no resident company. During the Cromwellian period the theatres were closed down, reopening at the Restoration in a celebratory blaze of freedom, under royal patronage and licensed by the Crown, but not subsidised by it. Increasingly, however, under the Hanoverian succession, the theatres took on the role of political satirists, savagely attacking the government (and indeed the monarchy). The establishment retaliated brutally with a draconian Licensing Act (1737), which effectively neutered the theatre; the Act was revised in 1843, further tightening the grip of the Lord Chamberlain over what could or could not be performed. The stage, far from being subsidised by the state, was apparently its sworn enemy.

The results of the legislation were disastrous: to anyone of a discriminating cast of mind, the British theatre of the mid-nineteenth century was an embarrassment. Ever more rigid censorship had driven gifted writers away from the theatre, principally into novel-writing; the rackety popular theatre, though often spectacular and brilliantly produced, was largely devoid of content, a mere diversion. Despite a succession of extraordinary leading actors, men and women, the general standard of acting was wretched – unsurprisingly, given the overwhelming focus on the star players. High-minded actor-managers like Charles Kean, Samuel Phelps and William Macready strove to improve the level, but the financial constraints were great. In 1847, Dramaticus, a pseudonymous pamphleteer, wrote a withering description of the condition of the contemporary theatre under the title *The Stage as It Is*; and the following year the publisher Effingham William Wilson wrote the first clear articulation of the case for a subsidised theatre in *A House for Shakespeare: A Proposition for the Consideration of the Nation*. Notions of theatrical reform naturally focused on Shakespeare, who since the mid-eighteenth century had been the acknowledged pride of the nation; there had been Shakespeare festivals and the plays were frequently revived, albeit in desperately corrupt texts. But the idea of a theatre exclusively dedicated to staging the canon was new, and the leaders of the profession rallied round, raising funds, until finally, in 1879, the Shakespeare

OPPOSITE The staircase – a fine example of Brutalist architecture.

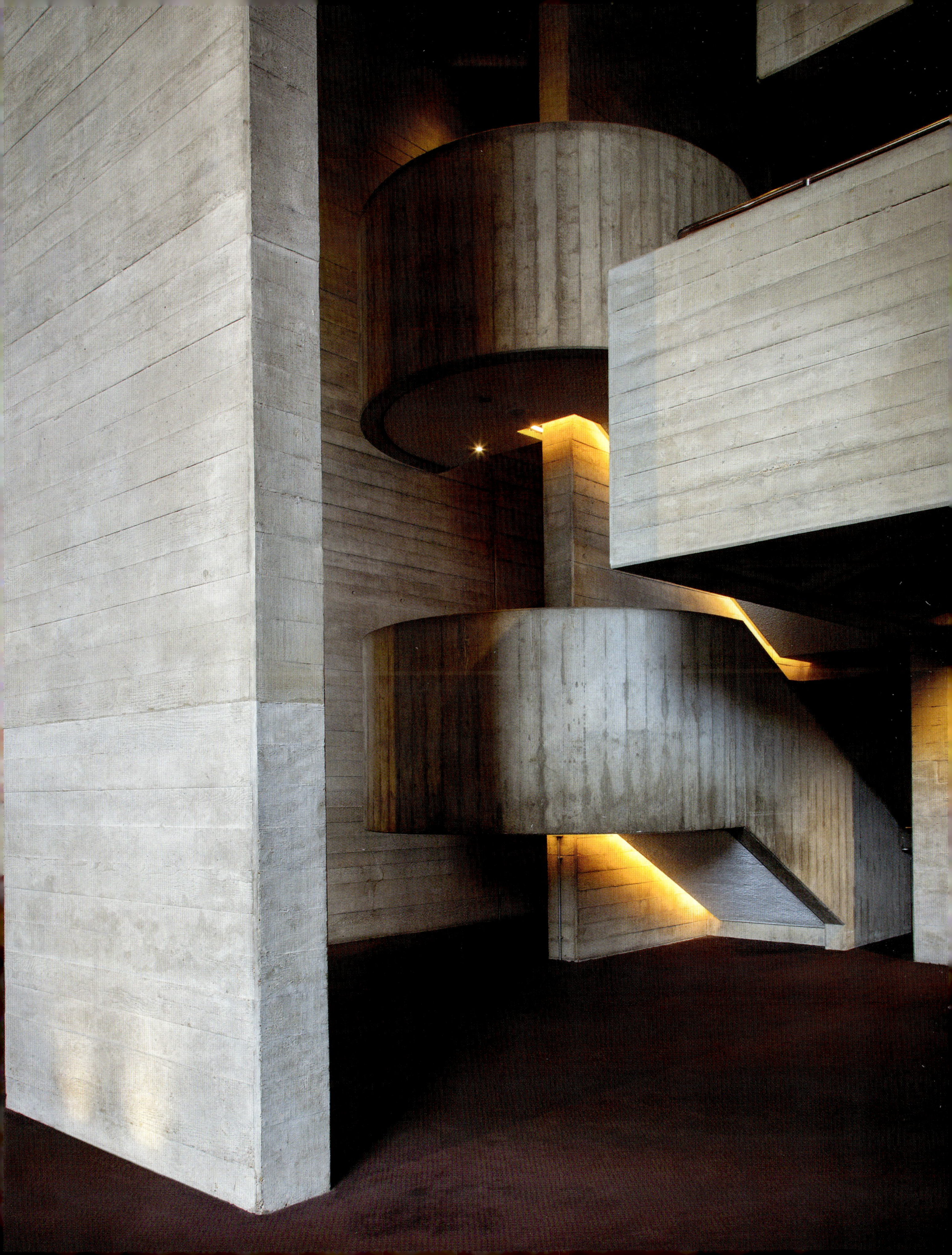

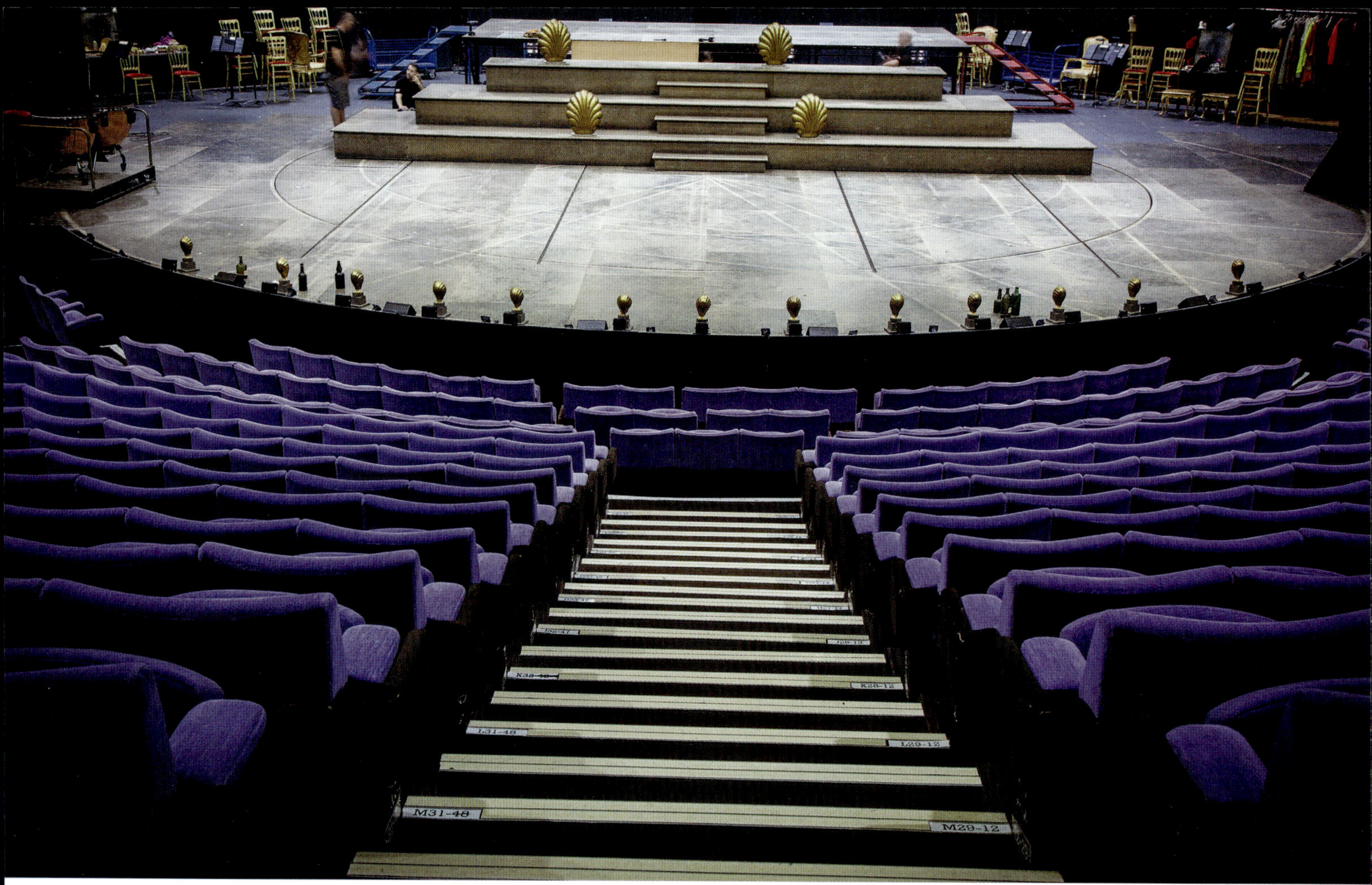

Memorial Theatre was opened in Stratford-upon-Avon on 23 April, the poet's supposed birthday, with the New Shakespeare Company in residence.

That same year, the London appearances of the Comédie-Française only served to underline what might be achieved with proper subsidy. There had never been a permanent company paid for by the state in Britain; the richness of the Continental tradition of court theatres, employing large numbers of actors, dancers, designers, directors and writers, with long rehearsal periods and standing repertoires, was evident in the works of those companies when they played in Britain. The company of the Duke of Saxe-Meiningen, patiently drilled over months into presentations that were daringly staged but also realistic and psychologically detailed, was a revelation; the great actor-managers Henry Irving and Herbert Beerbohm Tree strove to emulate their achievements, but in the end they were commercial entrepreneurs and the possibility of experiment was limited, as was time for rehearsal. Meanwhile, individuals like George Bernard Shaw, Harley Granville-Barker and William Archer toiled tirelessly to establish a British organisation that would field an ensemble of actors superb in quality from top to bottom to explore the dramatic riches of world literature – a 'Living Library' of plays, as they called it – and, equally importantly, provide a forum for new writing: they themselves, after all, were playwrights, resolved to present plays written by grown-ups, for grown-ups. 'Let us make up our minds', wrote Archer to Shaw, 'not to die, on any pretext whatever, until we have seen an English theatre worthy of the name.' All three of them died before the National Theatre was established – and Shaw lived until 1950.

ABOVE The auditorium of the Olivier stage. The 'rake' of the seats assures everyone of a good view.

In 1908, Barker and Archer had established what they called a Shakespeare Memorial National Theatre Committee, but its work was slow to show results. Parliament passed a private members' bill in 1913 to establish a National Theatre, only for it to be abandoned when the First World War broke out a year later. In the mid-1930s the Memorial Committee, still beavering away, eventually bought a plot of land for a National Theatre in South Kensington, opposite the Victoria and Albert Museum (the Ismaili Centre, by the architect Hugh Casson, now occupies the site). It was to be designed in tandem by Sir Edwin Lutyens, favourite architect of the British Raj, and Cecil Masey, who had co-designed the Phoenix Theatre in Charing Cross Road and was responsible for a number of magnificent Granada cinemas – an odd team, but possibly an inspired one, a shrewd combination of imagination and experience.

This too was not to be, falling foul of the Second World War. But during that war, the Old Vic, bombed out of its own building, took up residence at the New Theatre (now the Noël Coward), which under the triumvirate of two actors and a director – Laurence Olivier, Ralph Richardson and John Burrell – became a rallying point for national morale. 'The Old Vic', cried Olivier in 1946, in the introduction to a book about the theatre, 'has for some time been, in people's minds, the National Theatre; it is now destined to be in fact . . . let us hope that the rebirth of our theatre, both in the intrinsic artistic sense and in the fact of the general increase of interest in worthwhile plays, will be a feature of post-war Britain. For a nation which loves its theatre is a healthy nation.' Shortly after, he and Richardson were brutally dismissed from the Old Vic; the dream would be deferred for thirty years. A National Theatre Act was actually passed in 1949, finally committing the nation to realising the century-old idea, but despite having its foundation stone, on a site adjacent to County Hall on the South Bank of the Thames, officially unveiled by the newly crowned Queen Elizabeth II, successive governments wriggled out of their commitment; in 1955, the theatre critics Kenneth Tynan and Richard Findlater, in full mourning attire, held a much reported mock funeral for that same foundation stone, which they ceremonially draped in black.

'Must it again be urged', cried an anguished Tynan, 'that Britain is the only European country with a living theatrical tradition which lacks a national theatre . . . ?' Finally, in 1960, the Greater London Council and the government between them committed to building it, slightly further upriver. Laurence Olivier was appointed its first director and the high-flying modernist Denys Lasdun, who had never designed a theatre before, was nominated its architect. Lasdun undertook to consult with a huge range of theatre practitioners; Olivier threw himself into the process with the passion of a man who believes he is constructing his own monument: this, surely, would establish for all time his historic role in the British theatre. The quest of the consultants, spurred on by Olivier, was to create a theatre that would out-theatre all other theatres; that would be at once ultra-modern and also firmly plugged into the ritual roots of theatre; that would be adaptable to any form of play, from any period of history; and that would be a thing of beauty in itself, a beacon, a temple and a fun palace all rolled into one, a sort of triumphal arch of the theatre, all things to all men and women.

In 1967 Lasdun finally delivered his design, which was certainly bold, massive and grey, with its naked concrete and its vast glass windows, its imposing terraces and its looming flytower. At first it was intended that there would be two auditoriums, the Olivier, inspired by the mighty Greek theatre of Asclepius in Epidaurus, and the Lyttleton, a sort of bare, box-like proscenium arch theatre (named after Oliver Lyttelton, Lord Chandos, who as chairman of the National Theatre Board had been instrumental in securing government support for the project); but Peter Brook, one of the committee of consultants, insisted that there should be a smaller space reserved for more experimental work. It was Peter Hall,

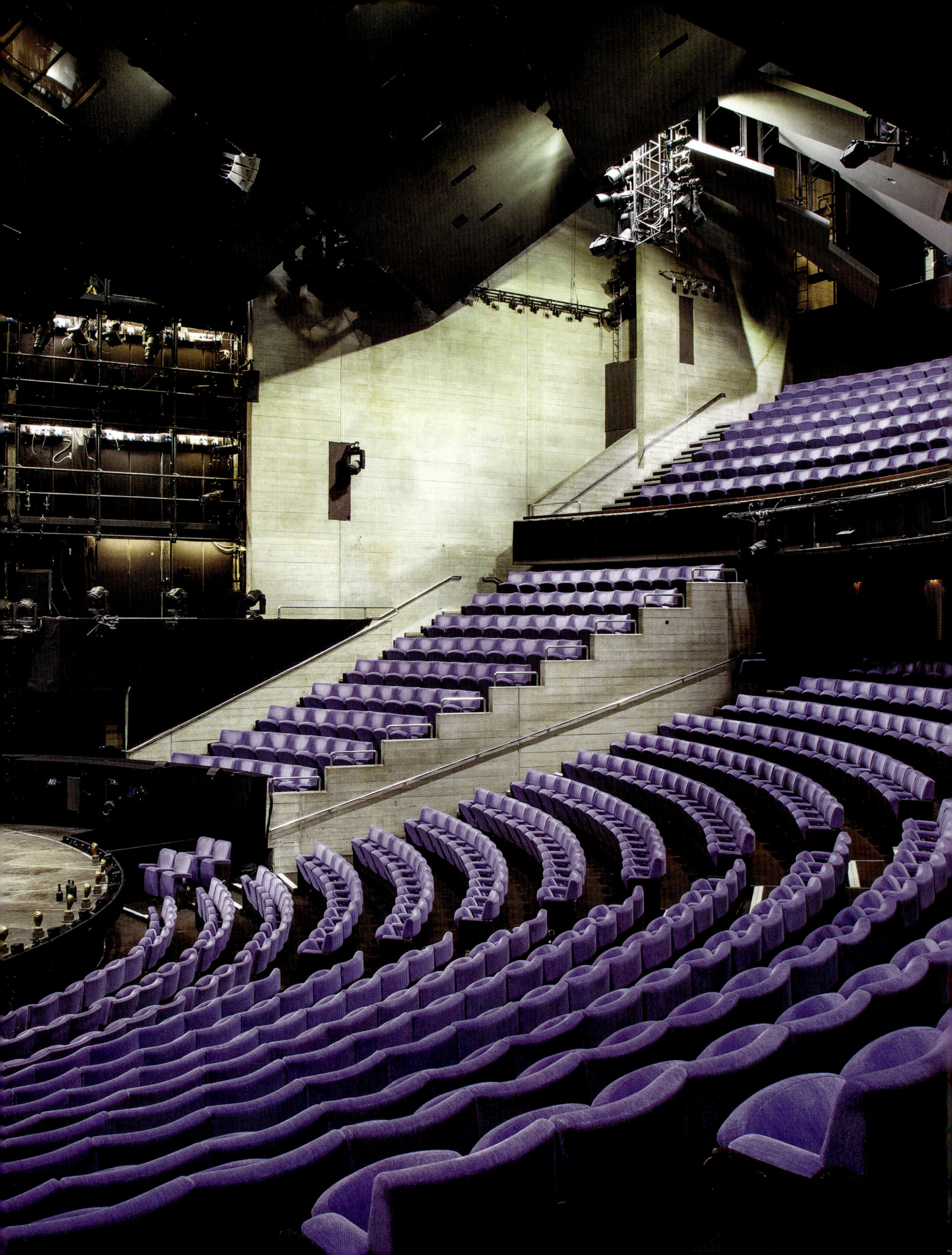

another consultant, who identified the space within the building which finally became the Cottesloe (named after the chairman of the Arts Council, whose support was also critical in getting the building built); it was designed – not, as it happens, by Lasdun but by the theatre consultant Iain Mackintosh – to approximate the form of an Elizabethan theatre while being as flexible as possible.

Lasdun's design met with the general approval of the architectural fraternity; the response of the theatrical community was more muted. But it had now become a matter of national pride at a time of economic and political uncertainty: 'Put shortly,' said Ian Nairn, one of the sharpest architectural commentators of the day, 'I believe in this design . . . it deserves to be started now, as an act of faith in our national potential, and even in the present gloomy financial climate there is one ray of hope – no major payments will be required in the next 18 months. And if we are not out of the wood by then, we will deserve a National Poorhouse, not a National Theatre.'

It was hoped that the new building would be ready in 1973. Meanwhile, until it was, Olivier continued to run the National Theatre Company from its temporary home, the Old Vic, as he had done since 1962. Its time there was a remarkable period in the history of the British theatre. This dazzling company, under the direction of some of the greatest directors in the world and led by the man generally acknowledged to be the greatest actor of his time, in a repertory of classics, rarities from all the storehouse of unknown masterpieces and knockout new plays by Shaffer, Stoppard and Peter Nichols among them, was everything that Barker and Shaw and Archer had dreamed of. But the Vic was strained to breaking point: the administration of this most glamorous of theatrical operations was done from a series of prefabricated huts in a car park just down the road from the Old Vic. A wartime mood of cheerful privation prevailed; but the extraordinary effort of creating a company and a repertory that rapidly became the envy of the world, while leading from the front as actor and director, took its toll on Olivier. As the move to the new theatre became imminent – or seemed to be – it was clear that it would be too much for him. The board decided that the pilot must be dropped, and Peter Hall was co-opted to take the National forward to the next stage in its destiny. The atmosphere became Shakespearean: Olivier was deeply resentful of being sidelined and lashed out on all sides, like Richard III at bay; Hall – witty and deep-revolving, like the Duke of Buckingham – was busy forging alliances and steering the company, slowly but surely, in a new direction.

This awkward and unhappy succession would have been difficult enough, but the new theatre itself was beset with construction problems, which delayed the opening. Finally, in 1976, Hall decided they must occupy it even though it was not entirely finished; indeed, none of the stages was ready to receive a production, so Hall boldly rehearsed Marlowe's *Tamburlaine* on the terraces. Astounded pedestrians found themselves in the fearsome presence of Albert Finney, breathing fire as the Mongol warlord. But even when the stages were ready to be occupied, the actors were prevented from doing their work by an arbitrary and politically motivated strike by the technicians' union. Hall proved to be their match, however, and finally saw them off. But it was not an auspicious start to the most ambitious, the most costly and the most radical statement ever made by the British theatre; even the royal opening was muted, with a poor production of a minor play by Carlo Goldoni. Each of the auditoriums had severe problems acoustically and technically; the great revolving drum in the Olivier was not activated for a full ten years after its installation. It took a while, too, for actors and directors to discover how to make the best of the individual theatres. Designers were constricted by a clause in Lasdun's contract that stipulated that he

OPPOSITE The Olivier Theatre. The bright mauve seats create an interesting contrast to the bleak concrete walls. A concession to frivolity?

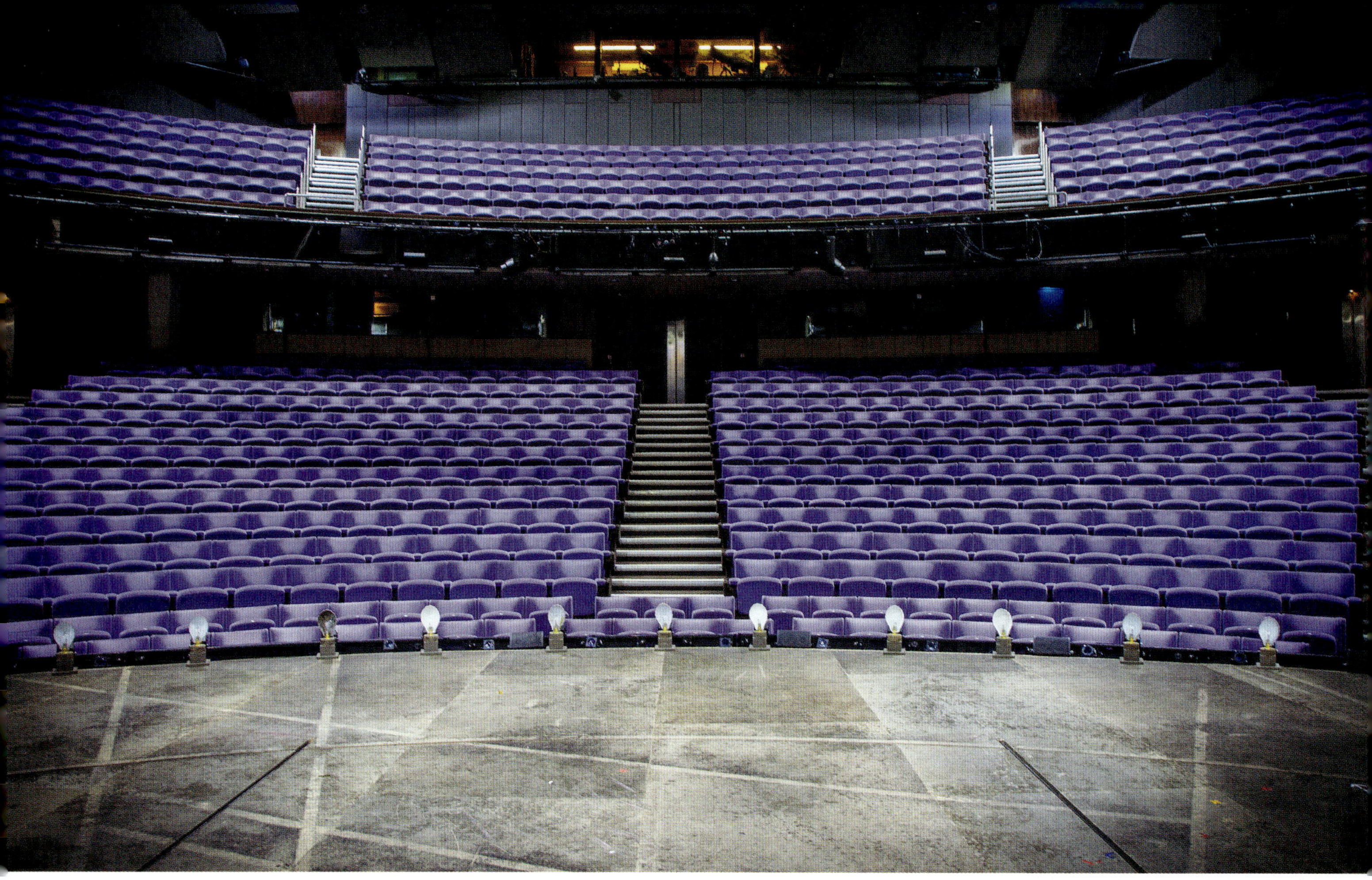

had the right of approval over their designs, which had to harmonise with the stark, bare walls; similarly, he had absolute control over the public spaces, the foyers and the terraces. The feeling of the National's workforce towards the building was not loving: it was hard to enjoy the cell-like dressing rooms, which looked out on to a well that resembled nothing so much as a prison yard; the dreary, grey, neon-lit corridors whose linoleum tiles started peeling off the floor almost immediately; the odd little airless and lightless rehearsal rooms.

But from the very beginning the public loved it, and loves it still. This enthusiasm was perhaps less aesthetic than practical: there was an underground car park, the foyers were spacious, the lavatories plentiful and salubrious, the bars numerous, the seats comfortable and easy of access. The front-of-house operation was efficient, cheerful and audience-friendly, and the views, looking out through the windows on to the Thames and, directly opposite the theatre, William Chambers's magnificent late eighteenth-century Somerset House, were marvellous; you could even, in those days, catch a glimpse of St Paul's Cathedral. And as the theatre got into its stride – an operation on a scale unparalleled in the British Isles – each auditorium found its defining triumph. There was *Amadeus* in the Olivier, David Hare's *Plenty* in the Lyttelton and medieval mystery plays in the Cottesloe, each of which fitted its theatre like a glove. Hall stayed at the National for ten years, presiding over a stupendous range of work, and not only simply plays – the nightly Platform performances were endlessly stimulating footnotes to the night's main event, and Hall's own *Oresteia*, in masks, was a staggering and radical achievement. His supreme triumph was in attracting the cream of British

ABOVE The Olivier Theatre auditorium from the stage.

theatrical talent – writers, designers, composers, directors – to the South Bank, which they turned into a continuous pageant of imagination, audacity and entertainment. Each of his four successors, sometimes subtly, sometimes radically, has shifted the emphasis, but in terms of box office success alone it is clear that the National Theatre on the South Bank has fulfilled its extremely ambitious remit: it has raised the general standard of playgoing; stimulated new artists, both performers and primary creators; and hugely encouraged, through its outreach and educational programmes, new and, most importantly, young audiences.

Successive directors, freed of the yoke of Lasdun's personal and very active presence (he died in 2001), have increasingly confronted the building's shortcomings. The Olivier auditorium has been reconfigured so that the actors are now closer to the audience and the ratio of empty space to the walls diminished; the Cottesloe has been entirely refurbished (and renamed as the Dorfman); and attempts have been made to improve the somewhat dead acoustics of the Lyttleton. The foyers have been reconfigured and, on the right side of the building facing the Thames, enlarged. There are new cafés and bars. Externally, everything has been done to cheer up the austere aspect of the building. It is to be feared that the late Sir Denys is more or less permanently revolving in his grave since the austere aspect of his great fortress has been flooded in coloured light, onto which various slogans are projected; a moving neon display on the front gives details of what's on that night; and whole nurseries of foliage have been encouraged to spread over the balconies. It now distinctly suggests a fun palace, which is splendid as far as it goes. But, paradoxically, Lasdun's original building was at its best at night, the *béton brut* surfaces of the flytower chastely lit with white light, somehow resembling the masterly designs for *Hamlet* by the Edwardian theatrical visionary Edward Gordon Craig (Peter Hall's hero, as it happens), all sculpted line, epic and awe-inspiring.

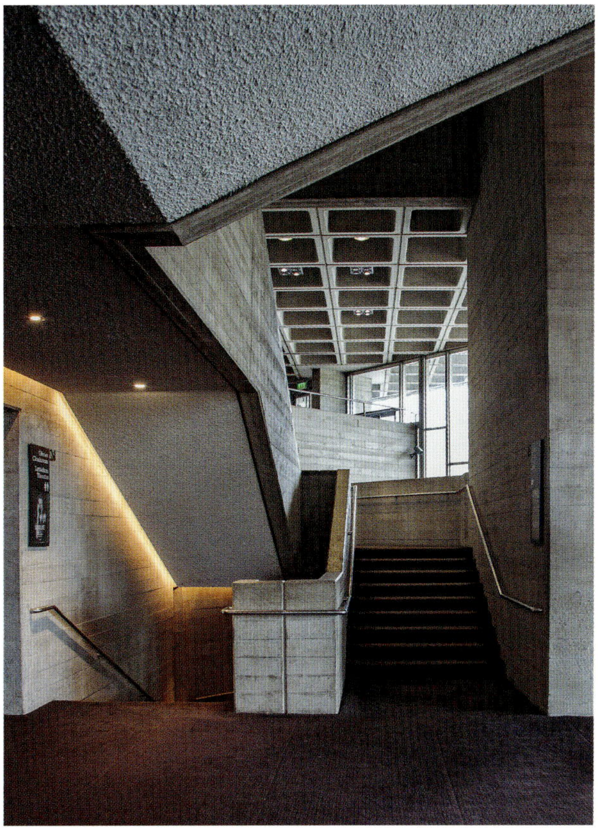

If this book has a theme at all, it is that the theatre – and indeed the theatres – are in constant evolution. Nothing is set in stone; everything adjusts to the pressures of the time. It exists to supply a need, and those needs change on an almost daily basis. The National Theatre is a unique institution, with unique obligations. Like everything else, it must change or die. The idea of theatre is much stronger than any individual manifestation of it. So its motto must be, as it always has been: watch this space.

ABOVE A staircase in the lobby. Another good example of Brutalism.

ACKNOWLEDGEMENTS

Firstly, I would like to thank all the owners of the theatres photographed for this book, also the various stage managers and public relations people, whose help has been invaluable. I would also like to thank my assistants, Katy Conover, Sinéad Bligh and Raffaella Matrone; my editors at Prestel, Lincoln Dexter and Anna Godfrey; and Peter Dawson and Alice Kennedy-Owen, whose patience and skill in designing the book have been exemplary. And, as always, particular thanks to Brent Wallace, whose help in editing the pictures as well as removing certain fire extinguishers and cables has been essential.

—Derry Moore

I must first acknowledge my predecessors in the field, the late Raymond Mander and Joe Mitchenson, whom I had the privilege of knowing and whose heroic and tireless spadework is the foundation of much of what we know about London's theatre today – all done without the internet. The stars of that astonishing resource are Arthur Lloyd, who has spent a lifetime gathering and then sharing, electronically, a mass of riveting primary material, and the many authors of the superb Survey of London (founded in 1894 and still continuing), which has been indispensable in reconstructing the history of the oldest theatres represented in this book.

Next, I must thank my editors, Anna Godfrey and Lincoln Dexter, for tolerating and accommodating an ever-expanding text. My publisher Andrew Hansen, for unflagging enthusiasm and patience, and Aimée Selby, for eagle-eyed attention to the text, rooting out factual errors and stylistic infelicities.

Finally, my deep gratitude to Derry Moore, for asking me in the first place, for instant, warm and witty responsiveness to the pieces as they slowly appeared, and for constantly inspiring me with the quality of his wonderful photographs.

—Simon Callow

Front cover: Theatre Royal Haymarket
Back cover: Apollo Victoria

Prestel Publishing Ltd.
14–17 Wells Street
London W1T 3PD

Prestel Publishing
900 Broadway, Suite 603
New York, NY 10003

Library of Congress Control Number is available; British Library Cataloguing-in-Publication Data: a catalogue record for this book is available from the British Library

Editorial direction: Anna Godfrey
Copyediting: Aimee Selby
Design and layout: Grade Design, gradedesign.com
Production management: Friederike Schirge
Separations: Ludwig Media, Zell am See
Printing and binding: DZS Grafik, d.o.o, Ljubljana
Paper: Profisilk

ISBN 978-3-7913-8386-6

9 783791 383866

Verlagsgruppe Random House FSC® N001967

Printed in Slovenia

ISBN 978-3-7913-8386-6

MIX
Paper from responsible sources
FSC® C106600

www.prestel.com